Mexico's Military on the Democratic Stage

Praeger Security International Advisory Board

Board Cochairs

Loch Johnson, Regents Professor of Public and International Affairs, School of Public and International Affairs, University of Georgia (U.S.A.)

Paul Wilkinson, Professor of International Relations and Chairman of the Advisory Board, Centre for the Study of Terrorism and Political Violence, University of St. Andrews (U.K.)

Members

Vice Admiral Arthur K. Cebrowski, USN (Ret.), former Director of Force Transformation, Office of the Secretary of Defense (U.S.A.)

Eliot A. Cohen, Robert E. Osgood Professor of Strategic Studies and Director, Philip Merrill Center for Strategic Studies, Paul H. Nitze School of Advanced International Studies, The Johns Hopkins University (U.S.A.)

Anthony H. Cordesman, Arleigh A. Burke Chair in Strategy, Center for Strategic and International Studies (U.S.A.)

Thérèse Delpech, Senior Research Fellow, CERI (Atomic Energy Commission), Paris (France)

Sir Michael Howard, former Professor of History of War, Oxford University, and Professor of Military and Naval History, Yale University (U.K.)

Lieutenant General Claudia J. Kennedy, USA (Ret.), former Deputy Chief of Staff for Intelligence, Headquarters, Department of the Army (U.S.A.)

Paul M. Kennedy, J. Richardson Dilworth Professor of History and Director, International Security Studies, Yale University (U.S.A.)

Robert J. O'Neill, former Chichele Professor of the History of War, All Souls College, Oxford University (Australia)

Jusuf Wanandi, co-founder and member, Board of Trustees, Centre for Strategic and International Studies (Indonesia)

Fareed Zakaria, Editor, Newsweek International (U.S.A.)

Mexico's Military on the Democratic Stage

Roderic Ai Camp

Foreword by Armand B. Peschard-Sverdrup

Published in cooperation with the Center for Strategic and International Studies, Washington, D.C.

PRAEGER SECURITY INTERNATIONAL
Westport, Connecticut • London

Library of Congress Cataloging-in-Publication Data

Camp, Roderic Ai
    Mexico's military on the democratic stage / Roderic Ai Camp; foreword by Armand B. Peschard-Sverdrup.
      p.   cm.
    Includes bibliographical references and index.
    ISBN 0-275-98810-4 (alk. paper)
    1. Mexico—Politics and government—1988– 2. Civil-military relations—Mexico—History—20th century. I. Title.
  F1236.C358 2005
  972.08'2—dc22   2005016705

British Library Cataloguing in Publication Data is available.

Copyright © 2005 by Roderic Ai Camp

All rights reserved. No portion of this book may be reproduced, by any process or technique, without the express written consent of the publisher.

Library of Congress Catalog Card Number: 2005016705
ISBN: 0-275-98810-4

First published in 2005

Praeger Security International, 88 Post Road West, Westport, CT 06881
An imprint of Greenwood Publishing Group, Inc.
www.praeger.com

Printed in the United States of America

The paper used in this book complies with the Permanent Paper Standard issued by the National Information Standards Organization (Z39.48–1984).

10 9 8 7 6 5 4 3 2 1

To the memory of Delal Baer,
Mexicanist and devoted mother.

Contents

Foreword by Armand B. Peschard-Sverdrup		ix
Preface		xvii
Acknowledgments		xxiii
1	Civil-Military Relations in a Democratic Mexico	1
2	Civil-Military Relations in Historical Context	15
3	The Sociology of Civil-Military Relations	43
4	Military-Civilian Interlocks, the Politicized Officer	73
5	Civilian Missions: Redefining Civil-Military Relations?	99
6	Citizen and Military Views of Civil-Military Relations	121
7	Educating the Officer Corps	149
8	Higher and Global Officer Education	173
9	Reaching the Top	205
10	Challenges to Civil-Military Relations in the 21st Century	245
Notes		277
Bibliographic Essay		335
Collective Biographical Data		351
Index		353

Foreword

In July 2000, Mexico experienced alternation of power in the office of the presidency. For the first time in over 70 years, an opposition party candidate captured the position. Leading up to that historic day, both the Mexican political elite and observers in the United States and elsewhere in the region were uncertain how the military would respond to the passing of the presidential sash from one party to another. The specific concern was whether the military would conduct itself in a professional, nonpartisan manner. The climate of uncertainty produced by the political transition was reinforced by the fact that one of the generals incoming President Vicente Fox had secretly met with prior to the election was reprimanded, stripped of his zone command, and reassigned to a desk job in the archives. The uncertainty with regard to the new relationship between civilian and political leadership was compounded by an immense lack of understanding of the Mexican military as an institution.

The 2000 presidential election brought with it an end to single party rule and the beginning of minority government. Mexico now faces the challenge of restructuring and refining a civil-military relationship molded by decades of authoritarian rule. In addition, there is the parallel challenge of adapting to the new global security environment brought on by the September 11 terrorist attacks in the United States and reinforced by the recent bombings in Madrid and London. Increasing emphasis has been placed on securing the border between Mexico and the United States. The Department of Homeland Security and the Pentagon have sought ways to engage the Mexican military in the fight to secure the border. Former Secretary of Homeland Security Tom Ridge met with Mexican Defense Secretary General Vega García in 2002. Chairman of the Joint Chiefs of Staff Richard Myers has taken an unprecedented number of trips to Mexico since 2001 in an attempt to cultivate a more robust military-to-military relationship. These efforts have, arguably, fallen short of expectations; Mexico's failure to understand its military extends to the military's relationship with the United States and other countries.

In *Mexico's Military on the Democratic Stage*, Roderic Ai Camp, a longtime student of the Mexican armed forces, has employed a wide variety of research methods to compile a uniquely comprehensive account of the development and direction of the Mexican military. Camp performed extensive field research, reviewed the latest published and unpublished works on the subject, conducted personal interviews with senior civilian government officials and high-ranking military officers, and leveraged Mexico's freedom of information act (*Ley Federal de Transparencia y Acceso a la Información Pública Gubernamental*) to obtain previously classified information. Camp's research is particularly impressive given the persistently closed and hermetic nature of the Mexican military.

Camp's analysis focuses on the evolution of civil-military relations in Mexico over the last century, placing emphasis on notable changes in the last decade and a half. His account provides the reader with a context to analyze the evolution of the Mexican armed forces in the new democratic political environment.

Mexico's Military on the Democratic Stage begins by examining the evolution of civil-military relations in Mexico during key presidencies in the late nineteenth and twentieth centuries. Camp analyzes the impact of the 31-year rule of President Porfirio Diaz (1876–1880 and 1984–1911) and the importance of the Mexican Revolution of 1910. He looks carefully at the post-revolutionary era and how it defined the military's development. He chronicles some of the specific measures that were adopted by Presidents Alvaro Obregón (1920–1924) and Plutarco Elias Calles (1924–1928) to distance the military from political activity. These measures were adopted not necessarily from a commitment to civilian supremacy but rather as a political survival tactic. Camp then focuses on the presidency of General Lázaro Cárdenas and his founding of the National Revolutionary Party (PNR). Cárdenas used the PNR as a vehicle to channel the military's political activity through a "monopolistic, state-controlled party." Camp also examines how, in 1938, Cárdenas further expanded the military's role in political affairs, renaming the PNR the Party of the Mexican Revolution (PRM) and formally incorporating the military into the government by naming it one of the party's four corporate sectors (the others were the labor, popular, and agrarian sectors). Despite this merger between the political party and the military,

Camp notes that Cárdenas's reforms also contributed to the development of military subordination to civilian authority.

Camp then addresses the role that President Manuel Ávila Camacho played in separating the military from politics and promoting Mexico's transition to civilian leadership. Ávila Camacho not only ordered the withdrawal of the military from the PRM at the beginning of his presidency, but also selected, for the first time in Mexican history, a civilian as the party's presidential candidate. President Miguel Alemán (1946–1952), in an effort to guarantee the military's loyalty to him, led a generational change within the military. Alemán purged the older, more politicized officers, promoted a new generation of officers, and created the presidential guard.

Camp offers a well-documented account of the government's decision-making process that led to the 1968 student massacre in Mexico City's Tlatelolco plaza. He also explores the communication between the political and military leadership. Although the events of Tlatelolco reaffirmed the military's subordination to civil authority, they also contributed to the military's perception of civilian fallibility. Camp notes that the incident had extensive repercussions on the way the military viewed civilian leadership, the way political leadership viewed the military, the way younger officers viewed older officers within the military, and the way society viewed the military.

Throughout the work, Camp's analysis places emphasis on the sociology of civil-military relations in Mexico, examining the role this variable played in fostering a military caste mentality. He tracks the generational changes that have occurred within the armed forces by differentiating three types of officers—the political-military officers, the "mustangs," and the regular career (orthodox professional) officers—and the influences each exerted within the institution. The political-military officers were the combat veterans of the Mexican Revolution of 1910, many of whom straddled careers in both the army and politics. Until the 1970s, these officers tended to restrict the rise of new generations of officers. The "mustangs" were predominantly from working class, rural backgrounds, rising from the enlisted ranks from the mid-1940s on. The regular career (orthodox professional) officers are the current generation of military leaders, born in the 1940s and educated at the *Heróico Colegio Militar,* the *Escuela Superior de Guerra* or the *Colegio de Defensa Nacional.* The sociological analysis of the interactions between these various castes is key to understanding how the military has evolved in the past century.

In Chapter 4, the book shifts its focus to an examination of the linkages between the military and society. Camp refers to these linkages as "military-civilian interlocks." He asserts that, over time, the Mexican civilian leadership employed different strategies to maintain equilibrium in civil-military relations. Even as governments pursued closer linkages with the armed forces, they were mindful of protecting their autonomous status. Some of the formal linkages developed included the incorporation of military leaders into national or state-level political positions and the expansion of the military's mission to include national security and other civilian-oriented responsibilities. Camp includes a table listing the political offices held by military officers between 1935 and 2004. The table illustrates the shift toward closer (but cautious) relations between the government and the armed forces. He also analyzes the informal linkages (such as family ties, educational backgrounds, and partisan politics) that have affected these "military-civilian interlocks." For example, he provides a fascinating historical account of how the relationship between the governing party and the military evolved from when the military was officially part of the government party (the PRM) to when the military was unofficially prevented from affiliating with any party other than the Institutional Revolutionary Party (PRI), the PRM's successor, to the election victory of Vicente Fox in 2000 and the possibility of having the military establish ties with various political parties.

In addition to the sociological and political influences explored in the early chapters, Camp highlights the changing mission of the armed forces as another key factor in the evolution of the civil-military relationship. Camp contends that the redefinition of the Mexican military's mission to adjust to the new national and international security context has been particularly consequential. He notes that, although the Mexican Constitution prohibits the military from performing any functions in peace time, the article has been violated since 1920 as the military has at various times performed a range of tasks traditionally associated with civilian actors (such as health education, medicine and dentistry, school and road construction, distribution of food supplies, and reforestation).

Despite the expansion of the military's role into civilian-oriented activities, Camp asserts that the greatest influence on the evolving mission of the Mexican military stemmed from its role as a guarantor of internal security. He cites numerous instances in which the military has been called upon to confront perceived threats to internal security. Examples include military involvement in suppressing the 1958–1959 railroad workers strike and the 1960 telephone and postal workers movement, in quelling the 1968 student movement in Mexico City, in the murder of guerrilla group leader Lucío Cabañas Barrientos in 1974, and in confronting the Zapatista rebellion in 1994. The increasingly dominant role of the Mexican military as a guarantor of national security was most recently exemplified in June 2005, when the military was ordered to assume law enforcement duties in the border city of Nuevo Laredo after the federal government temporarily relieved from duty hundreds of municipal police officers suspected of having ties to drug cartels.

Camp also looks at the increased role of the military in counter-narcotics efforts, noting that this is perhaps the most important "interlock" between the military and the political leadership. The justification for involving the armed forces in this particular mission has stemmed from the inability of civilian law enforcement agencies to adequately confront the problem, in large part due to the narco-corruption that has infiltrated federal, state, and municipal police. Concerns have been repeatedly raised over the possibility that exposing the military to the drug trade will make it susceptible to narco-corruption and compromise its institutional integrity. There is some evidence to justify these fears. In 1999, General Jesús Gutierrez Rebollo was found to be a drug czar and was implicated in narco-corruption. Camp concludes by noting that, while the expanded role of the military in counter-narcotics operations has strengthened its position in national security decision-making, the military's participation has remained subordinate to civilian control.

In Chapter 6, Camp examines the attitudes of the military toward society and vice versa. The principles of discipline, obedience, and loyalty that are instilled in the military's "socialization experience" have been extended to the civil-military relationship. With regard to civilian attitudes toward the armed forces, Camp points out that, despite notable cases of corruption and highly publicized examples of human rights abuses, Mexican society views the military favorably, and compared with other state institutions, downright positively. However, the respect most Mexicans have for the military stems partly from ignorance and fear. The decline in recent decades of civilian respect for civilian authorities has not transcended to the military; levels of respect for military authorities within the armed forces remain high. Camp makes the case that that the more heavily civilian leadership relies on the military to perform traditional civilian responsibilities, the greater legitimacy it gives the military and its mission, thus opening the door for an expanded role in the future.

Chapter 7 examines the evolution of career officer education and training because these are key to the military's professionalization and socialization and instrumental in forming military attitudes toward subordination to civilian rule. Camp compares the education of career officers at the various Mexican military academies with those of other countries in the hemisphere, including the prestigious United States military academy at West Point. He discusses the impact that education has had on career patterns, noting instances in which senior officers favored promoting graduates from their alma mater. He also offers a contrast between the education of career military officers and the education and training of Mexico's civilian political leadership.

In Chapter 8, Camp analyzes in more detail the higher and international education of the Mexican officer corps. Specifically, he examines officer formation at the *Escuela Superior de Guerra,* founded in 1932, and contrasts it with the *Colegio de Defensa Nacional,* founded in 1981. He considers such variables as the changing nature of the curriculums and the civil-military faculty ratio at each institution. Throughout the chapter, Camp draws parallels with the Mexican navy's *Centro de Estudios Superiores Navales,* founded in 1970. Camp notes that recent events (such as the disputed 1988 presidential election and the 1994 Chiapas uprising) have prompted the military to modify the structure and curriculum of the military's advanced educational system to include a broader range of subjects.

In recognition of the important role of military leadership in Mexican society and in the civil-military relationship, Camp devotes a significant amount of his research to an examination of the promotion process within the Mexican armed forces. Given that the appointment of senior command positions, including the Secretaries of Defense and Navy, is among the least-known aspects of the Mexican military, Camp's ninth chapter makes a significant contribution to the literature on this subject. In an attempt to determine the extent to which civilian political leadership—for example, a president—has influenced promotion processes, Camp looks carefully at all of the promotions to Colonel and General under each Mexican president since 1939. He examines all of the variables that are factored into the promotion process and then contrasts them as they apply to the two types of officers in the Mexican military: staff officers and troop commanders. While he finds civilian interference in the promotion process to be negligible, Camp provides examples of tensions that have surfaced within the military over cases of perceived favoritism and breach of typical promotion requirements. Camp concludes the chapter by cautioning readers about possible impacts of interservice rivalries between the navy and the army/air force. He points to the bold and progressive changes spearheaded by the navy since 2000 compared to only modest alterations in the army. Camp suggests it is only a matter of time before the Mexican congress and the media focus on the changes within the navy. He carefully notes the potential adverse impact this could have on the army's reputation in the civilian world.

After providing the reader with the necessary historical fundamentals to understand the Mexican armed forces, Camp examines the challenges to civil-military relations in the twenty-first century. He asserts that the performance of civilian democratic institutions may well be the most important variable in civil-military relations in the years ahead. The fact that, in February 2004, Mexican Secretary of Defense General Vega Garcia publicly called upon all political groups to negotiate their policy differences for the betterment of the nation seems evidence of this claim. Camp concedes, though, that these recent public statements may simply suggest the beginning of a newly defined civil-military relationship. Another factor in how the civil-military relationship will evolve in the coming years is the degree to which the military continues its tradition of isolation from civilian actors within the democratic setting. While some progress has been made toward a more open relationship since 1997, Camp recognizes that new ties and bridges will have to be forged through new relationships between representatives of the armed forces and members of the legislative and executive branches. He cautions that the lack of expertise on national security and military matters among civilian public officials remains a fundamental impediment to a more progressive civil-military relationship. Finally, Camp notes that the increasing role of the legislative branch in policymaking is also likely to alter the civil-military dynamic. Camp cites congressional oversight and appropriations procedures as mechanisms that will affect relations between the government and the military in the coming decades.

The approaching July 2006 presidential and congressional elections represent a critical juncture in civil-military relations in Mexico. Alternation of power in the executive branch will be accompanied by a generational change in the military and produce a large degree of uncertainty about the future of the civil-military relationship. The fact that a left-of-center candidate currently leads in the polls adds to this climate of uncertainty.

Civil-military relations in Mexico are a key variable in both the consolidation of Mexican democracy and in the ability of the United States to engage Mexico as an effective partner in confronting the security challenges of the twenty-first century. Thus, this book is required reading not only for those aspiring to the Mexican presidency or a seat in the Mexican congress, but also for U.S. policymakers with responsibility for U.S.-Mexico security and defense relations.

Armand B. Peschard-Sverdrup

Preface

A decade ago I published the first book-length work in English, and the first scholarly book in any language, on the contemporary role of the Mexican military.[1] Sadly, since that date, in spite of the extraordinary changes in the Mexican political setting, few serious contributions have emerged that attempt to assess the military's involvement in this dramatic transformation, the changes within the armed forces itself, or the implications both have for the civil-military relationship. Of all the leadership groups and all the institutions exercising political power in Mexico since the 1930s, none have been examined as sparsely as the armed forces. The present work, as distinct from the original, focuses precisely on the evolution of the civil-military relationship, emphasizing those themes that shed light on this relationship in a period of democratic transformation while providing a comprehensive revision of the substance, data, and arguments in the original work.[2]

The lack of attention paid to civil-military relations is remarkable considering the theoretical implications it offers as a case study of a Third World society that successfully limited the military's political involvement and established a longer reign of civilian supremacy than any other Third World country. In the context of the broader, comparative literature on military withdrawal, this neglect is unfortunate given the appraisal that generally "little has been published on a systematic, comparative basis."[3] A plethora of literature exists on civil-military relations for most individual Latin American countries, but Mexico continues to be ignored substantively and within the larger theoretical context of civil-military relations.[4]

The most recent comparative works on democracy and the Latin American military continue this neglectful pattern. More importantly, much of the theoretical literature in comparative politics generally, and civil-military relations specifically, draws on Western examples. This reinforces those biases in the theoretical literature, especially as it relates to civilian-military subordination issues.

I want it to be clearly understood that this work falls into a real world dynamic. Hopefully, it avoids forcing Mexico into an inappropriate, Western-built theoretical box.

Methodologically, the working hypotheses for this study were extracted from the general literature on civil-military relations, from Third World and Latin America case studies, and from my own work and that of others on the Mexican military in the 1970s, 1980s, and 1990s. The historical literature has been useful in producing valuable interpretations, but several other sources or approaches contribute to the overall thrust of this analysis. It is interesting that the literature on Latin America, with the exception of a few classic introductions to civil-military relations, excludes sociological studies of the U.S. armed forces, probably the best examined in the world. This is an unfortunate oversight. Although societally the United States has little in common with Mexico, remarkable similarities occur between any two military cultures, even in the broader context of civil-military relations. In particular, empirical examinations of officer values and origins are the most complete in the U.S. literature and, therefore, offer revealing comparative perspectives useful for this work.

Because the Mexican military erected obstacles to outside examination-obstacles which continue to the present-scholars resorted to different methodological approaches to acquire fresh data. This study focuses on the officer corps, specifically on the officers reaching the rank of two and three star generals (brigade and division generals in the Mexican Army), or their naval and air force equivalents. Such individuals exercise decision-making authority over the armed forces. Additionally, as Frank McCann suggests, officer generations are overlapping time lines that link the army to the past and project it into the future. Because such officers are on active duty the longest, they are the ones who give the institution direction and a sense of historical continuity. They set policy in the context of their accumulated professional experiences and intellectual baggage.[5] This linkage is further enhanced by the fact that Mexico's military leadership relies heavily on a mentoring process; most mentors of successful officers are themselves leading generals and admirals.[6]

A shifting pool of generals and national civilian politicians has largely determined the broader context of Mexican civil-military relations during recent decades, thus these two groups of leaders are compared and analyzed in some detail. The basis for some of these comparisons is collective biography. Collective biography provides only one element among this book's multiple resources. Collective biography also provides some original, empirical evidence in support of, and for disproving, certain assertions about the Mexican case.[7] Typically, prior analyses of the armed forces have focused on the army alone, but new more extensive data I have acquired on top naval and air force officers have made possible for the first time to introduce valuable *inter-service* comparisons. These comparisons are essential within the context of Mexico's democratic transformation since 2000, because the navy has instituted some radical changes in response to internal military criticisms and in recognition of the changing external societal setting. Theoretically, internal rivalries within and between services are among the most important explanations for military interventions in civilian politics.[8]

To facilitate increased attention on societal variables in civil-military relations, this book makes use of, also for the first time, general surveys of Mexican attitudes toward military intervention in politics. National poll results offer fresh significant insights into Mexican society. This book incorporates survey research on citizen attitudes towards political and other institutions, and the comparative position of the armed forces among those rated.

Finally, documentary evidence on internal military policies, especially in regard to promotion policies, is extracted from defense publications, Senate records, Presidential state of the union appendixes, official military web sites, the federal government transparency website, and the official army-air force magazine. Individual officer records shed considerable light on presidential policies toward promotion, affecting attitudes within the military with a potential for influencing civil-military relations. Similarly, frank political elite attitudes toward the broader relationship have been expressed publicly in the Senate *Memorias*, especially since 2000, as the Senate and Chamber of Deputies committees have taken their oversight responsibilities more seriously. These discussions reveal not only legislative attitudes toward the executive branch but the civilian political elite's views of the military.

The primary focus of this book is on civil-military relations over the last half century, but especially on notable changes in the 1990s and 2000s, as Mexico begins to transform itself into a functioning democracy. Mexico continues to provide a unique case study of the transformation of civil-military relations in a setting where military subordination was not the issue. The fundamental issue for Mexico is how pluralistic political institutions learn to interact with a state institution such as the armed forces, which has remained relatively closed and perpetuates, in many respects, a non-democratic internal institutional culture? In turn, an equally significant issue is how the armed forces makes the transition within a democratic setting when they have a long heritage of internal autonomy, despite subordinating themselves in general terms to civilian control? And finally, the theoretical importance of the Mexican case is how military subordination to civilian control continued under a semi-authoritarian model for decades, before democratic institutions took root.

This book was written to shed a penetrating light on the composition, experiences, background, and behavior of the officer corps, specifically the most influential generals and admirals, in Mexico. It also will provide—in many cases for the first time—fresh empirical data for testing claims and assumptions concerning civil-military relations. Finally, we hope to generate additional provocative hypotheses about the civil-military relationship generally and about such a relationship within the context of democratic transformation, as well as to raise theoretical questions that share some relevance to Third World experiences. Simultaneously, it is hoped that a more thorough understanding of consequences stemming from officer formation will provide convincing insights about the Mexican success story of military nonintervention in civilian politics.

Mexico is often cited in the literature as a key illustration of military subordination to civilian rule. Why, therefore, has the Mexican case been so neglected? Three decades ago, David Ronfeldt wrote, "the contemporary Mexican military may be the most difficult such institution to research in Latin America. Certainly it is the most difficult national institution to research in Mexico."[9] What is most remarkable about this statement is that in spite of the extraordinary political changes since 1994, this description still applies in the twenty-first century.

An important explanation for this void is the armed forces' intense desire to remain unexamined, indeed enigmatic. The Mexican military openly discourages analysts, domestic and foreign, from exploring its institutional behavior in the post-1946 era. Mexican scholars have paid it little attention because of the military's openly antagonistic attitude. Restricted access to historical archives has discouraged, even intimidated, scholars. Despite announcements to the contrary, scholars continue to experience difficulties after 2001. Indeed, James Smith, the former Mexico correspondent for the *Los Angeles Times*, noted that officials in the press department would not give their names, and that after months of faxing requests to speak to General Gerardo Clemente Vega García, Vicente Fox's secretary of national defense, Vega García told the reporter that "the only reason I am talking to you is that my president ordered me to do so."[10]

Mexico provides a unique example of a military leadership transforming itself into a civilian political elite, simultaneously transferring the basis of power from the army to a civil state. It accomplished this task in a nondemocratic setting. Importantly, the transfer of power occurred after a revolution, and regardless of how one classifies that particular revolution, similar upheavals have not occurred elsewhere, providing a unique historical context from which the Mexican pattern emerges. Some similarities can be found in the Chinese experience, where the role of a strong, centralized party allowed it to use the armed forces for extra-military missions while maintaining civilian control, which also had emerged originally from civilian, popular origins.[11]

Given the uniqueness of the Mexican case, it is fair to argue that the abundant literature on civil-military relations generally, and Latin American specifically, has little to offer. In some respects this assertion is true, because theorists largely have concerned themselves with authoritarian regimes where military-civil power is shared, or with more politically competitive societies where the military cyclically, if temporarily, involves itself directly in politics. Nevertheless, keeping in mind the many singular features of the Mexican case which suggests several valuable working hypotheses, it provides convincing theoretical arguments about military withdrawal from and military subordination to civil authority.

Acknowledgments

I benefited from the help of many colleagues in researching and writing the first version of this book on the Mexican military. A number of individuals assisted me in the ongoing research for this second book. They include General Gerardo Clemente Vega García, secretary of national defense 2000-2006, who answered questions frankly about his views of the armed forces and its role in Mexican society since the presidential election of 2000 and offered access to public information, and General Luis Garfias, who corrected a number of factual errors in the first book and provided numerous insights and differing interpretations on military matters. In the extensive revisions I undertook, I would like to thank Raúl Benitez Manaut for exchanging information with me. A number of reporters who cover military affairs in Mexico have been important and generous sources, including Jorge Luis Sierra, Hugo Martínez McNaught, Sam Dillon and James Smith. Finally, I would like to thank John Bailey and Sam Fitch for their careful and thoughtful criticisms of the manuscript, and Armand Peschard for bringing it to fruition.

CHAPTER ONE

Civil-Military Relations in a Democratic Mexico

A Revised Model of Mexican Civil-Military Relations

Recent analysts are correct in asserting that no single explanatory theory adequately interprets the removal of the Mexican military from direct participation in civilian politics, nor can it explain the predominant features of civil-military relations. The Mexican military has remained outside the civilian political arena for reasons that can be found in other cultures, but I will also argue that Mexico provides some original conditions uncommon to most other Third World societies. Among these is Mexico's extreme emphasis on subordination in officer-formation courses, incorporated in professionalization theory; the military's autonomy from civilian intervention in its *internal* affairs, notably promotion, an institutional theoretical argument; and the historic linkage provided by the "political-military" officer prior to the 1980s, an element of sociological civil-military relations theory.

Western intellectual tradition perceives the armed forces as apolitical and narrowly confined within their own institutional boundaries.[1] Sam Sarkesian, a leading theorist on civil-military relations, maintains that this view is misleading and that an equilibrium model is much more appropriate. This model, while imperfect, offers many qualities appropriate to the Mexican situation. "The requisites of a democratic ideology, it can be argued, do not provide for a separate subsystem removed from society. The legitimacy and credibility of any military system rests with its links to society and the reflection of basic social values," a basic perspective highly relevant to the Mexican setting.[2] A revised version of this view can be found in Douglas

Bland's "theory of shared responsibility," where he correctly suggests that "civil authorities are responsible and accountable for some aspects of control and military leaders are responsible and accountable for others."[3]

Given recent tensions between civilian leadership and the military, a number of authors sought to explore traditional civil-military theory emanating from the American experience. These appraisals are somewhat inconclusive, but they agree most on the weaknesses of earlier arguments, and on a somewhat rigid and therefore artificial division between military and civilian spheres.[4] The Sarkesian-Bland Model holds up well against recent criticisms.

This model is characterized by several important features. It is built upon the concept of interlocks, not only in personnel but values, between civil society and the military on one hand, and between the political leadership and the officer corps on the other. Their "partnership is an educational and socialization intermix, where values, morals, and ethics of military and civilian elites are congruent."[5] Scholars reinforce this argument for the democratic transformation in the 1990s, noting that civilian leaders must come to know enough about military affairs to gain sympathy for the military's professional requirements and perspectives.[6] This linkage raises an important dilemma in our analysis of Mexican political-military relations. The conventional wisdom has been that armed forces personnel, even in the industrialized world, have been isolated, suggesting that interrelationships between the officer corps and other members of society are infrequent and limited.

Our framework for analysis, which combines Bland's theory of shared responsibility with Sarkesian's original equilibrium model, can be described as a Modified Equilibrium Model, consisting of the following principles:

- Political actors or subsystems within a political model share the same values and agree upon the norms of behavior, while maintaining their own identity and integrity. The military and the larger society also share basic social values.

- Military and civilian leadership can be described as friendly adversaries who disagree with each other, but largely agree on the rules of the political game and the processes each will use in their interactions.

- Their relationship is asymmetrical, and the armed forces does not have a major role in determining the norms or boundaries of the political actors' power.

- Their relationship is dynamic, and does not envision isolation on the part of one actor from the other.

- Civil control of the military is managed and maintained through sharing of responsibility for control between civilian leaders and military officers. Civilian authorities are responsible and accountable for some aspects of control and military leaders are responsible and accountable for others.

- Regime differences between states are responsible for the particular national character of civil-military relations.
- Civilians outside of the military are the sole legitimate source for civil control of the military.

This model, as would be true of any other theory of civil-military relations, must address four fundamental responsibilities in the hands of civil authorities:

- To curb the military's political power and to manage civil-military relations once that power has been curbed
- To ensure that the military behaves without threatening society's interests
- To protect the armed forces from civilian politicians who might use their influence for partisan interests
- To figure out a way to obtain expertise on the armed forces without relying solely on the military.[7]

Within this modified framework I have developed working hypotheses that speculate about these issues, and test the broader principles of the revised model. The explanations most theorists have considered fall into two broad categories: the culture of the military, and the values or ideology society conveys about the military's role. I would add a third category: the views of leading politicians toward civil-military affairs. Given the political dominance by a small group of civilian leaders until 2000, this category takes on added importance. The intermixture of these three broad categories is likely to determine the fundamental qualities of civil-military relations. Historical experiences, institutional characteristics, structural patterns, and informal and formal behavior also condition the relationship.

Regime differences between states are responsible for the national character of civil-military relations. The most unusual circumstance from the Mexican perspective contributing to a different civil-military relationship is that contemporary Mexico is the product of a major social upheaval that occurred between 1910 and 1920. No analyst can understand Mexican society and attitudes without understanding the Mexican Revolution of 1910's impact. As I have argued elsewhere, it might be suggested that the military did not withdraw from politics in the 1930s and 1940s; rather, the post-revolutionary military had never, in the true sense of the word, intervened in political affairs in the first place. In the context of civil-military relations, the Revolution did not produce military intervention as traditionally understood but, instead, a civilian-grown army defeated the established military.

Violence became the only means through which the post-1910 generation of civilian leaders could express disagreement with established political authorities. Force developed into an essential tool of political life. The institutionalized military, the Federal Army, only briefly sustained its supremacy in the exercise of force once it came under the direction of a new civilian political leadership in 1912 (against a rebellion by a former revolutionary), and at the head of a coup against elected civilian authorities in 1913-1914. Those most politically skilled were not the Federal Army officer corps, nor its civilian political representatives, but leaders extracted from opposing popular forces. After 1920 forces loyal to victorious revolutionaries, having popular roots, put down rebellions by dissident peers vying for political control.

The point of my argument is that an army of *civilian* origin defeated an established, state-supported army, and, after 1920, *both* political and military leaders in Mexico shared revolutionary experiences. I hypothesize that this shared experience is the first of several variables that help explain the origins of civil-military relations in contemporary Mexico. This extraordinary experience also explains another component of the model: a set of shared values between civilian and military leadership. The fact that both Mexico's officer corps and its political leadership originate from a major revolutionary upheaval has several crucial implications. The first consequence is more exaggerated but offers certain similarities to the large-scale influx of "civilian officers" in the U.S. Army, notably during wartime, especially in World War II. The presence of civilian influence in the officer corps affects internal, hard core "professional" military values, certainly those attitudes involving civil-military relations.

The distinction between a revolutionary versus a regular army is extremely important because "such armies tend to incorporate every active element of a nation including many which are usually regarded as the antithesis of the regular soldier, such as the intellectual, the author and the politician."[8] Mexico's experience easily illustrates this argument. Not only did its most important politicians from 1920 through 1946 share this revolutionary background but so did many other leading figures, including novelist Martín Luis Guzmán and muralist David Alfaro Siqueiros.[9]

While similar patterns have occurred in other societies characterized by social revolution, such as China, in many other respects these cases are not comparable. For example, the Chinese borrowed an external ideology, one relying on a philosophy of authoritarian, civil control, institutionalizing civilian dominance through the *presence of political cadres* in the armed forces. Civil party political socialization became all-encompassing in the Chinese case, as did the overwhelming influence of a single, messianic leader.

Some scholars have argued that the essential explanatory variable for long-term military disengagement in a Third World culture is a social revolution and the rise of a coalition of classes.[10] It is true that social upheaval opens up political debate in a society, but it does not necessarily lead to elimination of any particular political practice unless a consensus develops to alter traditional political behavior. Brian Loveman convincingly demonstrates this fact in the persistence of legal and political impediments to consolidating democratic control in Latin America.[11] There is no question that militarism as a tradition feeds on itself.[12] This is only logical; political behavior is learned. The more the military has intervened, the more it is likely to intervene at some future point no matter what changes occur in the political arena. Unless a consensus emerges among military *and* political leaders to withdraw the use of force as a legitimate political tool (as occurred in Mexico) and eliminate the officer corps as a skilled political actor, permanent military withdrawal from political life is not likely.[13]

The Mexican Revolution produced a coterie of leaders who took charge of the government, although not without serious, almost victorious challenges from their dissenting revolutionary peers in the 1920s. Their very defense of that power led them, by 1928, to see the necessity of de-legitimizing military intervention, and to introduce some political and structural means for accomplishing that goal. A hypothesis is that the Revolution produced a coalition of groups that eventually evolved a revolutionary ideology or rhetoric that included the concept of military subordination to a central, civilian political leadership. This pattern marked the beginning of civilian and military actors evolving similar norms of behavior, a fundamental principle of our model.

I argue that many Mexicans, political leaders included, were favorably inclined toward such an attitude, not because of some philosophical or morally superior argument that civilian was preferable to military leadership, but because shared personal experiences with the tragic consequences of violence were deeply impressed on a generation. As I discovered from extensive interviews twenty years ago, "The most striking universal belief among the Mexican political leaders, a belief which refers to means rather than ends, is an almost universal emphasis on peace and order . . . when it comes to peace and order, the environment created by the Revolution is preeminent."[14] Thus, Mexican leadership sought a way to reestablish permanent order and peace without further resort to violence. The Revolution was critical to civil-military relations. It facilitated new leadership choices and, more important, made the desire for peace preeminent among leaders and the population generally.[15]

Prominent theorists have suggested that societal sources are one of two important categories in explaining civil-military relations, at least in terms of military political intervention. In the case of Latin America, the actual examination of societal, as distinct from elite, values concerning military political involvement, is practically negligible.[16] Some scholars, such as Sam Fitch, are only just beginning to cite newspaper polls about citizen preferences for a military government.[17] As a consequence of this void, the relevance of societal values is strongly suspected but little empirical evidence has been collected.

Underlying the first principle of the Modified Equilibrium Model is the extent of the linkage between society and the armed forces. I offer an additional hypothesis that argues that the most influential and the least examined variable is the level of permanent, societal support for the pillars of civil-military relations. It is impossible for any society, whether it maintains a more democratic or more authoritarian model, to achieve civilian control of the military if the average citizen believes the military should govern. Even in the United States, confidence in the armed forces as an institution declines with the level of contact civilians share with the military, as measured by their own military service.[18] With the assistance of survey research, citizen values concerning military intervention, confidence in the military as a state institution, and preferences for authoritarianism versus democracy will be explicitly developed in the Mexican case, and will be shown to have significant consequences for explaining the present civil-military relationship.[19]

For civilian leaders to maintain superiority in their relationship with the armed forces, and for the military to refrain from political intervention, another condition is necessary. That critical condition is what Alfred Stepan identified as a "political led strategy toward the military."[20] That strategy conforms to Bland's principle of shared responsibility in our model. Such a strategy, to be successful, requires that the chief executive's political powers as a leader be directed toward winning professional allies within the military establishment. The 1910 Revolution produced an unusual blend of military leaders with political skills. These post-revolutionary leaders skillfully executed such a philosophy, opening up the officer corps, and subsequently the rank of general, to men who would give their loyalty to the secretary of defense, to the president, and ultimately to the state. In effect, both civil and military leadership after 1929 agreed on the rules of the political game, another fundamental principle of our model, and developed processes by which they could interact with each other. Several presidents partially reversed the civilian strategy reinforcing military subordination to civilian rule, but overall Mexican leadership is remarkable for the level of consistency that it maintained in its civil-military patterns for seven decades, including under President Vicente Fox (2000–2006).

The specific strategy worked out by the civilian political leadership seems to be characterized by two other conditions: praise for the military and skillful patience. Throughout the evolutionary stages, during which the political leadership builds up gradual but firm support for civilian supremacy, it must constantly praise the military. As one major theorist argues, Mexico, as well as the more tenuous cases of Colombia and Venezuela, suggest the importance of honoring the military's individual, corporate, and ideological interests.[21] President Fox, well into the consolidation phase of Mexico's democracy, continues to emulate his predecessors in content and tone when he comments publicly about the armed forces and their loyalty to the government. The second condition, based on analyses of the Turkish and Mexican cases, is that the political-military leader must have the skill and the patience to pursue a slow, gradual, and protracted process to disentangle the armed forces from politics.[22]

The revolutionary origins of Mexico's post-1920s army has led observers to believe that the leaders successfully avoided dividing the military and political leadership into two disparate groups, especially in terms of class origin and values. As we have noted in the Modified Equilibrium Model, their relationship is dynamic. A hypothesis which might explain the ability of a society to both effect and sustain military nonintervention in politics is the elimination or prevention of a caste mentality on the part of the officer corps. C. Wright Mills first suggested this argument in terms of the social homogeneity of leadership, whether it be economic, intellectual, military, or political.[23] My own recent work demonstrates such a pattern among Mexican civilian politicians in the 1990s.[24]

Major historical evaluations of the Mexican case have accepted Mills' theory, arguing that the "middle-of-the-road governments of the past quarter century have been in tune with the social philosophy of the officer class."[25] Whether one can ascribe similar values and ideology to a leadership's shared social background is open to debate. In fact, except for the 1920s and 1930s, civilian politicians and the officer corps do not share the same social background. Nevertheless, this book provides some empirical comparisons of the highest ranks in the officer corps with top civilian politicians, examining the potential consequences of differences in background and the extent of their interlocks.[26] The Revolution itself provides the foundation for bridging these two elites because it has been assumed that both had firsthand revolutionary experience. It is convincing that the experience helped create a shared sense of legitimacy essential to the inculcation and acceptance of the doctrine of civilian supremacy.[27]

To a certain extent, the Mexican military has created its own version of a caste image, one reflected in its aggressive posture against probing examinations of its institutional characteristics and leadership. An extreme example of this is that in 1989, in an attempt to shut itself off from the prying eyes of outsiders, the military stopped distributing its official journal to the Library of Congress, the University of Texas, and the Colegio de México.[28] Their posture generally has led to social isolation, not only from the average Mexican but also from other elite groups, few of who know anything about the armed forces or can personally call a high ranking officer a close friend. Such patterns result in isolation, which contradicts our model's principles.

Scholars complain that a weakness among Latin American civilian cultures is their failure to incorporate military sociology and strategy into educational curricula. People in the areas of communications and politics should be knowledgeable about all aspects of military life because they are indispensable to military oversight, especially in the legislative branch. One author noted that the lack of interest in and preparation by individual members of congress about the Colombian armed forces as an institution of democratic governance is incredible given the military's deep and constant presence in so many facets of the country's life.[29]

Legislative oversight and increased expertise are critical variables if Mexico is to bring the armed forces into the twenty-first century and modernize the present civil-military relationship within a democratic context. Indeed, a number of Latin American defense secretaries told the U.S. secretary of defense that their greatest problem in gaining control of their ministries and the armed forces was the dearth of qualified civilian defense specialists.[30] This dearth makes the principle of civilians being responsible for civilian control—a principle of our civil-military relations model—more difficult to implement in a democratic Mexico. Prior to 2000, an attempt to carry out oversight by an independent congress might, in some respects, have threatened rather than strengthened one of the foundations of Mexican civilian supremacy.

Civilian leadership sets the basic parameters of Mexican military activity, including budget and size. The military, on the other hand, decides its own internal policies without civilian scrutiny. Interestingly, civilians have refrained from institutionalizing military studies throughout the civilian educational system, including university and graduate programs, while the military, at its most advanced levels, has recently allowed a highly select group of civilians to study within its ranks.

A hypothesis offering insight into the Mexican case is that, in pursuit of a political strategy, the political leadership created a rock-solid government party, providing the fundamental foundation for an intergenerational pool of civilian leaders from 1929 to 2000. This party was the institutional source of the asymmetrical relationship between civilian and military actors in the political arena. In the eyes of some historians, the strength and persistence of this civil institution alone has been a critical variable in sustaining civilian supremacy and maintaining the parameters of its civil-military relationship. This thesis is supported in this work.[31] The existence of a strong party and an executive branch bureaucracy reflects the larger theoretical argument that the inclination to intervene results from a lack of strong political institutions.[32] Scholars have made a similar argument in their analysis of Cuba since 1959, suggesting the party's importance in cementing an interlocking relationship between the military and civilian leadership.[33]

Huntington asserted that maximizing civilian power over governmental institutions as a means of maintaining control over the military offers limited effectiveness because civilians generally compete for power among themselves.[34] Mexico, however, gradually eliminated civilian competition, confining it to a monopolistic political leadership associated with the government party. An often neglected dimension of civil-military relations "concerns protecting the armed forces from political partisanship."[35] Naturally, the recent revival of democratic electoral competition has not only altered political behavior between the state and its political opposition, but also opened the possibility for changes in civil-military relations, an area where previously identifiable and strong open civilian divisions were rare.

Since 1997, Mexico has produced three national legislative sessions characterized by party pluralism, but this has not led to significant divisions in civilian attitudes toward the armed forces. Political pluralism has led to more open and heated discussions of military missions, internal military policies, and congress' own role toward the military, especially in the print media. This pluralism is creating the potential for deeper civilian political fissures, and, consequently, military alliances with differing civilian factions. The most likely of these divisions revolves around past human rights abuses in the 1970s.[36]

Mexico has been fortunate during the past sixty years; military officers in pursuit of political ambitions have not really been given the opportunity to make the distinction between loyalty to a government and loyalty to a nation. When such distinctions occur, the officer corps begins "to invent [its] own private notion of the national interest, and from this it is only a skip to the constrained substitution of this view for that of the civilian government."[37] Indeed, Mexican political leadership has engaged in a persistent effort to establish within its own ranks and among co-opted groups that loyalty to it is tantamount to loyalty to the state and to the nation. That leadership has been quick to accuse dissidents of any ideological stripe of treason, as if it alone had a monopoly on political loyalty. That feature of Mexican politics began to disappear under Ernesto Zedillo's administration (1994–2000), with heavy opposition representation in Congress, and disappeared altogether with Fox's electoral victory in 2000. The armed forces transferred their loyalty and subordination from one administration to another, having given it clearly to state institutions, not to parties or politicians per se. National defense secretaries publicly suggested prior to the 1994 and the 2000 presidential elections that they would support any party that won a fair election.[38]

The importance of professionalism provides the basis for an influential hypothesis in the Mexican case. In the literature on the potential for military intervention and withdrawal, especially in the case of Latin America, probably no single explanatory variable has received more attention than military professionalism. Professionalism would make the military a tool of the state, keeping it out of politics by granting it a certain amount of autonomy.[39] The shared responsibility premise, under which civilians and the military manage the relationship, grants the officer corps responsibility and accountability for some aspects of its behavior.

Protecting the military's autonomy from prying civilian eyes has been carried to an extreme in Mexico, but there is no question that such autonomy played a fundamental role in the stability of the civil-military relationship, as it does elsewhere.[40] While military autonomy may have been a strength in the evolution of civilian control of the armed forces, under a democratic model military autonomy could become a serious defect.

The most critical elements in the more traditional definition of professionalism—developing an institutional sense of identity and behavior—are the level of discipline conveyed in the officer's socialization process and the common agreement as to whom subordination is ultimately directed. Mexico has one of the highest levels of military discipline in the Third World. The military-imposed discipline in the Mexican academies and war colleges facilitated the formation of a homogeneous, obedient officer corps that shares an extreme sense of loyalty to superior authority, including that of the president.[41]

Ultimately, the quality of professionalism within the officer corps depends largely on their own self-perception.[42] Their self-perception has not included a desire for political power. Rather, their self-perception has included recognition of the officer corps' vital role in preserving internal order and defending national sovereignty. Officers also want their profession to be respected by citizens and politicians.[43] Long-term disengagement from politics requires officers to have favorable views of their appropriate roles and the actions of civilian politicians.[44] Civilians, of course, need to share similar views. Attitudes towards civil-military relations are transferred from one generation to the next within the political elite and the officer corps, becoming embedded in their respective institutional cultures.[45]

Professionalism, defined in terms of developing a strong sense of corporate identity and skills and knowledge about the area of expertise, does not preclude, as has been so clearly demonstrated, intervention by the military. In fact, professionalism may encourage intervention. If the military feels more competent than others to judge its internal characteristics, such as size, recruitment, and equipment, that predilection may bring it into competition with civilian authorities.

In earlier arguments about elimination of a caste mentality among the officer corps, the importance of a certain level of autonomy within the military was suggested. In Mexico, the lack of competitive opposition traditionally protected the military from civilian political intervention. An important hypothesis that the Mexican case appears to illustrate is that civilian leadership made a special attempt to refrain from interfering in what might be truly deemed "internal" military matters, such as promotion, discipline, and assignments.[46]

A significant working hypothesis posits the view that civilian interference in "internal" military matters prompts military political involvement in civilian arenas. This variable can be empirically tested to some degree. An examination of promotion records affords some important insights into one fundamental aspect of civil-military relations. It is possible to argue that military autonomy may have favored long term military subordination to civilian control.

The most unusual hypothesis emerging from the Mexican case, even more significant than the initial revolutionary origins of civil-military groups, is the controversial interpretation that the key to nonintervention "is to keep the army involved in politics. The military may become involved anyway, so individual officers might be encouraged (or at least permitted) to run for political office."[47] This argument implies that formal military involvement in politics has many positive consequences, including a bridge between political-military leaders, eliminating the ambitions of politically motivated officers, and limiting but maintaining a direct military presence in political leadership. Similarly, the Chinese purposely integrated retired military officers into important party posts.[48] Military representation in politics was extremely important as an explanatory variable in the transitional stages through the 1970s. This historic pattern did assist in the transformation of military *participation* in politics to military *influence* in politics.[49]

Another hypothesis—one that might be offered more appropriately as an explanation for the reintroduction of the military into politics rather than sustaining its exclusion from politics—is the military's importance to national security. Contemporary military power, according to one theorist, is centered largely on the military's ability to establish itself at the apex of the national security structure.[50] In Mexico, the military has always been part of the national security formula. However, a strong argument can be made that since the 1980s internal security issues in Mexico have multiplied, exacerbated by drugs, crime, and guerrillas, and that the military, called on to combat the more overt manifestations, has increased its presence in internal political matters.

The military's expanded role has contributed to a reformulation of its responsibilities politically and in the decision-making process; recent events have expanded its established position in civil-military relations, especially after the September 11, 2001 terrorist attacks.[51] Our model allows for changing roles, while simultaneously maintaining the superior position of civilian decision-makers. Civilian control is the ultimate determinant in the relationship. Although the assignment of non-military roles to the armed forces may produce some adverse effects, ultimately the crucial variable is who makes those decisions.[52]

One of the most important internal conditions, one which exerts an influential impact on civil-military relations, is the level of military factionalism. This hypotheses is not directly addressed in our model, unless one considers it to be included in the principle of maintaining institutional integrity. The hypothesis posits that factionalism is a characteristic of the armed forces that can lead to military alliances with civilian politicians and intervention in civilian affairs. Such fissures within the armed forces are composed of two broad categories. One typical pattern in South America focuses on differences between services, usually the army and the navy. The second pattern, much more relevant to the Mexican case, are factions which might emerge within a given service, most significantly in the army. As some authors have noted, these divisions take on the greatest importance during times of political crisis.[53]

The argument can also be made that during a democratic transition, when citizens typically express tenuous attitudes toward the legitimacy of such political models, the crisis explanation also applies.[54] We can obtain numerous insights regarding the level of dissatisfaction with internal structures and processes by assessing the self-criticisms which emerged in an Army/Air Force internal document in June 1995.[55] This document, which appeared in the press, highlighted such issues as overcentralized command, educational inadequacies, hiring civilians, addressing promotion processes, developing special forces, and improving public relations.

Lastly, a final hypothesis can be generated from the argument that international variables have exercised an influential impact on civil-military relations in Third World countries.[56] The proximity of the United States to Mexico has undoubtedly influenced Mexico's stability, the characteristics of its political model, its continuity, and its pattern of civil-military relations. In the Mexican case, at least until the 1990s, external explanations play a secondary role to internal variables.[57] For most of the history of recent civil-military relations in Latin America, the presence of the Cold War and then the subsequent demise of communism served as significant contextual variables.[58] These conditions have had some impact on Mexico, but much less so than elsewhere in the region because the Mexican armed forces maintained its distance from the American military. Mexican nationalism largely limited, but did not completely eliminate, these influences.

The United States may have exercised much greater influence indirectly. Over the long term, the U.S. military served as the most prevalent source of professional training as well as an intellectual source of foreign military textbooks. Therefore, the degree to which the United States helped mold the attitudes of the officer corps, and specifically attitudes toward appropriate missions and civilian supremacy, are critical sources of professional socialization worth exploring.[59] Finally, the United States is both the source of Mexico's number one national security problem, drug trafficking, as well as the strongest voice pushing the civilian leadership to assign the anti-drug trafficking mission to the armed forces. This will have numerous, influential consequences on Mexico's civil-military relations. In the most general terms, the democratic transformation itself, which potentially has forced changes in the civil-military relationship, cannot be understood without examining the presence of U.S. actors. International support for democracy is "not inconsequential."[60]

Each of the following chapters will examine one or more of these hypotheses, testing their validity in the Mexican context and drawing on comparative data from Latin American and United States case studies to explore their relevance to the Modified Equilibrium Model. Does this model provide an accurate picture of contemporary civil-military relations in Mexico? Some principles offer more explanatory power for Mexico than others. Certain hypotheses are extremely useful in understanding the past behavior of the officer corps and civil-military relations in general, rather than the contemporary scene.

Having approached a stage of democratic consolidation since 2000, Mexico now faces new challenges in restructuring and refining a relationship molded under an authoritarian regime. Among other topics, subsequent chapters explore the historical patterns in civil-military relations under successive presidents, the interlocks between civilian and military elites, the trends within the military leadership among all the services since 1946, the values and prestige of the officer corps through civilian and military eyes, the role of education and socialization in the military, domestic and foreign; the background of the officer corps and its consequences for civil-military relations; and global influences on the officer corps and the civil-military relationship. The final chapter provides speculative interpretations of the importance of some working hypotheses in understanding Mexico's military today in the dynamic context of altered political relationships characteristic of a neophyte, democratic polity, and the possible direction of civil-military relations further into the twenty-first century.

CHAPTER TWO

Civil-Military Relations in Historical Context

A country's historical setting sheds considerable light on existing political relationships. This is especially true for Mexico's civil-military patterns because modern Mexico is a product of one of the world's great social revolutions. All of the influential characteristics of Mexico's civil-military relationship since the 1920s are affected by Mexico's historical circumstances. Two influential themes stand out in the following analysis of presidential administrations and their posture toward the relationship.

First, unlike most of its counterparts in Latin America or the Third World, Mexico's social revolution created a unique setting in which civilian and military goals were wedded together within the larger context of a post-revolutionary social and political ideology.[1] Two preeminent features of this civilian-military collaboration are the establishment of a constitutional culture of civilian supremacy, gradually introduced in the 1920s and 1930s and firmly maintained since the mid-1940s; and the rare situation where political-military figures produced in the heart of the Revolution firmly push the state into the hands of civilian professional politicians.

From a comparative theoretical perspective, the second hallmark of Mexico's historical experience is the emergence of a strong, civilian organization, the National Revolutionary Party.[2] The party solidly integrated civilian and military leadership in the post-revolutionary decades, creating a strong, authoritarian state.

Rather than merely highlighting the general findings of the historical literature as a prelude to my analysis of the officer corps and civil-military relations in recent years, it is worthwhile to identify and evaluate the significance of selected presidential policies that contributed to the military's withdrawal from the decision-making arena, and its gradual subordination to civilian authority, changes which continue in the democratic era since 2000. These policies are crucial in explaining Mexican civil-military relations because they formed citizen attitudes as well as the attitudes of civilian and military leadership toward such relationships. The current officer corps and political leadership views on civil-military relations, like church-state relations, is a product of years of historical experience and interaction.

The nature of civil-military relations and the evils attributed to direct military participation in politics are generally associated with Porfirio Díaz (1884–1910). Like many post-1920 presidents, Díaz was a military officer. There is no question that Díaz and his collaborators used the Plan de Tuxtepec rebellion of 1876 to destroy the tenuous civilian control and legitimacy represented by Benito Juárez and his successor, Sebastián Lerdo de Tejada. Díaz had long harbored political ambitions for the presidency. When his political machinations failed, he resorted to the force of arms, instead of the ballot box, to achieve power.

Díaz contributed to the heritage of Mexican civil-military relations in several influential ways. He set back the possible evolution of civilian supremacy by at least half a century, although it is doubtful whether any single civilian politician possessed the skills and charisma to lead the polity in 1876 without resorting to violence. When Díaz arrived in the presidency, it was only natural that he brought some comrades in arms into the cabinet. Of all the politicians who served in Díaz's administrations from 1884 through 1910 who were of age to have participated in combat in the 19th century, 83 percent fought in one or more of the three major conflicts: the North American invasion of 1846–1848, the Liberal Conservative conflicts of the 1850s and 1860s, and the French Intervention from 1862 to 1867. Among the politicians in Porfirio Díaz's own generation (born between 1820 and 1839), two thirds fought against the North Americans. An even higher percentage (78 percent) fought in the French intervention.[3]

By incorporating large numbers of battle-hardened officers directly into politics, Díaz legitimized the military's political role and its supremacy over civilian leadership and over the rule of law. He contributed to the gradual strengthening of the presidency and the national executive branch.[4] These features of the Díaz era are well known and frequently discussed. What is less understood is that, over time, Díaz contributed to the expansion of civilian leadership at the national political level. His presidency reveals a gradual but persistent decline in career military backgrounds among his most influential collaborators. By the early twentieth century, prominent military figures were only a small minority among influential Mexican politicians. This pattern presages a similar decline in the 1920s and 1930s after the Mexican revolution.

The evidence suggests that Díaz selected individuals personally loyal to him on the basis of shared career experiences. Initially, these were combat-related experiences. However, politics relatively quickly became essentially a civilian occupation, and civilians ultimately constituted the lion's share of its practitioners. By 1910, only a fourth of his collaborators were career officers. This historical pattern suggests that, in Mexico and elsewhere, the military does not have sufficient human resources to provide continuous political leadership over time. Nor do military leaders themselves, even when firmly in control of political institutions, necessarily continue recruiting from military ranks to fill important political offices.[5]

The rapid decline of an overt military presence among Mexico's political leadership does not necessarily signify a decrease in the military's decision-making influence. On the other hand, it does indicate three important characteristics of the civil-military relationship. First, in Mexico and elsewhere, military officers must form an alliance with civilian sympathizers who have the skills and the inclination to be politically active. This was the case, for example, in Chile, Brazil, and Argentina in the 1970s and 1980s.

Second, physically removing the military from political office is a first step in conveying to the population, the political leadership, and the officer corps itself, that the political arena is the purview of civilians.

Third, Díaz created a large core of civilian loyalists to fill his top offices, men who had spent most of their lives in public office. In the context of the nineteenth century, it might be possible to describe this group of Mexicans as harbingers of "professional" politicians. These individuals understood that their successful pursuit of that career depended exclusively on their relationship to Porfirio Díaz.

Simultaneously, Díaz in his own way, began to professionalize the officer corps. By 1900, many of its top leaders were Colegio Militar graduates, and developing the beginnings of their own corporate identity. Their acquisition of a separate identity, regardless of whether or not it included subordination to civilian control, meant that Díaz initiated what others might consider a caste mentality, a characteristic which continues to affect civil-military relations in Mexico in the twenty-first century.

The composition of Mexico's political leadership and the civil-military relationship were altered by the rebellion of 1910 followed by full-scale violence in 1913. Francisco Madero (1911–1913), a civilian revolutionary who briefly replaced the Porfiriato leadership, ultimately contributed to this change. First, Madero legitimized a civilian presidency, the first since 1876. Second, a central theme of Madero's political platform attacked militarism. Later revolutionaries wanting civilian control over the political system could cite both Madero's leadership and his platform.[6]

Some lower-ranking Federal Army officers, sympathetic to the Revolution, joined forces with one of several popular armies, but those who did so and rose to senior rank after 1920 were exceptional. By 1920 most senior officers in the Federal Army had retired, died in combat, or been placed on inactive status. Elements of the victorious Constitutional Army replaced the establishment officer corps. Because presidential leadership from December 1920 to December 1946, with one exception, was military, the Revolution established the dominance of military leadership, albeit a type of leadership different from that of the Porfiriato; this military leadership boasted popular roots similar to those of its civilian counterpart.

By reintroducing military officers in large numbers from the president on down to political positions, the post revolutionary leadership not only established firm control of the decision-making apparatus but also once again legitimized for all Mexicans the military's direct role in politics. This post revolutionary heritage, constructed on the foundation Díaz introduced in his own rise to power, created a barrier to the goal of civilian supremacy later presidents hoped to achieve.

The Revolution also provided an additional critical ingredient to this proven formula: a desire for a lasting peace. Governments after 1920, like governments after 1871, had the advantage of a populace accepting of certain political deficiencies in return for domestic tranquility and stability.[7] The Revolution had claimed the lives of nearly a tenth of all Mexicans, a decimation that rendered the survivors especially sensitive to instability and violence. Even through the 1960s civilian governance justified its compromises and relationships, in part, as efforts to avoid violent confrontation.[8]

Post-Revolutionary Era of Civil-Military Relations

Immediately upon General Alvaro Obregón's accession to the presidency in 1920, he, like Díaz, began to recruit skilled civilians with college degrees for his cabinet. At the same time he tried further to limit overt military political activity, not necessarily because he believed in civilian supremacy but because the practicalities of remaining in power called for this strategy. Obregón made repeated attempts, mostly futile, to restrict officers to their military missions, ordering troop commanders not to talk to opposition politicians. Those who disobeyed were cashiered from the army. Obregón not only resorted to political blackmail and censorship but applied restraints from a more institutional angle. He improved upon Díaz's tried-and-tested procedure of circulating zone commanders (then called chief of military operations) when, in early 1923, he expanded the number of zones from twenty to thirty-five. He publicly justified decentralization by saying that, because rebels and bandits were under control, large troop concentrations were no longer required. His real reason was to further fragment sizeable, regional military commands, thus reducing challenges to the national government.[9]

President Plutarco Elias Calles (1924–1928), as he did in so many other areas of Mexican political life, introduced the most important changes to civil-military relations. He used a reconstituted Colegio Militar, which had reopened in 1920, to produce a generation of professionally trained officers and instituted important procedural changes to facilitate that policy.[10] In 1926 he passed a promotions law, ending some of the irregularities that had prevailed since 1910, including eliminating individuals promoted at the whim of a superior officer. Professional training and competitive examinations now determined advancement in the lower ranks.[11] Calles also reinforced Obregón's policies regarding officer behavior, penalizing officers sympathetic to the opposition, using the two service journals to denounce their political ambitions, and cashiering or transferring suspected opposition partisans.[12]

Most important, two months after General Obregón's assassination as president-elect, in September 1928, Calles told assembled leading generals that no army officer should become either provisional or permanent president because this would not only give the people an unfavorable impression of the army but would also split the army into rival factions, leading to violence. Instead, Calles suggested, the army and the Congress would make the final selection, agreeing beforehand on a candidate.[13] They chose Emilio Portes Gil, a lawyer, as interim president. His successor in 1929, Pascual Ortiz Rubio, although an officer of the rank of general in the latter years of the Revolution, had not been on active duty since 1920. Thus, for brief periods, 1928–1929 and 1929–1932, Calles, an important military figure, reintroduced governing through civilian leadership.

Many of Mexico's most important generals continued to hold influential political posts during the 1928–1934 period, but they did not use their power to unduly enhance the army's institutional interests. On the contrary, they recognized its contribution as larger than necessary.[14] Also, many prominent military leaders were thinking of their own political and personal interests rather than the military's interests as a corporate body. It was the younger, newly trained officers who, for the most part, developed a sense of institutional loyalty, in the same way that civilian politicians developed a similar sense of institutional loyalty to party and state. Nevertheless, the political-military officers, of whom Calles, General Lázaro Cárdenas, and lesser military lights were representative, made the switch to civilian supremacy possible by identifying themselves with the new civilian-dominated political leadership.

It cannot be overly stressed that Mexico's political-military leadership made the decision—of their own volition—to reassert civilian supremacy. By the end of the 1920s, the orientation of Calles, Cárdenas, and others toward the supremacy of civilian leadership distinguishes them from most of their colleagues elsewhere in Latin America.[15] This difference is explained, in part, by the popular roots of the post-1920s army and the fact that most of these generals did not pass through an organized socializing process that would have strengthened their institutional identity and loyalty. Moreover, the political-military officers in power during the 1920s confronted rebellion in their ranks, not incompetent or offensive civilian political leaders whom the military wished to replace. In the eyes of the military leadership desirous of institutionalizing the armed forces, the problems came not from the civilian sector but from their own officer ranks. Thus, a period of a decade or so was needed to permit a shaking out among remaining generals and troop commanders, leaving a smaller, more coherent pool of generals at the top.

During this same period of transition (1929), elements of the military, for the last time after 1920, rebelled in large numbers against the central government. As Gordon Schloming notes, the 1929 rebellion differed from its more comprehensive predecessors in 1923 and 1927: "It was the first time that a significant number of subunits under regional command preferred loyalty to the national government over a personal loyalty to their rebel generals. Apparently the professionalizing reforms . . . had indeed inculcated a national and institutional loyalty in important segments of the junior officer ranks."[16]

Calles laid the groundwork for the beginnings of the transition from a revolutionary to an institutionalized army, and from a military directly involved in politics to one functioning as a separate state actor. His effort provides both the essential foundation for contemporary civil-military relations, and the ingredients essential for such a relationship in a democratic setting. After the interim years (1928–1934), during which three men served as president, it was General Cárdenas who solidified what Calles had initiated: "His principal lasting contribution in this respect was to centralize the civilian pyramid of power by uniting governmental and party authority in the person of the President."[17]

Cárdenas used professionalization as a key for removing politically interested officers. Although his positive results have been exaggerated, he did set this pattern in motion. Shortly after taking office, in 1935, he ordered proficiency tests for all infantry officers below the rank of colonel. Those who failed the test were required to take remedial training, the results of which were to be the sole criterion for promotion. Cárdenas eliminated men who without any merit or military skill had risen in the ranks. Many officers with considerable ability had also received promotions on the basis of politics and favoritism, but they remained.[18]

Professionalization was integral to Cárdenas's ultimate political goals for the military. For Cárdenas, however, professionalization did not mean developing a separate caste identity, one that would encourage the military to act as an independent arbiter of political affairs. He clearly expressed his views in addressing the 1935 graduating class at the Colegio Militar: "We should not think of ourselves as professional soldiers . . . but rather as armed auxiliaries organized from the humble classes . . . it is the duty of young officers to broaden the collective spirit of the nation and help incorporate the humble into the whole program of the Revolution."[19]

To give future general officers a sense of institutional identity that was nonpolitical, and to retain a shared bond with civilian leaders, Cárdenas used professionalization techniques in several ways. As will be demonstrated, professionalization becomes essential to defining the civil-military relationship. First, Cárdenas encouraged the promotion of younger, academy-trained officers to positions of strategic command. Such men were not of sufficient rank to be zone or battalion commanders, but he used them to create a buffer between the troops and generals of dubious loyalty to the government.[20] Second, he encouraged the recruitment of cadet officers from the popular classes, promoting men from the ranks to cadet status, a program initiated by General Joaquín Amaro as secretary of war and navy and during his tenure as director of military education. Anyone serving in a battalion, regiment, or equivalent unit could be eligible. The program remained in effect until 1944.[21] Third, Cárdenas lowered maximum-age limits and reduced the maximum career span for an officer below the rank of general, forcing the retirement of some older generals.[22]

Cárdenas introduced a structural change having the potential for reducing the military's power. Initially, he changed the Secretariat of War and Navy to National Defense in 1937. On December 30, 1939, he established an autonomous Navy Department, thus dividing the Secretariat of National Defense into two separate ministries, the Secretariat of National Defense (army and air force) and on December 31, 1940, under Cárdenas's successor, the Secretariat of the Navy.[23]

The Party's Crucial Role in Civil-Military Relations

Cárdenas's most controversial and important contribution was his conception of the relationship between the military and the new civilian political institution, the National Revolutionary Party (PNR). His attitudes toward professionalism were tied to his views on the military's relationship to the party. Cárdenas believed that military professionalization should occur at a rate commensurate with party institutionalization. Such a strategy was essential to civilian control. However, political passivity or neutrality in the officer corps is a luxury regimes can afford only after they have achieved some minimal level of national integration that promotes an underlying value consensus on the fundamental nature of the regime. This integration was effectively achieved through the centralizing and institutionalizing power of the official party.[24] In other words, Cárdenas attempted a balancing act between professionalizing the officer corps and professionalizing civilian leadership. The party served as the umbrella organization, teaching loyalty, discipline, and skills through political experience. These qualities contributed to the party's role as a civilian counter-balance to the armed forces, thus strengthening civilian supremacy over the long term.

The party became the focus of civilian political loyalty for those hopeful of successful political careers after 1929, but Cárdenas could not foresee that the federal bureaucracy—not the party bureaucracy—would become the influential training ground for generations of future civilian leaders who received their education and influential values at the National University. A career in the federal bureaucracy determined most politicians' success in national politics. As de facto head of the party and the executive branch, Cárdenas effected an increasing centralization of power in the hands of the president thereby removing the possibility of competition from other sources, including dissident generals.

Cárdenas startled many Mexicans with his decision, in 1938, to rename the National Revolutionary Party the Party of the Mexican Revolution (PRM) and create four corporate sectors: labor, popular, agrarian, and military.[25] Many officers resisted direct incorporation into the government party because they supported the process, initiated under Calles and reinforced by Cárdenas, of eliminating direct political participation by military personnel. Now it seemed to them that Cárdenas had done an about-face, reversing what they had learned in military schools, in their journals, and on active duty since the early 1920s.[26]

Even his own secretary of defense, General Manuel Avila Camacho, faithful ally and later presidential successor, privately feared an eventual division within the armed forces because of this decision. Avila Camacho preferred the military's role as that of adviser rather than participant.[27] Cárdenas explained publicly why he took this controversial step; he announced that he did not want the officers in the new military sector to represent the armed forces as a special caste.[28] Again, Cárdenas seemed concerned that the military might differentiate itself socially; he believed such a military would act in its own interests, possibly those of a single class, as distinct from the interests of all Mexicans. Cárdenas had firm grounds for his concerns since such patterns were prevalent throughout Latin America.

Under the original National Revolutionary Party statutes, individuals from the army and navy were party members as citizens, not as representatives of the armed forces.[29] Yet, when incorporated into regular party ranks, the government imposed certain restrictions on military membership. Gradually, the party developed a corporatist quality, integrating constituencies from various occupational categories. These groups, such as organized labor, were deeply involved in political affairs, and their representatives, although not accurately reflecting the wishes of their constituencies, spoke precisely for those constituencies. According to another clause, all party members except the military were required to pay regular and extraordinary dues punctually, suggesting to Jorge Alberto Lozoya that the military entered the party unwillingly.[30]

I argue instead that these clauses suggest that the civilian leadership not only was sensitive to the military's resistance to joining but also could not make up its mind how to include the military within its corporatist framework. Unlike most other groups, the military was already incorporated directly into the state, and, during the formative years of the party, the military's political power was decisive.

Both before and after the addition of a military sector in the government party, officer participation in party leadership ranks added important elements to the party's own value system for many decades. The military ethos of rank, discipline, militancy, and loyalty—qualities that also are the hallmark of the party—can be traced back to military participation.[31]

With the division of a new party into four sectors, the officer corps had to choose its own representatives. The Secretariat of National Defense selected forty delegates, one from each of thirty-three military zones, one from each of the two naval zones, three from the department level at the secretariat, and two as personal representatives of Avila Camacho. The two leaders of the delegation, both loyal Cárdenistas, were General Juan José Ríos and General Heriberto Jara. The assembled delegates from all four party sectors chose three officers among their leaders, men suggestive of the direction the army was headed. Predictably, they selected Division General Heriberto Jara, representative of the revolutionary veterans, an important military figure who had pursued a political career, as vice-president of the assembly. They also selected Captain Alfonso Corona del Rosal, a young political-military officer critical to the future transformation and subordination of the military to civilian leadership, as secretary; and Brigadier General Edmundo M. Sánchez Cono, later the official military representative on the party's national executive committee in 1938, as a member of the statutes committee.[32] When the final composition of the constituent assembly of the new PRM became public, the military sector exceeded the other three sectors in strength.[33]

Even prior to Cárdenas's controversial decision, the party played a significant role in civil-military relations. Keeping in mind that political leadership during the 1920s attached themselves to various personalities, the most prominent of whom were Generals Obregón and Calles, the party helped to unify civilian and military elements, channeling their respective interests. The establishment of the party, primarily Calles' brainchild, provided the post revolutionary generation with a mechanism for forming a coalition.[34]

In anticipation of the presidential election of 1940, Cárdenas reinforced the channeling process, ordering all zone commanders to ban political activity at military installations and to participate through the party.[35] Enforcement of these orders was essential because the front-runners for the PRM presidential nomination, automatically Cárdenas's successor, were all military officers.[36] As the government party strengthened its role in the presidential election process, dissident officers, supporting a candidate other than the party's choice, were forced to seek a leave. The military sector of the PRM formally backed Avila Camacho for the nomination. During the campaign, thirty-four officers on active duty received extended leave to lobby for General Juan Andreu Almazán, Avila Camacho's strongest opponent, who became the opposition candidate of the Revolutionary Party of National Unification (PRUN).[37]

During the campaign Avila Camacho publicly revealed his private doubts about military participation in the party. In fact, in addition to his well-known posture as a national unification candidate, he personally represented the new nonpartisan military officer. Avila Camacho personified the military bureaucrat, an officer who earned his general's stars behind a desk, not on the battlefield. He bluntly told audiences that partisan participation of men in uniform would be a "return to the past."[38] Within a month of taking office in December 1940, he ordered the withdrawal of members of the army and navy from the organs "of political action to which they belong."[39] Avila Camacho's decision was a benchmark in civil-military relations, further cementing civilian supremacy over the armed forces. Not only had he reversed an institutional relationship, but he had established symbolically a different image of civilian-military relations for civilians and career officers.

Avila Camacho deserves equal credit with Cárdenas—perhaps greater credit than Cárdenas—for Mexico's transition to civilian leadership. He not only sensed strong dissatisfaction with Cárdenas's decision to incorporate the military within the government party but also took immediate steps to reverse it. Some scholars believe that in reversing this policy, Avila Camacho was more concerned about the image of the military's political involvement, rather than the reality of their participation.[40] President Cárdenas' own reaction is expressed in his diary. He believed that it closed a space for institutionalized political participation, again allowing military figures the possibility of political involvement without civilian control.[41]

President Camacho reinforced the shift toward diminished military influence in politics first by retiring many revolutionary generals who lacked the technical qualifications for modern warfare, and, second, by reducing military expenditures from 21 to 15 percent of the national budget by the end of his administration. The reduction was in line with the pattern of decline over two decades, but is surprising considering the armed forces' increased activity.[42] Avila Camacho strengthened his position during World War II by taking the unusual step of appointing former President Cárdenas secretary of national defense, the only time since 1932 that a president returned to the cabinet in that capacity.[43] The war also made it possible for Mexican officers, in much larger numbers than previously, to take advanced training in the United States, thus increasing professionalization on a technical level among future generals.[44] The President also applied the provisions of a 1936 law to retire 550 generals and colonels. By 1945, at the end of his administration, 12 division generals, 24 brigade generals and 48 brigadier generals remained on active duty.[45]

Civilian Adjustments to the Military's Civil-Military Heritage

The year 1946 marked the evolutionary process from military to civilian control in a symbolic and concrete fashion. General Avila Camacho selected Miguel Alemán, a young, civilian politician, as the party's presidential candidate. Ironically, Alemán's father, a revolutionary general, had died fighting against the government in the 1929 rebellion.

The choice of Alemán represents a another benchmark in Mexican civil-military relations. First, military leaders were instrumental in turning over absolute political leadership to a younger, civilian generation. Avila Camacho himself was the last serious official precandidate to come from the national defense secretariat. Second, Alemán's designation marked the advent of a new kind of professional politician: a university teacher, career bureaucrat, and civilian.[46]

When Alemán took office in December 1946, he not only personally symbolized the new civilian political generation but also surrounded himself with similar types in the most influential cabinet posts.[47] Parallel personnel changes occurred within the military. It has been asserted that Alemán promoted a new generation of officers to the rank of general, men similar to civilian politicians who had graduated from the reformed military academies in the 1920s and early 1930s. Alemán also promoted many younger officers rapidly through the ranks, although older generals continued to hold the most influential posts.

Symbolically, his appointment of Colonel Santiago Piña Soria as chief of the presidential staff, and of General Hermenegildo Cuenca Díaz as chief of staff of national defense, represented the ascendancy of the new generation, not, as some Mexican authors have asserted, the most significant change in the military structure since 1920.[48] Simultaneously, Alemán generated substantial resentment within the officer corps by giving close civilian friends the title of general, producing the degrading term "finger generals" among career officers.[49] Sergio Aguayo, a leading expert on Mexican national security, believes Alemán purposely awarded these military ranks to offend the military because of his father's death at their hands.[50]

Institutionally, Alemán created a presidential guard on February 27, 1947, which later developed into an elite unit within the armed forces. The creation of the presidential guard has had long-term consequences for civil-military relations, especially since 1968. Two infantry battalions had been functioning as presidential guards for many years. Alemán institutionalized their mission by formally creating a guard from the 28th and 42nd infantry battalions. His uncle commanded this unit, which was expanded to a brigade size of approximately 3,500 troops.[51] In order to consolidate presidential control over the military, he established a private telephone network with all of the individual zone commands.[52] The guard, whose chain of command goes directly to the president, was designed, according to some scholars, to restrain ambitious generals in the regular army.[53] However, Luis Garfias, author of an official history of the armed forces, argues instead that their size and lack of firepower to oppose regular forces makes that task unlikely.

Indicative of a more troublesome pattern, Alemán combined military and police functions for internal security purposes. This internal security role, and the military performance of civilian missions, anticipates its anti-drug and anti-crime missions in the 1980s and 1990s, and creates potential dangers for the established pattern in civil-military relations. For example, ten of the best graduates of the 1947 class from the Heroico Colegio Militar were incorporated into the recently founded Directorate of Federal Security in April of that year.[54] Military repression of civilians expanded during this period, especially against independent labor organizations.[55]

Alemán reportedly reconstructed the military's leadership with a new breed of officer, but his commitment was not necessarily to depoliticizing the military but, rather, to ensure the military's loyalty to him and his administration.[56] He used the armed forces, in tandem with civilian security forces, to carry out actions deemed necessary to guarantee the success of his political and economic programs. Hence, while purging the military of its older, more politicized officers, Alemán introduced the new generation of military leader to a different mission: the enforcement of internal security as politically defined by the president and his collaborators. Similar levels of military involvement in what typically had been civilian responsibilities did not reoccur until 1989, the first year of the Carlos Salinas administration.

The event that brought civil-military relations into sharper focus was the presidential succession in 1952. Two issues of importance to the armed forces came to the forefront. The first was whether Mexico should accept military aid from the United States. Alemán rejected a proposed bilateral military assistance pact; allegations that Mexico would subordinate itself to United States policies helped persuade the president.[57] It is also likely that Alemán did not sign the treaty because, although the military favored United States assistance, he needed to appease the populist wing of the party in order to strengthen the victory of his presidential candidate, Adolfo Ruiz Cortines.[58]

The second issue was how to deal with officers opposed to Alemán's choice of a successor. A sizeable group of officers, many of whom were Revolutionary veterans, wanted General Miguel Henríquez Guzmán as president. When the general did not receive the nomination from Alemán, he formed a popular electoral front to campaign openly for the office against the government party's candidate. Some observers suggest that support for Henríquez Guzmán went beyond a personal interest in the general, and was, instead, a strategy among older military officers opposed to Alemán's policies to ensure the ascendancy of their views.[59] Alemán confronted them in an extremely inflexible manner, instructing his national defense secretary to grant unlimited leaves–tantamount to discharging them from active duty– rather than the usual limited leave, to campaign. It was a clear message to the officer corps: support the government's candidate or leave the service. Military loyalists active in the government's own campaign were handsomely rewarded. Since then no group of officers has ever "sought to fulfill its political ambitions outside the PRI (Institutional Revolutionary Party)."[60]

From 1952 until 1968 no presidential decision regarding civil-military relations compared to those implemented by Calles, Cárdenas, Avila Camacho, and Alemán. The military was called in by successive presidents to control conflicts involving students and unions. Most notably these included the occupation of the National Polytechnic Institute in 1956, the replacement of striking telegraph workers in 1958, and the control of striking railroad workers in 1959. In the last instance, Military Camp No. 1 was virtually transformed into a political prison, a situation duplicated on a smaller but still unsavory scale in the 1970s and early 1980s.[61]

1968, A Transformation of Civil-Military Relations?

No single event from 1952 to the present, including the uprising of the Zapatistas in Chiapas in 1994, has affected the military and civil military relations more than the suppression of student activists in Tlatelolco plaza during the summer of 1968, immediately prior to the Olympic Games in Mexico City. Much speculation about the decision itself has been offered in academic and popular accounts. It is important to obtain as complete a picture as possible of the military's role in this decision because it serves as a case study both of military influence in political decision making and of the degree of clarity in the subordination of the military to civilian authorities.

It is crucial to understand that the army's involvement in the government's confrontation with the students extended back to July 30, 1968, when they were requested by the Secretary of Government to intervene. In General Marcelino García Barragán's memoirs, he argues that the request was based on false and exaggerated information, and suggested that the Preventative Police of the Federal District (the civilian agency responsible for maintaining internal order in the capital) was unable to control the student demonstrations and, therefore, unable to maintain order in the community.[62] The justification for the army's intervention is crucial; the alleged ineffectiveness of a civilian agency provides a strong historical precedent for the crime fighting and anti-drug missions.

It is equally important to understand that the armed forces, in performing such a task, realized that there might well be violence. Their operations orders (the specific orders under which these units were to be bound reveals a reasonable advance attitude and, given the potential situation, a tolerance for serious consequences. For example, it says if attacked with stones or Molotov cocktails, they should confront crowds man to man, but without the use of bayonets. More dramatically, the operations orders categorically state that, if they are fired upon by the students, fire should not be returned unless 5 or more soldiers go down. Finally, if gunfire is isolated and without consequences, only officers should respond, firing in the air.[63]

Accounts, based on interviews with individuals present at the decision, or having access to those who were, give a fascinating and significant interpretation of the events. Three basic versions exist: one with Díaz Ordaz out of the capital in order to avoid direct connection with the events; the second with Díaz Ordaz in the capital but unwilling to make the decision; and the third, and most convincing, with Díaz Ordaz planning the entire response, but without informing his national defense secretary, General Marcelino García Barragán. The first version has been presented as follows:

The situation was becoming serious, and it was decided that President Díaz Ordaz had to leave town. He was playing golf in a resort in Michoacán when the decision was made. General García Barragán had arrayed the troops, and he was in the Presidential Palace. Echeverría, who was the Interior Minister at the time, was down on the street with General Mario Ballesteros Prieto. Echeverría began giving orders to move the troops, and General Ballesteros interrupted him saying that General García Barragán was commander of the troops and that these orders would need to be cleared through him. So General Ballesteros Prieto called General García Barragán to explain the situation to him. General García Barragán's response was that Echeverría should keep his hands off Army matters. General Ballesteros Prieto then put Echeverría on the phone and that is when García Barragán told Echeverría what he could do. After that the order was given to clear the square. General García Barragán then went down to the golf course to tell Díaz Ordaz that the situation was all clear. Díaz Ordaz was scared because he thought the Army was about to tell him they had taken over. When he heard what General García Barragán had to say, he gave him an emotional embrace and told him he was a good soldier.[64]

The second version has Díaz Ordaz present but unable to make the decision, leaving it in the hands of his secretary of defense. Present were: Echeverría, General García Barragán, and three staff members. Reports of student strife were coming in. "OK, Mr. President, it is obvious something must be done. Unless you object, I am going to clear Tlatelolco." Then, General García Barragán turned to his two aides and said, "I want the place cleared out." After it was over, he reported to the president, "Mr. President, the situation is clear."[65]

The third and most convincing explanation, because its source is General García Barragán and because many elements are confirmed by newly released documentation, is disturbing for its crucial underlying implications for civil-military relations, and for the structural relationship between the executive branch, the armed forces, and the presidential military staff. President Díaz Ordaz himself orchestrated the repression. The most thorough analysis of the presidential mindset concludes that there can "be little doubt that Díaz Ordaz believed he was the target of a conspiracy. From his point of view the student movement had a number of ominous characteristics."[66] The President abused his command over his presidential staff to facilitate the repression of the student demonstrators.

From the beginning of his administration, Díaz Ordaz created the institutional setting for an awkward situation between the presidency and the secretariat of national defense, appointing a colonel, Luis Gutiérrez Oropeza, as his presidential chief of staff. Apparently, according to one account, the colonel gave his complete loyalty to the president.[67] Colonel Gutiérrez Oropeza took charge of three presidential guard battalions headed by generals. This overt violation of the military command structure produced serious tensions between the chief of staff and the battalion commanders, as well as with the national defense secretary, General García Barragán.[68] Gutiérrez Oropeza also alienated the national defense secretary by discussing promotions directly with the president, promotions which García Barragán refused to approve because he already had decided those promotions.[69] Furthermore, Gutiérrez Oropeza would not have been viewed in a positive light by his fellow officers since he rose rapidly in rank while on leave from active duty. Promotions while on leave were strictly prohibited by internal armed forces regulations. Oropeza joined Díaz Ordaz as secretary of government in 1958, as his chief of adjutants, with the rank of major; he became a colonel in 1964.

The president ordered his chief of staff to place a small number of snipers in surrounding apartment buildings, dressed in civilian clothes, to shoot at students massed in the Tlatelolco Plaza.[70] According to Sergio Aguayo, Díaz Ordaz previously crafted a similar scenario as governor of his home state, Puebla, involving a student demonstration in the state capital.[71] The group involved in the planning and implementation of this strategy, known as Cipol, were concentrated in Section 4, responsible for logistics in the presidential staff, under the direction of the second-in-command, Major Mata Valdés.[72]

García Barragán only discovered the deception accidentally, when one of the snipers was captured, and was identified as a member of the presidential guard and released through Gutiérrez Oropeza's intervention.[73] In his memoirs, García Barragán calls these officers from the presidential staff "terrorists."[74] As Aguayo reasonably concludes, it is difficult to believe that General Barragán would have acceded so easily to the request to release a detained lieutenant who fired on the students, possibly killing some of the soldiers too, without his belief that someone was obeying a direct, presidential order.[75] The national defense secretary's version of events is confirmed, in part, by a recently declassified U.S. Defense Intelligence Agency report that describes the army's mission on that fateful day:

> General García Barragán had instructed [Mario] Ballesteros [Prieto] to send troops to surround the Plaza of the Three Cultures, and to observe what was going on and prevent student demonstrations from spreading to other parts of the city. BLANK categorically stated that the Parachute Battalion's advance into the Plaza, which resulted in a violent confrontation with the students, *was not part of the planned military activity* [emphasis added]. BLANK stated that General García Barragán could not judge at the time whether General Ballesteros had

misinterpreted the orders or changed them deliberately; however, subsequent events convinced García Barragán that both General Ballesteros and Colonel Gutiérrez were bypassing his office and had, in fact, deliberately changed his orders.[76]

The repercussions of the decision were, in many respects, more important than the process itself. The consequences can be broadly categorized as:

- Altering the views of the military toward civilian leadership.
- Altering the views of the political leadership toward the military.
- Altering the views of the younger officers toward older officers within the military.
- Changing the views of the role of the military in Mexican society.

Probably the most important outcome, one that influenced many aspects of civil-military relations long after 1968, is how the officer corps looked upon political elites. The changes in generational views is fundamental to understanding civil-military relations in a democratic Mexico under President Fox since it is the younger generation formed by those events which has taken command since 2000.[77]

The retention of military subordination to civil authority was reaffirmed by these events. This can be seen as one of many positive reinforcements of the steadily evolving civil-military relationship since 1946. The reaffirmation is more astounding given General García Barragán's version of events. The president essentially betrayed the regular armed forces for his own purposes, placing the national defense secretary in a deeply awkward position. García Barragán never publicly revealed his version of events during his lifetime.[78] Even without that information, the overall image of civilian leadership took a nosedive in the officer corps' estimation, especially among younger officers.

The new generation deemed the events of 1968 clear evidence of civilian bungling. Increasingly, they viewed the leadership as politically incompetent and illegitimate.[79] That outlook led to the cadets' transfer from the Heroico Colegio Militar in Mexico City to Chetumal during the summer.[80] One officer who was a cadet at the time believed their commanders did not want them negatively influenced by events in the city; no mention was made to the cadets about the military's role in the disturbance.[81] Future officers would not be inclined to repeat such actions against large numbers of Mexicans, taking the blame for civilian incompetence. The military's perception of civilian fallibility led the military to reappraise its role in the internal security decision-making process.

It is not known whether the military pushed this new emphasis on civilian political elites, or whether political elites invited the military's increased involvement. To some degree, it is likely that both groups' views coincided on a revised internal security role. What is evident is that the civilian leadership realized that it could not unilaterally ask the military to perpetrate the "horror of slaughtering large numbers of countrymen in the future."[82] Analysts conclude that a shift in direction in national security matters can be traced directly to Tlatelolco Plaza.[83]

In practice, the new national security orientation involved increased political intelligence gathering on the part of the military against actual and perceived subversive groups. Joint cooperation between federal agents and the military became the norm. Most disturbing of all, elements of the military, with the knowledge and tolerance of the higher command, participated in paramilitary groups similar to those found throughout Latin America in the 1970s and 1980s. Mexico's version was referred to as the "Brigada Blanca" (White Brigade). It was a counterforce—comprised of select army and civilian personnel—to extreme left elements.[84]

An infusion of fresh leadership in the military officer corps was another effect of 1968. Some changes happened naturally through attrition, as younger officers took control of decision-making positions. It also occurred as a consequence of presidential promotion policies. Considerable dissension within the officer ranks existed. Instead of the usual ten to fifteen annual changes in medium- and high-level commands 1968 witnessed ninety-seven such appointments, including top commanders among the general staff and seven zone commanders.[85] According to insiders, 1968 produced a generational shift within the military, just as it did among civilian politicians. An instructor from the National Defense College noted a dramatic change:

> I have developed many close contacts with military officers, and one of the things I can tell you that has changed is that the younger officers are much less authoritarian than the older officers. I have seen them deal with the troops in a more flexible manner, instead of severely punishing someone for being late, they will be more generous in their reprimand. I attribute this different attitude to 1968. . . . I'm convinced that it has had an impact on their ideas, and there is a difference between this generation and the older generation.[86]

A long-term consequence of 1968 on the civilian-military relationship, one which could not have been foreseen until after the EZLN uprising of January 1, 1994, is the role of 1968 student activists in the Zapatista movement. Many students who participated in those events fled from Mexico City. A number of them ended up in rural Chiapas, where they began organizing peasant resistance.[87] Ironically, the groups which they helped create provided the foundation for the Zapatistas, and once again, for an encounter between the army and the civilian population. Given the complex circumstances of that confrontation, the army's suppression of the guerrillas produced similar consequences for civil-military relations and for the armed forces.

It is also valuable to keep in mind that the events of 1968 not only affected civil-military relations for the next three decades, but they also played a critical role in the democratization process and state-group relations generally. This conflict prompts leadership groups to question more openly the semi-authoritarian features of the Mexican political model, and its consequences for economic and social development. Thus, the doubts raised among a new generation of officers, appear among other leadership groups, especially intellectuals and politicians. In turn, this set in motion long-term trends which led to Fox's election in 2000.

The military realized the extent of the damage to its institutional reputation wrought by its actions in Tlatelolco Plaza. They demanded a high price from the government as compensation. That price is most readily apparent in structural and material changes within the armed forces. For the first time since Miguel Alemán's administration, the government created a new zone command, and it established three new battalions—infantry, parachute, and military police—as well as a new company of combat engineers in the presidential guards.[88] At the same time, half of the troops in the army were given new weapons, and the air force acquired thirty-seven new planes from the United States.[89]

The residue of 1968 tainted presidential attitudes toward the military throughout the next administration. Díaz Ordaz's successor was Luis Echeverría, a man intimately involved with those events. Echeverría never forgave the military for its violence in the plaza, because his attempts at moderation had been thwarted.[90] Elements in the military also intensely disliked the president. Echeverría told the author that, when he was speaking at the University of Michoacán as a presidential candidate, he asked for a moment of silence in memory of the students killed in 1968. When officers learned of this, they reportedly asked Díaz Ordaz to withdraw his candidacy.[91]

The officer corps, customarily acquiring little in the way of up-to-date weaponry, especially aircraft, tried to obtain new fighter planes during Echeverría's administration. The president consistently refused. Instead, the president concentrated on improving technical training, expanding military occupational specialty programs, and building new facilities.[92] He also increased the military's involvement in non-military, civic action programs. Yet, despite these tendencies, the military rapidly increased its presence in national security matters, confronting and ultimately eliminating several guerrilla groups. As a consequence, it did obtain valuable combat training and some prestige.[93]

Echeverría was to have his own, much smaller version of Tlatelolco. On June 10, 1971, a paramilitary organization, Los Halcones, at the instigation of political opponents within the cabinet, brutally suppressed a group of student demonstrators. At the time, it was reported that Echeverría appeared to have lost control over his own cabinet. This interpretation is not well supported and is typical of the rumors which tend to emerge during crisis situations in Mexico. Newly released documents from the United States embassy reveal that Echeverría clearly knew about the Halcones, and that Colonel Manuel Díaz Escobar, their leader, as well as the assistant secretary and secretary of foreign relations, José Gallastegui and Emilio Rabasa, all requested training for these men in the United States six months before the actual repression took place.[94]

Despite the military's loyalty to the president during the crisis, Echeverría still viewed the officers as potential competitors for political power, not as future loyalists. According to several scholars, the threat of a military coup, actually weighed on the president's mind. The possibility that the military might take the reins of power was most likely during the final months of Echeverría's administration. Despite the intensity of public rumors, including reports in the U.S. media, most authors, myself included, considered this a feat of public imagination rather than a real possibility.[95] The commander of the 3rd Artillery Regiment, stationed in the 1st Military Zone (which includes the Federal District), noted this was nothing more than a rumor. There were absolutely no indications of anything unusual going on in the zone. Moreover, the secretary of national defense was preoccupied with his possible candidacy as governor of Baja California, not with an alleged possible coup. Nevertheless, the rumors are significant, because of the degree to which they reflected a decline in presidential legitimacy and the established relationship between the military and political leadership. The relationship was sorely in need of repair.

Echeverría's handpicked successor, José López Portillo, was a dark-horse candidate with extremely limited political influence. His choice as the PRI standard-bearer led many Mexicans to believe that Echeverría, like Calles, hoped to become the gray eminence of his successor. In fact, rumors abounded that Echeverría might try to remain in power; similar rumors had received even wider currency during the last months of Alemán's administration. Michael Dziedzic asserts that a group of generals reportedly told the president, "'Were you to do anything against the Constitution, we would be forced to defend the Constitution.' In other words, if you try to stay in power, the Army will push you aside."[96]

López Portillo came into office with his sovereignty guaranteed by the military. He created an ambience much more favorable to substantive changes within the armed forces. López Portillo was the son of a career officer and graduate of the Colegio Militar who was incorporated into the Federal Army as a cadet during the Decena Trágica, and escorted President Madero on February 9, 1913. The President recalled conversations with his father about having been transferred from post to post in the course of his duties, and expressed considerable respect for his father's loyalty to the institution.[97] The tone of the president's comments and recollections suggests that his personal experience, more than that of any other president since 1946, may have inclined him to look favorably on military requests.[98]

During the López Portillo administration, the official attitude toward the armed forces changed in four general respects. First, the president encouraged the army to increase its role in the area of public security by taking over the protection of vital installations, including utilities and petroleum facilities. Second, he enlarged military involvement in the making of national security policy.[99] Third, López Portillo advanced modernization, not just in military education but also in arms and improved salaries. Fourth, he enhanced the public presence of the army.[100] In all cases, López Portillo himself initiated these expenditures without any pressure from the military. All of these decisions presage significant changes within the armed forces, most of which influenced the officer corps' relationship with civilian political leadership.

In the policy decision-making process, hidden from public view, the president was careful to include the secretary of national defense in all major consultations. In fact, the president informed the national defense secretary of his decision to nationalize the banks before he informed the treasury secretary, the only cabinet member asked to pledge his support for the measure the night before it was announced.[101] The military enhanced its image with an increased show of weaponry at military parades, although the president attributed this change to military leaders rather than to his office.[102] In his own public appearances, López Portillo praised the military more frequently than his predecessor.

When José López Portillo left office in November 1982, he left the political system, particularly the presidency, at its lowest ebb in many decades. His successor, Miguel de la Madrid, faced numerous problems, not the least of which was reviving the legitimacy of presidential and establishment leadership. It is not surprising, given these circumstances, that the president continued to curry favor with the military, perhaps in some respects more intensely than his two immediate predecessors. Again, the military's public presence became notable in what traditionally had been civilian parades, and presidential praise for the military incorporated such lavish terms as "cornerstone" of internal stability and "guardian" of society.[103]

The increased role of the military in anti-drug programs begun under López Portillo, continued under the de la Madrid administration. Analysts of the drug trade suggest that de la Madrid stressed the military as the "honest, dedicated phalanx of Mexico's campaña antidroga" at the expense of the civilian attorney general's office.[104] The emphasis reflected a growing participation by the military in internal security matters. Civilians had formerly laid out the military's role in the National Development Plan.[105] Also, events in Guatemala and Central America as a whole intensified security concerns along the southern border, brought about a stronger military presence there, and gave the military a more influential voice in foreign policy matters.[106]

The stabilizing trend in relations between civilian and military leaders hit a significant snag when de la Madrid limited the military's participation in emergency relief after Mexico City's major earthquake in 1985. Jorge Castañeda asserts that a split over the passive assignment occurred between older and younger officers, and between the younger officers and civilian leaders.[107] The younger officers wanted a much greater share of the emergency effort, as defined in the national disaster plans. De la Madrid's decision reflected the doubts many civilian leaders entertained concerning a more visible military role; they felt it could possibly place civilian leadership in an unfavorable light.

De la Madrid generally stabilized relations with the armed forces while simultaneously increasing their presence, but the political situation altered radically after 1988 when he left office. Civilian leadership's legitimacy had dropped to such a low level that, for the first time since the party was formed, a dissident from within the PRI, Cuauhtémoc Cárdenas, captured an extraordinary number of votes in the presidential election against Carlos Salinas de Gortari. This forced official tallies to reflect a substantial portion of the ballots cast in his favor. According to one source, because of the extent of the electoral fraud, and the PRI's victorious candidate's lack of legitimacy, Salinas went to an influential group of military physicians, including his uncle, to speak to different army factions to guarantee their support.[108]

The political consequences of the 1988 presidential election were many; for civil-military relations they were threefold. First, de la Madrid's successor, Carlos Salinas de Gortari, faced the daunting task of assembling a new set of constituencies in 1989. The traditional amalgam of interest groups had been shattered by preelection maneuverings and policy debates among the three leading presidential contenders. Within the first few months of his administration, Salinas included the armed forces as an important element in his new political formula.

Second, in recognition of his redefined constituencies, Salinas made extensive use of the military in executing some of his decisions.[109] For example, he directed the army—not the police—to move against a notorious drug trafficker, Miguel Angel Félix Gallardo.[110] In the largest such operation, he ordered a military takeover of the Cananea Corporation following an unresolved strike, which involved helicopters and two hundred soldiers.[111]

Third, as a consequence of well-organized opposition, local, state, and national elections were vigorously contested. Election violence, especially at the state and local level, became a hallmark of Salinas's administration. The government used troops to maintain order and, in some cases, to effect election fraud. Salinas further expanded the military's internal security role. He also gave prominence to a national security group within his cabinet headed by former Colonel Jorge Carrillo Olea, a longtime veteran of security affairs in the Secretariat of Government.

Salinas successfully improved the stature of the presidency, as well as his own image, until January 1, 1994. He relied on the armed forces, especially during the first year of his administration, to help him achieve his personal popularity. Second, Salinas institutionalized the role of the armed forces in internal security missions, most notably in anti-drug trafficking assignments. More importantly, the secretariats of national defense and the navy were represented at the cabinet level in the inter-agency group responsible for advising the president on national security.[112]

Chiapas, Shaking Up Civil-Military Relations

On January 1, 1994, the dramatic uprising of indigenous peasants in the poor, southern state of Chiapas shattered the careful image Salinas had created of an increasingly modernizing Mexico. They called themselves the Ejército Zapatista de Liberación Nacional (EZLN). The EZLN initially took control of several communities, but the army responded quickly and effectively, routing the guerrilla forces.[113] In the process, the army resorted in numerous cases to the excessive use of force, reviving memories of the anti-guerrilla actions of the 1970s, and the 1968 student massacre.[114] The president recognized that Mexican public opinion, and the national and international media, were sympathetic to the peasants' goals. He ordered the army to cease its offensive operations against the Zapatistas.

Like the events in 1968, the Chiapas rebellion was as significant to civil-military relations. The brief uprising itself, the authorities' reaction to it, and the Zapatista public relations' victory affected internal structures and policies within the armed forces. Once again events highlighted significant tensions between civilians and the officer corps in the making of and implementation of national security policy.

Given the army's traditional role of providing intelligence from rural areas, it had alerted the Salinas administration about the presence of guerrillas in Chiapas long before the actual uprising.[115] The civilian leadership not only prevented the army from cracking down on the rebel forces, but also denied publicly their existence.[116] Again, as in the 1968, the civilian leadership purposely put the army troops at risk, leaving them open to attack, and then relied on the army to confront the uprising. Military officers believed that their role in the decision-making process once again was negated. As was true 25 years earlier, the military had "grown increasingly disenchanted with having to clean up after politicians' mistakes."[117]

The authorities' reactions to the Zapatistas also reflected the same internal divisions between hardliners and soft-liners. The commander of the 31st military zone, responsible for the troops in this region, invited numerous reporters, including foreign correspondents, to his headquarters for a press conference. The general told the media that the best action would be for the army to take the offensive and wipe out the Zapatistas. The next day, he suggested that he had been misquoted and that he whole-heartedly supported the civilian leadership's strategy of a negotiated settlement.[118] Another general, a federal congressman, publicly criticized the government for using the armed forces in Chiapas, expressing the view that this was a political error and the executive branch and congress were responsible. Such a criticism was unheard of in the previous forty years of civil-military relations.[119]

The divisions were not confined to civilian-military relationships. Despite the briefness of the conflict, the Air Force, according to internal documents, claimed the most recognition for its actions in Chiapas, not only in requesting promotions, but also in the increased autonomy over its organization and budget, indicated by its procurement of airplanes. Resentment occurred within the army and the presidential guard toward officers who were being promoted to higher ranks that had not participated in the Chiapan campaign.[120]

Within the armed forces the uprising produced dramatic structural and strategic changes. Less than eighteen months after the rebellion, an internal document came to light in September 1995, reflecting the extent of dissatisfaction within the army over numerous issues, including the command structure, promotions, professionalization, public relations, training, strategic deployment, and technical competence.[121] It expanded the army's emphasis on special commando and coordinated air units, as well as increasing their logistical, intelligence and land and air transport units. The uprising set in motion the largest expansion in zone commands (two) and air bases (five) in decades.

The conflict between the armed forces and the Zapatistas also set in motion a significant change in the media's attitude regarding the military.

This change presages a much broader alteration in civil-military relations from a societal perspective. The media, for the first time, was willing to publish highly critical voices and commentary about the military, and actively sought out victims of army abuses.[122] Thus, society generally was exposed to a different view of the military, and its weaknesses and abuses were no longer shielded from public view.

At the same time, the military itself altered its attitude toward the media. The secretary of national defense, General Antonio Riviello Bazán, quickly grasped that the military was losing the war in the media, and "promptly appointed a public relations expert to deal with the press and set out to form new alliances. The Secretary of National Defense arranged meetings with journalists and academicians who had been critical of the army and made overtures to establish a more open dialogue."[123] Just days before Salinas left office, the army formalized their new emphasis on public relations by adding a department of communications to the secretariat of national defense.[124]

By not imposing a military solution, the army obtained recognition in the national and international context for subordinating itself to "civil opinion."[125] Mexican citizens overwhelmingly supported Zapatista social and economic goals, but they did not necessarily view the army in a totally negative light. According to a poll taken three years after the uprising, only 44 percent of the respondents believed that the EZLN represented the indigenous people, and 56 versus 32 percent believed that the army should withdraw from the indigenous communities.[126]

The Zapatista uprising, and the interactions between civilian and military authorities, as was true in 1968, contributed significantly to the pace of political change in Mexico, reinforcing patterns contributing to increased democratization. Among the most important of those patterns was a flowering of NGOs and civic organizations which publicly expressed their demands to the government, and encouraged greater levels of accountability among both politicians and the officer corps.

Civil-Military Relations in Mexico's Historical Setting

The Mexican historical record from the 1920s through 1994 suggests a number of variables important to the gradual withdrawal of the military from politics and the ascendancy of and belief in civilian political supremacy. Some of these variables can be found in other Third World contexts, but Mexico has developed its own formula for stable civil-military relations. It is worth summarizing the most influential variables. They are the product of Mexico's peculiar historical setting. We also need to keep their impact on the civil-military relationship in mind.

Even this brief outline of presidential attitudes and behavior toward the military through 1994 suggests several important phenomena. One of the most significant of these variables is the establishment of a major political organization, and its continued growth and legitimacy. From a comparative theoretical perspective, it suggests the continuing influence of institutions in explaining politics generally, Mexican politics specifically, and the civil-military relationship. Interestingly, the party's role in policy-making is minimal. Nevertheless it provided an institutional means through which a coherent and legitimate pool of political leaders could be identified. Initially, the most important figures were political-military leaders. These presidents, including Cárdenas and Avila Camacho, drew most of their key cabinet figures from among civilian professionals, not from the officer corps. Thus, they set in motion and reaffirmed the importance of civilian supremacy, and the use of the party and its institutional successors in maintaining a one-party state under civilian management. The degree of civilian unity engendered by the National Revolutionary Party contributed significantly to the development of military subordination to civilian authorities.

The military's withdrawal and the imposition of civilian supremacy, extending back many decades, are directly attributable to military, not civilian, presidents. These men, unlike most of their peers elsewhere in the world, came from revolutionary forces who although members of regular units in the Constitutional Army, shared roots with civilian leaders and retained a civilian rather than an institutionalized, professional military mentality. Because many of them had fought against the Porfiriato's militarism, and against Victoriano Huerta's collaborators, they had a natural aversion to instituting a new form of establishment militarism.

The Mexican Revolution generates a historical setting which has been duplicated only among a select number of societies, and therefore, can be viewed in the light of civil-military relations theory as a peculiar contribution of cultures undergoing revolutionary transformations, such as Nicaragua in the 1980s, or as a specifically Mexican experience. This might be viewed as a structural variable in that the socialization processes that provided them with a broader, shared mindset with their civilian peers was experiential. Their desire to produce a post-revolutionary leadership that was revolutionary in orientation but civilian in composition, established the principle of civilian supremacy in civil-military relations as part of the rhetoric of the revolution, a principle which seeped firmly into the mindset of the next generation of Mexicans.

Beginning with the administration of General Obregón, each successive presidency encouraged and expanded military professionalization, both in developing higher tactical skills and in imposing a strong sense of loyalty to the presidency and the secretary of national defense. The military's sense of discipline concerning political participation or association with the opposition, sometimes imposed through extreme measures, accompanied that of civilian political leaders, who developed an almost untouchable loyalty to and discipline toward a single party, the PNR and its successors.

The military professionalization process is a variable which has been touted by many authors to explain certain characteristics in civil-military relations found in numerous countries. What makes the pattern unique in Mexico is that the professional training, once implemented, placed a high value on civilian subordination. Moreover, politically ambitious civilians and military officers were forced to focus their political loyalties through a monopolistic, state-controlled party and its revolving leadership. The historic deficiency of a politically competitive party setting actually strengthened the ability of Mexico's politicians to maintain military subordination to civilian rule.

Political leadership, initially through military men in the presidency, imposed certain forms of behavior on the military, but civilian political leadership has allowed increasing degrees of autonomy within the military, even though the overall resources made available to the armed forces have declined considerably over time through the early 1990s. Civilian politicians and presidents traded excessive military budgetary influence, a condition found in almost every Third World country and in numerous First World countries, for numerous aspects of internal military autonomy.

Civilian leadership increased its dependence on the military for political support in the 1970s, 1980s, and 1990s, as the legitimacy of established political institutions, including the presidency itself, declined. Publicly, whether civilian reliance on the military has been greater or lesser, each president has lauded the military's loyalty and patriotism, not only conveying to the military the importance of its fealty but also reinforcing that value in the eyes of the general public. In return, the officer corps and the average Mexican have come to view subordination of authority to civilian leadership as natural and legitimate.

CHAPTER THREE

The Sociology of Civil-Military Relations

Most explorations of civil-military relations concentrate on institutional, structural, and historical experiences to explain the peculiarities of the relationship in a given society. As we have shown in the previous chapter, these influences are essential in understanding the Mexican case. Another contribution to filling in the pieces of the puzzle which explains civil-military relations is the sociology of the two leadership groups. This component has typically been neglected in the literature and there are few studies of any country which incorporates this variable. This gap is unfortunate because it excludes an essential ingredient in understanding the larger picture of civil-military relations in the twenty-first century, as well as critical contributions in its evolution.

An equally compelling argument has been made for understanding the sociology of the military. Sam Fitch notes that such studies are "urgently needed to better understand the social context of the military's understanding of and reaction to the unfolding events of a new century," because these variables will undoubtedly play in role in "understanding civil-military relations and future prospects for democratic consolidation" in Latin America. Fitch concludes that theoretical progress in the field can only be achieved if we give up the notion that the armed forces is a unitary actor with a single mentality and set of interests.[1]

Theorists have argued for more than four decades that leaders' social and geographic origins are critical variables in understanding the composition and behavior of elites. Such background variables interact with other characteristics to produce various socializing influences on individual leaders. Some studies concluded that an individual's closest circle of friends could alter a person's attitudes and perceptions.² Studies of American elites have provided evidence that a parent's occupation or childhood residence contribute to reinforcing their views.³ Still other students of elite socialization have argued that such variables as class background create an environment affecting elite behavior toward each other. This is the most relevant finding in assessing the importance of background characteristics on the relationship between civil and military elites.⁴ Studies of Mexican politicians confirm the importance of family and geographic origin as important sources of socialization, patterns which also are found among other Mexican leadership groups.⁵

Among elites, homogeneous backgrounds may have not only a psychological effect on their sense of community but also an effect on their recruitment. Mexican political leaders demonstrate the importance of generational criteria in elite recruitment; they recruit like types.⁶ A strong sense of regionalism prevails in Mexico and, although those differences have never been the primary basis of conflict among contemporary politicians, they were significant, especially after the Revolution. Urban and rural origins are becoming increasingly influential. Evidence from survey research in the 1990s and 2000s suggests important differences in the distribution of certain social and political attitudes (which have significant political consequences) between citizens residing in the poor, rural south, and those in the urban, industrialized capital and the north.⁷

The significance of background variables to the officer corps is its potential to foster a military caste mentality. Such a mentality would separate the military from not only the population, but also from other leadership groups, including civilian politicians. It would be a critical variable in civil-military relations if the military were to develop an identity of its own and, in that separateness, come to believe that it is superior to the civilians. Little attention has been paid to this issue, largely because its roots, as suggested earlier, can be traced to the popular armies during the Revolution (1910–1920). However, some scholars believe the potential for the officer corps to develop such a mentality in the twenty-first century is present as the officer corps takes on attributes differentiating it from other leadership groups.⁸

Political-Military Officer

Since the 1920s, three types of officers can be found in Mexico's military: political-military, mustang, and orthodox professional. Two of these types disappeared before the end of the twentieth century. The qualities of each officer type significantly influenced the homogeneity of the officer corps, its caste mentality, and the civil-military relationship. One of the most interesting features of the twentieth century Mexican military is the presence of the political-military officer, an individual who straddled two careers, one in the army and another in politics. Unlike his orthodox or regular military counterpart, he displayed an interest in and skills appropriate to politics. He was an officer whose career in politics was as important as a career in the military. Older political-military officers were Revolutionary combat veterans.

Presidents Obregón (1920–1924) and Calles (1924–1928), and Calles as a gray eminence in the early thirties, stiffened professional requirements through increasingly demanding educational programs. However, it was President Cárdenas who, in 1936, moved decisively to weed out large numbers of revolutionary officers, including many with political ambitions. He initiated legislation that shortened an officer's career span from thirty-five to twenty-five years. This change meant that all officers who had served before 1911 would be automatically retired, and that by 1940 (the end of Cárdenas's term) all officers who had served before 1915 would be gone.[9] If the legislation continued in effect, by 1946 no officers who had taken part in the Revolution should be among the military leadership.[10]

In reality revolutionary generals did not disappear after 1945. Nonpolitical and political-military officers who opted for advanced military training remained. The political-military officer survived much longer than expected for a variety of reasons. One significant structural means for accomplishing this end has not been previously recognized. Political leave time is excluded from computation regarding rank or retirement.[11] Therefore, into the 1950s and 1960s political-military officers were more likely to have had combat experience than their younger, orthodox career peers. Of the 466 generals in our sample through 1988, when such individuals all but disappeared from the officer corps, 176 (38 percent) were political-military officers (defined as having held a high-level national political office or a state governorship). Of those officers, nearly two-thirds experienced combat, almost all during the Revolution. Among nonpolitical officers during the same period, only 21 percent possessed combat records. Thus, leave time extended the influence of an older generation of political-military officers ten to fifteen years beyond their expected career span.

Phyllis Walker believes that after Miguel Alemán's administration (1946–1952), top leaders of the National Defense Secretariat were selected on the basis of their revolutionary credentials, bypassing younger officers. Such selections insured the military's support for political leadership after 1952 and its continued nonintervention in political affairs.[12] An examination of military leadership bears this out. The most influential field post in the army is that of zone commander. Of the nine regional zone commanders in 1951, seven were officers with revolutionary credentials and all but one had entered politics.[13] Essentially no change occurred between Alemán's and Adolfo Ruiz Cortines's (1952–1958) administrations.

Revolutionary officers have been most visibly represented among secretaries of national defense, the last of whom was Hermenegildo Cuenca Díaz (1970–1976)—which is stretching the connection, because he only had accompanied President Carranza as a cadet in 1920. His predecessor, Marcelino García Barragán, joined the Juárez Brigade, Division of the North, on May 14, 1915, as a second lieutenant under General Obregón, thus having served in the army for forty-nine years, excepting 1943 to 1947, when he was a state governor, and 1950 to 1958, when he left the army.[14] Interestingly, the symbolic importance of a combat veteran as a service leader was not stressed equally in the air force or the navy, neither of which were headed by an officer with such experience during comparable years.

The presence of the political-military officer introduced two features into Mexico's officer corps. The first, and most obvious, is the persistence of the commander with revolutionary roots or credentials. The second feature this type of officer brings to the officer corps is a politically interested and skilled individual. Mexico developed a cadre of career officers who through staff positions gained those political skills, and dominated command positions for some time. These individuals were for many decades largely political-military officers, men who obtained hands-on political experience in elective and appointive offices.

In many military organizations, a division develops between officers whose careers lie with field command, especially if their careers entail active combat, and those who are primarily staff officers administering troops from behind a desk. In Mexico, the division is complicated in two unique ways. First, Mexico opened up career opportunities for developing political skills outside the armed forces, thereby expanding the number of opportunities available to its potential commanders.[15] Second, political officers were veterans with premier combat credentials earned during the 1910 Revolution. These credentials were as important to the military officer's career in the 1940s and 1950s as World War II combat was to the U.S. officer's leadership potential after 1945.

The importance of the revolutionary credential and the extended influence of the politically experienced commander in the armed forces delayed the rise of the orthodox career officer. This created resentment on the part of the young professional officers toward older, combat veterans. The division between the two cohorts occurred quite soon after the Revolution, in fact under President Cárdenas, the prototype of the political-military combat veteran. "His professionalization and modernization program loosened the bonds between the revolutionary generals on the one hand and the junior officers and enlisted men on the other. The officers were interested in professional military careers. They came to feel that they were better qualified

The Sociology of Civil-Military Relations

to command—than the divisionarios [division generals], who were politicians rather than soldiers."[16]

From the 1940s through the early 1970s, the existence of this division in the military leadership, particularly the army, produced potential repercussions. Some scholars suggest that the political officer, lacking prestige among his more "professional" colleagues, could not serve as a significant political link between civilian and military elites.[17] This raised the possibility that in a serious crisis, the professional officers might not have had sufficient respect for their politically oriented leaders to obey specific commands.[18] That potential existed for many years, but it never materialized.

Since the mid-1970s the division in Mexican military leadership has disappeared as the political-military officer left the scene. In 1982, no officers with direct political experience outside the military bureaucracy, with one exception, were appointed to top posts. Since 1988 no politically experienced officers have been appointed to National Defense Secretariat posts. The same can be seen clearly in the data on military zone commanders. Political-military officers often dominated certain zone commands, especially in the 1940s and 1950s, and even well into the 1960s and 1970s. After the late 1970s, however, they ceased to appear among influential field commands.

The political-military officer disappears from the top staff and command posts because his type no longer exists in Mexico. The fading away of active duty generals with direct political experience reduced the likelihood of an internal military conflict but opened the door to a different, potentially more debilitating weakness, one seemingly present within the political leadership in the 1980s and early 1990s.[19] Neither the officer corps nor the civilian political elite could claim the mass-based political skills that characterize politicians who emerge from grass roots organizations and local and state elective offices.

The introduction of electoral democracy, and the competition for the presidency in 2000, brought to the forefront the type of politician more typical of Mexico in the 1950s and 1960s. These were individuals with experience in elective office, specifically in state governorships and congress. This is a pattern that is likely to continue after 2006. Thus, although a new kind of politician is emerging in response to the altered structure of Mexico's political model, such individuals among high-ranking officers have not reemerged.

The lack of political-military officers eliminated an important linkage in Mexico's civil-military relationship during the pre-democratic era. Political-military officers provided both leadership groups with greater insights to each other's views. This linkage served the interests of both groups. In a democratic setting, this peculiar linkage is less significant since other institutional channels, which increase access between the two groups, have increased in number. These include congressional and military relations, shared responsibilities in new missions such as the anti-drug task, and a civilian presence in the National Defense College.

The replacement for the traditional political-military officer is currently a junior officer who temporarily serves either as an aide to a prominent political figure in the executive branch or as a gubernatorial appointee. He is generally a captain or major. Many officers feel such an assignment has a negative repercussion on a military career, and that it is done for financial reasons. For example, Brigade General Domiro R. García Reyes, a garrison commander during the Fox administration, served as an aide to President Echeverría, and as chief of aides to President López Portillo. Division General Roberto Miranda Sánchez, a regional zone commander, also was assigned as an aide to President Echeverría.

Some observers assert that many junior officers hold lower level positions in the federal bureaucracy. However, an examination of middle-level posts in 1983, 1987, 1989, 1992, and 1994 reveals only one or two career military officers. Since 2000, a number of officers have served in the national bureaucracy, particularly in the Attorney General's office, in posts having responsibilities related to the drug war or anti-crime tasks. No empirical evidence exists on how many junior officers serve as aides; one officer estimated several hundred in the mid-1980s.[20] However, vestiges of the attitude that political experience lacks prestige must still be present within the military because only a small number of high-ranking officers who have served as politicians' aides mention this service in their public biographies.

Political-military officers added a number of characteristics to military leadership not found among contemporary officers. For most of the period since 1946, the political-military officer contributed substantially to the aging of Mexico's officer corps. Top officers were older than the leading politicians. Only 17 percent of top civilian politicians after 1935 had been born before 1900, compared to 58 percent of all political-military officers after 1946. Broken down by decade in which each was born, the differences become apparent. Top political and military leaders born in the 1880s accounted for nearly a fifth of all political-military officers, but only 4 percent of civilian politicians. Those born in the 1890s accounted for 13 percent among civilian politicians and nearly 40 percent of political-military officers.

Generational differences between political-military and regular officers have two consequences: they provide a generational division within the civilian leadership, between career civilian politicians and career officers who hold political posts, and a generational division within the military leadership. An examination of generations within the military suggests an equally divided leadership by career experience. The political-military officer, at least among generals in top command posts, retained substantial influence for a long period, and among younger generations. By the 1900s generation, generals did not exercise much influence over civilian political offices. Among the 1900s regular officer generation, however, more than half of the generals were transitional political-military careerists. Even among the 1910s generation, the politically experienced officer continued to exercise considerable influence within the officer corps.

Not until the 1920s generation does the political-military officer become a relic among his regular peers. In terms of generational background, top officers become younger and more homogeneous. Nevertheless, through 2000 they remained nearly a decade in age behind their civilian counterparts. For example, even navy brass, which is slightly younger than their army/air force peers, reflect this same comparative distortion. Among the top naval officers holding positions since 1988, 15 percent were born before the 1930s, 54 percent in the 1930s, and 31 percent in the 1940s. In contrast, in Salinas' administration alone (1988–1994), 63 percent of his top collaborators were born after 1940. Since the Fox administration, many of the top officers now are the same age as their civilian counterparts, including President Fox (born in 1942).[21] Officers begin their careers at a very young age, but time in rank now requires approximately thirty years to reach the rank of brigadier general, and longer for the two- and three-star ranks, which make up our sample. Consequently, top officers in the recent past were likely to be ten years older than prominent politicians, having more in common with an older generation than with the youngest generation of political elites. That appears to be changing in the 2000s.

The demise of the political-military officer has consequences for the broader civil-military relationship. Plenty of evidence exists in generational literature that age can affect an individual's attitudes. The elimination of the political-military officer has decreased the average age of top career officers, bringing them in much closer sync with their civilian counterparts. Sharing a similar generational experience is particularly significant in times of political change. Since older voters were most resistant to supporting Fox, and since he was viewed by the electorate as representing a change in the political system, the presence of two dominant but different age cohorts among civilian and political leadership offers the potential for greater disagreement on political and economic issues.[22]

Political-military officers also influenced the homogeneity of the officer corps in other important ways. Place of origin is a background variable which long has interested analysts of leadership. Regionalism has played a historic role in Mexico, more so than generational differences, at least through the 1940s. The centralization of political power in Mexico City, especially in the post-revolutionary period, eliminated regionalism's national political impact relatively quickly as measured in terms of states' or regions' abilities to operate autonomously from the center. Cárdenas's suppression of the last military rebellion, in San Luis Potosí in 1939, consolidated, once and for all, military power in the hands of the federal government.

Nevertheless, beginning in the mid-1980s, political events suggest that regionalism is likely to reassert itself, not through independent military means but through electoral participation and violence. Considerable resentment exists in various regions toward the federal government and toward politicians in Mexico City.[23] This resentment reached its apex with the Zapatista rebellion in 1994 in Chiapas, a region located in the poor, indigenous south. The continued dominance of civilian leaders who were Mexico City-born, reaching nearly half of all prominent national politicians by 1990, helped to inflame that resentment. Fox's election in 2000, however, introduced a significant, and potentially long-lasting reversal in this long-term trend.

In 2000, measured by the backgrounds of members of the executive branch, the percentage of individuals coming from provincial cities and state capitals has increased significantly, and those from Mexico City have declined. Mexico's conversion to a competitive democracy, in which the legislative branch has become a significant actor in the policy-making process, and state governors have become autonomous political actors in their own right, established a fundamental structural change. This change reinforces the reversal of increasing numbers of politicians coming from the nation's capital and replicates a pattern which had occurred under Diaz's administrations but was broken by the Mexican Revolution.[24]

Political-military officers helped temper the dominance of Mexico City natives among national political leaders and in the officer corps itself. Because they were older, they automatically better represented the regional pre-revolutionary distribution of the population. For example, 18 percent of all prominent civilian politicians from 1935 to 1994 were from the Federal District. Yet, at no time from 1910 to 1950, did the population of the capital account for more than 12 percent of the population. These figures demonstrate that, at least since the 1930s, the capital has been significantly overrepresented when measured by politicians' backgrounds. However, among politicians who were career military officers, only 8 percent were from the Federal District. Political-military officers also tended to give stronger representation to the West and the North, providing those regions with a fairer share of national political representation. The political-military officer's elimination served to help swell the figures of recent politicians born in the capital. Among younger, middle-level individuals in the federal bureaucracy, a whopping 51 percent come from Mexico City.[25]

The Sociology of Civil-Military Relations

Regional strengths introduced by politically active military officers are repeated within the officer corps itself. Regular officers reaching the rank of brigade general tend to come from three regions in descending order of importance, the Federal District, the North, and the Gulf. In fact, 22 percent of regular officers, several percentage points higher than the percentage for civilian leaders, are slightly more strongly from the Federal District than are national politicians generally since the mid 1930s. The North is somewhat over-represented, too, because of its importance to the Revolution and the predominance of two generations of political-military leaders from northern states, especially Coahuila, Sonora, and Chihuahua. The Gulf is well represented because an extraordinary number of naval officers come from Veracruz, Mexico's principal port. Political-military officers contributed to exaggerating the North's importance; one out of five came from that region. They also provided a strong counterbalance to generals from the east-central and western states.[26]

Political-military officers also introduced another source of diversity into the origin of military and political leaders. Mexico has been characterized by increasing urbanization. Leadership, regardless of sector, has increasingly tended to come disproportionately from metropolitan areas. Again, political-military officers were more representative of the general population, specifically rural Mexicans. Among all politicians, fewer than one in three comes from a rural area, and among nonpolitical officers, fewer than one in four does so. Half of all political-military officers grew up in rural surroundings, in part, of course, because they were from an older generation.

The political-military officer also represented a different social class among civilian and military leaders. Perhaps more than any background variable, class has a potential impact on the development of a caste mentality. Whether one looks at regular military or civilian politicians, the political-military officer is socially atypical. Over the years, 55 percent came from working-class backgrounds. Among orthodox officers, only 15 percent are known to have come from such backgrounds, and among politicians, 35 percent come from the masses.

The political-military officer contributed to the heterogeneity of civilian and military leadership because of differences in his educational background. For the military, these differences were important because they delayed the impact of military academies on both the socialization and recruitment of the officer corps. It is important to recall that many of these generals controlled command posts necessary to career advancement. One out of three political-military officers never went beyond preparatory school, a characteristic shared by only 2 percent of regular officers. By the

1890s generation, all regular army officers had graduated from the Colegio Militar, or had pursued further professional military studies. This was the case for only two-thirds of political-military officers.

For early generations, a political-military career was the means by which the self-made battlefield commander without formal education could climb the military and political ladder. By the 1900s generation, with revolutionary experience eliminated from their backgrounds, political-military officers increasingly blended in educationally with their regular officer counterparts. Only a third of the officers from this generation can be considered political, but 97 percent were graduates of the Colegio Militar and nearly half completed the staff and command program at the Escuela Superior de Guerra. All regular officers were graduates, and nearly two-thirds had completed the advanced course. By the 1920s and 1930s generations, political-military men had declined to about 20 and 10 percent, respectively, of all top generals. A higher proportion, three-quarters, were Escuela Superior de Guerra graduates. This figure suggests that the younger political officer was the product of a homogeneous military training, and that to achieve a political career, he would also require a level of military education more competitive with that of successful civilian politicians.

Educationally, the political-military officer added diversity to civilian leadership. As was true within the military, the political-military officer allowed a politically ambitious individual, usually from a lower socioeconomic background, to rise to the top of the political ladder. Without the political-military officer's presence in national politics, the leadership would have been further restricted to college-educated, middle- and upper-class individuals. Furthermore, with the exception of physicians, none of the political-military officers who reached national political office received advanced degrees, a credential possessed by 12 percent of the civilian leadership.

Without political-military officers in Mexican politics, the likelihood of a civilian politician's having a military degree is essentially non-existent. This is currently the case. Of the more than fifteen hundred national civilian political figures about whom we have information, only 1 percent graduated from the Heroico Colegio Militar and they had resigned their commissions to pursue other careers. Economics is a field second only to law in politicians' educational credentials; it is absent altogether in military officers' preparation. Only two officers holding national political office have some background in public accounting or economics. This suggests a lack of emphasis on, as well as a need for, such training. Their particularized education bars military men from moving into many of the most influential cabinet agencies, including Treasury, Economic Development, and Commerce, and stands in the way of their flexibility as generalists.

The Sociology of Civil-Military Relations 53

The elimination of political-military officers, given the differences in their backgrounds from regular officers, also has the potential for affecting civil-military relations. Its demise has contributed to both civilian politicians and top officers being more homogeneous, but less like each other. The heterogeneity the political-military officer added to the make up of the typical leading member of the officer corps, contributed to reducing the potential for a caste mentality, a quality which can be a significant obstacle to positive civil-military relationships.

Mustangs

One of the remarkable characteristics of the Mexican officer corps since 1946 has been the presence of the "mustang," an individual, similar to his U.S. Army counterpart, who achieves a commission after starting out in the enlisted ranks. Nearly one in four men reaching the rank of general began his career as an enlisted soldier. This fact gives substantial credence to the belief that officers are a product of the masses. Analysts have pointed to revolutionary origins as the source of the popular roots of the officer corps, but mustangs have produced greater long-term effects. No other country in the region can claim the level of representation achieved by Mustangs or their equivalent in the Mexican armed forces. In his examination of Ecuador, Fitch only could identify a single such officer from the 1930s and 1940s who reached the rank of general.[27]

The presence of a significant percentage of mustangs has potentially important implications for civil-military relations in Mexico and elsewhere. Fitch speculates that such a group of officers might feel more indebted to the political leadership, having been given access to an upwardly mobile career, and would be resistant to military intervention. Given the size of this group within the Mexican military, one could speculate that they may have helped reinforce military subordination. I would argue, however, that these officers, instead of feeling indebted to civilian leadership for such an opportunity, would credit the military for legitimizing its values and beliefs, which in Mexico includes subordination to civilian rule.

The surviving revolutionary officer, more often than not a political-military general, and the enlisted soldier who makes officer rank were often one and the same in the early years. Among officers born in the 1880s and 1890s who saw combat in the Revolution, nearly half joined the revolutionary forces as ordinary soldiers. They were promoted on the basis of leadership and combat skills, essentially battlefield promotions. This type of officer in the next generation, that is the generation born in the first decade of the twentieth century, declined to 17 percent. Increased professionalization in the 1920s further separated officers from the enlisted ranks. Had this pattern continued, mustangs might have disappeared altogether.

Instead, President Cárdenas formally instituted what had happened informally during the revolutionary decade. In 1935, in an address to the Colegio Militar, he explained to the cadets that officers "should not think of ourselves as professional soldiers . . . but rather as armed auxiliaries organized from the humble classes."[28] He also announced that a substantial number of the Colegio's cadets would henceforth be drawn from enlisted ranks. Two years later, when the government realized that sufficient junior officers were not available for police duty in remote rural regions, the Centro de Instrución de Jefes y Oficiales was set up to train noncommissioned officers of proven ability for service as officers.[29]

The enrollment of enlisted soldiers as cadets at the Heroico Colegio Militar officially lasted until 1944, although actual examples had stopped several years prior to that date.[30] The program led to two influential generations of mustangs in the officer corps. Generals born between 1910 and 1929 dominated the armed forces in the 1960s, 1970s, and 1980s. Of their numbers, nearly one in four could claim mustang status. This is an even more remarkable figure given the fact that during the years the program was in effect at the military academy, only 12 to 16 percent of the cadets enrolled had begun their careers as enlisted soldiers. These percentages indicate that the success rate of cadets from enlisted backgrounds was far higher than that of the usual cadets.

Termination of the program in 1944 resulted in eliminating mustangs among general officers born after 1930. In 1955, after much debate, the Secretariat of National Defense instituted a limited version of the original program. For the first time a select number of first sergeants who had both graduated from the noncommissioned officers school and demonstrated exceptional leadership ability were chosen for a one-year program at the Heroico Colegio Militar.[31] However, I have found among leading generals no graduates of the 1955 program.[32] In 1966 another change occurred. The regular cadet program was extended to four years. From 1966 to 1978 first sergeants selected for the program were required to enroll for four years. After 1978 first sergeants were allowed to take one year of special training and then a one-year program at the Heroico Colegio Militar to become second lieutenants. That program occasioned resentment on the part of regular cadet officers, who perceived its graduates as adversely affecting their own promotion rates.[33] An expanded program was instituted in the 1980s, when de la Madrid's modest modernization program produced an unmet demand for officer cadets. Top officers who began as enlisted personnel, generally as a means of upward social mobility, can still be found in the communications

The Sociology of Civil-Military Relations

specialty. In fact, nearly half of the recent promotions to brigadier general in that specialty were officers who enlisted as privates. The most recent case in our sample of an officer who enlisted as a private is that of a general in the cavalry who was serving as a zone commander in 2003, having joined the army in 1972.[34]

Mustangs have not only risen to the rank of general but have achieved other top posts in the armed forces. They often take several years longer to achieve general rank but are no less successful than typical cadets. "In fact, as a percentage of all officer candidates at the Heroic Military College, the cadet who entered the army originally as an enlisted man has, in the past, greater success reaching the rank of general than his peers."[35] One reason for the accomplishment may be that their completion rate is higher than that of their civilian counterparts who enlist directly as cadets at the Heroico Colegio Militar and customarily have had no previous exposure to military life. The discipline and extreme authoritarian environment at the Heroico Colegio Militar and later at the Escuela Superior de Guerra are more difficult hurdles than the academic challenge, and enlisted men often cope more easily than do relative novices with these challenges.

Mustangs reached their heyday in the 1982–1988 administration, especially in holding top posts in the National Defense Secretariat. Four secretaries of national defense from 1946 to 1964 can claim enlisted origins, but Juan Arévalo Gardoqui's colleagues best exemplify the success of this group. Among his top upper-echelon department heads, of whom only nineteen were old enough to have attended the Heroico Colegio Militar during those years, ten were mustangs. Such predominance is attributable to his second- and third-ranking officials, both of whom were mustangs in the 1930s.

Mustangs have been important to the officer corps for several reasons. The socioeconomic makeup of the officer corps is in large measure a result of their presence. A much larger percentage of mustangs come from the working class than from the middle class. In fact, although the majority of officers whose social origins are known to have been middle class, the proportion of officers from working class origins who enlist in the military as cadets is much higher. If mustangs are excluded from the ranks of generals, only 14 percent come from lower socioeconomic classes. Among mustangs alone, however, half are products of a working class background. The disappearance of mustangs from the officer corps increases the social homogeneity of the generals. Given the increased educational credentials necessary to enroll in the Heroico Colegio Militar since 1995, the social effects are even more pronounced. It also helps to distance officers further from the masses in terms of roots and contributes to the potential for a new caste mentality, which, if it developed, potentially could affect civil-military relations significantly.

The military, in contrast to civilian structures, provides an important channel for upward social mobility through the enlisted officer program. To this day, the only other elite group in Mexico providing such opportunities is the clergy. Many leading bishops, given the access of children from humble families to seminary schools, share similar social origins with military mustangs.[36] The civilian with political ambitions who comes from a working-class background comparable to that of the mustang must survive financially and intellectually in a middle-class academic environment. Few do. Civilian public institutions of higher education are numerous and diverse, and many working-class applicants enroll in them, but few graduate.[37]

Why, then, did the Secretariat of National Defense drop the enlisted officer program? No official explanation has been given, but several possibilities come to mind. First, by the mid-1940s, political authorities were trying to reduce the size of the officer corps. Closing off one possible channel for recruits was a means of limiting the cadet pool. Second, Cárdenas' definition of the officer corps was part of his larger populist political platform advocating stronger ties between the state and the masses, incorporated into a sophisticated, corporatist political structure. A residue of his philosophy has been a fixture of the political system until 2000, but his successor, General Manuel Avila Camacho, de-emphasized this orientation on many fronts, including state-military relations. Possibly, the enlisted officer program was a victim of that new direction.

John J. Johnson offers a more practical assessment, based on an interview with an officer from the period: "One of the chief reasons his nation felt obliged to suspend the practice of permitting able non-commissioned officers to win regular commissions was that their wives simply could not make the social transition: this made them unacceptable to the wives of the regular commissioned officers and an embarrassment to their own husbands, all of which led to family difficulties."[38] If Johnson's source is correct, it explains why the military quietly eliminated the program. It could never be discussed publicly because the rationale contradicts the military's projected populist image and the lack of class conflict that Mexican leadership stresses.

The mustang's elimination also alters the geographical composition of the officer corps. Proportionately, mustangs provide much stronger representation for rural Mexicans than do high-ranking officers in general. Enlisted men are drawn from many regions, but cadets have had to transport themselves, in the past, to Mexico City. Consequently, only 28 percent of the officers from cadet origins were born in rural villages compared with nearly half of the officers who enlisted before becoming cadets. Elimination of the mustang not only increased the officer corps' urban bias but emphasized certain regions. Most important, like political-military officers, mustangs also did not come disproportionately from the Federal District, as does the officer corps as a whole. Nearly twice as many regular officers as mustangs, one in four, were born in the Federal District. Mustangs provided stronger representation for both the North and the East Central regions and over-represented the South, the poorest region and the least-well-represented among politicians and other leadership groups. Also, the officer corps, partly because of the influence of naval officer candidates, who are not mustangs, strongly over-represents the Gulf, a region significantly underrepresented among mustangs. Without mustangs, top-ranking officers as a whole take on many of the social and geographic background variables, including both strengths and weaknesses, of Mexican politicians.

Within the armed forces, mustangs affect the prominence of career military occupational specialties (MOS) among its leadership. Two patterns became clear. First, because many of them emerged from the Revolution, more than half were infantry. Generally speaking, the more sophisticated the training, the less likely mustangs will be found. For example, they are underrepresented in artillery, and most significant, five times as many regular officers as mustangs pursue engineering and medicine. Second, mustangs overwhelmingly dominate one specialty, communications. Nearly three-quarters of all generals in our sample with a communications background are mustangs. A large percentage of recent generals in this field enrolled in the army as privates, before becoming officers. They typically graduate from the Communications School, not the Heroico Colegio Militar. In the early years mustangs were extremely well represented in the infantry, the core of the army. As the army professionalized educationally and technically, cavalry, artillery, and engineering increased in importance. Communications, on the other hand, never acquired the critical mass of the other three fields, thus affecting its leaders' potential to influence future military policy decisions. It remains defined as a service field, and officers on active duty in this specialty can only be promoted to brigade general rank.[39]

Mustangs, similar to political-military officers, produce similar potential consequences for civil-military relations. Mustangs were far more significant, however, in emphasizing the differences in social composition between the civilian and military leadership. Sharp differences in social class origins, even more so than those differences in urban and rural backgrounds, enhances the possibility of different outlooks between these two groups, as well as different perceptions each group shares of their peers. Johnson's observations about the difficulties class backgrounds generated within the officer corps are potentially equally significant between civilian and military leadership.

Regular Career (Orthodox Professional) Officers

The political-military officers and mustangs, two subgroups with special characteristics, dramatically affected the composition of the Mexican officer corps. However, it is the officer corps as a whole, especially since these two types of officers have disappeared altogether in the last two decades (except communications), that must be analyzed in order to understand the image it projects and the significance of its composition. What are the important consequences of age, geography, class, and family military background among the typical high-ranking officers, and what, if any differences are there between the services?

Why look at generals and admirals on the basis of age? Generational experiences, especially in a society that has undergone significant changes politically and structurally in the twentieth century, can affect the outlook of leadership groups.[40] In the case of Mexico, the Revolution is a natural dividing line between pre- and post-1910 generations.[41] Some of Mexico's most astute historians believe that individuals born after 1920 "do not have the slightest idea of the difficult realities which the Revolution brought."[42] A national security expert who has taught for a number of years at the Colegio de Defensa Nacional believes the military is divided into four important groups or generations: the first consists of revolutionary generals; the second is the generation formed during World War II; the third is graduates of the staff and command school at the Escuela Superior de Guerra and the fourth is a new generation of graduates of the Colegio de Defensa Nacional. This generational pattern is confirmed by none other than Fox's secretary of national defense, General Gerardo Clemente Vega García, a graduate of the fifth Colegio de Defensa Nacional class (1986), who described his generation as "marking a fundamental change from the previous group." He noted in 2004 that only two division generals from an older generation remained on active duty and characterized most of his group as graduates of this highest level institution.[43]

Some of these distinctions are valuable, but the rationales for the distinctions are somewhat different from those provided above. For so many reasons, including those that differentiated the political-military general from the rest of the generals, the pre-1900 generations constitute a clear grouping of men who shared the comradeship of combat. That experience is all pervasive when one considers that only 2 of the more than 134 generals and admirals born before 1900 had not actually fought in the Revolution. That shared experience itself helped to serve as a bridge to civilian politicians, many of whom also participated in the Revolution but did not choose the military as a career. The pre-1900 generation put its stamp on the officer corps and flavored both the armed forces' composition and self-image far beyond its own expected lifespan. Its members were politically ambitious; three-quarters of their numbers also successfully pursued political office.

The second group of officers (born from 1900 to 1919) is more difficult to describe. Many of them were the first to be trained not only in the Heroico Colegio Militar but also in the Escuela Superior de Guerra. About 20 percent fought in the Revolution, but most of them with combat experience (34 percent) earned their spurs during the rebellions of 1923, 1927, 1929, and 1939. They were a transitional generation reflecting the qualities of officers to come, and they dominated the armed forces leadership in the 1950s and 1960s. They were molded during the political system's adolescence, many being called to defend the state against fellow officers, typically from the pre-1900 generation.

The third generation, born in the 1920s, was shaped almost completely through higher military education and technical training abroad. Nearly all its members were graduates of the Escuela Superior de Guerra, the most universal of their shared professional experiences. In that sense, surviving the rigors of Escuela Superior de Guerra, which has a dropout rate no less severe than combat mortality rates, replaced combat as a key socializing experience. Whereas 98 percent of the pre-1900 generation fought in the Revolution, exactly 98 percent of the 1920s generation saw no combat. Many also were mustangs, having started their careers in the enlisted ranks.[44] It is true that many were trained or grew up during World War II, but the war itself had little impact on their formation,[45] other than increasing the prestige of the U.S. military in Mexico, and probably influencing Mexican security concerns within the context of the post-1945 cold war mentality. They were a decisive generation in post-1946 leadership because they accounted for a fourth of all commanding officers controlling top posts in the 1970s and 1980s.

The fourth generation, the 1930s–1940s generation, which has been called the Colegio de Defensa Nacional group, is the one we understand least. Its members are the officers now in control of the armed forces, and have been in control since the 1990s. Their full impact on the military and civil-military relations is yet to come, but the younger members of that group, born in the 1940s, have introduced a number of significant changes, especially in the navy, since 2000. They tend to have urban middle-class backgrounds, to have lived in Mexico City, and to have followed staff careers.

The civil-military relationship in Mexico has been affected by an artificial separation between the military and civilian leaders sustained by their differences in age. Conservatism and a strong association with the values arising from the shared experiences of the revolutionary and post-revolutionary generations naturally persisted longer among military than political leaders because of age differences. This difference can be demonstrated dramatically when comparing presidents and their national defense secretaries by date of birth. In some cases, these individuals have been separated by age differences of 15 years or more and, only in the case of President Fox and General Vega García in the last half century, are they the same age. Also, different age groups emphasize other elite background characteristics more strongly, including regional origins, birthplace, and education. If these varying backgrounds produce differing ideas, as some authors have asserted, then an older generation of officers at the top of the military hierarchy may have contributed to a source of friction between the two groups.[46]

A trend toward younger senior officers was brought about by the elimination of the political-military officer and the officer with revolutionary roots. This change may well increase the military's influence because "younger officers will have more in common with the generally younger civilian leadership."[47] The trade-off for bringing the two groups closer together in terms of age, implying shared backgrounds and generational experiences, is that the traditional political-military leadership interlock, and the benefits ascribed to it, disappeared.

In addition to generational differences, geography has a potentially significant influence on civil-military relations. For example, in some Latin American countries certain regions dominate political and military leadership and are resented by other regions. Frank McCann found an extremely influential geographical pattern in Brazil. At the turn of the century only 5 percent of military cadets came from the politically important state of Rio Grande de Sul, but 49 percent of the officers of that generation who became generals were from Rio Grande de Sul.[48] McCann's data suggest that place of origin affects promotion.

Prior to the 1940s only one significant geographic pattern is present among all Mexican military officers: overrepresentation of the North. More than a fourth of all officers came from the North, a statistic explained by the fact that nearly one in three revolutionary generals did so. But an analysis of the post-1946 military leadership suggests two influential regional patterns: increasing dominance of the Federal District and under-representation of the West Central region.

Mexico City is the most important locale geographically speaking in officers' birthplaces. The predominance of the capital city is a phenomenon found among other Latin American militaries. Approximately 38 to 47 percent of each Argentine military graduating class were from the Buenos Aires metropolitan area.[49] Mexican data from the mid-1950s suggest a comparable figure: 39 percent of cadet aspirants were from the Federal District.[50] These are the same cadets who control the secretariat of national defense in the 2000s. Forty-one percent of Brazil's recent cadets are from Rio de Janeiro, the historic capital, rather than Brasilia.[51]

Over the history of the officer corps, the proportion of officers from Mexico City has been several times the proportion of the population living there (19 percent versus 5 percent respectively). Figures for generals born since 1930—in 1930 only 7 percent of the population lived in Mexico City—show a ratio of 5 to 1. It appears that the military has become sensitive to the imbalance; of the 245 spaces for cadets in the 1991 Heroico Colegio Militar class, only 18 percent have been allotted to the Federal District.[52] This pattern may well have been introduced among earlier cadet classes. For the first time in many generations, the 1940s cohort, who are still comparatively smaller in numbers than earlier generations, show a significant decline in officers from the Federal District. The youngest generation of top officers have the smallest percentage from the Federal District of any generation in the twentieth century. The reduced numbers of cadets from the Federal District in the 1991 class may produce a decline in Federal District birthplaces among top officers in 2020 or, as McCann discovered in Brazil, officers from the capital may be promoted disproportionately. However, members of the 1992 Escuela Superior de Guerra class, who will become the next generals in several decades, still over-represent the Federal District at 39 percent of the class.[53]

Generational data for Federal District birthplace demonstrate that the 1900 generation is a key group because the capital city birthplaces escalate dramatically from 3 to 24 percent, an eightfold increase in just ten years, and remains at a quarter of high ranking officers until the 1930s generation. Scholars argue that in Mexico and elsewhere the geographic concentration of military units also affects the recruitment of enlisted men.[54] Prospective Mexican officers had to apply in the capital, thus imposing a financial and geographic hurdle for applicants from more distant regions. In the late 1990s, as part of the recommended internal changes, the application procedures were diversified geographically. Also, it has been said that the availability of superior preparatory education and the visible presence of the academies in Mexico City have contributed to attracting greater numbers of applications from the Federal District.[55] The effect of this pattern is accentuated by the fact that now all cadets must have completed a preparatory education before enrolling in the Heroico Colegio Militar.[56]

The dominance of Mexico City in the backgrounds of Mexico's generals has several implications. All Mexican elite groups seriously under-represent other regions. Considerable provincial resentment exists against Mexico City because of its authoritarian exercise of political and economic power prior to 2000. That is translated into resentment against people from Mexico City. In the past the military, more than other leadership groups excepting the clergy, provided broader geographic representation and alternative channels for upward mobility to ambitious provincials.

The third geographical trend with considerable significance revealed by data regarding the birthplaces of Mexican officers is the sizable under-representation of the West Central region, one of Mexico's most populous, and to a lesser extent, the South. Twenty-one percent of the population lived in the West Central region in 1910, but it produced only 8 percent of the top officers. We have no explanation for why this might be so for early generations, but one possible interpretation for low representation among subsequent groups of generals is the role of the army in suppressing the bitter Cristero rebellion against the government in the 1920s. An oral history of peasants in the region suggests that they see military zone commanders as opponents of land reform.[57] General Garfias Magaña, who represented Lagos de Moreno, Jalisco in congress, a locale in the heart of the Cristero rebellion, reported experiencing this resentment personally.[58] According to contemporary military observers, the military purposely maintains a low profile there.[59]

The military, as an institution, reinforces its historic role in the region as part of its self-image. An examination of individual officer records and the military's own publications suggests that the Cristeros' suppression was considered an important contribution to national unification and a demonstration of military loyalty to the state.[60] As if to mirror the revolt's importance in the generals' formation, it plays a similar role, for opposite reasons, among leading Mexican clergy. Mexican bishops come disproportionately from the West Central region, but surviving priests and bishops remember well their persecution as seminary students in the late 1920s.[61]

One other region stands out in the birthplaces of high-ranking Mexican officers. The Gulf was over-represented, although not significantly so until the post-1930s generations. The Gulf's high level of representation occurs largely because naval officers have been disproportionately from the Veracruz area. The primary naval academy is located in Veracruz. Of the military officers from the Gulf in the 1900, 1910, and 1920 generations, 38, 71 and 53 percent, respectively, were navy officers. Of all naval officers in our sample, nearly half are from the Gulf, most from Veracruz; 7 percent are from the Federal District, and the remainder are from all other regions combined. Veracruz is to the navy what the Federal District is to the army. The army recruits and enlisted and officer ranks are most heavily from Veracruz and Tabasco. In 2003, those two states alone accounted for 24 percent of Mexicans who enlisted in the army and air force, while representing fewer than 10 percent of the population.

Officers in each of the two major services come disproportionately from a particular region, and each is substantially different from the other in terms of geographic composition. There is no evidence that these geographic circumstances exacerbate inter-service rivalries, but they create some potential in that direction. More important, younger generals and admirals, like younger politicians, are coming from these two regions in increasing numbers. Half of the national executive branch division heads, the lieutenant colonels and colonels of the civilian political elite, came from the Federal District in the 1990s, and Veracruz was the only other state with a reasonably strong representation in their birthplaces.[62]

A second broad geographic variable in regard to birthplace and early residence of military officers is size of their native town, a variable which has potential implications for civil-military relations. Studies of Third World countries reveal that most elites have rural backgrounds because the societies are rural. Proportionately, however, rural birthplaces among the military have been over-represented. Officers' birthplaces worldwide tend to over-represent smaller cites.[63] A combination of the provincial, lower-middle-class origins contributes to the military's "fundamentalist" orientation and lack of integration with other elites, especially the political elite.[64]

Our empirical data can provide a generational picture of urban and rural origins. The trends imply a significant contrast between Mexican political and military elites among the oldest generations. Mexico's military leadership, in contrast to what Morris Janowitz found elsewhere, is not a rural-based elite, nor does it differ substantially from the civilian leadership in the last three generations.[65] Historically, the officer corps always has been disproportionately urban, although much less so than political leadership. Prior to 1935, during most of the Porfiriato, only slightly more than half the officers came from rural backgrounds, and with few exceptions, that figure was relatively consistent from the 1820s generations to the turn of the century. Only two-fifths of their civilian counterparts were from rural communities. In fact, rather than a natural decline in rural birthplaces because of urbanization, the 1910 Revolution provided many ambitious rural men with an opportunity to use popular armies as a channel for upward mobility, especially those from the 1880s generation, and to a lesser extent, the 1890s generation. Again, the 1900s generation becomes a benchmark generation for both politicians and general officers, as a sudden drop in rural birthplaces becomes apparent for the post-revolutionary generation.

Contrary to popular belief, the military urbanized at a faster rate than the civilian political leadership. Sixty-seven percent of all generals in our study came from urban communities. From 1900 to 1910, an extraordinary decline in military rural backgrounds to only 16 percent occurred; fewer than half as many as the previous generation, a change not equaled or exceeded by either leadership group until the present (1940s) leadership generation. The military's rural backgrounds increased again in the 1920s generation, equal to its political counterpart, largely because President Cárdenas introduced the mustang in the 1930s. Only 5 percent of the post-1940s generations of generals and politicians boast rural origins.

Many professional armies, as a consequence of constituents' rural birthplaces, have an anti-urban outlook, and the officer corps develops a critical attitude toward upper-class urban values.[66] Of course, because the Mexican officer corps has been predominantly urban, it does not express such an attitude. Furthermore, the military rarely has identified with peasant or rural interests despite its original rural origins and positive rhetoric toward peasants.[67] This bias is typically attributed to political elites too.

Generational and geographic differences within and between the officer corps and the political leadership have received relatively little attention in Latin America. In contrast, since José Nun's theory regarding the middle class military coup, the general literature on social class origins has paid close attention to this variable as a source of divisions within the military and a basis for political intervention.[68] Several variations on these theories exist. The first is that the military is likely to support, or intervene in support of, policies advocated by its own class. In Mexico, this is not a likely source of division between the two leadership groups. More important, some scholars believe that social origin contributes strongly to officers' social and political attitudes. Marion Levy, Jr. argues that: "Given the general isolation of armed forces personnel . . . the general social origin of the personnel has a special relevance for their behavior while members. . . . These opinions are of great importance when members of the armed force organizations operate in contexts other than those strictly military ones."[69]

In the Kourvetaris and Debratz survey, the authors could not find a universal relationship in the officer corps between social origin and political participation.[70] Nevertheless, persuasive arguments suggest that comparable class origins within military and political leaders eliminate social-class differences as a source of friction between the two groups.[71] The 1910 Revolution created some shared roots between the military and the masses. The military's post-1940s modernization, however, has gradually increased the social distance between the officer corps and the ordinary Mexican. "Some analysts have emphasized that modernization is also giving the military a distinctive social status which tends to isolate soldiers from the rest of society. It does this by creating a centralized command structure, full-time soldiers, bureaucratization, specialized high esprit de corps, technical sophistication, a corporate identity, and professional responsibility."[72]

The Sociology of Civil-Military Relations

Still another reason that class origin is thought to be important is its ideological implications, especially in terms of attitudes toward democracy versus authoritarianism. It is probably true that social origin seems to be more consequential in Third World countries than in industrialized nations in shaping the military's political perspectives.[73] Nevertheless, a general assumption is that individuals from lower socioeconomic backgrounds (people who typically are victims of the military's "political" activities) would be strongly opposed to such authoritarian abuses. Frederick Nunn is not convinced that lower-class officers would evince ideals any more democratic than officers from different social backgrounds.[74] However, a study of authoritarian attitudes among Mexican children conducted by Rafael Segovia unequivocally found that as socioeconomic status increases, authoritarianism decreases.[75] These findings have been confirmed in a recent comprehensive exploration of citizen democratic attitudes in Mexico.[76]

Segovia also discovered that as education increases, authoritarianism decreases. In Mexico, as in most other societies, increased education would be associated with individuals of higher socioeconomic status. For military officers, the level of education is not likely to be associated with a decline in authoritarianism but, rather, its increase. First, the content of the education is more important than level, especially in terms of obedience to authority. Second, the higher the educational level in the Mexican military system the more complete the subordination to authority.

Social origin is not particularly important to Latin American military officers because of the socialization process through which all officers must pass. The process instills obliviousness to class, a strong set of values that determines organizational behavior, and, most important, the primacy of institutional over personal or political interests.[77] Socialization processes can eliminate the significance of social class origin; on the other hand, the Mexican military can stress values and organizational behavior that give officers a closer identification with the masses and build a strong sense of subordination to civil authority.

Lower-middle-class origins of the Mexican officer corps and the middle- and upper-middle-class origins of politicians have fundamentally affected civil-military relations. Several generals have indicated that they believe middle-class professionals in the public sector perceive them as ignorant. One officer who served in the Chamber of Deputies concluded, "My fellow members in the chamber seemed to think that military officers couldn't think or write."[78] Numerous anecdotes suggest that they are seen as socially inferior. This phenomenon, perhaps more than any other variable, has encouraged distance between civilian and military groups.

The Mexican officer corps, like any elite group, never has been representative of the population. Prior to 1935, only 38 percent of the officers came from the working class, whereas more than 91 percent of the population were working class. During the same period, 46 percent of the officers came from the middle classes, from which no more than 8 percent of the population were drawn. Fifteen percent of the officer corps came from the upper class, the class represented by only 1 percent of the population. In percentage terms, of course, the upper class was most over-represented in the officer corps.[79]

The Mexican Revolution temporarily altered the socioeconomic composition of the officer corps. The 1880s generation was most important, and of this age cohort, nearly two-thirds of the officers came from working-class families compared with nine-tenths of the population. At no other time in the past century has the working class been better represented, numerically or proportionately, in the officer corps. Even in the following generation, although their numbers declined, working-class officers still accounted for almost half of those reaching the rank of brigade general or vice-admiral. As has been true of all other background characteristics, a sharp distinction occurs between the nineteenth and twentieth centuries. In the 1900s cohort nearly four-fifths came from the middle and upper classes (upper-class origins were negligible), at a time when only one-tenth of the population was classified as middle or upper class.

Politicians have been much more representative of the population as a whole than have top military officers, except the oldest generations who are not numerically significant among post-1940s leaders. The youngest political generations, like the military, reflect the nearly complete disappearance of leaders from the working class, even though in the 1940s and 1950s the working class still accounted for 80 percent of the population.[80] Most of the individuals desirous of upward social mobility born in the 1920s and 1930s would have found greater opportunities in a political rather than a military career. Among the 1940s generation, while the national political elite has become almost exclusively middle class, the officer corps still retains more opportunities for working class aspirants. In fact, if we compare the hundred most influential politicians with an equal number of influential officers from 1970 through 2000, a third of the officer corps, compared to only a fifth of politicians, came from these socio-economic origins.[81]

The figures regarding the socioeconomic background of military officers are extremely important given the military's public attitude about who it is and what it represents socially in Mexico. General Félix Galván, a former secretary of national defense, best expresses this view: "The army comes from the people. I myself am a product of campesinos. We, truthfully—this isn't a word, a phrase or posture—truthfully, we are the people of the people. The enlisted men are campesino boys who we recruit; the officers also come from the popular classes."[82] The irony of this statement is that Galván, according to an officer who knew him, was actually a product of a lower middle class family. His father owned a print shop. This fact reinforces the desire of the army to emphasize these origins; even of the secretary of national defense has to tell a white lie about his own social background.

William S. Ackroyd found that officers he interviewed considered their social identity to be toward the lower end of the socioeconomic scale.[83] The discrepancy between actual and perceived class backgrounds can be explained in two ways. First, a wide range exists in the empirical categorization of the middle classes. The same criteria were applied to both politicians and officers, but it is fair to say that a far greater number of politicians come from upper-middle-class or professional backgrounds, whereas officers come from the bottom of the middle class.[84] Second, an increasingly large percentage of middle-class officers are the children of career military. Their parents' incomes, however, do not put them in the same category as politicians' children. Technically they are middle class, but these men share their fathers' perception that they, too, are from the "people."

It is also possible that the socioeconomic backgrounds of the officer corps as a whole does not accurately reflect those of high-ranking generals. A study of U.S. officers found this to be the case. Although working-class backgrounds were underrepresented in the U.S. military, the discrepancy was much less among all officers, suggesting that middle-class origins, for whatever reason, assist officers in reaching the top ranks.[85] Graduates of Mexico's Escuela Superior de Guerra were disproportionately from the middle class relative to cadets graduating from the Heroico Colegio Militar.[86] Graduation from the Escuela Superior de Guerra is typical of almost all general officers, but especially two and three star ranks, who make up our sample. Interestingly, recent Escuela Superior de Guerra graduates not only suggest that most of their peers are from the working class, but they are proud of that fact. This suggests the importance of working class origins as part of the officer corps' own self definition.[87]

The overrepresentation of the lower middle class in the backgrounds of the Mexican officer corps can be explained largely by the economic advantages it offers. Admission fees of both the Heroico Colegio Militar and the Colegio Aire initially screened out lower income applicants. Because applicants were tested in the Federal District for most of the century, they must also have been able to pay travel expenses to get there.[88] However, since the late 1980s, the secretariat of national defense decentralized its test, and its current website lists the various locations where the entrance tests can be taken. Also, the required competitive examination is a social screening device. Whereas members of the lower middle class can more readily obtain the preparatory education necessary to pass the examination, those from lower socioeconomic backgrounds often cannot.[89]

Indeed, the armed forces' attempt to place itself on par with civilians educationally and professionally may have a serious adverse effect on its social composition as an organization, and potentially on civil-military relations. Since the publication of the 1995 internal report, a preparatory credential became required for admission to the Heroico Colegio Militar. "The imposition of preparatory education would surely improve the caliber of cadets, but it would also act as a deterrent to many potential working-class recruits who now have access to the military, drastically altering the officer corps' social composition. Since few working-class families have alternative upwardly-mobile social channels to pursue, narrowing access to military careers may adversely affect political stability."[90]

It is possible that in the future the officer corps will become more rather than less representative of the population, something that has already occurred in the United States.[91] Since World War II sons of the lower-middle and working classes have had greater opportunities to become officers.[92] The reason for this is that as the economy grew, lower-middle-class children had a wider range of opportunities for upward social mobility, and working-class children received better educations, which enabled them to compete more effectively. However, less prosperous times in Mexico since the late 1970s have considerably reduced middle-class growth. Consequently, higher educational requirements, not increased access, is likely to produce the only foreseeable source of change in the officer corps' social composition.

Studies of other nations suggest that most individuals join the military as a means of upward social and economic mobility. Most newly independent nations recruit for the military among the middle and lower-middle classes. The United States, with the smallest working class, recruits two-thirds of its military officers from the lower-middle and working classes,[93] and the officer's social background is likely to determine his or her persistence in the military. Lifetime careerists tend to come from lower socioeconomic strata than do those who resign their commissions. Thus, "the striking implication was that young men from less privileged social backgrounds are finding opportunities for increased social status in the military career more attractive than in civilian careers."[94]

Upward social mobility as a basis for choosing a military career has been important for Mexicans with little formal education but strong political ambitions. They had a greater chance for success in the military than did their civilian counterparts with equivalent educational credentials.[95] This circumstance applied only to the revolutionary generation. Individuals born in the 1880s and 1890s without advanced education had fewer chances of rising to the top of the political ladder through a career in politics than through a career in the officer corps. Many officers believe that this "revolutionary" origin alters the social composition of the Mexican officer corps, especially relative to other Latin American militaries.[96]

For the revolutionary generation, especially those who chose politics, the military was attractive to the lower socioeconomic classes and to individuals in rural areas. At "that specific historic juncture, then, the military appears to have provided routes of access for socially deprived campesinos" to the political elite.[97] But looking at high-ranking officers in general rather than just political-military officers, one sees a military more open to urban than rural poor, even though more mustangs (who are generally from the working classes) come from rural areas. Rural working-class Mexicans are less likely than their urban counterparts to pursue a military career because the latter have greater access to primary and secondary education.[98] This pattern will only be enhanced with the recent requirement that cadets at the Heroico Colegio Militar have completed a preparatory education.

One additional background variable, whether or not an individual's father is in the military, has significant bearing on the characteristics of the officer corps. This is true in terms of both its self-image and its relationship to civilian political leadership. In fact, other than upward social mobility, the reason given by the largest remaining number of officer aspirants to the Heroico Colegio Militar is to follow in the footsteps of their father or other relatives.[99] In Brazil, for example, 30 percent of the cadets at the army academy were sons of career military personnel.[100] Cadets entering the Heroico Colegio Militar because of an intrinsic desire for a service career are for the most part sons of army personnel.

Second- or even third-generation army men are extremely important because they indicate the emergence of a self-perpetuating officer corps.[101] Among leading members of the officer corps during the last three decades, 36 percent were the children of career officers. The officer corps is the most ingrown of leadership groups except for capitalists. Family ties are a significant source of networking among elite circles in Mexico. For the cream of the crop from the officer corps, they are the least important primarily because the officer corps comes disproportionately from military family backgrounds. These are people who inter-marry with other military families, thus reducing their opportunities to form kinship and social ties with representatives of other elite groups.[102]

Military fathers always have been well represented in the backgrounds of the Mexican officer corps. The fathers of prominent officers born in the decades of the 1880s through the 1930s came primarily from three important backgrounds: peasant or laborer (33 percent), military (18 percent), and professional (16 percent). The figure for working-class parents, however, is deceptive. Revolutionary officers account for four-fifths of the fathers who were peasants or laborers; this means that among all other generations of top officers prior to 1935, fewer than one in ten had a working-class father. What these figures suggest is that the revolutionary generation was extremely important in contributing to the contemporary military's popular roots, but that its contribution was short-lived.[103] Again, if we look at that more selective group of influential officers from 1970 to 2000, those who come from parents who were peasants or laborers drops to 13 percent, and professional and white collar occupations become increasingly common in parental backgrounds.[104]

The pre-1935 generations, except for the revolutionary group, were not only the children of military fathers but often came from prominent military, political, or landowning families (14 percent). A larger percentage also were otherwise related to prominent political figures (23 percent) or military figures (5 percent). The revolutionary generation gave birth to a new military, most of whose members had no familial roots in the established military. This did not, as might be expected, eliminate the caste aspect of the military. Rather, it initiated an entirely new set of parental sources for officers in the second half of the twentieth century. In the mid-1950s, one in five parents of aspirants to the Heroico Colegio Militar was in the military.[105] It is estimated that military families constituted about 20 percent of the total number of cadets, and that double that figure had extended family members serving in or affiliated with the armed forces.[106]

Data from our survey of Mexican generals and admirals reveal that one in three is the child of a career military father, typically an officer.[107] In addition to reestablishing the importance of military parentage, generals with military fathers since 1946 are more numerous than in any previous period. The phenomenon does not appear to be unusual for Latin America. Forty percent of the entering cadets in Brazil's Academia Militar das Agulhas Negras (AMAN) were sons of military men in the 1960s; nearly three-quarters of them were sons of corporals or sergeants.[108]

If about one in five Mexican cadets has a career military father, the fact that one in three of such cadets actually reaches the rank of general is significant.[109] U.S. military observers suggest that one aid to surviving the rigors of the Escuela Superior de Guerra, a hurdle that most officers who go on to general must overcome, is kinship with a prominent officer. If junior officers who are the children of officers are more likely to achieve the highest ranks, whether on their own merits or those of a father, a potential for resentment among officers without such blood ties exists. Among U.S. military cadets, a direct correlation exists between career military parentage, academic success, and lower attrition rates.[110] Nevertheless, two in three Mexican officers de not have officer fathers. Substantial upward mobility within the service still is the norm for officers without such fathers.

The Impact of Origins on Civil-Military Relations

The gradual decline and nearly complete elimination of political-military and mustang officers among Mexican generals has had considerable impact on the officer corps and on civil-military relations. No longer does a large percentage of officers having personal experience with and ties among civilian politicians serve as a bridge between the two leadership groups. Other means will have to substitute for maintaining adequate communication and exchange. The absence of political-military officers and mustangs also directly affects the caste quality of the military, encouraging it to become more homogeneous and potentially more isolated from civilian leaders. Differences in social origins, and in some cases geography, helped to diversify the military and, in some cases, increased its comparability to the civilian political leadership. The increasing homogeneity in officer backgrounds facilitates the military's tilt toward developing a stronger caste mentality, differentiating it from, and possibly complicating its relations with, civilian leaders. The most important of these patterns is the percentage of top officers in the army, navy, and air force whose fathers also were career officers.

Other trends in the backgrounds of the officer corps, however, offer a countervailing influence on its composition and its relationship with other leadership groups. The decline in working class backgrounds in the social origins of the officer corps, while eliminating an important vehicle for upward social mobility among humble Mexicans, has clearly increased the social compatibility of the officer corps with other leadership groups, specifically civilian politicians, who come largely from middle class professional occupations. In other parts of Latin America, lower socio-economic origins appear to be on the increase.[111]

In the past, the officer corps has perceived itself to be socially inferior to their civilian counterparts or, at the very least, to believe that the politicians do not perceive them as social equals. The changing social composition of the younger members of officer corps, which reflects more closely a similar composition among politicians, in combination with a dramatic increase in professional educational credentials, places the new generation of generals and admirals in a more comparable position with their civilian peers.

Overall, the impact of the two earlier types of officers, but especially the political-military officer, and the changing background variables among the typical officer, specifically their age and social origins, can be viewed as a neutral exchange in terms of its potential influence on civil-military relations. The military remains the least integrated with other leadership groups, largely because it must rely almost exclusively on its career contacts since family accounts for only 6 percent of its friendships with other influential figures, and education, given its largely internalized educational system, for only 22 percent of its contacts.[112]

The fact that three-quarters of Mexico's influential officers are most likely to develop ties with other elites, and that politicians are the most likely group with whom they would associate through institutional and career contacts, means that formal organizational structures, and their relationships to civilian institutions, are essential for understanding a crucial element in the civil-military relationship. Three important organizational sources of contact between the officer corps and politicians exist in Mexico. The most significant of these has been the presidential staff. In the last thirty years, nearly three out of ten top officers held a post in this organization. Second, embassy posts, especially in the United States, France, and the United Kingdom, have brought a select group of younger officers into contact with prominent public figures. Finally, nearly every successful officer who reaches the rank of admiral or general has served on the general staff. It is in these positions where they not only make crucial contacts with current high-ranking officers, but also associate with the staffs of cabinet members and other influential political figures who have government business with these agencies. It is these organizational contacts, and the evolution of new points of contact between federal legislative liaisons and congressional committee members and, possibly, with state governors, that will in the future exert more influence on the civil-military relationship than will social variables.

CHAPTER FOUR

Military-Civilian Interlocks, the Politicized Officer

In societies where military service is widespread and numerous civilians have extensive contact with the armed forces, the level of military integration in civilian life evolves naturally. For example, in the United States, hundreds of firms employ thousands of employees who produce products directly for military use. These firms employ former military personnel and civilians who share similar professional interests. In countries like Mexico, where the armed forces as a profession is largely limited to military careerists and where the enlisted and non-commissioned officers receive little respect and exercise almost no influence on military institutions, the vehicles through which civilians and military personnel come to know each other, and share similar attitudes and values, is severely limited in scope.

Mexican presidents succeeded in imposing civilian supremacy over the armed forces by legitimizing civilian leadership, by creating and institutionalizing a single, monolithic political party, and by voluntarily removing power from the hands of prominent revolutionary figures and placing it into those of younger, civilian professional politicians. These patterns were set in motion at a price: creating military institutions set apart from their civilian counterparts. Mexico's leadership created a dangerous situation in which the military isolated themselves professionally and personally. Such isolation may contribute to the growth of a caste mentality, where civilians and the officer corps pursue different paths in defining the military's mission, describing the responsibilities of individual officers, and establishing the extent of military participation in civilian affairs. Over time, Mexican leadership evolved different strategies to maintain civilian supremacy, simultaneously reinforcing closer linkages to the armed forces while protecting their autonomous status. The formal, institutional strategies involved military participation in national political positions, the incorporation of the officer corps in the state political party, and defining the military's mission broadly to include national security and civic action responsibilities. Informally, the degree to which career officers and influential political and economic elites share social and kinship ties can also impact on their relationships and their perceptions of the other groups' roles in society.

Numerous interpretations have been offered on the level of interchange between military officers and the political system, and its impact on civil-military relations. It has been asserted that a limited but important presence of military officers in political posts has, in Mexico's case, actually guaranteed military subservience to civilian leadership. Basically, if one considers the Mexican political system from Lázaro Cárdenas' presidency to Vicente Fox's electoral victory in 2000 to have taken on corporatist qualities, then various forms of military interlocks might be viewed as formal means of civilian cooptation.[1]

Formal Linkages—Officers as Politicians

Franklin Margiotta first offered the theory that political office holding by the military explained the persistence of civilian supremacy in Mexico.[2] He contended that the political system allocated a certain percentage of positions to high-ranking military officers, thereby providing a channel for politically ambitious officers. It was his belief that this "informal, individualized military representation has been sustained at fairly even levels in the last twenty years [1950–1970], thus giving the military a direct stake in the political system and personal ties to their political counterparts."[3] Margiotta's thesis remained valid through the early 1960s, but the data he used to support his argument after that date are flawed.

Historically, political office holding by military officers in Mexico was quite common. This is not surprising. During many periods of the country's history, as elsewhere in Latin America, military men were in charge of the presidency. Beginning with General Porfirio Díaz (1884) until 1989, of 2,612 nationally prominent politicians and state governors, one in five had risen to the rank of lieutenant colonel or higher in the National Guard or armed forces.[4]

Individuals, including politicians, undergoing the same experience, typically develop personal bonds based on their shared experience. The more harrowing the experience (i.e., combat), the stronger the bond.[5]

The four events having the strongest impact on politicians from 1884 to the present are:

- the North American invasion of 1846–1848
- the Liberal-Conservative conflicts of the 1850s and 1860s
- the French intervention from 1862–1867
- the Mexican Revolution of 1910–1920.

All four of these events share certain characteristics that distinguish them from others which might have been expected to exert some influence over future Mexican politicians. These characteristics are:

- each involved considerable violence
- each attracted numerous Mexicans from a wide geographic area
- each was strongly linked to politics

Three of the four events involved the direct participation of politicians. The majority of Mexicans were not combatants in these events, but the majority of national political leaders were.

The impact of violent events on civil-military relations, as measured by the level of involvement among Mexican politicians, is comparable to post-revolutionary leaders in China, Cuba, and the Soviet Union.[6] Of all nineteenth-century Mexican politicians who were of an age to fight, four-fifths fought in one or more of the century's three major events.

What is important to emphasize is the shared combat experience of politicians, civilian and career military alike, in the Revolution of 1910. Among first-time national office-holders from 1920 to 1935, 58 percent participated in the Revolution of 1910. This fact explains why among the generation (1880–1899) of Generals Alvaro Obregón and Plutarco Elias Calles,[7] the military's representation in national political office averaged 37 percent. Like Díaz, Presidents Obregón and Calles recruited many collaborators from their wartime experiences.[8] Furthermore, the presidents who succeeded them, notably Pascual Ortiz Rubio, Abelardo Rodríguez, Lázaro Cárdenas, and Manuel Avila Camacho, were themselves generals who had fought in these battles, often under these two mentors.

The post-revolutionary generation (1900–1919) led by Miguel Alemán, the first elected civilian President since Madero, marked a significant drop in career military officers in national politics, at only 9 percent. The possibility of a military career leading to political success drops again in the next generation of politicians (1920–1939), with only 4 percent of national politicians having military backgrounds.

Alemán was the perfect figure to carry out this task. Many of his supporters expected him to institute such a policy, and recall with pride his appointment of young, well-educated civilian professionals to political office.[9] This antimilitary attitude stems from the 1929 presidential campaign, during which many of Alemán's collaborators were supporters of José Vasconcelos, the prominent civilian opponent against the government's candidate.[10]

Military officers held fewer than 2 percent of all-important political posts in Mexico in the late 1990s and 2000s. In the executive branch, from midlevel to the top, only 4 percent claimed service in the army, air force, and navy as their occupation.[11] Qualitatively, the influence of military officers has declined even further than Margiotta's thesis would suggest. Military officers have found certain types of political posts more attractive or available than others: those having the least say in policy-making (see Table 4-1).

Table 4.1 Political Offices Held by Mexican Military Officers

Administration	Cabinet %	Governor %	Senator %	Deputy %
1935–1940	12	48	18	–
1940–1946	12	40	20	–
1946–1952	0	13	5	3
1952–1958	2	23	17	11
1958–1964	0	23	20	11
1964–1970	4	3	15	3
1970–1976	2	5	12	2
1976–1982	0	3	5	3
1982–1988	1	5	3	1
1988–1994	0	0	2	1
1994–2000	0	0	3	1
2000–2005	2	0	2	1

Excluding the secretaries of National Defense and of the Navy and the Department of the Air Force, military men have not been significant in cabinet-level agencies for years, basically since Alemán's administration. Fox's appointment of a brigadier general as his attorney general in 2000 received significant attention in the media because it was the first time in decades that an officer was appointed to a top, non-military cabinet agency.[12] On the state level they have persisted much longer as governors, accounting for one in four state chief executives from 1953 through 1964. Again Alemán accounted for a precipitous drop, from 40 to 13 percent. Whereas Alemán reduced the military's presence across the board in the legislative and executive branches, his successors revived the military's presence in the legislative branch, especially the Senate, to pre-1946 levels. The Senate, the least influential of the two legislative bodies, retained the military presence longest. By 1976, when Luis Echeverría took office, the military, in terms of holding political office, essentially had disappeared from the political scene.

The qualitative distribution of military officers among influential political positions has a long history in Mexico. From 1884 to 1934, officers accounted for only 14 percent of the cabinet posts (including defense agencies), not much different from the figures for the post-1935 era (12 percent). Officers were also well represented among national elective offices: 38 percent of the deputies and 21 percent of the senators came from military backgrounds. Military officers actually dominated politics at the state level. Two-thirds of military officers who rose to national political office previously held state political posts. More important, of the 365 officers during this period who were prominent politically, 57 percent were state governors. Of the officers who reached national political office after 1935, 39 percent served as governors compared to only 18 percent of the civilian politicians.

Why have military officers been so well represented in governorships and what does it imply for civil-military relations? Career military officers were often recruited to state governorships because of unsettled political conditions in those states. If one thinks of these conditions as security issues at the state level, it suggests the importance civilian leadership placed on the ability of military officers to solve security problems. This is a significant pattern given the military's gradual expansion of anti-drug and security-related missions at the behest of civilian politicians in the 1980s, 1990s, and 2000s. The historical precedent already existed in the provincial security context, as distinct from the national security context, for military officers to address these problems.

Not only have officers declined proportionately among political elites, no longer holding important political posts, but, starting in the 1980s, the kinds of officers who occupy legislative posts are different. In the 1982 legislature, four deputies were career officers, all brigadier generals or higher. Two other officers also held seats, but they were no longer on active duty. Several former enlisted men were in the lower chamber, two of whom were members of the Mexican Communist Party (PCM) and the Unified Socialist Party of Mexico (PSUM). Only two senators came from military backgrounds: one was a former cavalry major, the other an active duty naval officer with the rank of corvette captain (lieutenant colonel).[13] In the 1985 legislature, five deputies claimed military backgrounds, but only three were known to be on active duty, two of whom were senior officers.[14] The other two were a major and a lieutenant.

In the 1988 legislature, only two active duty officers were deputies: one was a captain and military lawyer; the other was an air force graduate of the Colegio de Defensa National. There were also two engineers who had left the service and one retired division general.[15] Only three officers represented the armed forces in the Senate: one retired, the second a brigadier general and Colegio de Defensa Nacional graduate, and the third an active duty admiral. In the 1991–1994 session, military representation dropped further, and only two individuals in the senate, a retired admiral and retired army general, could be considered high-ranking career officers. In the legislature, of the five individuals with military careers, only one, a division general, had exceeded the rank of colonel.[16] By the 2000–2003 session, only two officers were represented in the Chamber of Deputies, and one in the Senate. According to the candidate lists submitted by the parties for the 2003 congressional elections, PRI nominated no military officers and only one candidate from any party was a former officer.[17]

In sum, high-ranking, active duty officers in Mexico are rarely present in either legislative house. Most significant, they have lost control over the national defense committees in both chambers. From the 1930s through the 1980s, national defense committee members were typically active duty or retired military officers. Since 1990s, other parties have been well represented on these committees and, since 1997, have even chaired them. For example, a member of the National Action Party headed the Senate National Defense Committee in the 1997–2000 session.[18]

The political activities of Mexico's generals since 1946 suggest some interesting patterns about which top officers have chosen political careers and the political offices they have held. Among the generals in our sample of 670 division and brigade generals or their air force and naval equivalent, 30 percent held some type of political office. Of officers born before 1910, more than half successfully pursued political careers. Of those born after 1920, the proportion was only one-tenth, although individuals born after 1920 account for more than two-fifths of the generals in our sample.

The army medical corps plays an important role in the interchange between politicians and military officers. This is somewhat analogous to the role bankers played between the private sector and public officials. (Among businesspeople bankers were a key channel for communication with the political world.)[19] Its impact, however, is limited by its members' importance in the officer corps itself. Medical officers have not held influential commands and only rarely do they achieve staff positions in the national defense secretariat. A significant initial link was provided by Gustavo Baz, a distinguished physician who interrupted his studies at the Military Medical School to fight in the Revolution and then returned to the National Medical School to complete his program with a generation of distinguished physicians and politicians.[20] Baz, who later directed both of his alma maters, had become a friend of General Cárdenas earlier in his career, and served as president of the National University during the Cárdenas administration.

The importance of the Military Medical School as a special channel for political contacts remains to this day.[21] Jesús Kumate Rodríguez, one of Mexico's leading medical researchers, followed in Baz's footsteps. He graduated from the Military Medical School in 1946, taught there in the 1940s and 1950s, and was appointed secretary of public health in 1988.[22] President Salinas maintained a circle of military physicians through his uncle on his mother's side, a graduate of the Medical Military School.[23]

Contrary to the views of Margiotta and others, some analysts believe that military office holding since 1946 is not indicative of military political influence because the "decisive question is whether the officer is selected by and represents the military institutions or whether he seeks or holds office because of his personal motivations and acts according to impulses from the party and/or a civilian constituency."[24] There is no evidence whatsoever that the national defense secretariat pressures civilian leadership to include officers in any political posts. In fact, it seems likely that the Secretariat of National Defense has little interest in its officers holding government posts. According to Division General Luis Garfías, who was appointed Ambassador to Paraguay in 1986, it was the president who took the initiative:

> "General Arévalo called me in and said, 'what did I want to become an ambassador for?' I told him 'I would consider it to be an honor to serve my country in this capacity abroad.' He was extremely negative about it. Then I suggested to him that the President, who was the commander in chief, would be the one to decide whether I would be given this honor. Two days later I was informed by the Secretary of National Defense that I had been chosen as ambassador."[25] If, however, one accepted the view that the military leadership aggressively sought these assignments, the decline in military representation would be indicative of its decreased level of influence.

Political office-holding by military officers may be more important theoretically on civil-military relations not because the military has historically played some role in determining its level of representation but because of its long-term impact on military professionalism. It could be argued, for example, that the persistence of politically active officers reduces the potential of the military's becoming caste conscious.[26] In other words, individuals with military careers and political ambitions would be treated in the same manner as lawyers, businesspersons, or intellectuals. Some prominent politicians, including recent presidents, believe their political representation is significant for just this reason. Miguel de la Madrid wanted to have more military officers in the Chamber of Deputies, and several more as governors: "Unfortunately, I had to remove General Alpuche [governor of Yucatán] because the party said it would never be able to win the elections after his continued performance in office. I wasn't able to replace him with someone else from the military, and I never received any pressure from the military to replace him with one of its own. I personally believe that *having some officers in political office is very helpful to the relationship*" (emphasis added).[27]

Fewer military officers in top political offices eliminates the military's direct influence in policy-making and decreases ties between political and military figures at the highest levels, but these effects may be tempered by the presence of junior officers as aides to high-level politicians and moonlighters. For example, a cabinet secretary may ask the presidential chief of staff for a major or lieutenant colonel to act as a liaison between the secretary and the staff. This would be a special request; it is not a general rule. One former secretary remarked, "I thought this was silly and unnecessary myself. . . . I think it has to do with the presidential relationship. In other words, the closer the relationship between the secretary and the president, the less need to have a special link to presidential military staff."[28]

It has been said that moonlighting is common among younger officers, especially in the public sector. Moonlighting is illegal, but one source asserted that, in the mid-1960s, an officer had estimated that as many as one fourth or more of the officer corps held second jobs.[29] A secretary of planning and budgeting who attempted to stop double employment in the public sector in the late 1970s was told to desist.[30] The military condoned the practice, probably because large numbers of younger officers resign their commissions over low pay. Some civilian officials believe low pay tends to lead military men into other activities. A former secretary of government properties was so concerned about inadequate military compensation that he gave military aides in his agency a separate salary, a practice which violated both civil and military regulations.[31]

Today, moonlighting is not widespread. In fact, Vicente Fox's secretary of national defense, General Gerardo Clemente Vega García, told the author in the early 1990s that:

> As far as I am concerned, moonlighting has basically ended in the military. Of course, as you know, it is legally prohibited, but even more importantly, most high-ranking officers just would not have the time to hold another job because we are on duty for long hours each day including weekends. Now, it is true that they would allow officers who desire it the opportunity to obtain additional education from a civilian institution. I did this on weekends when I was a young officer. So in that sense, the military was very liberal in allowing me the opportunities which improved my credentials and benefited my technical knowledge. One has been given extra time, but not the time to hold another job.[32]

Certain specialists, such as military physicians who work in nonmilitary hospitals after completing their daily assignments, are common. Ironically, moonlighting was one of the violations which the military lodged against Lt. Colonel Hildegardo Bacilio Gómez, a military physician who, in 1998, organized an informal movement of dissident, lower-ranking officers to voice their complaints against the internal military justice system.[33] Other officers who are unassigned often take additional jobs or start small family businesses on the side, often with their spouses. Their wives operate these businesses when they are on active duty.[34]

Another important channel for political-military communication, one more broadly affecting civil-military relations, is the civilian world of embassies abroad. The linkage is especially important at the Mexican embassy in Washington, D.C. Postings to the United Kingdom, Russia, and France also are significant since those ambassadorial posts often have been awarded to influential political figures. Carlos Tello, the son of a former ambassador and secretary of foreign relations who served as ambassador to Russia, believes this can be a significant source of contact:

> But, I had a very special circumstance in getting to know military men even sooner. When my father was ambassador to the United States, we had a number of attachés at the embassy. . . . In Washington we had five or six attachés and of the five or six whom I came to know personally, two became secretaries of national defense. The present secretary of the navy served in the embassy in Peru. Most cabinet secretaries did not have this experience in getting to know these military men, so they have to rely on their contacts with the presidential staff. The embassy is a world unto itself. There is a close relationship between the ambassador and the military staff.[35]

The current national defense secretary, General Vega García, served as military attaché in Russia.[36] As later evidence suggests, these assignments are career plums for would-be generals. Numerous top-ranking officers from all the services have served in the Washington embassy as attachés, assistant attachés, or adjutants. They have included two secretaries of national defense, three navy secretaries, and two air force directors. Both the official mayor of the Navy in 2003, and the chief of staff of the national defense secretariat from 2000 to 2002 served in the Mexican embassy in Washington. Because of the level of formal socializing, there is a very close relationship between the ambassador and the military staff. Such socializing often produces strong friendships.[37]

In recent years the military has developed a beneficial relationship with the Secretariat of Foreign Relations. Attachés have become a critical means of cementing ties between that secretariat and the defense and navy ministries.[38] These ties have policy implications because the secretariat of foreign relations and the national defense and naval secretariats are among the few agencies which make up the national security sub-cabinet. Their collaboration jointly strengthens their influence within the national security group, and their ability to influence the direction and definition of national security concerns.

As if to reinforce the significance of these informal contacts, the *Diario Oficial* announced in 1990 that, as part of the military's enhanced responsibilities for national development, the selection of military attachés would henceforth be more formalized, and that they would come more directly under the authority of the Secretariat of Foreign Relations.[39] The ruling does not compromise attachés' obedience to naval or defense regulations, but it marks a basic shift in ties between the secretariat and the military and, more important, between the civilian political world and the officer corps. This linkage is further reinforced by the fact that in recent years a number of foreign service officers have graduated from the National Defense College, some of whom serve alongside the military in these posts.

According to Article 174 of the military code, special leaves are given to officers (1) to hold popularly elected posts; (2) to carry out a presidentially designated activity outside military service, and (3) to carry out civil activities or employment in executive agencies of the national government, state governments, the Department of the Federal District, municipalities, decentralized agencies, or state-owned enterprises and other public institutions.[40] Of the fourteen thousand officers on active duty in the mid-1980s, probably no more than 8 percent received leaves to work in government agencies or the PRI.[41] By 2003, this pattern had changed dramatically. Only four officers had requested leaves during the first nine months of that year (two captains, one lieutenant colonel, and a brigadier general).[42]

The leave policy has been abused in several ways. Leave time is not to be counted toward time in grade, but many officers were given credit for time spent in civilian jobs when they returned to active duty.[43] Rear Admiral Miguel Angel Barberena, who held civilian posts for twenty-two of twenty-six years, was a case in point. According to the Organic Law, officers are not permitted leaves for party positions, unless the president appoints them. During the 1994 presidential campaign, members of the presidential staff provided security for Zedillo and for Cecilia Soto, the Labor Party candidate. As of 2000, this no longer is an issue since neither Mr. Fox nor Mr. Labastida involved presidential military staff in their campaigns.[44]

Other Linkages Influencing Civil-Military Relations

The gradual but persistent decline of important officers in politics since 1946 increases the potential for greater isolation of the military from other groups, including politicians, and the development of a caste mentality. In Mexico, there are basically three important channels for establishing personal ties among leadership groups. Typically, these occur through education, careers, and family. If we explore the networking ties of the most influential Mexicans in the last three decades, it is apparent that leading officers rely heavily on making contacts with other elite Mexicans through their careers, not through educational experiences or family ties and kinship. Family connections and common schooling are important vehicles for bringing together politicians, capitalists, and intellectuals in Mexico. But for clergy and the officer corps, career contacts are overwhelmingly significant.

Organizationally, through institutional linkages, no overlap exists among Mexican leadership in the last three decades. Of the 398 elites examined during this period, only seven—a minuscule 2 percent—exercised direct influence across any two of the five leadership groups studied.[45] As I suggested in this study, this is "convincing evidence against the existence of positional, institutional elite interlocks across Mexican leadership categories, and this type of power elite."[46] The interlocking relationships which do exist, however, are the consequences of informal relationship and friendships resulting from other forms of contact, rather than from holding a position in another elite institution. The importance of these sources of contacts varies from one leadership group to another depending on their peculiar qualities.

Informal Networking Interlocks—Family

The officer corps and Catholic bishops share certain characteristics which accentuate their insular qualities. In terms of their immediate family, military officers are only second to capitalists in the high levels of relatives who share the same occupational background. Sixty percent of top officers' immediate family members were in the armed forces, compared to only 10 percent who were employed in governmental careers.[47] Over a third of leading officers were the children of career military, thus replicating military values within the family structure. Furthermore, the officer corps' social class background is more representative of the working class than that of any other leadership group, reducing the potential for influential family social contacts. The family origins of the officer corps have implications for networking and for socialization, passing on insular values contributing to a caste mentality. The broad differences in social origins have produced resentment, and a lack of social confidence, on the part of the military, toward politicians. As one prominent figure remarked: "A general told me that once they were having a meeting with civilian politicians, and that the government officials treated them as though they were waiters. He said that one of the officers commented that 'all we needed was a napkin and we would become like waiters before these politicians'."[48]

The institutional character of the armed forces has limited its informal ties with other influential leaders. This insular quality from other non-state groups sets the Mexican military apart from many Latin American peers. Indeed, this unique quality is a significant explanatory variable in the evolution and continuity of military subordination to civil rule. Analysts of the Latin American military have long argued that to be successful in politics, the officer corps requires political allies. The strength of the PRI and its monolithic nature has prevented, until the 1990s, the establishment of possible partisan, political allies. Yet, other, potential groups remain, notably capitalists, the Catholic episcopate, and intellectuals.

Ties to private sector leaders are significant because, in the majority of countries where the military has intervened politically, alliances between businesspeople and the military have been fundamental.[49] Miguel Basáñez believes the Mexican military could not engineer a coup because it lacks strong ties with leading entrepreneurs.[50] Military leadership also shares equally few ties with cultural leaders and influential clergy, further limiting its links to politically important groups. In Argentina, for example, the use of Catholic military chaplains and the social and ideological ties between clergy and the armed forces, contributed to the perpetuation of the repressive military government and implied Church complicity in the "dirty war."[51] No evidence exists to support the view that conservative interests have penetrated the armed forces in Mexico.[52]

Historically, the military has shared ties, on at least a personal level, with the political world. Prior to 1935, when the military was the dominant force in politics, nearly one in three officers was related to a prominent political figure, but few claimed kinship ties with other leadership groups. One-tenth of the officers were sons of prominent, national political figures. From 1935 to 1990, the proportion of officers related to intellectual and entrepreneurial groups slipped to less than 3 percent. However, the percentage of those with relatives in politics remained strong: 38 percent.

If we explore only the most influential officers from 1970–2000, and their equally notable peers among capitalists, the clergy, intellectuals and politicians, none of one-hundred leading officers from those decades is the son of a politician or a wealthy businessman. As far as extended kinship ties, the leading officers had no relatives in their immediate family from the clergy, and only one was related to a capitalist family. Only one in ten was related to a politician or an intellectual. On the other hand, 60 percent counted military officers among their extended family.[53]

The concrete impact of these informal ties between the military leaders and civilian political leaders, in terms of civil-military relations, is difficult to measure. It is apparent that the proximity of other professions in a military officer's family background does influence their professional orientation. A predisposition exists among the children of professional people in many cultures, including the United States, to pursue the same profession. The actual importance can be seen empirically in the Mexican context. The officers most likely to pursue political careers come from politically active families. In fact, of generals with known family backgrounds, three out of four who held national political office were related to someone who held an equivalent post. Regardless of the nature of the personal relationship, it serves as an invaluable communication channel between the political and military worlds.

On both the institutional and personal levels, the interlock between the military and the civilian leaderships can be examined from another perspective. Political figures, for reasons explained elsewhere, do not produce military offspring. The most important contributing factor is the middle-class and upper-middle class origins of politicians, who would therefore view a military career as a less attractive choice from a socio-economic perspective. Of the 1,113 individuals in top executive-branch positions in the 1990s, only 43 (less than 4 percent) identified their fathers as career military officers. In the legislative branch, only one percent claimed fathers in the military. And of the more than 200 federal judges, only one came from a military background. Two percent of governors and their top personnel were the children of fathers who pursued military careers.[54]

Some members of the military can be found serving in influential civilian posts, but the reverse in Mexico has never occurred. The military maintained some visibility in public political offices, at least until the 1970s, and President Fox, as noted earlier, even appointed a brigadier general as his attorney general in 2000, but civilians have rarely been allowed to hold posts reserved for the military. In other words, unlike the U.S. Department of Defense, the Mexican Secretariats of the Navy and of National Defense do not fill decision-making or advisory posts with civilians.

The navy led the way in culling the political-military officer from its membership, thus "purifying" its leadership. In that sense, it could be said to be the first service to have placed strictly "orthodox" career officers in control, that is, officers who had not dabbled directly in politics. On the other hand, it is the only service since 1940 to have been led, however briefly, by a civilian as well as by career army officers who held numerous political posts. Perhaps this abuse by successive presidents helped motivate the navy to pursue such professionalization of its leadership.

This issue of little or no civilian professionals in appropriate administrative military posts in the Mexican armed forces finally received official recognition in 1995, with the publication of the internal document *Army and Air Force Development Program*. Among its many, controversial recommendations, it decries the lack of civilian expertise:

[F]or the first time in its history the military requested an immediate study of recruiting and hiring civilian specialists and professionals. The military obviously believes it is deficient in a number of specialties, and this request complements its desire to expand the number of university careers available to the officer corps. . . . Increasing the civilian component in the military, while expanding its capabilities and expertise and increasing its ties to the civilian community, also adds to the diversity of influences to which the military would be exposed more directly.[55]

Informal Networking Interlocks–Education

Education is the other means by which civilians can come in contact with the Mexican officer corps and visa versa. In the United States, prominent political figures are frequently alumni of the service academies, often having studied there during wartime. Jimmy Carter, for one, an engineering graduate of Annapolis, had close personal ties to navy brass. George Bush senior flew missions during World War II. In Mexico, however, few civilian politicians are products of the service academies or, since the Revolution, combat experiences. Only 7 percent of Salinas's appointees were alumni of military schools. These were roughly divided between the Escuela Superior de Guerra and the Heroico Escuela Naval. All but ten (1 percent) were career officers in the National Defense or Navy Secretariats. Fewer than 3 percent of his appointees pursued graduate studies at the Centro de Estudios Navales Superiores, the Colegio de Defensa Nacional, and/or the Escuela Médico Militar.

These figures will change in future administrations because, since 1989, the national defense secretariat has encouraged expanded contact between civilian and military students at its premier academy, the Colegio de Defensa Nacional. Lieutenant colonels are among the faculty, and colonels and generals, and their naval and air force equivalents, are among the student body. According to the instructors, civilian and military students, and civilian and military instructors frequently socialize. A few civilians began attending in 1989, but numerous civilians from all walks of life have taught there for many years, and civilian directors general, assistant secretaries, and secretaries lecture regularly.[56] In the early 1990s, civilians typically accounted for 17–19 percent of most classes. By 1998, the director of the Colegio de Defensa Nacional expanded the proportion of civilian students dramatically, to a fourth of each class.[57]

The director of the Colegio de Defensa Nacional in 1990 was General Gerardo Clemente Vega García, the secretary of National Defense under Vicente Fox. Vega García later directed the Military Education Department, responsible for all the army and air force educational institutions. Vega

García described to the author how in its brief history from 1981, it achieved such an impact on the officer corps and on civil-military relations:

> One of the major changes since 1988 is the establishment of informal cabinet groups. One of those groups established by law, in addition to the political and economic cabinet is the national security cabinet consisting of the President, and the secretaries of government, foreign relations, national defense, navy, and the attorney general. The secretary of national defense, who plays an important role in this cabinet, obtains his information from the staff at the Secretary of National Defense, and from the National Defense College. The impact of the National Defense College in its short life has been extraordinary. Since 1981, we have graduated 200 officers. Today, most of the three star generals on active duty are graduates of the National Defense College, as are nearly all of the zone commanders. The ambassador from the 1989 class is now a personal adviser to the secretary of foreign relations. This is another example of how we can improve our relations with the civilian agencies through representatives of this program who have contact with leading military officers.[58]

The only field in which considerable contact between officers and civilians is maintained through higher education is military law, although some notable cases have occurred in secondary and preparatory level institutions. A small percentage of officers pursuing careers in military law graduate from the National University after completing their military education. A notable example is General Max Notholt Rosales who, as a retired officer, was director general of naval legal affairs under two secretaries of the navy, from 1977 to 1988. He graduated from the Heroico Colegio Militar in 1947 and from the National School of Law in 1967.[59] The most notable example of military and civilian contacts between future prominent politicians and a leading military officer is that of José María Rios de Hoyos, who completed a law degree from the National School of Law in the same class as Mario Moya Palencia, future secretary of government and presidential contender; Porfirio Muñoz Ledo, former president of PRI and leader of the PRD; Pedro Ojeda Paullada, another president of PRI; and Carlos Fuentes, world renowned novelist. General Rios de Hoyos was a zone commander and president of the Supreme Court of Military Justice in the 1980s.[60]

It is possible that the number of contacts between civilians and members of the officer corps through public education may actually increase in the future. The Army and Air Force implemented higher educational standards as part of the 1995 internal report, requiring that all officer cadets now have a preparatory education before enrolling in the Heroico Colegio Militar, which had previously served as the equivalent of a preparatory credential. Younger officers could potentially have increased contacts, for greater lengths of time, with their civilian counterparts at preparatory schools, which are the academic track for college bound professional students in Mexico. This pattern is counteracted, however, by a notable shift in the educational origins of politicians and capitalists, most of whom now graduate from private, preparatory schools. Military officers, because of their social origins, have not shared in these significant educational experiences; such educational experiences are bound to have long-term consequences on differing socialization patterns among future Mexican elites.

The lack of substantial military contact with future prominent civilians leads to numerous possible consequences for civil-military relations. It has been alleged, for instance, that military officers tend to share a uniform point of view in regard to social problems, and are often at odds with the majority of the population This homogeneity in attitudes, observers say, originates in military discipline and/or indoctrination at the military academies, a point which will be expanded considerably in the chapter on domestic military education. Marion Levy argues, however, that it is the absence of general social contact and isolation from civilian settings that may be at the root of the uniformity, not the training itself.[61] I would argue that both conditions contribute in important ways to such patterns.

The insularity of the Mexican military not only limits civilian occupancy of top posts in the secretariats, but has also contributed to the significant lack of civilian expertise on the military and low civilian interest in the military. Structurally, this pattern also produced an unusual impact on the top military's leadership. It is worth noting that the secretariat of national defense is the only cabinet agency since 1946 which has not had a change in secretary mid-way through an administration. The top leadership of the military is characterized by extraordinary stability, and the secretary of national defense always has been a senior officer.[62]

This is just one illustration of how the political elite has sought to discourage military intervention. It hopes that by not politicizing officer corps leadership, pitting one officer against another, and leaving military affairs to its own cabinet leadership, it eliminates another possible reason for military intervention. The continuity in military leadership suggests that the president, who frequently plays musical chairs with or removes other cabinet figures, does not tinker with the armed forces. Salinas's abrupt dismissal of Admiral Mauricio Schleske as secretary of the navy in 1990 was an exceptional, necessary intervention.[63]

In granting the military autonomy in personnel matters, however, the civilian leadership simultaneously encouraged the artificial separation of military and civilian leaders, resulting in a tradeoff between encouraging and discouraging possible military intervention. The lack of contact between the two groups increases some risks associated with military intervention, while the distance civil leadership persistently maintained from internal military affairs decreased other risks.

Informal Interlocks–Partisan Politics

Mexico's civilian leadership sought to maintain civilian supremacy in civil-military relations through another means. At the same time that President Cárdenas and other revolutionary leaders were reducing the politically active officer corps, Cárdenas altered the structure of the government party—the Mexican Revolutionary Party (PRM)—to incorporate the military as a special sector, as discussed in detail earlier. Previously, the party had three sectors, agrarian, labor, and popular, and the military was one of many groups in the popular sector. Cárdenas created the military sector to bring the officers into the open and force them to channel their political activities through the party. In this position, the military sector could be kept in check by other sectors.[64] Fortunately for Mexico, ambitious generals who responded to Cárdenas's challenge chose to engage in combat on the electoral level.[65]

Cárdenas, of course, was criticized for deliberately trying to involve the military in party politics. His motivations seem clear in his blunt response: "We are not involving the army in politics, it is already involved. In fact, it has dominated the situation, and we are reducing its influence to one out of four votes."[66]

The military sector was short-lived (from 1938 to 1940), but it is not its potential policy influence as a separate party sector alone that is important to consider.[67] In the first place, the party per se was not a vehicle for that kind of policy influence, which instead occurred within the executive branch. Making the military a visible component of the corporatist structure through the party was important mainly for psychological reasons. Cárdenas's reasoning makes sense, particularly in the electoral arena, but an argument could be made that by highlighting its influence in such fashion, the government added to the military's prestige, recognizing it as an equal of the three larger, traditional civilian sectors.

Strategically, the military's inclusion can be viewed as a serious political error. The case of the private sector is instructive. The Mexican entrepreneurial leadership has always felt politically limited and inferior to other groups, especially labor, because it had never been formally incorporated within the party.[68] It participated individually as part of the popular sector, which since 1943 the military did, too. But the fact that the business community never received its own official recognition in the party promoted a mistaken belief that labor exercised more influence on the decision-making process. This belief was unsupported in fact and, more significantly, encouraged businessmen to remain apolitical in a partisan sense, until the 1990s.[69]

In terms of civil-military relations, the elimination of the military's official representation in the party sent a broader message to the populace that the officer corps had no legitimate reason to be involved in electoral politics, and that the state did not recognize its formal participation as acceptable. The socialization of succeeding generations of Mexicans, civilians and military alike, to the fact that the military's task fundamentally was nonpolitical, benefited from this perception.

When the government withdrew the military's official representation in the party, it did so with great care, leaving a talented and politically ambitious officer in the position of secretary of popular action, the party's top representative of the popular, or middle-class professional sector. The officer, Major Antonio Nava Castillo, co-founded and later served as first secretary general of the National Federation of Popular Organizations, the most influential umbrella organization in the popular sector. He served as a military aide to Manuel Avila Camacho, ultimately rising to the rank of division general in 1961.[70] Later, Leandro Valle, an organization made up almost entirely of retired and active officers, or their closest relatives, informally replaced the abolished military sector. Many of Mexico's leading political-military officers, such as Generals Hermenegildo Cuenca Díaz and Fernando Pámanes Escobedo, were its members or leaders. Despite the caliber of its membership, it never achieved much visibility or exercised any influence within the party leadership.[71] In 1954 those officers looking for an electoral vehicle more to their liking, established the Authentic Party of the Mexican Revolution (PARM), a co-opted offshoot of the PRI (which replaced PRM in 1946) financed by the government. The PARM has generally been led by retired army officers and, in the 1970s and 1980s, admirals. It joined Cuauhtémoc Cárdenas's electoral alliance, becoming part of the populist opposition in 1988.[72]

When Alemán ran for the presidency in 1946, he tried to impose his "civilianizing" pattern on the party, too. He not only revised its name but also imposed an unknown and unpopular figure as president of the National Executive Committee. In less than a year he appointed General Rodolfo Sánchez Taboada, a former aide to Lázaro Cárdenas, to the post. From December 1946 to December 1964, four generals, among Mexico's most important political-military officers, directed the government's party. It is also no accident that, after 1946, military officers led the party during the same years the military was most prominently represented in national political offices. Even if important only symbolically; the military was better represented in the party (six of its twenty-one presidents since 1935) than in the executive branch leadership.

A liaison group of prominent military officers evolved as a substitute for the military sector after 1952. General Alfonso Corona del Rosal, along with other high-ranking officers, headed this group within the PRI for years, and the group was the only link between the army and the civilian leadership, especially the PRI, through which top officers could voice personal and institutional demands.[73] This pattern was formalized in more recent years in the military's selection of talented and ambitious young officers as assistants on the PRI president's staff, but they never had any policy input, practically speaking, and that practice has ceased.[74]

The military tended to remain aloof from party activities, especially since 1952. Until the 1990s, opposition groups until did not have special ties to, nor did they attempt to elicit support from, the military. In this respect Mexico has been unique among most Latin American countries. Cooptation "in a multiparty system encourages military intervention," but in a single-dominant-party system intervention is discouraged.[75] In part, this pattern is a by-product of two things: a modified one-party state and the continuous relationship between an established civilian leadership and the officer corps.[76] Until 1987 a permanent opposition party with widespread support among various sectors of the population did not exist. Hence the government party remained unchallenged in co-opting the military. Among military officers in national political office between 1935 and 1987, only one was a member of an opposition party.

The political cooptation of the military, through socialization, persuasion, threats, rewards and where necessary, brute force, underwent an arduous process in the 1920s and 1930s, setting a series of precedents for later decades. After the Revolution elements of the military, in alliance with civilian groups, tried to wrest control from the established political leadership, but their efforts tapered off gradually until 1952. Military leadership employed various socializing means to convey a message of nonparticipation. For example, the May 1927 issue of the army's official *Revista del Ejército*, reprinted an editorial from the government-controlled newspaper *El Universal* that condemned the political ambitions of Generals Arnulfo R. Gómez and Francisco R. Serrano, both of whom were presidential hopefuls.[77] Obregón, who ran a second time, forced Gómez to rebel, capturing and executing him. Serrano, Obregón's political disciple, and Serrano's closest civilian aides, were murdered on Obregón's orders.

Serrano's death is extremely important because it served as a severe, cautionary message to present and future officers who might consider pursuing political ambitions "outside" the system. The ruthless massacre of Serrano's campaign staff also sent a chilling message to civilians who also might be giving thought to associating themselves with military-political opponents of the regime.

It is often forgotten that the key figure in establishing many aspects of current civil-military relations, Miguel Alemán, was a student supporter of General Gómez, and that Alemán and many of his peers went on to become important figures in politics from 1946 through 1970.[78] Their strong antimilitarism stemmed from events associated with the 1927 and 1929 presidential campaigns.

A military rebellion occurred in 1929 and again, on a minuscule scale, in 1939. Forces loyal to the civilian political elite easily suppressed both attempts. It was not until 1940 that an important faction within the officer corps joined a splinter group from the political establishment to support General Juan Almazán's presidential candidacy. Inevitably, although Almazán attracted supporters from other sectors as well, he was unsuccessful in his bid. Officers who supported Almazán were granted a leave to campaign for him, but the national defense secretary announced on September 13 that they had until October 1 to return to active duty or face charges of desertion, an order that considerably circumscribed their political choices.[79]

The last presidential hopeful to attract numerous followers from within the officer corps was General Miguel Henríquez Guzmán, who tried for the official party nomination in 1945 and 1951. In the 1946 presidential succession, the establishment civilian leadership under President Avila Camacho viewed his potential candidacy as reflecting military and civilian regional interests against the economic interests and federal bureaucracy Miguel Alemán represented.[80] The candidacy of two other generals, and the pre-candidacy of Henríquez Guzmán, represented those military figures who were not in agreement with the leadership's strategy of turning over political power to a non-revolutionary, civilian elite.[81] The general, whose family was friends of the martyred President Francisco I. Madero, ironically, had helped suppress Almazán's supporters as the Monterrey zone commander. Civilian elites were not even tolerant of his 1945 pre-candidacy. They removed one of his supporters, General Marcelino García Barragán, who was on leave from active duty and serving as governor of Jalisco, from office nearly a year early, as punishment for supporting Henríquez Guzmán.[82]

In 1951, after again failing to obtain the PRI's presidential nomination, Henríquez Guzmán formed his own party, the Federation of Peoples Party of Mexico. García Barragán, along with numerous other military officers, was active in this new party.[83] Interestingly, Cuauhtémoc Cárdenas, the president's son—and the only Mexican to produce a popular opposition movement in many decades until 1988—was a student supporter of Henríquez Guzmán in 1951. This upset PRI leaders because it gave the public the impression that General Cárdenas personally supported his campaign.[84]

Elisa Servín identifies many factors which contributed to the resurgence of military support for someone other than the PRI official candidate. Besides the personal prestige of Henríquez Guzmán and García Barragán, the general's platform promised improved benefits for the military. At the time, lower ranking officers and enlisted personnel also were dissatisfied with their salaries. Among high-ranking officers, many favored Henriquismo because of Alemán's abuse of the promotion process. Indeed, a United States consular report suggested that corruption within the Army had reached its highest levels, and that one could actually purchase promotions, with the price of promotion to major and lieutenant colonel going for two thousand pesos. Finally, the conflict between the secretary of national defense, Gilberto Limón, and General Santiago Piña Soria, head of the presidential staff, further alienated the military from Alemán's government.[85] In June 1951, the national defense secretariat announced that approximately seventy generals would be retired.

Throughout the Henríquez Guzmán campaign, which attracted considerable public support, the secretariat of national defense responded capriciously and aggressively by threatening or punishing active duty officers who favored his campaign or that of any other opponent, while permitting wide latitude to those officers who supported PRI's official candidate, Adolfo Ruiz Cortines. The secretariat's techniques included reassigning officers to remote posts. According to an intelligence report prepared by the Federal Security Department, 383 officers, including 5 division generals, 52 brigade generals, 15 brigadiers, 51 colonels, 61 lieutenant colonels, 29 mayors, 98 captains, and 72 first and second lieutenants sympathized or actively supported the Henríquez Guzmán campaign. As least a third were on active duty.[86] The most notable of these supporters was Division General Antonio Sánchez Acevedo, then the army's chief of staff, who was reassigned as the military attaché to Turkey because of his personal friendship with the general.[87] The secretariat of national defense pursued a similar strategy with General Cristóbal Guzmán Cárdenas, who also had held the post of chief of staff in the last two years of Avila Camacho's administration. Guzmán Cárdenas was sent to Yugoslavia as ambassador, but similar to Sánchez Acevedo, was promoted to division general in November 1953 and served as military attaché to the United States in 1957. He held a top national defense post in the 1958–1964 administration.[88]

From 1952 to the early 1990s, almost no officers spoke out against the government or supported a political candidate or opposition party. The PRI and its antecedents generated as much discipline in controlling their members' political ambitions as did military institutions, a remarkable achievement in the civil-military relationship. The military and civilian leaders' success in limiting the political activity of officers can be illustrated empirically. Given the presence of opposition parties after 1920, and the establishment elite's limited legitimacy, one might expect many civilian and military leaders to have joined those parties. Yet, from 1920 to 1934 only 5 percent of the politically active officers were leaders of opposition parties and fewer than 6 percent were members. Among politically active civilians, the proportions were even smaller.

Officers who joined opposition parties were not sympathizers of Díaz or Huerta. They were revolutionaries who supported alternative revolutionary choices. However, joining opposition movements quickly disappeared as a career experience among successful generals; since 1946, only 3 percent have done so, and of those, all but one were born before 1900. No general born after 1910 was been an active member or leader of an opposition party until Alberto Quintanar López announced on September 20, 1990 that he had joined the Democratic Revolutionary Party (PRD) as an adviser. The son of a chauffeur, the former troop commander and director general of infantry under de la Madrid was on retired status.[89] General Quintanar López's decision presaged a pattern among other retired officers who joined the PRI. In 1997, three brigadier generals, one admiral, three vice-admirals, and two rear admirals announced that they too were joining the PRD.[90] Later that same year, Division General Luis Garfias Magaña, who twice served as a federal deputy from PRI, also joined the PRD. PAN's more limited direct link with the military occurred through Brigadier General Mario A. Huerta Carrascosa, an Escuela Superior de Guerra graduate who ran for congress on the party's ticket in 1985.[91]

The government and the military seem to have applied an informal rule preventing military officers, even on leave, from involving themselves with parties other than the PRI. In fact, from 1952 to 2000, only one active duty general worked for an opposition civilian presidential hopeful. Even though he was a military lawyer and not a traditional career officer,[92] the military tried Octavio Véjar Vázquez, who had become vice-president of the Popular Party in 1951. He was prosecuted under article 17 of the 1945 law of military discipline, which held that an officer "on active duty is strictly prohibited from involving himself in political affairs or work, directly or indirectly, without losing the rights given by the Constitution."[93] According to Lieuwen, the many officers who participated in the PRI campaign equally violated Article 17.[94] Véjar Vázquez should be considered a notable figure because he served on the 1945 army reorganization committee and, at the time of his arrest, presided over the College of Military Lawyers.[95] His trial clearly raised the question of whether career officers with leave really were free to participate in politics, specifically, opposition politics.[96] In practice, the secretariat of national defense made it clear that it would violate its own regulations to prevent such behavior.

Observers of the Mexican political scene have witnessed the military's involvement in successive PRI presidential campaigns. These troops and junior officers obviously were not on leave to perform these activities, directly contrary to the prohibitions set forth in the organic military law. According to insiders, the pattern of military involvement in the election process was on the decline before 2000. As one division general, whose career spanned the 1950s through the 1990s concluded: "[W]e are actually intervening fewer times today than we did when I first joined the service. We were always involved in some kind of election duty when I started out as a lieutenant."[97]

Fox's electoral victory in 2000 destroyed this form of direct military political involvement. Nevertheless, although no military officers participated in his campaign, Fox maintained the long-established tradition of the military being in charge of presidential logistics and security. His chief of presidential staff is General José A. Tamayo Casillas, a man who previously served as assistant chief of operations on the presidential staff, as chief of staff of the presidential guards, and as a presidential aide. Tamayo Casillas is a graduate of the Colegio Nacional de Defensa and completed the U.S. Army's prestigious staff and command course at Fort Leavenworth, Kansas in 1983.[98]

Military officers establish contact with future prominent political figures and presidents through the campaign staff. Equally important, Mexican presidents become acquainted with high-ranking officers on the campaign trail. President José López Portillo, before he ran for president, considered his contact with the military to be "superficial and exceptional in the case of general officers, including General Félix Galván López [who became his national defense secretary], prior to my presidential campaign. . . . During my presidential campaign it [contact with the officer corps] was systematic. I had meetings with all of the military zone commanders and got to know a little bit about them personally and about their service records. . . . I picked four of these zone commanders who made the strongest impression on me, and then I studied their careers rather carefully. I picked out Galván as my secretary of national defense. In my opinion he was an excellent secretary, and performed a great service for the military. President Echeverría proposed this selection process to me."[99]

Numerous examples can be cited of highly successful military careers which are linked to significant contacts with presidents and influential cabinet members. These provide a channel for civil-military relations. It is critical to understand that simple personal contact with influential civilians is not the most significant variable in determining career success. One officer supports this view with a frank revelation: "Look, I was an aide to President . . . for many years. But without the kind of attitude that the military hierarchy wishes to see, you will never rise up the promotion ladder, even if you are well thought of by an incumbent president. I have been in the service for 25 years and look at my present rank. I am an example of a nonconformist, and the harsh consequences that it produces within the military in Mexico.[100]

In understanding the larger context of civil-military relations, the officer's revelation is significant for two reasons. In recent decades, the Mexican military places a more significant value on conformity and the acceptance of the prevailing military culture than on personal linkages with outside civilians, including those involving close ties with individual presidents. Equally significant, the officer's own career demonstrates the limited influence exercised by prominent civilians, including presidents, on internal military affairs, of which the most selfishly guarded is the promotion process. Numerous abuses exist in the process, but the military—not civilian politicians—are responsible for those conditions.

Traditionally, the PAN was the only long-lived opposition party with which the military might have had some ongoing contact, and possibly some ideological affinity. Some analysts speculated about a possible alliance between the PAN and conservative military officers in the mid-1980s, but there is no empirical evidence of such a connection either then or now.[101] However, according to one analyst, the majority of the military voted for Vicente Fox's Alliance for Change in 2000.[102]

After Cuauhtémoc Cárdenas established a popular opposition party in 1987, he told the press that he was not looking for an open and direct relationship with those in command of the armed forces in spite of the fact that "when any military person expresses his sympathy with the FDN [now the PRD], he is removed from his post and various charges are brought against him."[103] However, following the political violence in Michoacán and Guerrero in early 1990, Cárdenas did call for the military to prevent such actions and to protect his sympathizers. At that time PAN representatives made no public declaration, but the other parties represented in the lower chamber, including the PRI, the Authentic Party of the Mexican Revolution (PARM), the Popular Socialist Party (PPS), and the Cardenista splinter group, the Party of the Cardenista Front of National Reconstruction (PFCRN), rejected his call for intervention, saying it would cause political instability. In response to Cárdenas, the secretary of national defense claimed that the military intervenes in political conflicts only when constitutional order disappears.[104]

Prior to 2000 no active duty officers are known to have shown any inclination to contravene informal military policy by involving himself or herself with the PAN or PRD during an election. Plenty of evidence exists that numerous officers and enlisted men were and are sympathetic to both parties, and have been voting for the opposition for decades.[105]

In the 1988 elections, the leftist magazine *Proceso* assigned a number of its reporters to individual polling stations serving largely military voters. In President Cárdenas' home state, Michoacán, in the polling station adjacent to the general barracks of the military zone command in Morelia, the general's son received 502 votes to 156 for Salinas and 156 for Manuel Clouthier (the PAN candidate). On the air base in Zapopan, Jalisco, the location of the air force academy, Salinas received 752 votes to 193 for Clouthier and 77 for Cárdenas. In a number of Oaxacan polling stations covered by the magazine, including those in military residential zones, Cárdenas received more votes than Salinas.[106]

Mexico provides a fascinating case study of formal and informal interlocks between the officer corps and civilian political leadership. The most important of these interlocks, which disappeared by the 1980s, was the continued presence of prominent officers, ones who can be considered political-military officers, in nationally important political posts. In a sense, Mexican leadership informally implemented President Cárdenas' original idea of keeping politically interested officers visible and active in national political offices, but without allowing them access, with a few exceptions, to influential executive branch posts. Thus, civilian leadership strengthened its bonds to prominent military officers while at the same time reducing pressures among those officers with strong political ambitions to pursue alternative political routes outside the government party. The elimination of this group of officers from Mexico's political leadership not only reduced the regular contact between certain politicians and leading officers, but also eliminated a formalized, institutional channel linking the two leadership groups together. On the other hand, the military's behavior in the last fifteen years demonstrates that this linkage, while unquestionably important to the civil-military relationship which emerged in the last half century and a proven influential linkage which deserves consideration in theory building regarding civil-military relations generally, is no longer necessary to maintain civilian supremacy in Mexico.

It is equally clear from an examination of informal linkages that few prominent Mexican political figures have developed close friendships with career officers, or the reverse. Socially and educationally, more obstacles to establishing such networks exist than there are channels which might encourage them. The exception to this in recent years is that a number of public servants, most of them from the secretariat of foreign relations, have begun attending the year-long course at the Colegio de Defensa Nacional, the premier military educational institution which produces many of the top generals and admirals in Mexico. For example, the first class of 1981–1982 produced twenty-one division generals, four admirals, and four brigade and brigadier generals. Those recent contacts will serve to replace some of the previous ones lost through the disappearance of the political-military officer.

Finally, the years of effort by the government and the official party to prevent partisan military support of other political parties ended abruptly with the electoral victory of Vicente Fox.[107] This does not imply that high-ranking career officers will suddenly appear on the campaign trail with their preferred party's candidates. What it does mean is that individuals can and will express their preferences for candidates from all political parties. If a military officer harbors political ambitions, he may take a leave to run for or hold office. However, as recent patterns of civil-military interlocks make abundantly clear, pursuing a political career as part of one's military career will not contribute positively to moving up the rank structure in the armed forces. As of 2000, what Mexico has accomplished as part of the larger civil-military relationship is the elimination of formalized representation by the military in national political office while simultaneously creating an open arena for partisan political preferences and, therefore, the likely expansion of closer ties among top military and different types of leadership groups from various political parties.

CHAPTER FIVE

Civilian Missions: Redefining Civil-Military Relations?

Direct military involvement in national political office or in partisan political activities affected linkages with both civilians and the larger civil-military structure, especially prior to 2000s Mexico moves onto the stage of democratic consolidation, it has eliminated the political model which encouraged previous patterns. Mexico has also removed two prominent forms of contact between military and civilian leaders. Other characteristics of armed forces behavior currently offer a greater potential for influencing civil-military affairs in the twenty-first century. Perhaps the most important of these potential influences in the late 1990s and 2000s is a shift in armed forces missions within the broader context of redefined national security priorities to non-traditional tasks typically performed by civilian agencies. In Mexico, the extent to which the armed forces is involved in national security decision making and drug control enforcement missions, is controversial. These two roles affect the established civil-military relationship.

The general literature on the consequences of the Latin American military taking on such roles, especially since democratization reemerges in the region, has focused on two opposing arguments. Most analysts, and especially those from Latin America, argued that these new missions enhance the prestige and influence of the armed forces and increase their potential for creating an imbalance in the tenuous democratic civil-military relationship.[1] In Mexico, scholars provocatively label this influence as the militarization of civil society, a phrase that describes the growing role of the armed forces in tasks that civilian agencies traditionally performed.[2] Columbia is, of course, the most extreme example of this scenario in the region. The opposing view is that the negative impact of the armed forces performing such tasks has been exaggerated.[3]

Formally, the Mexican military's mission is delineated in four defense plans known as DN-I through DN-IV. DN-I sets forth the Secretariat of National Defense's strategy in case of invasion, an approach relying on a people's militia and protracted guerrilla warfare. Some members of the armed forces have frankly suggested that Mexico is not an army of national defense, but an army of national security, because they do not have the capacity to defend Mexico from external attack.[4] Plans II through IV, however, open the door for non-traditional military responsibilities, all involving internal, civilian-related responsibilities and all potentially affecting long-term civil-military relations.

DN-II responds to internal problems, including insurgencies, strikes, and other civil disturbances. It calls for an immediate reaction and isolation of the instigators. This plan generates the most debate among the public, the media, and among the military and the politicians. The plan justifies both the use of the armed forces' intelligence services and preventative measures in responding to civilian actions deemed as internal threats.[5] DN-III, which has been implemented on several occasions, responds to natural disasters to avert the country's becoming vulnerable to internal or external enemies.[6] The newest of these plans, DN-IV, organizes and legitimizes the military's anti-drug mission. It was implemented at the end of the Zedillo administration and continued under President Fox.[7]

The Military as a Civic Actor

Civic action is another element in the residual political roles of the military. Civic action is generally composed of a variety of developmental-type projects and brings the officer corps into contact with rural poverty and ordinary Mexicans. The specific nature of civic action programs depends on the needs and priorities given to them by individual states. The military often represents the federal government in the hinterland through these missions, thus performing apolitical functions for the political leadership.[8]

What role does civic action play in the larger context of civil-military relations? For years, analysts have argued that assigning the military responsibilities that typically are performed by civilian agencies blurs the line between civilian-military missions and civilian leadership.[9] When the citizenry views the military performing such roles on a continuing basis, it tends to define the role as part of the armed forces' professional responsibilities. Such a perception also introduces the image of civilian incompetence or inadequacy in performing such tasks. Unlike many of the interlocks analyzed previously, this particular quality impacts strongly on the views of ordinary citizens rather than the views of the elites.

The scope of the military's civic action, including its responsibilities in the anti-drug campaign, are prescribed by the Mexican Constitution: "No military authority may, in time of peace, perform any functions other than those that are directly connected with military affairs. There shall be fixed and permanent military commands only in the castles, forts, and warehouses immediately subordinate to the Government of the Union; or in encampments, barracks, or arsenals established for the quartering of troops outside towns."[10] Strictly speaking, the military has been violating portions of this article since 1920. Its programs have included health education; applied medicine (from dentistry to minor surgery); school and road construction and repairs; the dispensing of food supplies and utensils; and reforestation.[11]

Mexican military civic action did not originate as a counterinsurgency measure but as a component of the armed forces revolutionary tradition. According to historians, in 1921 General Obregón created nineteen labor battalions to be employed in road construction, irrigation projects, railroad maintenance, and telegraph repairs. These functions were continued under his successor and legitimized in the army's organic law, as long as they had some connection to military needs.[12] Considering the military's actual activities, "needs" have obviously been broadly defined. Given this historical legacy, the argument could be made that civic action has a long tradition in the armed forces' mission in Mexico. It has little effect on the issue of civilian leadership in the civil-military relationship.

The military itself gives various forms of civic action high priority. The idea, according to one analyst, is to convey a benign image to the public. The army and air force assigns it significant attention in the official *Revista de Ejército y Fuerza Aérea*.[13] By the 1950s the military was involved in such public relations functions as Little League baseball and transportation of anti-malaria drugs. And even in that decade it was cooperating with civilian police against drug smuggling and drug sales.[14] In the 1960s, 60 percent of its budget was devoted to these types of projects. During the following decade, military officers with engineering and communications skills were recruited to a pilot development program known as Plan Huicot.[15] In the 1990s the military continued its health programs which, in addition to checkups and inoculations, also involved the distribution of potable water, veterinary checkups, and actual surgical procedures. By the mid 1990s, the army typically conducted two civic action visits per military zone per month. In Chiapas, however, the civic action battalion was permanently on duty.[16] Their activities continued to be summarized in the official army/air force journal, and in President Fox's state of the union reports.

The army was put in charge of coordinating disaster relief in 1966, an assignment reflected in the aforementioned DN-III-E national security plan. The military's performance in this role increased citizen esteem for the military and added legitimacy to and respect for the government.[17] During the major earthquake in Mexico City in the fall of 1985, instead of giving the military overall responsibility, civilian authorities took control. The military's role was to provide security:

> [I]n so doing, it occasionally impeded spontaneous civilian ventures thereby damaging the reputation—a fact that embittered many generals toward the *técnicos* who had restrained them. At the same time, the navy's image sparkled because, after its ministry building collapsed, blue-uniformed officers were seen relentlessly hunting for survivors in the ruins of its own and nearby buildings.[18] Overall, the de la Madrid administration was viewed by the average Mexico City resident as incompetent and untrustworthy during the disaster relief activities in the capital. Their perceived incompetence was so noteworthy that it produced significant political consequences, including the emergence and growth of non-governmental organizations in Mexico.[19]

On the face of it, of the three types of missions the Mexican armed forces are authorized to perform, disaster relief would be viewed as the least threatening to civil supremacy over the military. Yet the 1985 earthquake illustrates how a single action can have enormous political consequences on civilian legitimacy as well as on the civil-military relationship. It is essential to consider, however, that legitimacy issues already faced the de la Madrid administration, and that civilian authorities, through their own incompetence, were even more important than the military itself in putting the armed forces in a favorable light.

The Military as an Internal Policeman: Internal vs. National Security?

The military's involvement in disaster and civic action relief, while having the clear potential of influencing the public's opinion of its residual missions and its position in the broader civil-military relationship, pales in significance compared to the role the military plays in national security. The military's participation in office-holding, campaigns, elections, and opposition parties is the most obvious means of direct political involvement in Mexico. Indirect means, given the dramatic decline in direct participation since Vicente Fox's electoral victory in 2000, equally affect the military's self-image and potential political involvement, both in decision-making and in the application of national security policies.

As suggested by one of the working hypotheses, the military's potential affect on civil-military relations through the vehicle of national security is dependant on the manner in which civilian and military leaders define national security. Phyllis Walker offers an interesting hypothesis: "The national security doctrines designed by the armed forces of other Latin American countries—in particular, those of the Southern Cone—to deal with perceived threats were not developed in Mexico. Moreover, the absence of such a doctrine may represent a partial explanation for the military's continuing nonintervention in political affairs throughout the post-World War II era."[20]

It has been suggested that in other countries (notably Brazil from 1964 to 1974), that the military's primary concern was domestic subversion and that the officers educated in this "ideology of internal warfare" at the Higher War College were the primary architects of the March 1964 coup against the civilian government.[21] In Latin America, most specifically in the Southern Cone, the armed forces strongly subscribed to a "national security doctrine" in which the individual armed forces shared numerous commonalities.[22]

The trend toward an armed forces national security function is universal. Some theorists expect it to become a primary function of the military in most countries.[23] The orientation of the Mexican armed forces toward internal security missions rather than toward external defense is complicated by the fact that the United States, in its relations with Latin America, has not articulated a notion of internal security that incorporates a society's level of economic and social development.[24] Mexico's proximity to the United States, the long history of U.S. aggression against Mexico, and the fact that Mexico is the only country in which the majority of U.S. officers say they would willingly fight against domestic insurgents, encouraged the Mexican armed forces to pursue an external defense strategy until the 1980s.[25]

In the last twenty years, Mexico has moved in the direction of the armed forces playing a growing national security role. In the post-World War II era, Mexico's definition of national security was influenced by the cold war mentality of the United States. The 1952 edition of the basic text on military ethics changed the order of Mexico's military objectives. This text placed the preservation of internal order first and defense of national territory third.[26] In 1965, after an armed group attempted to assault the military barracks in Ciudad Madera, Chihuahua, references to special or guerrilla warfare appeared in military publications.[27] Colonel Jorge Carrillo Olea, former director of Mexico's Department of Federal Security defined it in this manner:

Number one, Mexico does not have external military enemies.... The unsatisfied demands of the people are the first element to attend to: services, education, justice.... To ignore these will produce a more polarized society. Mexico's problems are inside its borders, recognizing that the source of many of these originate from outside the country and have a great deal to do with social justice. Which are the groups on the margin at truly insupportable extremes? Where is the government not capable of guaranteeing average standard measures and norms of justice and of democracy? This is the problem of national security.[28]

The linkage between internal security and the military has a long history in Mexico, even though the military's own internal security role, in many respects, remained undefined until the mid-1980s. Their connection to national security tasks, through civilian leadership, occurred through the venue of Mexico's national security agency, the Federal Security Department. This agency is a cross between the United States Federal Bureau of Investigation and the Central Intelligence Agency. The Federal Security Department (DFS), which disbanded in 1985,[29] had been headed from 1946 to 1970 (except 1958–1959) by an active duty or retired officer. It is important to note that the agency was founded in 1946 during the Alemán administration. The president ordered the secretary of national defense to pick ten top young officers to organize the Federal Security Department.[30] Most of these officers were from the 1947 Escuela Superior de Guerra graduating class. The class included Fernando Gutiérrez Barrios, a key figure in Mexico's national security agencies, and Silvino Ramírez Michel, the brother of the army's attorney general during the Salinas administration.[31] The relationship was further complicated by the fact that those officers who joined the Federal Security Department were simultaneously commissioned on the presidential staff.[32]

Its first director, General Marcelino Iñurreta, who had studied with the U.S. Federal Bureau of Investigation, organized the department.[33] His assistant director was a lieutenant colonel. Once again, Alemán, while reducing the military's overt role in politics, simultaneously provided the means for insuring its involvement in national security issues at the enforcement level. This decision affected the evolution of civil-military relations generally.

General Iñurreta was replaced in 1952 by Colonel Leandro Castillo Venegas, whose second-in-command was Gilberto Suárez Torres. Suárez Torres was a lawyer, special federal agent, and later attorney general of the Federal District. He directed the agency briefly from 1958–1959. In 1959 Colonel Manuel Rangel Escamilla, who had relatives among senior officers, took over, with Gutiérrez Barrios, a graduate of the Heroico Colegio Militar, as his assistant. Gutiérrez Barrios replaced his boss in 1964. Captain Luis de la

Barreda, one the first ten officers who joined the department in 1947, and a fellow classmate of Gutiérrez Barrios, replaced Gutiérrez Barrios in 1970, bringing along Miguel Nazar Haro, as his assistant director. Nazar Haro was not, however, a regular officer, and never graduated from the Heroico Colegio Militar. He held no rank until 1980, and received the rank of lieutenant colonel in military justice courtesy of General Arévalo Gardoqui, the secretary of national defense (1982–1988), through a special promotion.[34]

In 1977, the first experienced politician, Javier García Paniagua, was appointed director. He left after two years to become assistant secretary of government. However, he maintained strong connections with the military, having been a student supporter of General Miguel Henríquez Guzmán in 1952. Most important, García Paniagua was the son of General Marcelino García Barragán, secretary of national defense. Miguel Nazar Haro took over the post in 1978. His successor, Antonio Zorrilla Pérez, the third civilian to head the agency, took charge in 1982.[35] Both Zorrilla Pérez (who was charged as the intellectual author in the murder of prominent newspaperman Manuel Buendía) and Nazar Haro (who was indicted by a U.S. grand jury on a list of charges including grand theft auto) imparted an unsavory image to the agency.[36] More recently, another former director, Captain Luis de la Barreda (1970–1977), was charged with the murder of three leftists from this period.[37]

Despite the military's reorientation from external defense to internal security affairs, national security experts suggest that the military itself had little to do with the change. This is significant because it reinforces the argument that we have made in our theoretical framework that the fundamental issue in civil-military relations is who remains in control, and not the redefinition of military tasks.[38] "One outstanding feature of the national security issue in Mexico is the slight participation of the military sector both in the definition of the concept of national security itself and in the decision as to the most appropriate means of confronting the dangers that threaten it."[39] General Félix Galván López, national defense secretary from 1976 to 1982, suggested that the essence of national security, the ideology that inspires it, the relations among the classes that facilitate it, and the respective share of power to each group were not matters for the army to decide.[40]

In 1985, the Secretariat of Government quietly established an agency known as the General Directorate of Investigation and National Security (1985–1989). Its first and only head was Pedro Vásquez Colmenares, a veteran civilian politician. Phyllis Walker observed that his appointment signaled the military's inability to translate its influence into a more active role in national security policy-making.[41]

At first glance, Vázquez Colmenares' appointment might seem to reflect civilian dominance over security affairs, but it is worth noting that his superior was Jorge Carrillo Olea, a colonel and assistant secretary in charge of all government secretariat security-oriented agencies. Carrillo Olea was the only active duty officer holding a position at that level in a civilian government agency from 1982 to 1989. Equally interesting is the fact that Carrillo Olea's brother, a career officer, served as chief of Section 1 (human resources) on the staff at the secretary of national defense, from 1982–1984, providing an unusual personal bridge between civilian intelligence and the military.[42]

Within a week of taking office in 1988, Salinas appointed José Córdoba, his chief of staff, to direct a technical cabinet comprising five sections. Four of the sections—economic, agricultural, social welfare, and foreign relations—had been established previously by de la Madrid, but Salinas, as previously noted, added a fifth: national security, composed of the Secretariat of National Defense, the Secretariat of the Navy, the Secretariat of Government, the Secretariat of Foreign Relations, and the Attorney General.[43]

This is the first time that both the navy and the national defense secretariats were formally represented in national security matters at the cabinet level. Some observers believed that national defense replaced government as the most important voice in this sub cabinet. Despite this new cabinet level structure, responsibilities for national security decisions remained divided, and military intelligence was not shared with civilian intelligence.[44] Under the Fox administration, the national security cabinet became more fully integrated after structural reforms were introduced in April 2003. Its mission is clearly defined to include social cohesion, protection of rights, and "preservation of democracy based on economic, social and political development of the country and its citizens." Its members consists of the Secretariats of Government, of National Defense, of the Navy, of Public Security, of the Treasury, and the Controller, the Attorney General, and the director general of the Center for Research and National Security (CISEN), who serves as the executive secretary.[45]

Intelligence sharing between the military and civilian agencies has improved dramatically, especially as it relates to the pursuit of drug trafficking, a central national security mission. The potential contributions of the Secretariat of National Defense to government intelligence is suggested by the fact that 272 individuals are now assigned to Section 2 (intelligence) on the general staff.[46] The extent of the cooperation can also be measured by the presence, in 2004, of 186 members of the armed forces employed in the attorney general's office, and more significantly, 5,326 individuals in the Secretariat of Public Security.[47]

In 1989, Carrillo Olea, promoted to general, replaced Vázquez Colmenares as director of a new agency, the Center for Research and National Security (CISEN), located in the secretariat of government. With that appointment, Carrillo Olea again became the only active duty officer holding a director general position or higher in a civilian, federal agency. Carrillo Olea, unlike previous active duty officers on leave or retired, actually used his military title. A graduate of the Escuela Superior de Guerra, he trained in the United States at Fort Knox. He held the key political-military intelligence post as head of intelligence for the presidential staff, where he served with five future prominent generals, including two presidential chiefs of staff.[48]

Carrillo Olea's predecessor as assistant secretary of government, Fernando Gutiérrez Barrios, who retained equally close ties to the military, went on to become the government secretary in 1988, after a long history in the Federal Security Department. Gutiérrez Barrios, of course, is a former officer, the son of a Revolutionary colonel, and a graduate of Heroico Colegio Militar who resigned his commission as a captain in 1959. From 1990 through 2000, however, civilians exclusively led CISEN.[49]

An internal security focus also took hold in the National Defense Secretariat at the higher echelons during this period, a focus reflected in the backgrounds of some of its top brass. The oficial mayor of the secretariat from 1988–1994 received added training in intelligence gathering, counter insurgency, and psychological warfare in the United States.[50] The assistant secretary of national defense from 1994–1998 directed the intelligence section (2) on the staff of the secretariat of national defense from 1973–1974, the highpoint of the antiguerrilla war in Guerrero.[51] Fox's secretary of national defense graduated from the counterinsurgency course at Fort Gulick, Panama Canal Zone, and is a military expert on national security and the author of a manual on the subject used at the Escuela Superior de Guerra.[52]

The armed forces have ties to the civilian intelligence community through their affiliation with intelligence agencies. This is the most indirect linkage the armed forces have maintained in the broad arena of national security issues. Traditionally, the armed forces have been involved directly in national security assignments involving the suppression of organized opposition, whether they relied on political or violent techniques. The 1968 student massacre serves as a notable example of this. With the redefinition of the armed forces missions in the 1980s and 1990s, two other tasks linked the military explicitly to civilian responsibilities and reshaped the military's role. These were personal security and crime and the anti-drug mission.

Internal Suppression

The military plays a significant internal political role as part of Mexico's security formula. Its scope has included civic action projects, drug eradication, and political suppression. When the civilian leadership fails to negotiate a satisfactory solution in a political dispute and finds the use of other threats unproductive, it may take recourse in a military solution. Typically, Mexican politicians have not resorted to the military except in extreme cases; however, such cases occur far more often than one might think. The more civilian leadership relies on the military to carry out politicized, internal police functions, the more the military itself expects to have a voice in political decision making, and, equally important, the more society, including future civilian and military leaders, defines intervention in these civilian responsibilities as a legitimate military responsibility.

The military played a primary role in suppressing the railroad workers strikes of 1958–1959, the telephone and postal workers movement in 1960, a student movement in Mexico City in 1961, and, of course, the student demonstration in Tlatelolco Plaza in 1968. The military was also implicated in the death of an important peasant leader, Rubén Jaramillo. This case was hushed up, and the involvement of the army high command and the national leadership was impossible to ascertain.[53] The military has been used to shut down critical presses, too. The presidential guard arrested the editor of *Política*, a left-wing publication, in the early 1960s.

The military's most frequent—and least documented—use has been to control numerous rural political disturbances. To maintain order in the countryside, the military relies on small detachments of soldiers, each generally led by a lieutenant, that are assigned to the more inaccessible regions.[54] A U.S. officer's report in the early 1980s noted that a detachment's most common task is to mediate land disputes in small Indian villages and to investigate murders and other potentially explosive situations.[55] The privatization of the ejido land system in the countryside, beginning at the end of Salinas' administration, is likely to have an adverse effect on this system. Prior to privatization, a small cadre of active duty officers commanded rurales, groups of peasants associated with the individual village lands. These relationships maintained an important link between peasants and the army and provided the army with a source of intelligence that helped them anticipate potentially volatile situations.[56]

Shortly after Echeverría became president in 1970, the country faced a number of urban and rural guerrilla movements. The military received national attention when a guerrilla group led by Lucio Cabañas Barrientos kidnapped Rúben Figueroa, the PRI candidate for governor of Guerrero. The military fought the guerrillas, and ultimately freed Figueroa, but Cabañas Barrientos, under murky circumstances, was killed by the military in December of 1974. Military censorship prevailed over other activities in the anti-guerrilla campaign, too. As one participant recalled, "One incident that has never been revealed publicly, . . . someone accidentally set off a firefight between a parachute battalion and an infantry unit, and a number of soldiers were killed by our own troops."[57]

The military effectively eliminated guerrilla activity in the early 1970s, committing numerous human rights violations in the process. These violations, long known to analysts, are now becoming familiar to the general public as a result of the reform of freedom of information statutes and access to federal archives under the Fox administration. Equally important, one similar to the army's experience in the student massacre in 1968, their missions disturbed many younger officers. As one officer recalled:

> One of the most extraordinary consequences of my experience there was seeing elderly peasants tied up and blindfolded, and beginning to wonder what actually we were doing there, and why were these people being treated this way. This was not only my feeling, although I tended to express it more openly, but the attitude of many other, younger officers. In fact, the feeling of dissatisfaction with the military's mission in Guerrero became so widespread that many officers were not assigned to Guerrero or Oaxaca. The national defense secretariat purposely separated us after this assignment so we could not form a cohesive group to express our dissatisfaction and to question what went on there.[58]

Experienced guerrilla groups remained dormant or ineffective until the 1990s, when the Zapatista rebellion brought to the forefront the level of rural dissatisfaction with government policies nationally and locally. In addition to the conflict in Chiapas, the military responded to another guerrilla organization calling itself the Popular Revolutionary Army. It is believed to have been organized May 1, 1994 by fourteen armed organizations, some of whose origins date back to the 1960s.[59] Its political structure is governed by a central committee, which is responsible for both military and political activities, and calls itself the Revolutionary Popular Democratic Party (PDRP).[60] It has been most active in the poor, rural south, specifically in Guerrero and Oaxaca. Its active members at the time of its foundation probably numbered between 150 and 200 guerrillas. It does not attract nearly the same level of support in Mexico as the Zapatistas because it relies largely on violent tactics.[61] According to knowledgeable Mexicans, "these attacks have been greatly underreported. Ambushes and raids have inflicted military and police casualties in prime ERP operating areas and elsewhere."[62] Their comparative danger to that of the Zapatistas is reflected by the comment of an Escuela Superior de Guerra graduate who, while attending a reunion of his classmates, heard many of them report that it was much safer to be assigned duty in Chiapas rather than in states where the ERP operated.[63]

The government's response to the 1996 outburst of violence from the ERP is reflected in President Zedillo's state of the union address (delivered on

September 1, 1996) after their activities were reported in the media, Zedillo told congress and the Mexican people that his administration would, "employ all the force of the Army to defeat them."[64] Near the end of his administration, the secretariat of national defense identified the probable existence of 16 armed groups operating in at least 16 states in Mexico. (These groups claimed the support of 167 political and social organizations).[65] The Secretariat of National Defense identified only two armed groups operating in Mexico as of 2003, the EZLN in Chiapas and the ERP in Oaxaca and Guerrero.[66]

The Military as a Drug Enforcement Agency?

In the past two decades, the single most important linkage between the Mexican military and the political leadership is the fight against the drug trade. This single task provides the greatest amount of evidence for supporters of the view that the armed forces' performance of traditional civilian missions endangers civilian supremacy. The dilemmas that this task poses for Mexico within the context of constructing a fledgling democracy have been well stated:

> [T]he policies of building democratic political systems and eliminating drug traffic have not been easily reconcilable. Within the rubric of military subordination to civilian authority, the dangers of the drug war as a military mission are obvious. As with the counterinsurgency activities of the 1960s, direct Latin American military involvement in the drug war would involve military in policy tasks that are technically within the civilian domain; it would also require mastery of a complex combination of political and military skills, likely necessitating the expansion of military intelligence operations; it would blur the line between appropriate and inappropriate domains for professional actions; it would expand the managerial roles played by the military in society; and it would increase the role military men play in national politics and political decision making.[67]

The military has a long history of eradicating drug production, but, until the 1970s, it had to cope only with individual farmers, not cartels. The South Florida Task Force, created in 1981, successfully interdicted the flow of drugs through the Caribbean Sea, which prompted the South American cartels to begin shipping drugs through Mexico. This change produced a devastating impact. By the end of the century, 70 percent of all drugs entering the United States passed through Mexico.[68] Furthermore, the number of peasants growing associated crops in Mexico increased tremendously, complicating the military's relationship with the rural population. The military likes to think of itself as deriving from the masses, and it realizes that most peasants are only trying to survive, not to profit from criminality. Under these conditions, it becomes difficult to destroy crops.[69]

Salinas reinforced the importance of drugs as a national security issue in his first state of the union address: "The drug trafficker has become a grave risk for the national security and the health of Mexicans."[70] He committed the state to combating it. The military's involvement, especially since implementation of the Condor Plan in 1977, has serious implications for Mexico's civilian leaders and for the military's political role. Among the issues raised are:

- inter-institutional coordination (the program is in the hands of the attorney general)
- exposure of the army to the extensive corruption that accompanies the drug trade
- increased contact between U.S. officers, government officials, and the Mexican officer corps
- constitutional questions raised by the military's strategy
- supremacy of the military over civilian control in various regions
- enhancement of the military's public image compared to that of civilian officials.[71]

The United States is responsible, in large part, for the presence of drug traffickers in Mexico. It has pushed the Mexican government to involve its armed forces in the interdiction process. By the end of 1994, the U.S. government was spending 20 percent of its anti-drug budget on interdiction and enforcement, despite the fact that study after study has shown after a decade of effort that such policies fail to staunch the flow of narcotics across the border.[72] In the mid-1990s, the United States army began training over 1,000 officers at more than a dozen bases in drug interdiction tactics. In addition, the Central Intelligence Agency provided extensive intelligence courses to about 90 officers who became part of the new counter-drug force in Mexico.[73] To enhance their capabilities in performing the anti-drug tasks, the Mexican military has acquired the type of military technologies that Pentagon theorists in the military establishment consider essential to information war capabilities.[74] In 2000, the Secretariat of National Defense created a new electronic information service to improve and develop army and air force technological norms.[75]

As early as 1985, 20 generals, 120 high-ranking officers, and 25,000 soldiers—18 percent of the active duty army—were engaged in anti-drug work. From 1976 through 1985, 315 military men had died in the anti-drug campaign.[76] By 2003, the number of soldiers who had lost their lives in the drug war reached 439, including 2 generals; 11 colonels, lieutenant colonels and majors; and 70 officers.[77] In 1991, Salinas established the Drug Control

Planning Center (CENDRO), making the Secretariat of National Defense responsible for increased air space surveillance.[78] Reportedly a majority of officers would have preferred to devote themselves to traditional military pursuits.[79] Sensing the officers' resentment, Salinas narrowed the scope of military anti-drug work to destroying drugs rather than combating dealers.[80]

This narrow definition changed to a much broader assignment under Zedillo, a policy continued into the Fox administration. The president asserted that the secretariat of national defense would, "contribute to a reduction in violence generated by organized crime related to illegal drug trafficking, precursor drugs, and weapons by intensifying" its search for drug producing sites.[81] As of 2003, an average of 30,000 officers and troops are assigned to a permanent campaign against drug traffickers.[82] Support for the broad drug enforcement mission can be found in the army's own internal 1995 document, which on this issue is unequivocal and succinct: "the anti-drug mission should be permanent." This recommendation suggests that the higher command agreed with President Zedillo that drug trafficking and drug-related corruption are major national security issues. Indeed, General Vega García, the secretary of national defense, told the author in 2004 that drug trafficking was one of the two leading threats to Mexico's national security.[83] The fact that this mission is not analyzed in any way in the report suggests their level of commitment to this task.[84] This is surprising given the fact that many individual officers express reservations about performing such a mission.[85] As a brigade general told the author:

> Yes, it is true that most young generals do not want to be involved in any way in combating drugs. I think this whole issue is a point of dispute within our country. We really run the risk of increasing corruption in the military because of the amounts of money involved, and that is the main reason that the military wants to get out of this activity. . . . Actually, we didn't define this as our function, but our activity in the anti-drug program stems from the organic military law. Under that law, our responsibility includes . . . guaranteeing internal security, which the President has defined as including drugs.[86]

It can be argued that drug enforcement missions have provided more combat experience in the armed forces than any other form of activity, including anti-guerrilla campaigns. The continuous use of large numbers of troops and officers in day-to-day operations permits the armed forces to practice anti-guerrilla techniques as their anti-drug strategy.[87] The intertwining of drugs and guerrillas, especially elsewhere in South America, is central to new definitions of national security.[88] In fact, although he did not intertwine them, Mexico's secretary of national defense considered violent guerrillas to be the other major nation security threat under Fox.[89]

Civilian Missions: Redefining Civil-Military Relations? 113

A significant justification for involving the armed forces in the anti-drug task stemmed from the inability of civilian agencies to adequately perform these functions. Civilian limitations can be explained in large part by the extensive corruption found at all levels of civilian police agencies, federal, state and local. Many analysts warned that similar levels of corruption would taint the military.[90] According to many observers, drug-driven corruption undermined the government's own credibility in the late 1980s.[91] The linkage became more visible in the first year of the Salinas administration, when the former head of the Department of Federal Security (indicted for the murder of journalist Manuel Buendia) was said to have ties to the drug trade.

As the military became more involved in anti-drug trafficking tasks, the level of corruption reached even more serious levels in their high command. The army became so concerned with drugs corrupting its leadership that it stepped up internal intelligence, including increased tapping of phones.[92] Under President Salinas, the alleged involvement of the Navy high command in drug-related corruption led to the president firing the naval secretary. In another incident, the armed forces were involved in a deadly firefight in Veracruz with federal agents from the Attorney General's office while protecting the landing zone for a drug shipment.[93] According to one analyst, 1992 marked the beginning of the "limousine service in which the military, federal agents, and state judicial police officials began providing protection for drug shipments to the border area."[94]

Besides high-level cases of military corruption, the military has received increasing attention for its civil rights abuses while implementing its drug-related missions. The Supreme Court ruled that, despite accusations against the military of confessions obtained under torture, the ability of the military to make arrests and to take confessions was legal.[95] However, according to the 1990 Americas Watch Report on Mexico, torture and political killings were still "institutionalized in the military" and by federal and state police.[96] In response to this characterization, the Salinas administration created the National Commission on Human Rights.[97] Of the seventy formal complaints processed in its first two months, only one involved the military.[98] Following that report, the Catholic Church's Centro de Derechos Humanos Fray Bartolomé de las Casas alleged that soldiers interrogated and beat peasants in search of marijuana fields.[99]

Zedillo inherited a difficult situation from his predecessor. Drug-related corruption had become more extensive among civilian and military officials.[100] Symbolically, the case of Division General Jesús Gutiérrez Rebollo, which received substantial coverage in the United States media, was the pinnacle of known corruption in the military. Gutiérrez Rebollo reputedly was one of the army's most successful commanders in the drug war. Based on his reputation, in 1997 the secretary of national defense recommended Gutiérrez Rebollo to president Zedillo to become his first drug czar, a recommendation passed on to General Barry McCaffrey, president Clinton's drug chief.

Less than three weeks after taking office, Gutiérrez Rebollo was arrested on charges of drug-related corruption, embarrassing the national defense secretariat, the presidency of Mexico, and General McCaffrey.[101] What is noteworthy about the case is that Gutiérrez Rebollo's alleged ties were well-known and had been going on for years. By 1999, Mexico's attorney general admitted that "economic power and the level of corruption of organized crime dedicated to [narcotics] has reached the armed forces," and that "it is the principal threat to national security and democratic institutions."[102] In a classified report prepared for Attorney General Janet Reno, the web of corruption linking top generals and drug traffickers was much broader than had been publicly acknowledged.[103]

The public's concern with general criminality and public safety complemented the penetration of drug-related corruption and violence at all levels of society. The number one policy issue in the 1994 presidential race was personal security. That fact led President Zedillo to establish a comprehensive National Public Security System designed to coordinate anti-crime and drug efforts among 2,000 police agencies in December 1995.[104] He created a National Public Security Council that included the secretaries of national defense and navy. This decision is highly significant because it provided, for the first time, a role for the armed forces in domestic public security issues, a role distinct from national security issues.[105]

An important consequence of the increasing crime rates in urban locales was a dramatic expansion of military involvement in traditional police activities. In 1996, the Federal District appointed an army general to take over a corrupt civilian police. He was not the first army officer to run the Mexico City police, but he became the first chief to appoint more than 150 fellow officers to high and middle-level positions in the police force.[106] His appointments included 15 generals and 50 colonels.[107] The government also experimented with a pilot program in the northern state of Chihuahua. This pilot program incorporated individuals with military training into 50 percent of the posts in the federal judicial police in Chihuahua, a notoriously corrupt agency.[108] The Supreme Court, in March, 1996, concluded that the "army, air force and navy may intervene in public security matters as long as a civilian authority, even the government itself, requests it."[109] By the end of the Zedillo administration, *El Universal*, a Mexico City daily, reported that 37 percent of the army was involved in police functions or anti-narcotics mis-

Civilian Missions: Redefining Civil-Military Relations? 115

sions.[110] A growing presence of the military, most of whom were on leave or retired, could also be found among state and municipal security forces.[111]

The military was not in agreement in the performance of these broader police functions in the late 1990s, as distinct from the issue of combating drugs. "This role acceptance has not been whole-hearted, and there continues to be some underlying dissent among top ranking military leaders over this expanded role.... This is a source of tension within the military institution itself."[112] As one of the few recent military members of congress (2000–2003), General José A. Vallarta Ceceña suggested that the armed forces believed it was necessary to help with police work, but that the military hoped it would end quickly.[113]

In the last few months of his administration, Zedillo's government and the armed forces were rocked with a second major drug-related scandal. Two active duty generals, Francisco Quirós Hermosillo and Mario A. Acosta Chaparro, were arrested August 31, 2000, on drug trafficking charges. Apparently, military intelligence knew about their activities and that of a former director of the Directorate of Federal Security since 1997.[114] They were not tried until November 1, 2002, two years into the Fox administration. Their trial was the first trial opened to the public by the armed forces, unlike the closed trial of the officers responsible for the murder of Mexican federal agents in Veracruz during the Salinas administration. They received stiff prison terms,[115] and in the course of their testimony they admitted knowing a leading drug cartel figure, Amado Carrillo, since 1992.[116]

Since 1995, the secretariat of national defense committed 25 percent of its budget to the fight against drug trafficking. As of December 1, 1996, 1,493 troops were trained to work with the Attorney General. By the end of his administration, the secretariat of national defense had committed 36,341 soldiers and officers to the drug mission, a threefold increase in 9 years.[117] Troops used in these operations averaged 25,000 during the entirety of his administration.[118] The air force restructured its units into three broad regions to increase its efficiency in the battle against drug trafficking in 1999.[119]

The anti-drug campaign has made the military the supreme authority or, in some cases, the only authority in parts of such states as Oaxaca, Sinaloa, Jalisco, and Guerrero.[120] The long-term effect of this is, of course, to subvert civilian political supremacy, and give the military a taste of political control on a regional level. Yet, there is absolutely no evidence that the military either desires or would like to expand this assignment. Its increased visibility has been largely positive, despite its own prominent cases of high-level corruption. There does not seem to be public resistance to its exercising such a role, opening up the possibility of the military engaging in other non-traditional roles in the future.[121] A poll of 14,000 citizens taken by Televisa suggests that ordinary Mexicans wanted the armed forces to assume control of the anti-drug efforts.[122] An argument could be made that its alleged successes in this venue made it more appealing to civilian politicians to request its greater involvement in fighting crime generally.

When Vicente Fox campaigned for the presidency in 2000, one of his campaign promises was to eliminate the military's role in drug enforcement. Instead of taking the military out of drug enforcement tasks, Fox actually deepened their role. Furthermore, representatives of the military, including the director of the Colegio de Defensa Nacional, the military's premier institution for the study of national security policy, publicly defined the drug mission as a national security issue, contradicting the position of Fox's national security advisers before the election.[123]

Fox took the unprecedented step of appointing a brigadier general as his Attorney General. This was an effort to control corruption within the key civilian agency responsible for fighting crime and to enhance cooperation between the armed forces and federal agents. While confronting the same issues faced by the military under Fox's two immediate predecessors, the armed forces, even with corruption in its ranks, has become a more effective tool in the drug war. The special mobile forces units (GAFE's)[124] were responsible for capturing major drug cartel leaders.[125] Those forces are made up of three brigades, consisting of nine battalions and a rapid reaction force.[126] The United States exerted a significant influence on their training. Between 1940 and 2002, 120 soldiers completed special forces training.[127] The secretary of national defense, General Vega García, made an unprecedented appearance on the nation's top evening newscast in 2002 to explain how the army nabbed Benjamín Arellano Félix, the alleged leader of the violent Tijuana drug cartel.[128]

The armed forces can claim some notable successes in tracking down and arresting key drug kingpins under Fox, far more than his predecessors, but corruption in military and civilian agencies continues unabated. In the initial months of his administration, the military set off an international incident when Mexican soldiers in Humvees shot at U.S. border patrol agents on the American side of the border. As one analyst charged, "the absolutely brazen manner in which armed detachments and individual members of the Mexican army can operate in a coordinated manner in American territory is a source of continual amazement. What is even more disconcerting, however, is the fact that they can commit their nefarious criminal acts with impunity."[129] According to one source, the chief of the Gulf Cartel, Osiel Cárdenas Guillén, had a personal security force made up of 14 deserters from GAFE after they abandoned a select team as part of the Special Prosecutor Against Drug Crimes (FEADS) in Tamaulipas.[130] The following month, the Attorney

Civilian Missions: Redefining Civil-Military Relations?   117

General requested that the military withdraw the soldiers assigned to guarding the Special Prosecutor's facility and its archives.[131] The Attorney General eventual shut down this office in January of 2003 for corruption, and replaced it with a new agency.[132]

Much more devastating to the image of the armed forces, however, was the discovery that another general and his aides were arrested for allegedly providing protection to drug traffickers.[133] Shortly after that revelation came to light, the armed forces announced that the entire 65th Infantry Battalion, stationed in Guamúchil, Sinaloa, was being tested for drug use and investigated for drug-related corruption. Of the 600 soldiers, 48 were detained by the military. As of 2003, only 26 individuals have been tried and convicted in the army for drug-related charges since the Fox administration took office.[134]

The militarization of the drug war in Mexico generates numerous consequences, some for civil-military relations and others for the armed forces itself.[135] In spite of its improved track record under Fox, the inability of the combined efforts of the attorney general's office, state police, and the armed forces to rein in drug trafficking in the last twenty years suggests that the government has a geopolitical security problem, and that its territorial hegemony is incomplete. Richard Craig asserts that either through intimidation or corruption, drug lords exercised de facto power in portions of Sinaloa, Durango, Chihuahua, Guerrero, Veracruz, and Oaxaca in the 1980s and 1990s.[136] It is unlikely that such control has been fully eliminated by the armed forces, as suggested by the fact that more troops had to be assigned to the U.S. border region in 2005.

A second consequence of the expanded military role in drug interdiction having national security implications is the greater possibility of increased United States military involvement and intervention.[137] Unlike South America, the American military has not been and is not directly involved in this mission on Mexican national territory. However, the Mexican military has increased its training in American bases, thus expanding their influence on the professionalization of Mexican personnel.[138]

Within the military, the drug enforcement mission increased tensions between the services. Piñeyro cites an example of the Navy viewing the Army as being given preference in this task, after organizing its own Special Forces Amphibious Groups in 1999, and requesting 70 high speed boats for intercepting drug traffickers, but only receiving 40.[139] On the other hand, even more recent scholarship, and the national defense secretary himself, describe closer cooperation between the navy and the army since 2001 as a result of having a general as attorney general.[140]

From a sociological perspective, a more complex and possible long-term consequence within the army is a functional disjuncture for military officers assigned to the Attorney General. Officers were allocated assignments based on their competence, not on their military grade. Such experiences might create problems for military discipline among those officers who come to view their civilian status as taking precedence over their military rank.[141]

In addition to the continued and expanded role of the armed forces in anti-narcotics missions, the military continued its high visibility in other anti-crime tasks. Just as it had been in Zedillo's campaign, the extent of crime and lack of personal security was the single-most important campaign issue in 2000. Fox took a more dramatic step than his predecessor; he created a new cabinet-level agency, the secretariat for Public Security. He appointed the Mexico City police chief, a former law school dean and prosecutor, as his first secretary of the new agency. This agency was in charge of the Federal Preventative Police,[142] a civilian agency created in December 1998 that combined the federal highway, immigration and tax police. Its charge included working closely with the military and the Attorney General on organized crime and drug trafficking. In the last year of the Zedillo administration, army officers were integrated into this force, then under the control of the secretariat of government. Eight hundred intelligence personnel were transferred from the Center for Research and National Security, to a new Directorate for Intelligence.[143] The secretariat of national defense loaned 4,899 soldiers from the 3rd Military Police Brigade and 352 Humvees, allowing them to help this agency from July through the end of December 1999.[144]

Under Fox, a similar pattern of military involvement continued. Two years into his administration, 826 members of the Mexican army joined the secretariat of public security.[145] Little progress has been made in eliminating corruption from the civilian police culture. The secretariat of national defense, in recognition of what has become a permanent public security mission, made transparent their security and defense polices in a published white paper.[146] The army alone used 33,794 troops monthly in 2001 for national security operations, a 47 percent increase over 2000.[147]

The officer corps has involved itself politically in many ways, both in structural roles assigned to it by the civilian leadership and in extra-military posts held by officers. As the latter declined, the military has expanded its nontraditional activities, most notably in the anti-drug campaigns. Its enhanced role in defining and fulfilling national security missions, including anti-crime and anti-drug tasks, has undoubtedly enhanced its visibility and given it additional prestige to the detriment of civilian agencies traditionally responsible for carrying out those assignments. Nevertheless, the military has not sought either of those non-traditional roles; indeed, there exists con-

Civilian Missions: Redefining Civil-Military Relations? 119

siderable evidence that many officers would like to withdraw from them altogether.

The officer corps, at the behest of civilian leaders (including president Fox), has responded to the request that such missions are required of the armed forces, at least until newly professionalized civilian agencies can perform those tasks. While these missions have strengthened the armed forces role in national security decisions, their contributions to the decision-making process remain subordinate to civilian control and civilian input in determining the broad outlines of national security missions.[148] The Mexican case therefore, strongly supports the conclusion that the performance of some civilian tasks, when a strong sense of subordination to civil authority prevails, does not threaten the balance in civil-military relations.[149]

CHAPTER SIX

Citizen and Military Views of Civil-Military Relations

The military, depending on how analysts evaluate its potential influence, has remained an unknown quantity in the civil-military relationship and, more broadly, in the transformation of Mexican politics. Questions remain, not because the armed forces have behaved in a threatening manner, but primarily because few Mexicans or outside observers have a feel for officer corps attitudes, values, and beliefs.[1] This statement remains accurate even though the pattern has started to change in the last few years. Similarly, little attempt has been made to understand how civilian political leaders view the armed forces or how their attitudes toward the relationship correspond to those of military officers. Because both political and military leaders are themselves products of the larger citizen culture, it is important to understand the attitudes of the average Mexican toward the military as an institution and toward its professional mission. Civilian ignorance of the military in Latin America is generally a serious obstacle to readjusting military missions within the context of a "redemocratized" continent.[2]

Understanding the attitudes of the officer corps is important in the larger context of Mexican politics because of their historic role in the political arena. Despite the military's having stayed away from direct involvement in the political arena since 1946 (that is, not controlling the presidency), most observers are unsure of what its conduct would be in a future political crisis. This situation has been accentuated by Mexico's dramatic transformation into an electoral democracy in 2000, by the missions the Fox administration has asked the armed forces to perform, and by different institutional strategies between the Navy and the Army pursued within the officer corps. In the recent past, many Mexicans believed that the military might be inclined to impose its own authoritarian order should it deem such action necessary. I would argue that Mexican civilians have reached this invalid conclusion because of their unfamiliarity with the armed forces leadership. This ignorance suggests a wide social and professional separation between civilians and the officer corps.[3]

Military Attitudes, Tenets of Mexican Professionalism

Military officers, just like accountants, doctors, economists and professors, are considered to be professionals. According to organizational theorists, a profession must include five attributes:

- it must be based upon a body of systematic theory (for example, theories of warfare)
- its members must possess differentiating expertise (for example, knowledge of military strategy)
- it must incorporate certain powers and privileges granted by society (for example, the military exercises autonomous control over its training)
- it must subscribe to a code of ethics (the most critical variable for the military because a code governs intra- and inter-group relationships)
- its culture, including values, norms, and symbols, must convey its mystique and distinctions.[4]

The degree to which the officer corps obeys higher civilian political authority, and the nature and scope of its attitudes toward political participation, are incorporated into the military's code of ethics and culture. It is sometimes forgotten, in stressing the insularity of the officer corps in Latin American countries, that professional perspectives and values are not developed in a vacuum. As Sam Sarkesian has noted, "Military systems, to remain legitimate, reflect society and, thus, professional ethics, attitudes, and beliefs developed from roots deep within the political-social system."[5]

Officer attitudes are an element worth assessing in detail because professional thought and self-perception within the armed forces are critical to civil-military relations in a democratic context.[6] Another issue is one regarding the unity of Mexico's military organizations. Can one set of values can be attributed to the organization as a whole? Because of the low level of general citizen familiarity with the military, it is extremely unlikely that most outsiders would know of any internal differences. McAlister believed that, in the 1960s, a younger group of officers, whom he called the pencillinos, were highly critical of government ineffectiveness in correcting important social and economic failures. The young officers were resentful of having to perform associated political and quasi-military tasks.⁷ This attitude never reached the higher ranks. These officers were members of the general staff at the secretariat of national defense, and they included then major Héctor Portillo Jurado, who became the assistant secretary of national defense from 1980–1982.⁸ These attitudes came to a head in 1995 with the publication of the secretariat of national defense document *Army and Air Force Development Program*, the first time officer criticisms became known to the general public. This document included criticisms of the command structure, the army's missions, its national security definition, its level of professionalism, its social communications, and its social development, among other issues.⁹ It is quite possible that younger officers, at various times, do not share the attitudes of generals toward military and governmental policies. The process of officer formation in Mexico, however, does have far-reaching effects on moderating such differences.

The only other public airing of military attitudes toward broader societal issues occurred in November 2004, when the newspaper *Milenio* published part of the results of the army's own internal survey. The survey revealed, among other findings, that 44 percent of the respondents, made up of enlisted personnel and officers, were dissatisfied with the Fox administration's performance and abilities.¹⁰ Since we don't have comparable responses from civilians, it is difficult to assess whether or not the army and air force were more critical of the administration's failures than civilians generally. Fox's personal approval ratings at this time hovered around 50 percent.

The level of military integration remains an unknown quantity. This has important internal implications and external repercussions. This separateness, according to some analysts, has not led to a caste tradition. Those who support this interpretation argue that revolutionary and popular origins, notwithstanding subsequent professionalization, have imprinted themselves on officer corps values.¹¹ It is true that Mexico's military leadership likes to convey that self-image.

Whether or not the officer corps shares its social origins with the people will be empirically examined, but a linkage to the lower or middle-classes is questionable. In the first place, members of organizations that are highly institutionalized, with rigorous prescriptions for behavior, tend to comply with the institution's rules, regardless of their social background; more often than not they internalize the rules.¹² Another weakness of the presumed military-class linkage is that Mexican officers, "once professionalized, are remarkably critical of the bourgeoisie. Allegations of middle-sector origins notwithstanding, officers do not look kindly on the sociocultural regalia of the bourgeois world–this despite aspiring to the same economic lifestyles."¹³

The issue of unity extends beyond ideology and class origin to the military's corporate strength, that is the degree to which Mexican officers operate in their own interests or the institution's interests. Mexican military literature promotes group sacrifice for country, but the way in which the professionalization process actually works, as distinct from its content, suggests an opposing interpretation. The presence of group cheating at the Escuela Superior de Guerra is more compatible with turning out individuals willing to break rules in return for personal advancement than individuals willing to sacrifice for their country.[14] In other words, military professionalization does not necessarily instill a monolithic sense of corporate solidarity.

A circumstance that might help to explain professional dishonesty is the importance of self-interest and institutional integrity in the population as a whole. Is such behavior tolerated or encouraged in civilian institutions or solely in the military culture? Is the environment of most civilians different from that of junior officers? The larger social context may exert far more influence on behavior than any other condition or experience, military or civilian.

As I have argued elsewhere, "organizational studies from different professions suggest that individuals who succeed inside an institutional structure are more likely to have been socialized by their profession's norms."[15] A study of cadets at the Royal Canadian Military College concluded that those promoted to higher positions changed their values in a direction congruent with military professionalization. Those changes occurred in a chronological progression based on time spent within the organization, but "the values and professional orientation the individual brings to an organization are more important than what the individual learns from the socialization process within an institutional atmosphere."[16]

Whatever the source of officer attitudes, the attitudes that govern officers' behavior, especially their relationship to civilian authorities, have an obvious influence on civil-military relations. Socialization becomes a key variable in explaining civilian supremacy over the military. Perhaps most important in this respect are military attitudes toward discipline and loyalty. From an institutional point of view, the idea that the army should be changed from a vehicle for advancing individuals' political aims into a nonpolitical institution whose sole task would be to defend against internal and external threats stemmed from General Joaquín Amaro's modernizing mission in the 1920s. He sought to instill a new sense of discipline and of obedience to civil authority among younger officers.[17] Officers who increasingly achieved top rank in the military had been trained at the Escuela Superior de Guerra. The founding principles of the Escuela Superior de Guerra include a description of the officer's respect for authority: "The professors will be particularly exacting with their students in the practice and exercise of all the habits that contribute to the development of affection for the army and an enhancement of military spirit; any tendency to depreciate military studies or *put down the discipline and prestige of the army will be severely reprimanded*" (emphasis added).[18]

The Heroico Colegio Militar, which graduates most army officers, warns cadets that it expects similar discipline and loyalty. The 1965 admissions pamphlet, when most of Mexico's senior officers in the 1990s attended that academy, demonstrates that each cadet lives in an environment in which his activities have been carefully planned to develop the personal qualities the institution wants to instill, particularly loyalty.[19] Its fundamental goal was unquestioning subordination to authority: "The Heroico Colegio Militar is essentially a brainwashing school. Its most important goal is to produce unthinking officers who will obey authority; really robots I would say."[20] Fifteen years later the 1980 admissions pamphlet emphasized even more strongly that "discipline is the norm which the military must subject its conduct; it has as its foundations obedience . . . and the exact completion of those duties prescribed by military laws and relations."[21]

Military academies everywhere socialize students through intense indoctrination programs and remold them within their institutional framework.[22] Among the values which can be commonly found are the acceptance of an all-pervasive hierarchy and patterns of deference.[23] Individuals who choose military careers typically affect the socialization process through self-selection. For example, secondary school graduates in the United States who "expect to serve in the military are more pro-military than those who do not, and those who anticipate military careers are the most pro-military."[24] Officer cadets who are the children of fathers in the military, and/or who have been previously exposed to the military, are more likely to share the military ethos.[25]

In the discussion on educational socialization, it will be argued that the Mexican officer corps, even by U.S. standards, is subject to extreme forms of military discipline and authority. In the Mexican context, military discipline means unquestioning, unyielding deference and obedience to superiors. No order is questioned and no action is taken independently of a superior.[26] The extent to which this attitude is imbued is illustrated by several recent examples.

One consequence of this exaggerated discipline is the centralization of authority in the hands of a few superior officers, most notably the secretary of national defense. One officer provides an apt recollection of a conversation with his superior reflecting the prevailing military culture: "I remember once that the assistant secretary of defense told me that I had a problem. I asked the general what my problem was. He said 'I was thinking too much, and that in this army we don't think.' Really, in this country, *the secretary of defense is like a small god* in terms of how he can send someone here or send someone there, or change their assignment, without any appeal whatsoever" (emphasis added).[27]

The procedural characteristics of internal military decision making both severely limit individual officer initiative and reinforce obedience to higher authority. Officers who openly take issue with a superior's decision are blackballed for having an "attitude" problem. Such treatment can dog their entire careers; they either resign or accept the prospect of a severely limited career.[28]

One of the few cases where it is known that the secretary of national defense actually relinquished direct control occurred during the events of 1968, suggesting once again the importance of the student movement in the eyes of Mexico's political and military leadership. According to the United States Defense Intelligence Agency, the secretary of national defense "sent instructions to all zone commanders authorizing the commanders everywhere in the country to act against student disturbances without waiting for instructions from the capital."[29]

The 1995 *Army and Air Force Development Plan* included a number of recommendations involving the simplification of the administrative structure and the decentralization of the command hierarchy. It specifically used the language "delegate administrative functions, logistics, training, and operations to regional and zone commanders," implying that such responsibilities should be removed from the national defense secretariat. The report recommended that technical responsibilities be delegated from the secretary of national defense personally directly into the hands of the appropriate department heads, typically headed by two and three star generals. Overall, the report argues for decentralization within the national defense administrative structure at the national level, and among zone commanders at the regional level.[30]

Within several years of the report, the army had implemented a process of decentralization. According to one observer, the new system granted each of Mexico's zone commanders sufficient autonomy to make decisions about logistics, training, and special forces missions, three areas specifically identified in the report as deserving of reform.[31]

It is important to note that the decentralization of control from the secretary of national defense to zone commanders does not always lead to positive consequences. In the worst case scenario, a corrupt officer who is more autonomous is given greater opportunities to commit criminal acts. This can be seen in the career of Division General Jesús Gutiérrez Rebollo. Contrary to established army policy, he was allowed to command the 15th military zone in Jalisco as well as the 12th regional command for nearly five years. Allegedly he used both posts to promote his own drug-related criminal activities. Another consequence, impacting on how national defense policy unity is perceived, emanates from the ability of zone commanders to make public policy-related statements. The most notable example is that of Division General Miguel A. Godínez Bravo, commander of the forces against the EZLN in Chiapas, who called his own press conference and announced military policy in the region to the domestic and international media.[32]

Discipline is another value instilled during the military socialization experience. Mexican officers expect strict discipline not only in their peers and subordinates but also in the populace. General Juan de Dios Calleros Aviña, a two-time zone commander, told a reporter that discipline is born in the home, is affirmed in the classroom, and should become a habit of the ordinary citizen.[33]

The officer corps' view of their own qualities has been transferred to the general civilian population's view of the army. When asked what attributes they associated most strongly with the military, over four-fifths of all Mexicans in 2004 mentioned discipline, solidarity, and order.[34]

A leading Mexican intellectual has noted the importance of discipline in the cultural worlds of civilians and military officers. Of the many changes that have occurred in his country during the 1980s and 1990s, he believes that one of the most significant is the extraordinary decline in respect for civilian authorities among civilians as compared to the military's respect for its superiors. This is a view confirmed in numerous public opinion polls., He describes its impact in this way: "But in the military, respect for authority remains very strong and traditional. For example, let's take the use of language as an illustration of this in civilian culture. The use of *usted* and *tu* has changed tremendously during this period. The use of these two forms of address is part of the culture of hierarchy in Mexico. The elimination of the *usted* and the use of the familiar form with people who are recent acquaintances is a change in the hierarchical structure within the civilian community."[35]

Intense discipline and loyalty are inextricably intertwined in the military. Acceptance of this level of discipline relies on absolute loyalty to the institution and to superior officers who represent the institution's decisions. The loyalty of high-ranking officers to civilian authorities reinforces military loyalty to civilian leaders. This sense of loyalty to national political institutions has been repeatedly reinforced in the military textbooks and academies since the early 1930s. In an interesting exchange between a Panista congressman and General Gerardo Clemente Vega García, Fox's secretary of national defense, the congressman complained that the current leader of the

National Defense Committee in congress, a retired division general, had turned his back on the President during the fourth State of the Union address in September 2004, thus disobeying his supreme commander, the president of Mexico. The congressman argued that he showed a lack of respect for his superiors and violated the military's statues on discipline.[36]

The Mexican military is not alone in its demand for loyalty. All political systems have their version of the "team player." It can be argued, however, that the Mexican political system, under the dominance of a single party and leadership group until 2000, encouraged a stronger sense of institutional loyalty than is found in most competitive political systems. Until recently, it was rare for a politician within the PRI-controlled Mexican system to publicly criticize it or its leaders.[37] Generalized silence was not always the norm. Historically, political arguments were intense, just as they have become since the late 1990s.

The subsequent self-imposed discipline of Mexican politicians is likely to have impressed the officer corps. It can be argued that the discipline PRI imposed, because of the positive view it generated among some officers, may well have been a positive contribution to civil-military relations. It is also fair to suggest that the most influential element in retaining military loyalty is the officers' belief in the civilian leadership's ability to maintain order. As long as the government demonstrates that ability and retains at least limited popular respect, the military will support civil authority.[38]

When an officer publicly doubts civilian abilities, as in certain crisis situations, it leads to trouble. One of the most notable recent cases of an officer's openly questioning civilian competence took place in the 1970s during the confrontation between the army and Lucio Cabañas's guerrillas. The officer in charge, Division General Salvador Rangel Medina, told the press after he had been criticized repeatedly for not capturing Cabañas, that he would be happy to do just that as soon as he received a government order to that effect. The secretary of national defense immediately removed him from his post.[39] Not only the commander, but many junior officers serving in the campaign against Cabañas questioned government policy.[40]

By the late 1990s, dissatisfaction within the officer corps reached its apex. According to an American army officer well-connected to the Mexican military: "Nor is this discontent restricted to general officers. There is considerable unhappiness in the mid-level officer corps with the way the country is being run. A lot of lieutenant colonels are disgusted with the corruption and incompetence they see both among civilians and within the military itself . . . and they are frustrated with a promotion system which, as they see it, is designed to weed out the best elements in their ranks and co-opt the opportunists."[41]

Like many other Mexicans, the officer corps hoped that the 2000 presidential elections would bring substantial political change and that the Fox administration, through a democratic transformation, would eliminate some of the growing political problems. By 2005, the extent of the stalemate between the legislative and executive branch encouraged General Vega García, the secretary of national defense, to offer an unique public criticism during an army day speech before Fox and other cabinet figures. General García Vega called on political leadership from all sides to work out compromises and address Mexico's outstanding policy issues.

The military's attitude toward discipline impacts its perception of order and societal behavior. "The military ethic emphasizes the permanence of irrationality, weakness and evil in human nature. It stresses the supremacy of society over the individual and the importance of order, hierarchy, and division of function."[42] The officer corps has often transferred their view of human nature generally to that of politicians specifically, producing important consequences for civil-military relations. Military officers rarely establish close friendships with politicians. According to one politician:

> In my experience, my military acquaintances have never allowed me to get close to them. I think this is not only due to the social differences, but also something they, themselves, initiate. They are much more closed in terms of their attitudes. I think it's that attitude, even more so than social differences, that prevents the development of close friendships between civilians and military personnel. You never really know for sure how they will react to something. For example, you can't be totally frank with most of these military acquaintances because if you were to criticize the President, you might believe they would react in such a way that they would consider what you said to be treasonable, and report you to the authorities. This attitude would never be true of a civilian peer.[43]

In the past, this attitude seems to have affected their general behavior in public. This behavior is illustrated by my own experience. I was giving a lecture on civil-military relations in Mexico in the early 1990s. Instead of sending someone to hear my lecture, a civilian colleague known to me, who lectured at the military academies, was asked to attend and tape record my talk. He told me privately that they were strongly interested in the lecture, but did not want to be seen. Another time, during the same decade, they actually sent an officer, but he "disguised" himself in civilian clothes.

Acceptance of the importance of discipline, loyalty and order to a degree typically not encountered in society as a whole is enhanced by a self-selecting process as officers move up the ladder in rank. Most professional officers in the U.S. who enrolled in an academy with the intention of making the army a career, come from family backgrounds in which the father is conservative.[44]

Officers who remain in the services usually continue to characterize themselves as conservative. In another study, nearly half describe their ideologies as conservative; a third are in the middle of the spectrum; and only 15 percent label their views liberal.[45] Other studies reveal that twice as many liberals resign their commissions as remain, whereas the majority of conservatives stay on active duty.[46] Thus, the higher one rises in the rank structure, the more likely one is to be ideologically conservative.[47]

An interesting pattern in the backgrounds of the most influential generals, one which sheds some light on parental ideological influence and conservatism, was that junior officers promoted from enlisted ranks ("mustangs") reach the rank of general in disproportionate numbers. I have argued that the reason is that "mustangs," more than any other group of officers, experienced extreme superior-subordinate relationships as enlisted soldiers. The overwhelming origin of mustangs is from lower socioeconomic backgrounds. The usual thinking in regard to these groups in Mexico is that their family structure is hierarchical, extremely authoritarian, and socially conservative, suggesting that the enlisted officer may be more likely to possess the traditional military values, and to be a more well-adjusted and career-oriented professional.[48]

The fundamental attitude deserving the closest attention is the inclination of the Mexican officer corps to intervene militarily in civilian matters. In recent years, the Mexican army likes to tell outsiders that it functions as an impartial institution and, as such, does not express opinions on political matters but only complies with the dispositions of the government, offering guarantees to all political parties and to all the citizenry.[49] More important, this is the image the military conveys to its own future leaders.

A more modest posture can be subsumed under the view that the armed forces should play an increased role in the decision-making process. This view too was rejected in the 1980s and early 1990s. In 1983, at the beginning of the de la Madrid administration, one of Mexico's leading generals, then chief of staff, used the Army Day official ceremony to criticize those within the military who believed it should assume a greater role in political decisions: "In the army there is no place for anyone giving advice on national decisions because we are not and have no wish to be judges."[50] This strong statement can be interpreted two ways, both of which are accurate. First, it reinforces and repeats the military's official stance for at least the previous four decades. Second, it can be deduced from the statement itself and the occasion that the leadership, military and civilian alike, sensed an undercurrent of opinion within the officer corps favoring a more activist military posture in political affairs.

To moderate the desire of the officer corps for an active political role and to inculcate disinterest in politics, the military uses its training programs and official journals to socialize officers to subordinate themselves to civilian authority. Attempts to depoliticize the military through such means also affect officer interest regarding external political and social matters. In the United States most officers prefer to focus on social problems within the military itself and not on the broader range of social issues outside the military.[51]

According to one analysis, only 2 percent of the Mexican army/air force journal articles from 1973 to 1976 had some political content; whereas 16 percent concentrated on the theme of loyalty to the nation and its institutions.[52] Boils reported a change in political and social content from 2 to 18 percent in the same magazine from 1969–shortly after the date of the student massacre in the Tlatelolco Plaza–to 1973.[53] By the mid-1970s, some analysts were detecting changes in the military's conceptualization of its political role. They viewed officer education and training as preparation for broader activities. It was argued that enhanced administrative skills made possible by development of the National Defense College in the early 1980s could lead to greater participation in the formulation of national security and development policies.[54] As anticipated, the military did expand its decision-making role in the late 1990s and during the Fox administration.

The expanded role of the military did not originate only from their broader training. It also came at the insistence and invitation of civilian leadership. The extent of their decision-making role will be analyzed later. Underlying this expanded role, however, is the notion that by the 1980s the military's views on national security had changed. According to one of the few students of Mexico's national security policy, national security has meant defending national sovereignty. In 1983, with the announcement of Miguel de la Madrid's National Development Plan, national security acquired another dimension when it was placed in the context of internal and international politics. Thereafter, military and civilian leaders began to rethink their national security functions. Under Carlos Salinas de Gortari, the concept broadened further, to include multiple facets of security, including financial, technological, social, and political, and more specifically a "permanent condition of peace, liberty, and social justice within the law."[55]

The reconceptualization of national security has taken the military in two directions. First, it expanded its role in the foreign policy realm. As Mexico began to act as a regional broker between the United States and Nicaragua in the 1980s, and to express its views on U.S. policies in Central America and the Caribbean, the military, both materially and politically, appeared to demonstrate increasing interest in this external focus. Some observers viewed the military as inclined to raise its expectations concerning their role in this arena.[56]

The national government's international forays could indirectly increase the scope of the military in political affairs, as will be seen in the area of humanitarian missions abroad. Changes in its conception of internal security have produced deeper consequences for civil-military relations in the 1990s and 2000s. The importance of internal security to national security is given high visibility in the Organic Law of the Mexican Army and Air Force, Article 1, Section 2, and in the Organic Law of the Mexican Navy, revised in the first years of the Fox administration.[57] In 2004, the Supreme Court ruled that the participation of the army and navy in the National Council of Public Security did not violate the constitution. This emphasis is the consequence of the paradoxical contradiction between what the military has traditionally concentrated upon in its training programs and the tasks civilian leaders have requested it to perform since the 1970s.

Civilian leadership runs two risks in ordering the military to perform tasks normally thought to be within the purview of the police or other civil authorities. First, "as officers trained primarily for military pursuits, they have been forced into the political task of containing extremist dissidence on a growing scale. The conflict between the apolitical training and their increasingly political role causes contradictions and doubts in the minds of the younger generations of officers."[58] Second, when the government called upon the army to deal with civil disputes (for example, in connection with electoral fraud), it encouraged the view of a politicized army.[59] If the populace had come to accept such an army, the officer corps, a product of that very populace, might have adopted a similar view. Fortunately, it is not likely that it will be asked to perform such a task in the next decade.

Civilian Attitudes, the Building Blocks of Military Professionalism

The military's self-conceptualization of its role and the extent to which it might alter civil-military relations are influenced by general societal norms. Societal attitudes are important because they provide the greatest reinforcement of the military ethos, particularly regarding its relationship to civil authority. A professional culture depends on a discernible professional ethos. In the United States, however, social and political ideologies conflict with the professional military's ideology. "The military ideology demands authority, honor, and obedience; the political ideology consensus, expediency, and compromise. . . . Moreover, the liberal ideology challenges the military profession directly by regarding professional soldiers as a threat to liberty, democracy, and economic prosperity."[60] As the democratic transformation took hold in Mexico in the 1990s, a similar confrontation between these differing sets of attitudes emerged.

Societal attitudes are the fundamental determinant of civil-military relations specifically and values engendered among the officer corps generally, but it is striking how little exploration of this relationship has been reported in the Latin American military literature: "[I]t is important to emphasize that prevailing levels of political culture, including loyalty and public acceptance of civil institutions—from public approval of procedures involving the transfer of power, to public recognition as to who holds sovereign authority—play an important role in the long-term viability of civilian supremacy."[61] The tendency is to examine the military isolated from its general societal origins even though it is society that legitimizes the military through acceptance of its purpose, and whose own social norms are closely linked to the military's professional ethics and behavior.[62]

Generally, how do Mexicans perceive the military? More particularly, how does the public view the military as an institution? How do young Mexicans view the military as a career? And how does the ordinary citizen view the military as a component of society?

The ordinary Mexican's lack of connectedness to the armed forces might lead to more than mere ignorance of the military; it might lead to a fear or distaste for the military as an institution. This view is also borne out in interviews, with both Mexican politicians and intellectuals, and with general officers. As one officer concluded, "I would say that the higher classes in Mexico respect us, but they don't like us. I would say the middle-class, including most politicians, basically are fearful of us."[63] In 2004, a fifth of Mexicans reported they were fearful of the military.[64] The general's view is reflected in a curious incident involving my efforts to publish the previus version of this book in Mexico. I approached the publisher who had already published half-a-dozen of my books. The review committee for my book was made up of two prominent intellectuals, two PRI politicians, and a senior military officer, and was chaired by former president Miguel de la Madrid, the editor-in-chief of the press. All of the members of the committee were in favor of publishing the book, except for the two politicians; they opposed it because they thought it might somehow offend the officer corps, in spite of the fact that the military representative favored its publication.[65]

If well-educated Mexicans, including those active in political life, are ignorant of the military, the knowledge among the general public is even more limited. Javier Oliva, who has taught for many years at the Colegio de Defensa Nacional and is an expert on national security, describes the dual implications of ignorance and fear:

In terms of the respect with which society in general has for the military, I would say there are two very important factors. One factor is that most people don't really know anything about the military. In fact, one of the ways to illustrate this is that they don't even have any idea what the insignia rank of most military officers means. The second reason is that there is a considerable amount of respect for the military, not out of ignorance, but as a consequence of fear. The military, to many Mexicans, represents the use of force, and consequently, the use of force is seen as a threat to one's security. One of the things most Mexicans know is that when the military is called in to replace the police, then matters have become deeply serious. Consequently, they are taken far more seriously than are the police in Mexico, The third reason, which relates to the first, is that the military itself doesn't want them to know too much about the armed forces as an institution, and therefore, they helped to perpetuate the ignorance on the part of society as a whole.[66]

Surprisingly, in the 1990s, the situation Oliva described remained unchanged. Prominent persons and intellectuals were woefully ignorant concerning the military and readily admitted it.[67] Military funding and the military role are, in large measure, not part of the public discourse. This omission only began to change after 1997, and changed more dramatically after 2000, when the Fox administration took office. Nevertheless, the average Mexican remains uninformed about the armed forces.

Comparatively, ignorance appears to have benefited society's view of Mexico's armed forces. As early as the 1980s, when the first survey data on citizen attitudes toward Mexican institutions became available, the military's institutional image in certain respects was quite favorable, especially when compared with images of civilian institutions. When Mexicans were asked in a national poll to identify individuals most deserving of respect, they chose parents, teachers, and priests, thus indirectly praising family, school, and the church. The persons least deserving of respect were political bosses, politicians, military men, and bankers.[68] However, when Mexicans were asked to rank institutions, as distinct from individuals or occupations, the military scored more positively than all political organizations. Again, schools and the church were at the top of the list, but strongly entrenched in the middle of the ranking, along with the legal system, was the military.[69]

By the late 1990s, the military established itself as a respected institution compared to any governmental agency, private sector business, or political interest group. This level of confidence in the armed forces has continued through the Fox administration. In 2003, a Gallup poll reported that 56 percent of Mexicans interviewed expressed confidence in the army.[70] In 2004, 60 percent of Mexicans expressed a view favorable of the military, a number equal to that of the Federal Electoral Institute and only 3 percentage points behind the Catholic Church.[71]

A survey of younger Americans yielded a pattern similar to that found in Mexico: the military ranked fourth, after colleges, churches, and the media but well above political institutions in levels of respect.[72] Some observers believe the military had strengthened its institutional image in the early 1980s by its rescue operations during the El Chichón volcanic eruption and, more importantly, in the Mexico City earthquake, as well as its campaign against drug traffickers.[73] This interpretation is confirmed by the fact that, in 1993, 72 percent of Mexicans interviewed believed that the army acted well or very well in the 1985 earthquake, and an equally large percentage (73), thought it was performing well or very well against drug traffickers.

In the 1990s, the secretariat of national defense commissioned its own survey to determine how it was viewed by Mexican citizens. This action suggests that it began to take its public image seriously, and were seeking ways to respond to increasing criticisms of missions assigned to it by civilian leadership.[74] This survey is much more comprehensive and reveals more details about Mexican attitudes towards the armed forces. It also confirms numerous interpretations offered by Mexican cultural, political and military elites.

In the first place, nearly six out of ten Mexicans do not know anyone in the military, which helps to explain why society generally has no link to the military and is therefore largely ignorant of it on a personal and institutional level. On the other hand, a sizable minority, 17 percent, had a family member in the armed forces.

In the broadest sense, specific views of the armed forces confirm the solid levels of confidence Mexicans express in their military as an institution. Nearly three out of four Mexicans view it as bringing benefits to Mexico, and, when they compared their armed forces to other countries, over half rank it as better or much better than other countries' military. An additional fifth of those surveyed describe it as somewhat better.

Mexican citizens, based on the data from this survey, have accepted the broader and newer missions assigned to it by the civilian political leadership. When asked to describe its mission, combating drug trafficking (31 percent) ranks ahead of protecting the country (26 percent), the traditional task assigned to armed forces universally. In the 2004 Bimsa poll, both combating crime (39 percent) and controlling drug trafficking (19 percent) ranked ahead of external defense. These primary tasks are followed by assisting in national disasters (10 percent), rescues (2 percent), and reforestation (1 percent). Its anti-drug mission has been accepted, and has been viewed positively by many Mexicans, but it is also the source of its greatest perceived weakness, the level of corruption found in the military. Slightly more than half of all Mexicans view the military as being characterized by a lot or some corruption.

Perhaps most interesting of all, Mexicans view the military's performance as government agencies in a positive light. President Fox received considerable criticism in the media for appointing a career officer as his first Attorney General. Yet, two years after his administration began, when Mexicans were asked to rank the performance of his cabinet members, General Vega García, the secretary of national defense, ranked number one in 2002 (as he did in 2001), and the secretary of navy and the attorney general ranked second and third.[75] Thus, career military officers are viewed positively as administrators compared to their civilian peers, whether they are leading military or civilian agencies. Citizens' favorable reviews of the military's performance in these positions does raise an important question about the potential broader effects of career officers performing civilian political tasks more competently than civilians and, consequently, the established balance in civil-military relations.

How society views the military as a career and, more important, its prestige as an occupation indirectly affects how the institution is perceived compared to other organizations. The Mexican military has been a magnet for certain working-class groups for much of the period under study. The earliest survey of occupational preferences, conducted two years after Alemán entered the presidency, found that lower- and lower-middle-income groups found owning or managing a business and military careers the most attractive.[76] Becoming an officer would appeal to Mexicans from lower-income groups for two reasons. First, an officer is considered a professional, and professional status in a society is important to upwardly mobile persons. Second, the military subsidizes higher education through a master's degree, enables career success through regularized promotions, and provides exceptional job security, an especially rare attribute in a developing economy.[77] In 2004, the poorest Mexicans are most likely to see a military career as an attractive choice.[78]

Middle- and upper-middle-class Mexicans see a military career in an entirely different light. Johnson asserted that, in the 1960s, civilian leaders exhibited considerable prejudice against the military. He suggested that they considered military officers as "definite inferiors," who were socially unacceptable and with whom social contact should ordinarily be limited to official functions.[79] When asked whether they had thought of the military as a career, most had never regarded it as a viable option, believing it to be low in status and offering few economic rewards compared with other available occupations.[80] In the 2004 survey, when given a choice of recommending a career among four professions to a family member, 47 percent said they would recommend the military compared to 92, 80 and 78 percent who would recommend medicine, teaching, and the law. U.S. youth have similar reactions, ranking it lowest among their choices.[81]

This view of the military as a career option continued into the 1990s. Most elite Mexicans, who are the products of middle-class families, never considered the military as an option, nor were they encouraged by their parents to explore such a career. Politicians, in particular, have not encouraged their sons to follow military careers. The names of sons of successful politicians cannot be found in the graduation lists of the Heroico Colegio Militar.[82] On the other hand, examples can be found among notable politicians who are the children of high-ranking officers.[83] One well-connected Mexican, whose uncle was a three star air force general, and one of his best childhood friends, the son of a former zone commander, expressed an explanation offered by numerous other elite figures: "I believe there is a universal impression that military officers are socially inferior to the civilian upper middle-class, and that they come from a lower social extraction. I don't think the military is seen as a professional alternative in most middle-class families. It's not really something you think about as an alternate to most professions that are pursued by middle-class college graduates.[84]

This deep social divide, although declining, has produced a number of significant consequences. Perhaps most importantly, it exacerbates the lack of contact between politicians and the officer corps. As one former government official explained, "I know other officers from my jobs in government. They are professional friends, but they never become true social friends. They like to take their civilian friends to the military club where they are invited to go horseback riding and to shoot on the pistol range. But beyond that they never really develop the kind of closeness necessary to create long-lasting friendships."[85]

For whatever reason, depending on class background, the typical educated Mexican sees the military officer as the social inferior of the civilian politician. Another possible consequence of this inequality is the officer's tendency to defer to the socially superior civilian politician. Belief in this would reinforce the officers' perception that they are not thought of as professional equals. Psychologically, this puts them at a disadvantage with civilian politicians.

The nature of citizen attitudes toward the military and its role in society are crucial to civilian political elites, who cannot on their own impose hegemony over the military. They need the strong support of the citizenry and the support of the officer corps itself. To date, the Mexican military has accepted a fairly narrow, if growing, range of responsibilities. There has never been any indication, however, of any change in elite perceptions of military subordination to civilian rule.

Historically civilian leaders have used the budget as a means to limit the military's size and political influence. In recent years, civilian attitudes toward expanding military prestige have fluctuated. A case in point was President Miguel de la Madrid's decision not to allow the army to fully implement its DN-III (E) emergency plan in response to the September 19–20, 1985 earthquakes, even though the carefully devised scheme had worked well in other disasters, such as the 1982 El Chichón volcano eruption in Chiapas. Reportedly, the head of the Federal District Department persuaded the president to limit the role of the armed forces in a tragedy that consumed 20,000 lives lest an effective performance whet their appetite for greater political involvement.[86]

Civilian leaders may have been concerned about enhancing the military's civic-action image and thereby reducing their own visible role in earthquake relief, but during De la Madrid's administration they expanded the military's share of the anti-drug effort. Shortly after Salinas became president, he increased the military's internal security work, which served to elevate its visibility and further politicize its functions. The president's repeated use of military units to carry out executive political decisions attracted some criticism, but only from Mexico's most outspoken commentators. Few elites have commented publicly on the armed forces, especially depreciatively.[87] By the end of the Zedillo administration, the media began to discuss and to explore controversial issues involving civil-military relations, including the definition of military missions and the execution of its tasks. By the late 1990s, strong indications existed that the print media were being much more aggressive about covering the armed forces and that it no longer was a taboo subject.[88]

The armed forces, recognizing the importance of the media in shaping its image in society, has, since the EZLN uprising in Chiapas, sought to improve its communication skills. It hoped to use responsible organizations and well-placed officers in the chamber of deputies and the senate, to accomplish this goal.[89] According to one analyst, it never loses the opportunity to express in public and private meetings its desire to establish a channel of communication. The military's goal is having society know its soldiers, its means, and its missions. In practice, they have not opened their doors to the media.[90] Indeed, one author claims that military intelligence proposed a more nefarious strategy vis-á-vis the media, one that included buying off journalists, personal surveillance, and the acquisition of information about reporters and essayists identified as "critical" of the armed forces.[91] No other evidence exists that supports such a proposition or its implementation. During this same period, the secretary of national defense, General Enrique Cervantes Aguirre, actually held several public discussions of the military's role in Mexican society. However, as the scholar who raised the point noted, it remained to be seen whether that was a short-term tactic for dealing with concerns among some Mexicans about the military's growing roles and responsibilities or whether it represented a longer-term shift in their actual behavior.[92] Since 2000, military leadership has moved modestly in this same direction.

From a societal perspective, the fundamental issue is how do Mexicans view the military as a political actor? A recent analysis argues that a strong antimilitary bias on the part of the general public—a characteristic distinguishing Mexico's political culture from that of many Latin American and Third World countries—has likely served to inhibit greater military participation in the political arena.[93] This and other assessments of public attitudes are largely informal and speculative, but three public opinion polls in the 1980s and 2000s offer some hard evidence.

An April 1983 national survey of 7,051 Mexicans from fifteen occupational groups and thirty-two states (with a margin of error of less than 2 percent) discovered that 26 percent of the respondents thought the military should participate in government; 24 percent thought it should sometimes participate; and 30 percent thought it should never participate.[94] In 1987 the same question in a national poll of 9,028 Mexicans elicited these responses: 22 percent thought the military should participate in government; 16 percent, sometimes; and 62 percent never. This is a dramatic decline in support.[95] Class differences were apparent. It might be supposed that the wealthy would strongly favor military protection of private property in times of political instability, but they were the cohort most opposed to it in both 1983 and 1987. The other group definitely against military participation in government was college-educated Mexicans.

Strong sentiment against military involvement in the political arena, especially in the 1987 poll, is encouraging because it suggests society strongly favors limiting the military's political activities. Nevertheless, between 38 and 50 percent of Mexicans in the 1980s believed the military should have some political role. This suggests that a sizeable body of public opinion might be more receptive to increased military participation under certain circumstances. No surveys taken in the 1990s or 2000s have included precisely this same question, so there is no empirical evidence on whether or not support for governmental participation has decreased, remained the same, or increased. However, in the 2004 Bimsa poll, respondents were asked three similar questions:

- Do you support military participation in the country's political affairs?
- Do you support military candidates running for elective office?
- Do you support military participation in partisan politics?

Thirty-eight percent of Mexicans believed it is acceptable for the army to participate in political affairs. Although this is not the same question, it is possible that the increased percentages from the 1980s reflect the fact that the armed forces are already more involved in national security decisions. The response to the second and third questions was 29 and 28 percent respectively. On the other hand, since President Fox campaigned successfully on the issue of removing the military from its anti-drug mission, its most successful task in the eyes of the population, little resistance existed to removing its most overt form of participation.

Interestingly, in the 1980s polls it is the least educated, those with only a primary education, who take this pro-military in government stance. These are the same Mexicans who see the military as a potential career in a much more favorable light. It is quite possible that because the military provides opportunities for upward social mobility, the least educated perceive military leaders as sharing their goals and concerns. Older Mexicans also were more favorably inclined toward military involvement in government. Not surprisingly, Mexicans who have a positive image of the police, generally the least respected institution in Mexico, and those who care about security as a social issue, lean more strongly in that direction.

In 2004, more than 17 years after the last poll on the military was taken, the responses are completely the opposite. This is a surprising and highly significant finding, especially because the percentage differences between those with a sixth grade education, or those with a university degree, are significant. More than half of college-educated Mexicans believe the military should participate in political affairs, and nearly two-thirds believe that they should be allowed to run for elective office and be involved in partisan politics. The fact that these figures are highest among well-educated Mexicans, and that the differences in responses from primary school graduates are at least 32 percent higher, suggest that the most sophisticated and knowledgeable Mexicans have accepted the armed forces' role to a much great degree than they did in the 1980s. This dramatic change may also be a reflection of the larger civil-military relationship in which a democratically elected president is now the commander in chief rather than viewing the military as linked to a specific leadership group.

Mexicans who most endorsed the status quo under PRI in the 1980s were also more supportive of military involvement compared to those who opted for change. A dichotomy between occupational groups appeared between peasants and laborers on one hand, ironically the most positive toward military intervention, and intellectuals, government officials, and private-sector management on the other, the most opposed. These breakdowns suggest how successful the military has been in sustaining its image as an institution of the masses. True, peasants had the most "don't know" responses to the question, indicative of the possibility that their minds could change quickly if future personal experiences were negative. The responses also suggest that political leaders were highly satisfied with the civil-military balance as it was then constituted.

Some interesting political attitudes affect Mexican responses to military participation in government. If attitudes toward bringing the Catholic Church back into politics are taken into account, the results are significant. Remembering that the other key corporate institution, the Catholic Church, has a long history of political intervention in Mexico and the region, one could expect the same Mexicans not to differentiate the traditional corporate functions of the church and the military from fuzzier political ones. Of those strongly in favor of Church involvement, an overwhelming percentage favored military participation. However, this group of respondents is a tiny percentage of the population. On the other hand, those most strongly opposed to Church involvement are equally opposed to military participation, which suggests that they see intervention by outside institutions as a much broader and more sophisticated governance issue.

Mexicans were much more definite about the Church staying out of politics than the military staying out of politics. The comparison is important because it suggests the impact of educational socialization and experience. The much higher number of persons opposed to an expanded Church role is not surprising because several civil wars were fought over this issue. But more important, the 1917 Constitution incorporated numerous restrictions on the Church and denied it legal status. The Church was the only institution treated in this fashion; no comparable provisions constrained the military despite historical efforts to remove it from politics. Since these polls were taken, revisions to the Constitution in 1992 have eased up these restrictions.[96] The difference between how the two institutions are handled, constitutionally and societally, are conveyed by the fact that the Constitution says that a legislator cannot be a minister of a religious faith but can be a member of the armed forces (on leave from active duty).[97]

In some Latin American countries, institutional alliances with political parties have been almost as important to civil-military relations as direct military participation in the executive branch. Such alliances can serve as a path for indirect and direct control over governmental processes. Many observers have made numerous assertions about alliances between certain institutions and Mexican opposition parties prior to 2000. The most common allegation is that an alliance exists between the National Action Party (PAN), once considered the opposition party of the ideological Right, and the Catholic church. Like many such assertions in Mexican politics, such a linkage has not occurred.[98] Furthermore, PRI since the late 1990s is perceived by the voting public to be on the ideological right of PAN, thus negating an important component underlying the logic of these assertions.

Much less clear, but occasionally implied, is the potential for an alliance between the Right and the military, and, again, a potential linkage between PAN and the armed forces. No such linkage has existed or currently exists. Polling data do not support such assertions. Basically, no difference on the issue of military intervention exists among PRI or PAN sympathizers or party members. A partisan difference does exist but, ironically, it is between the PRD supporters and the other two leading parties. The PRD partisans are the citizens who gave the strongest support in 2004 to all measures of military political involvement, with over half responding favorably to such participation.[99]

Two other phenomena may have a bearing on the self-conceptualization by the officer corps of its role and other professional values, thus affecting civil-military relations. A small number of civilians can have a direct influence on the military through involvement with the officer corps or through other means. In the United States armed forces, the non-career officer lessened the potential for a caste mentality, and "democratized" officer corps values. Mexico, of course, does not recruit officers outside the military academies. It does, on rare occasions, give direct commissions to individuals who have special expertise it requires. For example, Article 152 of the Organic Law states that "professional or technical personnel required on active duty whose specialties do not exist in schools or military formation courses should be recruited from graduates of civilian schools and universities."[100] In the navy, individuals offered direct commissions are not indoctrinated in a special or regular training course but are assigned to units where they receive on-the-job professionalization.[101] Among the generals in our sample, there is no one with a direct commission.

Since the publication of the army internal document in 1995, however, the armed forces, for the first time in its history, "requested an immediate study of recruiting and hiring civilian specialists and professionals. The military obviously believes it is deficient in a number of specialties, and this request complements its desire to expand the number of university careers available to the officer corps . . . increasing the civilian component in the military, while expanding its capabilities and expertise and increasing its ties to the civilian community, also adds to the diversity of influences to which the military would be exposed more directly."[102]

Presently, the number of civilian professionals incorporated as officers are so few that their potential capacity to introduce civilian attitudes into the officer corps' value system is negligible. A more important vehicle for conveying civilian values is the president, especially because military subordination to him as the supreme commander is drilled into junior officers. Presidents use public occasions to lavish encomiums upon the military as a loyal and patriotic institution, thereby reinforcing its self-conception. Many officers have expressed deep personal respect, at times approaching reverence, for individual presidents. "Presidential concern for military status seems to have had a salutary effect upon civil-military relations in Mexico and may have helped insure political stability."[103] This hypothesis was introduced earlier. However, Mexican presidents have not encouraged or permitted visible displays of military power. Most Mexicans still have an ingrained antipathy toward such displays.[104]

The other source of potential influence on officer corps values related to civil-military relations is external. The proximity of Mexico to the United States places the U.S. military in a position to have an effect through military assistance and training programs. A foreign country can influence a military's professionalization and value system in those and several other ways. In many Latin American countries, foreign military missions were an essential ingredient in bringing about a domestic armed forces' self-definition and evolution.[105]

Great care should be taken in transferring the experience of South American militaries to that of Mexico's in the twentieth century. The Mexican military's professionalization is unique. For example, unlike the situation in Brazil, Mexico's professionalization was internally generated and focused; it was not a product of Europe or the United States.[106] Soon after the Revolution, General Amaro sent his brightest lieutenants and captains to military academies in France, Spain, Italy, and the United States. He also assigned them to embassies. On their return, they planned and led a professional program without direct foreign assistance. During World War II, Mexico did accept Lend Lease credits of some $39 million for training scholarships, defense factories, and weaponry.[107]

The general literature on the Mexican military conveys the notion that the military itself has taken the initiative to insure an autonomous position vis-à-vis the U.S. military despite fairly friendly cooperation during World War II.[108] The military has been fastidious in maintaining independence from the United States, and has had relatively little intercourse with their U.S. counterparts.[109] Mexico has no defense assistance pact with any foreign power, and since the 1960s, among the larger Latin American countries, only Mexico and Cuba have not hosted a major U.S. military advisory group.[110]

The U.S. military maintains attaches in our embassy in Mexico City, as does the Mexican military in its embassy in Washington, D.C. Yet, for many decades, American officers have consistently found it difficult to develop close relations with their Mexican counterparts.[111] "The Mexican military carefully controls personal contact between its officers and U.S. military attachés, going so far as to require formal authorization for social contacts with U.S. officers."[112] The Mexican government has on occasion expelled U.S. attachés for gathering information too aggressively and imposed early retirement on senior Mexican officers who had become too friendly with the U.S. mission.

The United States exerts some influence on Mexico. It exerts this influence indirectly through two channels, professional training in the United States, and its role in encouraging and funding the armed forces' anti-drug trafficking mission.[113] As Jay Cope noted, "service academies began exchanging language (or culture) instructors in the 1950s. A substitution in the air force of instructor pilots started in the 1980s. Mexican officers have routinely studied and taught at the U.S. Army School of the Americas and attended all U.S. senior service (war) colleges."[114]

Historically, the one exception Mexico has made in refusing United States monies for national defense is their acceptance of grants from the International Military Education and Training (IMET) funds. "Between 1950 and 1993, the U.S. allocated $6.7 million for 2,061 students (primarily officers) to receive professional instruction or technical training in the United States; over 800 have attended courses during the last ten years, many of them at the U.S. Army School of the Americas or in programs tied to counter-narcotics operations."[115] It is clear from top generals and admirals in our sample that many, especially more recent ones, have received technical training above the border. The training is given to the officers with the greatest potential for command and, consequently, a much higher proportion of officers reaching the rank of general or admiral are educated in the United States than the figures for the entire officer corps would suggest. For example, the Mexican navy has placed an officer in every U.S. Navy Command College class since 1960. Of those officers, thirty-three have risen to flag rank and, more importantly, six have gone on to become secretary of the navy.[116]

The only comprehensive examination of the effectiveness of international military training in the United States, and the most comprehensive evaluation of socializing consequences of this training, concluded that it has almost no influence over civil-military relations.[117] Perhaps the most significant contribution which U.S. training has made to Mexican military values is related to the learning process itself, that is, the open way in which learning goes on in U.S. institutions. This learning pattern, which is totally foreign to Mexican military education below the Colegio de Defensa Nacional level, is complementary to the new democratic political model undertaken by the society, which values debate and discussion in determining policy preferences.

A second element to consider when analyzing U.S. influence on the armed forces is the degree to which the military actually desired isolation from the United States. Some of the historic examples of the military's desire to stand on its own are misleading. In 1948 the United States proposed a hemispheric defense council at the Organization of American States meeting in Bogota, Colombia. Mexico's officer corps supported the proposal but civilian authorities vetoed it.[118] In 1951 the United States offered mutual defense assistance pacts to eight Latin American nations, under which they were to receive military assistance in exchange for assuming hemisphere defense responsibilities. Mexico's armed forces welcomed the offer, but again the civilian-dominated administration of Miguel Alemán refused.[119]

It may be that the incidents do not reflect subsequent military attitudes, but an insider's view of recent regional meetings does suggest the continuation of Mexican military aloofness from the United States. Mexico is the only major Latin American nation in the 1990s to send a token representation to the biennial Conference of American Armies. Most armies send their top commanders. Instead, the Mexicans usually have their resident attaché, a colonel or sometimes a brigadier general, attend.[120] At the Inter-American Defense Board meetings, "on sensitive issues, their delegation was under the strict control of the Ambassador. They admitted that they would often abstain on votes on important issues before the IADB because they had received instructions from their Embassy. Often, even if the head of the delegation, Brigadier General _____, spoke out strongly on some issue being debated, he would abstain on the vote (to my surprise)."[121]

A far more definitive source of U.S. influence on the Mexican military, and on civilian strategies incorporating the military in newly defined national security missions, is the impact of the U.S. government on the drug trafficking mission. This influence, more than any other, including international terrorism in the wake of the attack on New York City, is likely to affect military values and behavior for decades to come. It has already produced a decisive impact on civil-military relations. The United States played a determinant role in pressuring the Mexican executive branch to involve the military in combating drugs, and in extending its role well beyond the modest task of destroying drug producing sites in Mexico. By encouraging this multi-faceted mission, by funding it (the only other major source of monies which the armed forces accepts from the United States), and by training the armed forces in techniques to be used in the war on drugs, the U.S. impact is notable.

The military's drug-related missions only raise the possibility of other consequences for civil-military relations. The most definitive impact to date is the extent to which the anti-drug mission has contributed to important levels of corruption within the institution. Corruption has tainted the political world for many decades and, in many respects, contributed to the declining legitimacy of political institutions and the successful rise of political opposition, culminating in Fox's electoral victory in 2000. The military, while having its own problems with corruption, until very recently has been able to maintain a generally favorable public image, at least more so than civilian political institutions. One danger of increased corruption is its potential contribution to the military's declining prestige as an institution, which to date it has avoided. A second danger is that increased internal corruption will bring greater civilian interest and involvement in the military, altering the autonomy the military has earned since the Revolution. The greater transparency introduced by the government after 2000 has increased interest in the media and public. A third danger is the growing dissatisfaction among honest officers with institutional immorality and questionable leadership, factors that can quickly demoralize from within.

The persistent demand in the United States for drugs, even without U.S. interference in drug interdiction policy on Mexican territory, would have affected Mexico's society, internal security, and national defense strategies. By 1990, the secretary of national defense, attempting to dispel the military's influence, declared that the "Mexican army is at the margin of all anti-drug trafficking; we help only in those zones in which there are insufficient federal judicial police personnel."[122] In truth, the impact on the military itself up to that date was in no way marginal. At that time it was primarily involved in destroying drug caches, yet just during one month of 1990 it caught and arrested 89 presumed traffickers, destroyed 96 secret airfields, and confiscated 312 arms and 26 vehicles.[123]

In the last decade, the extent of drug-related corruption in the military has become far more visible. The secretary of the navy, Admiral Mauricio Schleske Sánchez, resigned in June 1990, giving family reasons. His departure was not voluntary according to media sources. The president had fired the secretary and other top officers. These naval officers, including the director general of the merchant marine (an admiral), were accused of possessing "inexplicable wealth," assets unreported on their statements to the controller general, the source of which was allegedly drugs.[124] A group of naval officers arrested for trafficking in drugs accused the former secretary of using naval intelligence as a clandestine police force under his personal command.[125] A source within the Mexican military suggested that the secretary of national defense was so concerned with drug corruption that he was rotating zone commanders more frequently to prevent senior officers from having sustained contact with the same people.[126] Since 1996, the removal of President Zedillo's drug czar just weeks after his appointment, the arrest of two former zone commanders during his administration, and the dismantling of a northern army battalion in 2002—all on charges of drug corruption—is plentiful evidence of its continued presence.

The allegations of corruption among high-ranking officers have an impact on the presidency's role in civil-military relations. President José López Portillo suggests why:

> One of the characteristics of presidentialism in Mexico is that he is really the head of the military. The person who understands the military situation best is, of course, the secretary of national defense. But when a difficult situation arises involving the military, it is the president who ultimately has to make the decision. There are occasions when a military zone commander has been corrupted by drug traffickers or more commonly is under the influence of some important landowners or ranchers in the region, and then the president, receiving this intelligence information from his political agencies, must tell the secretary of national defense to either remove this individual, or to watch him more closely for moral and/or political reasons.[127]

The drug mission, when it introduces high-level corruption, creates the potential danger for upsetting the delicate balance between the presidency and the armed forces.

Conclusions

The military's image is complex and fragile. It is formed through its professionalization process within the context of societal attitudes toward the officer corps as a profession and the military as an institution. One of the most noteworthy consequences of professionalization is the extreme level of discipline and subordination to authority imposed on young officers. The structure not only washes out officers who lack the "right attitude" but also insures unquestioning loyalty to commanding officers. It has also socialized officers, as part of the larger professionalization process, to accept civilian control, and discourages interest in political affairs.

Society's view of the military, despite notable cases of corruption and publicized examples of human rights abuses, is generally favorable. Compared with the image of other state institutions, the military image is downright positive. Ordinary Mexicans have personal experiences with high levels of crime and its consequences. It is probably these experiences that explain why Mexican citizens exhibit a lack of confidence in the police to reestablish acceptable levels of public safety and have accepted an expanded armed forces mission to actively pursue drug traffickers and an integration of the military in civilian agencies whose primary tasks are to improve internal security. The Mexican military has withdrawn from overt forms of political activity, including holding public office and supporting presidential candidates.

There is absolutely no evidence within the officer corps of the existence of doubts about or criticism of their subordination to civilian authority. This attitude remains a bedrock of military professionalism in Mexico. A small percentage of Mexicans believe that the military should be involved in government, and that minority may be increasing in response to its existing role in internal security.

The only danger to civil-military relations in the perceptions of Mexican citizens stems from the persistent stranglehold which organized crime and drug traffickers maintain over Mexico in the first decade of the twenty-first century. The Fox administration, in using the military more widely, has achieved greater success against individual drug lords. Nevertheless, U.S. demand for drugs has not receded, nor has Mexico or the United States achieved any success in reducing the movement from and production of drugs in Mexico, suggesting the persistence of this problem as a permanent, serious national security threat. Because society views military participation in this task as acceptable and perceives their performance of the task as positive, it encourages the armed forces to perform other non-traditional national security tasks. It is not unreasonable to make the case that the more heavily civilian leadership relies on the military to perform traditional civilian responsibilities, the greater legitimacy it contributes to the armed forces capabilities. This opens the door for a role which might alter the established accepted balance in civil-military relations.

CHAPTER SEVEN

Educating the Officer Corps

Formal training is integral to the professionalization of career officers including their attitudes toward subordination to civilian rule. Military academies typically perform three interrelated functions: to increase professional competence, a cognitive function; to mold values among cadets and lower-ranking officers, a socialization function; and to establish personal ties and peer trust crucial to future command, a recruitment function. There exists considerable discussion on the cognitive function, a cursory examination of the socialization function, and almost no analysis or empirical evidence of the recruitment function. The latter two functions contribute significantly to civil-military relations in Mexico.

This chapter evaluates the changing trends in military education, comparing new directions with patterns occurring among Mexican civilian leadership, especially since the 1990s. Useful conclusions can be drawn solely from studying the levels of military education, but the primary focus of this analysis is on the socialization and recruitment functions, the implications of these functions for the successful career officer, their contrasts with civilian political leadership, and their decisive effects on civil-military relationships.

Evolution of Mexico's Military Education

Historically, little prestige has been associated with Mexico's military educational system. The majority of officers in the pre-revolutionary federal army, or its antecedent national guard in the nineteenth century, did not graduate from specialized military training programs. Between "1876 and 1910 the army fared little better in the institutional, professional sense; the

Porfiriato did little to perpetuate the military past—and less to assure the army's future. Officers were only marginally prepared."[1] Furthermore, those reaching the rank of general could be distinguished educationally from all other officers in the army. Nearly all of the generals were nonprofessionals, and most of them were quite elderly by 1900.[2] Nevertheless, the number of officers attending the Colegio Militar did gradually increase from the 1870s through 1900.

It would be fair to say that Porfirio Díaz contributed to the military's institutionalization during his administration. He created both the Applied Military Medical School, the antecedent to the notable Escuela Médico Militar, and the Cadet Military School. His officers were increasingly trained at the Colegio Militar, where they actually pursued four years of technical studies in the arts of modern warfare. This was a length of military education unequaled until the 1940s. Enrollments at the Colegio Militar averaged 300, with 60 cadets graduating annually. By 1892, 30 percent of all officers were Colegio Militar graduates; by 1900, that figure reached approximately 50 percent.[3] The Colegio Militar began its modern operation in 1869,[4] which explains why many officers were graduates. This also explains why most generals, who began their careers before the 1860s, were without formal military education. In 1882, fourteen years after the founding of the Colegio Militar, only 19 (11 percent) of the 170 army generals, and 48 (7 percent) of the colonels were graduates.[5]

After the Revolution, renewed emphasis was placed on military education. The evolution of each military academy and its individual role in officer education, formation, and recruitment are examined subsequently. Here it is important to identify the general educational trends. Both military and political leaders have increasingly valued technical expertise. As indicated by their informal recruitment practices, these leaders, especially civilian politicians, have sought out and promoted disciples with specific, formal credentials.

This upward educational trend can be seen quite clearly through a general analysis of top officers since 1940. Among revolutionary contemporaries of Generals Alvaro Obregón and Plutarco Elías Calles, both of whom continued to hold command positions after 1940, only a third obtained formal military training or university education. Of those, more than half were graduates of the Colegio Militar, some attending as higher-ranking officers. For example, Adrián Castrejón, who first joined the Maderistas as a guerrilla on July 2, 1911, matriculated in the Colegio Militar's cavalry program as a brigadier general on April 11, 1921. He graduated in 1923, and was promoted to brigade general in 1924 while serving as commander of the 24th military zone in Guerrero.[6]

A crucial change in educational patterns among high-ranking military officers occurs between the 1890s and 1900s generations. More than half the officers born during the 1890s attended a military or civilian college; of that number, 63 percent attended the Colegio Militar and 14 percent graduated from the naval academy in Veracruz. Characteristics of the 1890s generation suggest not only an increase in level of education but also an important shift from civilian to purely military alma maters.

It is the post-revolutionary generation, born in the first decade of the twentieth century, who determines the future composition of the officer corps. Only one of the officers in our sample of sixty from that decade had not attended either a military school or a civilian university. More importantly, 90 percent had graduated from a military school. This figure alone does not tell the entire story. Half of all officers from the 1900s generation are graduates of the Escuela Superior de Guerra; only a miniscule 2 percent of the 1890s generation had done so. The Escuela Superior de Guerra, founded to prepare junior officers for staff and command positions, suddenly became an extraordinary presence in the educational background of Mexico's generals. The timing of this dramatic change can be explained by the fact that the school was established in the early 1930s.

The 1900s generation is a unique group among top officers and politicians for other reasons. In our discussion of civilian and military interlocks, we demonstrated that educational institutions—particularly the Heroico Colegio Militar and the National University—played a principal role. Among college-educated generals of the 1880s generation, 25 percent graduated from the National University. Among the 1900s generation, only 15 percent had done so and they were last generation in which a large minority of officers were National University alumni. Only 5 percent of all generals and admirals from all generations have attended the National University.

The 1900s generation also can be considered a crucial generation for the military because the "transitional political-military officer" reached an apex among that group. The political-military soldier can be described as an individual characterized by many professional qualities, not the least of which were training and advanced studies. These men pursued successful political careers outside of the armed forces. A decisive change occurs when the best-educated officers with political ambitions reaching the rank of general or admiral fade away and are replaced by equally well educated but more orthodox career officers. After 1910 superior education is the mark, not of the political-military officer, but of the true career professional. Ironically, it is the highly educated political-military officer in control of the military bureaucracy who raises fellow officers to this educational level.

From the 1900 generation onward, all officers of the rank of general or admiral had attained similar educational levels. In effect, officers born after 1910 who hope to become generals must attend the military academies or a civilian university. At the war college level, figures remain nearly constant among the three successive generations: about 60 percent of the top ranks have staff and command diplomas from the Escuela Superior de Guerra and the Centro de Estudios Superiores Navales or its foreign equivalent. Such levels of military education are high even by industrialized countries' standards. For example, in the mid-1960s only 28 percent of Czechoslovakian officers and 24 percent of Poland's officers were military academy graduates.[7]

By the late 1950s and 1960s, when Mexicans born in the 1940s entered the officer corps as cadets, another educational change occurred. Attending the Escuela Superior de Guerra or the Centro de Estudios Superiores Navales replaced attending the Heroico Colegio Militar or the Heroica Escuela Naval Militar as an informal credential in obtaining the rank of general or admiral. The 1940s generation, which reached two and three star rank in the 2000s, has graduated from these two institutions in much larger percentages. If we exclude military law and the medical corps from our 1940s sample, 100 percent of army and air force generals hold staff and command diplomas from the Escuela Superior de Guerra.

Naval graduates are even better educated. They have received an equivalent university degree in engineering from the Heroica Escuela Naval Militar for decades.[8] The Centro de Estudios Superiores Navales awards MAs and PhDs. All but two of the admirals graduated from their advanced naval war college, and those individuals received M.A.'s in other specialties. Many admirals from the 1940s generation hold PhDs, too. For example, Fox's appointee as secretary of the Navy, Admiral Antonio Peyrot González, holds two masters' degrees, one from the prestigious Colegio de Defensa Nacional in national security, and the other in diplomacy from the Matías Romero Institute, Mexico's Foreign Service school.[9]

Higher education in non-military institutions serves as another source of contact with civilians. In 1980, only 18 officers were enrolled in such MA or PhD specialty programs. In 1985 the number had increased to 40, in 1995 to 68, and by 1998 to 142. These officers were enrolled at UNAM, National Polytechnic Institute, Ibero-American University, and Anahuac, all located in the capital.[10] Among the 1940s generation, two and three star officers from all the services have essentially established an MA degree as the new educational norm. All naval officers have obtained this level of professional education or higher. Among army and air force officers from this generation, 60 percent have graduated from the Colegio de Defensa Nacional or its equivalent in Mexico or abroad.

By the 1980s, according to secretary of national defense figures, during a typical year 2,080 soldiers were enrolled in military schools, including 614 cadets in officer-training academies, 512 noncommissioned and junior officers in applied schools, 396 officers, colonels, and generals in higher war schools (including 7 naval officers), 38 civilians, and 12 foreigners.[11] By the late 1990s, those figures had risen dramatically. According to state of the union statistics, 4,650 officers were in various military schools.[12] In just four short years, the renewed interest of the officer corps in education and training is suggested by the figure for enrollments in all military schools in Mexico in 2001; it stood at 14,243.[13]

In recognition of the growing importance of various military training programs, on January 1, 1976, the Secretariat of National Defense established the Army and Air Force University to coordinate the army and air force academies and numerous specialty schools.[14] The reason for its departmental status in the ministry was "to lend continuity, uniformity and congruence to the doctrine and ideology of the military education programs."[15] By 1985 the military's umbrella university supervised twenty-three schools. Some observers believe that such diversity and technical competence enhance the military's capacity to perform political functions if the need were to arise.[16] In terms of day-to-day training, the other significant change introduced after publication of the *Army and Air Force Development Program* in 1995, was assigning training responsibilities to local zone commanders, who could then tailor training to the needs of their specific regional assignments.[17]

Perhaps more than anything else, the complexity and quality of military education suggest its increasing prestige compared with civilian institutions. In 2000 outside evaluators ranked the Escuela Médico Militar, which had boasted a strong reputation for many years, as number one among Mexican medical schools. In engineering, the Heroica Escuela Naval Militar Antón Lizardo ranked number five.[18]

As officers' educational attainments rose, the military budget fell. One might infer an inverse relationship between professionalization and the military's political influence.[19] There is, however, no evidence that the two trends are associated. In fact, the literature on the Latin American military repeatedly demonstrates that as professionalization (measured in terms of education) increases, so do budgetary allotments. Why is Mexico an exception?

Mexico's civil-military relations are unique for many reasons and serve to set it apart from most of the Third World. Higher levels of military education did not in and of themselves produce less political influence. Rather, the political leadership (who at the time of growing professionalization were military men) decided on a course of action that included reducing the size of the military, cutting government outlays, and producing well-qualified officers without ties to revolutionary generals. This policy led to a new kind of officer corps represented by the post-1910 generations. However, it was not the increasing *levels* of education that contributed to diminished political influence but their curricula, a program which emphasized loyalty and subordination to civil leadership and modest outlays for weaponry. Only in the sense that each level of education repeated its antecedent's message could it be argued that more education produced greater subordination to civilian authorities and strongly contributed to eliminating politically ambitious soldiers from the officer corps.

A comparison of the educational attainments of Mexico's top officers from 1970 to 2000 with those of other leading elite actors, suggests that the officer corps is actually better educated formally than Mexico's most influential capitalists and cultural elites. Only the clergy, who are the best-educated group of leaders (nearly half have obtained doctorates), and the politicians (one-out-of-five has a PhD) have more formal education.

The education of politicians and top officers in the 1990s reveals one significant difference. The more extensive the education of the politicians, the more diverse it became. The majority of younger politicians are obtaining their undergraduate degree from influential private universities and their graduate training from foreign universities and colleges, most of which are located in the United States. In contrast, in spite of more extensive military education (for example, at the separate Colegio Aire for pilots and the Colegio de Defensa Nacional for national security training for all the services), officers generally had to "advance through a fixed set of educational choices."[20] As the national political leadership chooses among private and public Mexican institutions of higher education and foreign universities, the military is receiving its additional education within a domestic, mandated curriculum that enhances its homogeneity.

This increased level of education has implications for the socialization function, a quality we have alluded to in the previous chapter on officer corps values. Officer socialization is critical to the civil-military relationship. As officers spend a greater percentage of their entire military career within the confines of the armed forces' educational system, they receive greater exposure to those attitudes and values which the military leadership wishes to impart. The broader literature on military socialization notes that while Mexican military cadets are a self-selecting group of high school or preparatory school seniors, their preconceived attitudes alone do not account for their professional beliefs.[21]

What does affect their attitudes, to some degree, is educational socialization. As a study of the United States Air Force Academy concluded "the total immersion in institutional values is a central feature of the overall socialization process. The typical cadet day starts before 0600, finishes after 2300, and is filled with exposure to all these elements."[22] The same pattern of socialization influence was observed in cadets at the Royal Canadian Military College.[23] Not surprisingly, military cadets have been found to score higher on measures of political conservatism and intolerance compared to civilian students.[24] Studies suggest that some, but not all, cadet attitudes are altered by these immersions in military educational environments, and that some of the changes move in the direction of traditional variables found universally in the military ethos.[25]

Studying is only one of the two important ways in which military education performs cognitive, socializing, and recruitment functions. The other equally important component of military education, one that has grown in importance paralleling the increased level of education, is teaching.

Teaching is a significant responsibility in the military and its prevalence in the careers of Mexican officers is striking. Nearly two thirds of the top generals and admirals since 1940 have taught compared with 45 percent of all political leaders since 1935. Among recent generals and admirals, more than 90 percent have taught in the military academies, many of them in two or more institutions. A large percentage of naval and army officers have served as directors, assistant directors, or course chiefs for the leading military academies. If one combines the years a top Mexican officer spends in a military educational environment as a student with their years as an instructor, it would not be uncommon for a top officer to have spent one-fourth to one-third of his entire career in some form of military education.

Teaching as an integral experience in an officer's career acquired importance beginning with the 1900 generation. Again, we see that officers who had been born in the first decade of the twentieth century are the swing cohort in the evolution of the military's educational training and instruction. An examination by generations suggests the decisiveness of the change. The change from pre-1900 to post-1900 is marked; about three-quarters of the surviving revolutionary generals never had taught but were replaced by a group half of which had taught, a dramatic switch. The teaching pattern held for years, changing only with the present generation of generals (those fifty and younger) for whom teaching is a nearly universal experience.

When the teaching experiences of all prominent generals and admirals since 1940 are looked at in the aggregate, an important aspect becomes apparent. Slightly more than half of the nearly two-thirds of all officers since World War II who have taught did so at the four major military schools; one in ten, at an applied school; and 4 percent elsewhere. Teaching is more common among officers than politicians, but it is extremely narrow in scope. Generals have rarely taught outside the hallowed halls of military academies.

Thus, teaching as a channel for military-civilian contact is negligible. Teaching's recruitment and advancement function, while highly significant, is limited to the military's own institutions and personnel.

The early prestige of the military teaching experience is most obviously exemplified in the careers of the officers who directed the Heroico Colegio Militar. Numerous directors reached the highest positions in the Secretariat of National Defense. Three secretaries of defense, three assistant secretaries, one oficial mayor, and two chiefs of staff directed the Heroico Colegio Militar during the years 1920 to 2004. An equal number had previously served in similar top posts before becoming director.

Officer Formation at the Heroico Colegio Militar

The Colegio Militar was the most important military educational experience for successive generations of cadets. President Carranza reopened the Colegio Militar after it had been closed under his predecessor on February 5, 1920. In 1925 it closed temporarily for repairs. The school reopened in 1926 with a new staff of instructors who had either been trained in the United States or Europe or who were former members of the Federal Army who had joined the revolutionaries after 1911.[26] The word Heroico was added to the name Colegio Militar in 1947 during the celebration of the 100th anniversary of the Mexican-American War. The renaming was a recognition of the cadets' defense of Chapultepec in 1847.

The potential influence of the Heroico Colegio Militar as a locus of recruitment is enhanced by its relatively limited student body. If we think of it as a college, its small size becomes apparent. In size the Heroico Colegio Militar parallels a small, liberal arts college in the United States. In 1925, it graduated 200 officers, mostly second lieutenants. In 1934, only 137 cadets graduated; in 1944, the figure rose to 289. In 1954, enrollment was 584, and in 1955, 166 cadets graduated. During the 1960's, graduating classes ranged from 200 to 290. For example, in mid-decade, 204 officer cadets graduated, 18 percent of whom were first sergeants (mustangs). In 2000, most of the top generals in the army and air force graduated in the late 1950s or early 1960s.[27] Based on enrollment figures, graduation figures suggest class sizes of 175 to 200 in the late 1990s and early 2000s. Enrollments ranged from 725 cadets in 1997 to a high of 977 in 2001. The number of cadets dropped to 730 in 2002.[28]

A new facility opened in 1976 with a capacity for three thousand cadets. Enrollments in the 1990s filled less than half that capacity.[29] The facility is modest. It includes 54 general classrooms, each with room for 35 students. The size of each class is significant because, after three years (presently four years) of training together, most cadets in a single class know one another personally. Cadets grouped together by military occupational specialty (MOS) form even smaller units. For example, throughout the 1960s, graduating classes specializing in mechanized cavalry never exceeded fifty; artillery second lieutenants numbered in the twenties; and administrative specialists were fewer than twenty per class.

The Heroico Colegio Militar recruits from a constituency that is markedly different from that of civilian universities. Prior to the mid-1900s, most applicants had completed only a secondary education; in one study, only a handful of aspirants could claim a preparatory education, a background now required for enrollment.[30] Some applicants have private primary or secondary school educations, but the vast majority are public school or vocational school graduates.[31]

In Mexico, a preparatory education is the first requisite to pursue a college degree. In 1947, a cadet with a secondary education who studied at the Heroico Colegio Militar for four years would receive the equivalent of a preparatory degree from the National University.[32] The military dropped the program the following year. It did not reestablish a preparatory equivalent until 1966.[33] From the 1960s through the 1990s, the Heroico Colegio Militar diploma functioned as the equivalent of a preparatory education. The only exceptions were pilots, who completed two years at the Heroico Colegio Militar and two years at the Colegio de Aire in Guadalajara, thereby earning a college degree. Since the inception of major educational reforms in the mid-1990s, cadets are now required to have a preparatory certificate before enrolling. Graduates of the Heroico Colegio Militar, like graduates of West Point in the United States, are second lieutenants with a college degree.

Prospective cadets are selected on the basis of examinations. In the mid-1950s, 223 of 450 applicants were admitted,[34] a rate comparable to Brazil's leading military academy.[35] By 1965, according to one source, applicants to Mexico's military and naval academies outnumbered admissions by proportions of six to one and fifteen to one, respectively.[36] By 2004, 479 cadets out of 2,787 applicants (17 percent) were admitted. In the first sergeant intensive program, only 26 out of 308 applicants were enrolled (8 percent).[37] Applicants can come from civilian life or they may be enlisted personnel with the rank of corporal and above. The entrance exams are now offered at 26 different military zones from June through July.[38] Civilian applicants may not be older than 21 or younger than 16; they must be male and Mexican nationals by birth.[39]

Education at the Heroico Colegio Militar is significant not only because nearly all army and air force officers pass through its classrooms but also because of the time spent there. Most cadets entered the academy between the ages of fifteen and nineteen before preparatory education was imposed.⁴⁰ In the case of army generals, I found the typical age to have been between seventeen and eighteen. During the four-year program, the cadet is provided food, clothing, and shelter, and the academy controls about four-fifths of the cadet's time, seven days a week. Cadets are allowed to visit family or friends from midday Saturday to 9:00 PM Sunday.⁴¹

The university education of politicians (they typically live at home or with a guardian) is much more open to diverse influences than that of the officers, both in and out of the classroom. University education for politicans is comparable to the education of a university student in the United States. One of the most important differences between the educations of politicians and officers is that the environment of the former is more varied and intellectual. Politicians have pointed to the significance of learning experiences in the homes of other students and professors, as well as in the ambience of the capital.⁴²

The increased educational requirements for cadets add a new dimension to officer socialization. This may, therefore, contribute to altering civil-military relationships. In the next several decades, a new generation of high-ranking officers will have had some opportunity to have a limited number of the experiences alluded to by politicians and intellectuals. Moreover, they will even have a greater opportunity to connect with fellow students with other career interests. By requiring that recent cadets complete their preparatory education before enrolling, the military has increased the average entrance age among cadets. Today's cadets are older and somewhat less susceptible to military socialization.They also bring greater intellectual diversity to their professional preparation through prepatory exposure to a civilian, academic experience.

Officers, once enrolled in the Heroico Colegio Militar or in the Heroica Escuela Naval Militar, rarely share these types of experiences since their free time is more limited. The impact of the Heroico Colegio Militar is intensified by the fact that cadets are almost wholly removed from their families and other civilians. Their isolation typically is reinforced by a post-graduation assignment to the provinces. Unlike the Brazilian model, it is not just the formal education, per se, but also the imposition of a common set of experiences for all army and air force officers that is critical.⁴³ The military controls cadets and young officers during their late teens and early twenties, a period when values and behavior are being formed.⁴⁴

The Heroico Colegio Militar experience is shared by a group of young men who have other things in common. (Women serve in the army but are not allowed in the regular academy programs except the military medical, nursing, and dental schools. Recently, however, several women attended the Escuela Superior de Guerra Applied Arms and Services course.)[45] As discussed earlier, many cadets come from lower-middle-class provincial backgrounds.[46] Unlike Brazilian cadets, most of whom come from secondary military academies where they have been educated from twelve to fourteen years of age, Mexican cadets have diverse educational backgrounds.[47]

According to one source, based on conversations held over eighteen months with some forty field grade officers at the Escuela Superior de Guerra, the typical rural applicant has "seen notices and heard about the Military College in Mexico City. The military often advertised over the radio or distributed flyers extolling the merits of the Military College."[48] These cadets hope to earn improved economic and social status. The current secretariat of national defense website lists as benefits of enrollment: food, lodging, spending money, and health care for a cadet's parents. This last benefit is a privilege for most Mexicans. Another reason for enrollment is a familial one; they hope to follow in the footsteps of a father or uncle.[49]

When the Colegio Militar was reestablished after the Revolution, the training program was expanded from eighteen months to three years. This program offered separate courses for infantry, cavalry, artillery, engineers, combat engineers, and administration.[50] In the mid-1920s, the Secretariat of National Defense began sending officers to study in the United States, Spain, France, and Italy. Upon their return, these officers often became instructors. By 1929 the Colegio Militar retained a professoriate composed of seventy-eight officers and forty-eight civilians.[51] The typical cadet was exposed to civilian professors, but most of the civilians provided instruction in a limited number of courses in Philosophy and Language. In the 1990s the majority of instructors were still career military officers.

In contrast, "the Navy and Air Force always have maintained much greater contact with civilians through their military educational programs. Three-quarters of the instructors at the Heroica Escuela Naval in the port of Veracruz, and the Colegio Aire in Jalisco, are civilian. . . . Because no detailed histories of the establishment and evolution of their academies exist, it is difficult to explain why that is the case. It can be suggested that their more recent origins chronologically, and their heavier reliance on technology from abroad, which increased their contacts with American programs, increased their openness to both foreign and civilian expertise."[52] From the 1920s though the 1970s, military education in the army remained virtually static and confined to strictly military subjects.[53] In 1952, at the educational midpoint of most of our generals, the curriculum—with the exception of general culture, geography, history, and civics—consisted exclusively of military science.[54] In contrast, most future political leaders carried a broad range of liberal arts courses, often with a heavy dose of political science and economics. Officers received little exposure to such subjects at the Heroico Colegio Militar.

Today, a cadet's four-year program includes a larger component of general studies but not much in the way of economics and political science. In the "first year a common program is studied; during the remaining years the cadet engages in specialized study for entry to the infantry, cavalry, artillery, combat engineers, or administration."[55] In the 1980s, only about 10 percent of the courses offered at the Heroico Colegio Militar were devoted to the social sciences, and only 5 percent incorporated any political content. Another 5 percent were devoted to the behavior of officers in relation to the military and society.[56]

The other source of diversity in civilian education not found in the military is course materials. The Mexican military makes use of U.S. Army field manuals but the texts used in the regular courses are by Mexicans. In the 1950s, no texts by foreign authors were used, a situation now atypical at the Escuela Superior de Guerra but still basically the case at the Heroico Colegio Militar. In 1991, all Escuela Superior de Guerra texts, except constitutional law, were foreign (with Mexican covers) but edited by an Escuela Superior de Guerra graduate. Since the 1920s many of the texts used in institutions attended by future politicians have also been foreign in origin, especially from France, the United States, and Spain.[57]

Thus, by means of curriculum and staff, Mexico's military provides an extremely homogeneous environment for the officer's educational socialization. This environment is far more hermetic than the environment in which the politician's or intellectual's educational socialization takes place. It is likely that the Heroica Escuela Naval Militar in Veracruz, which educates most of Mexico's high-ranking naval and marine officers, is somewhat more open in curriculum and staff, if its direct commission and foreign training policies are indicative of its educational philosophy. According to recent regulations, its civilian staff is selected by competitive examination and contracted to teach nonmilitary subjects. It also accepts foreign civilian cadets.[58] Nevertheless, there is no question that Mexican officers, regardless of rank or service, pass through a more nationalistic educational process than do their civilian counterparts.

What exactly does this type of training produce? Most important, the training imparts values that shape the behavior of officers, especially their attitudes toward political institutions. Furthermore, the experience at the Heroico Colegio Militar, as is the case at many U.S. military academies, is not always a pleasant one. This unpleasant experience helps to develop remarkable unity among a cadet generation, a unity that has many implications for their values and career trajectories.[59] A recent graduate (early

1990s) provides this frank and telling assessment: "Those four years as a cadet were most of the time a living hell for me (mostly when I was in my second year in Cavalry) and I wish that there had been a way to get a little bit less abuse for all of us, both physically and mentally. I believe that being in the army means getting many virtues such as discipline, courage, respect, etc., and that tough training is needed, but I don't agree with treating a human being worst than an animal. There were days when I wasn't able to sit down because my butt hurt so badly."[60]

Studies of West Point, the most comparable U.S. army institution, concluded that cadets underwent a transformation of values, but that the transformation "rested on adoption of primary values of military subculture," which produce "overt, patterned ways of behaving, feeling and reacting."[61] Furthermore, at the United States Military Academy, the changes that do occur are not universal. Cadets from military and civilian backgrounds, who initially differ somewhat in their attitudes, come closer together after four years but, on certain issues, no single attitude pattern exists.[62]

Of all the means of professionalization, military education most deeply affects behavior. Cadets learn behavior from their military superiors. Nearly all junior officers' superiors, whether in the barracks or in the classroom, are professional military men who have already passed through the same environment. In the civilian sector, some professors are politicians or intellectuals with political ambitions. Hence, from the 1920s through the 1970s, Mexican civilian politicians achieved a remarkable cohesiveness in regard to values passed from one generation to the next. These values have contributed markedly to pragmatism.[63] In that sense, the civilian politicians share certain qualities with their military peers. It is possible that Mexican civilian leaders have more in common with Mexican military leaders than some other Latin American military officers have in common with Mexican officers.

In contrast, during the twentieth century, officers in the Brazilian military attended many different schools. Changes in location, number, and function of the schools were matched by changes in curricula, instructors, and training facilities. Such variety made "it difficult to develop lasting traditions and a sense of commonality in the officer corps. The changes and the variety of educational backgrounds necessarily deepened generational divisions."[64] This diverse pattern may have contributed to the junior officers' rebelling against their seniors in the 1920s. Such internal division would be highly unlikely in Mexico. One Mexican graduate described his military training at the Heroico Colegio Militar as having one primary function: "how to conform to authority."[65] As the junior officer advances, he learns the value of discipline and obedience to authority. This is not altogether unlike the traditional Mexican politician, who acquired from his superiors a similar set of values through experiential socialization in a semi-authoritarian, one-party system.

My own studies of mentoring among Mexico's most influential leaders in the last three decades demonstrates clearly the importance of mentors to career success and, even more remarkable, the fact that Mexican leadership—including the officer corps—are the product of elite mentors. The individuals who serve as mentors to future top leaders have held equally influential positions of power in Mexico. There are no exceptions to this pattern among three star generals and full admirals. Top military officers share these mentoring characteristics with both influential Catholic bishops and civilian politicians. Where do Mexican leaders encounter their mentors? Among leading intellectuals, clergy, and politicians, education is the most influential source of mentors, providing 76, 63, and 45 percent of their mentors respectively. Even in the officer corps, among whom career contacts are more significant, nearly a third of all mentor relationships develop within an educational setting.[66]

If the "key to understanding military behavior, therefore, resides in the Mexican military educational system, the country's primary agent of military professionalization, the Heroico Colegio Militar, is only the first step in a well-established process."[67] Three other Mexican institutions play a role in the army and air force training and socialization process: the applied schools, the Escuela Superior de Guerra, and the Colegio de Defensa Nacional. At least three years after graduating from the Heroico Colegio Militar, officers attend mandatory six month tactical and command courses in infantry, artillery, engineering, cavalry or administration. These courses are now a prerequisite for attendance at the Escuela Superior de Guerra.[68]

For naval officers, the educational experience is somewhat less homogeneous. While most naval officers do pass through the naval college followed by the naval equivalent of the Escuela Superior de Guerra, the Centro de Estudios Superiores Navales, and the Colegio de Defensa Nacional, they are exposed to a greater variety of fellow students and instructors, most of whom are civilians. Approximately one in six high-ranking military officers is from the navy. The navy "accepts lateral entry for both enlisted and officer ranks from civilians, giving them a rank on the basis of their education and/or skill. The professionals are usually dentists, engineers, accountants, and lawyers. The army and air force only in special situations accept lateral entry for officers."[69] The navy's lateral entry program introduces the potential for diverse influences on the mission of the officer corps, influences likely to be somewhat liberalizing. Because the number of lateral entrants is small, and because often they are not in main-line command positions, they are not apt to greatly impact officer values as a whole.

Educational institutions have long been thought to play important roles in elite cognitive skills and the formation of values.[70] Only on the basis of recent scholarship has it been shown that universities were critical to the initial recruitment of future politicians.[71] In the case of military officers, scholars have suspected for years the importance of military academies in the upward mobility of career officers. In the United States, it was no accident that, in the 1970s, 90 percent of all generals with two or more stars were West Point graduates.[72] Today, however, the majority of generals are products of civilian college ROTC programs. It has been supposed that military schools are crucial to the formation of officer coteries in Mexico, but no evidence documented this supposition because military careers and relationships were not discussed in the Mexican press.[73] Among three star generals and admirals in the last thirty years, educational settings account for two-thirds of networking ties, and these networks are typically where recruitment occurs.[74]

Historically, the Colegio Militar functioned as a locus of leadership recruitment. Among the military leaders who commanded troops in the field, headed military zones, and took on cabinet and gubernatorial posts in the early part of the Porfiriato, combat was their training ground and their means of establishing ties of trust and friendship. An examination of battlefield commands under Porfirio Díaz makes the origins of his later political loyalties quite clear.[75] The peace of the Porfiriato augmented the relative importance of the Colegio Militar in the backgrounds of the Mexican officer corps, both as a training center and as a source of recruitment. Consequently, when General Victoriano Huerta came to power in 1913 (after murdering the constitutional president), he naturally recruited his loyalists from Federal Army officers—many of whom, like him, were Colegio Militar graduates, including his own cadet class of combat engineers.[76]

The same pattern continued after 1920. The military academy took on the recruitment function because "one of the most important things that one gets out of four years at the Heroico Colegio Militar is a lasting relationship with his classmates. A fraternal bond is developed among the individuals who persevere through four years together. It is a bond that lasts throughout a career."[77] That is also the case in other Latin American and Third World countries.[78] The most important group in an officer's career is his own graduating class, particularly in his own specialty. It is clear from an analysis of leading army generals that key specializations are infantry, mechanized cavalry, and artillery followed, to a much lesser extent, by engineering and administration. Some authors have speculated that personal relationships and ties to a graduating class improve promotions, but they have offered no supportive evidence.[79] It does appear, however, that who one knows clearly affects where and when an officer holds certain influential or prestigious posts.

Personal ties can be ascertained by analyzing the friendships of all recent national defense secretaries and their top associates. Such analysis of the six most recent national defense secretaries revealed important characteristics of officer recruitment in Mexico. It is not only the class ties of the secretary that are important but also those of his second, third and fourth in command (the assistant secretary, oficial mayor, and chief of staff). These individuals take on added importance when the secretary of national defense is from a generation older than most of his active duty contemporaries for it is from his active duty contemporaries that a leader must select his collaborators. This can be seen with General Hermenegildo Cuenca Díaz (1970–1976), who was twenty years older than the president who appointed him, and who attended the Colegio Militar from 1920 to 1922 (ten to fifteen years before most of his top subordinates). He was the last secretary of national defense to have served in the Revolution having, as a young cadet, accompanied president Carranza on his flight from the capital to Veracruz. One of his zone commanders, Agustín Carreño Gutiérrez, a fellow student with Cuenca Díaz, also accompanied Carranza. But a much larger group of his subordinates (11) attended the Heroico Colegio Militar at the same time as his closest collaborators, his assistant secretaries and oficial mayor. His contacts with the two oficial mayores occurred through their concurrent attendance at the Escuela Superior de Guerra.

Recruitment at the Heroico Colegio Militar occurs through peers and through teaching. Among his top collaborators, several taught together at the school, and one of his assistant secretaries was a cadet commander of four of his appointees. Such patterns are equally true among politicians. Generally, fellow students have been important collaborators in a successful peer's administration, notably a president, but teachers have been far more important in starting the budding politician on a successful career path.[80] Military officer recruitment differs from political recruitment because of the homogeneous environment of the educational institution. All individuals attending the Heroico Colegio Militar already have chosen the same career, and most of their instructors are successful officers. Among students at the National University and other schools important to politicians' recruitment, future public officials are a minority, as are their ambitious professors. This is becoming typical for future politicians. Growing numbers of politicians are graduating from elite, private universities in Mexico. For example, President Vicente Fox is an alumnus of the Jesuit Ibero-American University in Mexico City.

There is a major difference in top leadership in Mexico and the United States. This difference is strongly linked to the differing educational patterns in the two nations. In the United States corporate executives and, to a lesser extent, military officers often hold top political posts. One explanation for this interchange among the three careers was the lack of a genuine U.S. civil service with its own training and recruitment program. The absence of a civil service meant the U.S. government needed to seek out talent from many professions.[81] In Mexico, the government created its own informal civil training and recruitment facility in the guise of the National University. Through the 1970s, the National University was where its careerists taught and recruited the best and brightest. Educationally, it produced a professional politician, or better said, political bureaucrat, followed by the political technocrat. Unlike the United States, which recruits many officers through the Reserve Officer Training Corps (ROTC) on private and public college campuses nationally, Mexican military officers and corporate figures were largely trained in state supported institutions. For officers that meant strictly within the military institutions. Although some officer graduates resigned their commissions because of an attraction to politics, they rarely persuaded their peers to do likewise.

In the 1920s and 1930s, entrepreneurs achieved more contact with political peers. The military also increased their contracts with entrepreneurs but, as the private sector expanded and modernized, it financed institutions whose ideology and methodology were more to its liking and appropriate for teaching the needed new entrepreneurial skills. Thus, over time businesspeople, like officers, decreased their educational linkages with politicians. In recent years, however, as future politicians moved away from public universities, they have begun to attend some of the same private universities as entrepreneurs, including such schools as the Monterrey Technological Institute of Higher Studies in Nuevo León and the Autonomous Technological Institute of Mexico in the nation's capital. A number of cabinet members in the Fox administration are products of these two schools, as well as Fox's own alma mater, the Ibero-American University.

The potential of schools to serve as recruitment centers for career officers and politicians is reduced by the extent each individual undergoes pre-university or professional training. In Mexico in the early part of the century, education provided a key shared experience for many. Even as university education became more diverse, private preparatory schools became increasingly common in the backgrounds of future politicians and top business people. Military officers, however, because cadets required only a secondary education, attended an "exclusive" preparatory school, the Heroico Colegio Militar. Because they embarked on a separate educational track at a younger age, their opportunities for contacts with future politicians and businessmen were fewer. However, with the change in entrance requirements in the 1990s (cadets must now have a preparatory credential in hand), future officers will have, for the first time in decades a greater likelihood that they will come in contact with other future professionals. This expectation is strongly tempered by the fact that fewer and fewer politicians and businesspeople attend public preparatory schools, while most future officer cadets are more likely to graduate from just such institutions.

In its early years, the Heroico Colegio Militar included additional characteristics advantageous to future military careers. During a brief but important period from 1923 to 1940, many higher-ranking officers attended the Colegio Militar. For example, the class of 1923, included future Secretary of National Defense Marcelino Garcia Barragán (1964–1970), who himself was a major. Graduates in that class also included colonels and one brigadier general. Naturally, an older officer who assumed a command position soon after graduating would have the opportunity to request fellow cadets as his subordinates. In a recruiting sense, older officer cadets functioned in a manner similar to teachers rather than as fellow students.

The Heroico Colegio Militar temporarily closed in 1925, thereby collapsing the cadet classes entering in 1923 and 1924. As a result, the 1925 graduating class introduced an extraordinarily large and important generation. Some individuals, hoping to obtain more than one military occupational specialty, actually graduated in two separate classes. Javier Jiménez Segura, a premier early model of a military technocrat, graduated both as an artillery lieutenant on December 21, 1924 and then as a military industrial engineer on October 1, 1925. He guided the National Defense military industry in the 1970s.

Teachers or cadet troop commanders at the Heroico Colegio Militar were equally important in the recruitment process. Military instructors often assist favored students later in their careers. Héctor Camargo Figueroa, who was assistant secretary in the 1970s, commanded the 1st Company of cadets in 1930–1931, when four members of Cuenca Díaz's administrative team were students. The Heroico Colegio Militar also serves to link instructors who were in different graduating classes as students. Two of Cuenca Díaz's collaborators served together at the Heroico Colegio Militar as director and cadet commander, respectively, and three department heads actually taught together. Gerardo Clemente Vega García, secretary of national defense in the Fox administration, provides a more recent example. He commanded the 1st Cadet Company from 1968 to 1970, while his commander of the 3rd Military Region in 2003, was a squadron leader in the same company.

The same patterns are found in the following administration, when General Félix Galván López served as secretary of national defense (1976–1982). Galván López, who graduated from the Heroico Colegio Militar, appointed five classmates from his class to top-ranked positions, including two of his three oficial mayores. He would also have known one of his assistant secretaries, who graduated a year after him in 1935. Two of his appointees came in contact with each other as members of the academy's football team between 1934 and 1938.

If we explore the backgrounds of individuals in the last four administrations, the importance of Heroico Colegio Militar class ties to future defense posts becomes even more apparent. Juan Arévalo Gardoqui was the secretary of national defense under Miguel de la Madrid (1982–1988). Of the twenty-seven top staff and department heads in the Secretariat of National Defense between 1982 to 1988, fifteen (56 percent) were held by generals who had overlapped as cadets with him at the Heroico Colegio Militar. These men included his assistant secretary and official mayor, both of whom were in subsequent cadet classes. Three officers were actually part of Arévalo Gardoqui's 1940–1943 class. Again, teaching at the Heroico Colegio Militar expanded contacts among other officers. An important explanation for why the Heroico Colegio Militar is so influential as a source of collaborators in this administration is that larger numbers of officers are closer in age to the national defense secretary. Arévalo Gardoqui's collaborators are also distinguishable from their predecessors because, for the first time, graduates of the Colegio de Defensa Nacional, the top tier institution and most prestigious school in the Mexican armed forces, held top posts in the Secretariat of National Defense. It is remarkable that a fourth of his collaborators had attended that institution, considering it only graduated several dozen officers yearly beginning in 1981–1982, and many of those graduates came from the navy and air force.

In the 1988–1994 administration, the Secretary of National Defense, Antonio Riviello Bazán, returned to the more traditional pattern. He was older than most of his collaborators, and therefore, as under Cuenca Díaz, it is his assistant secretary and oficial mayor who recruit his collaborators from their cadet classes. Sixty-five of the eighty-nine top officials in Riviello Bazán's administration overlapped their Heroico Colegio Militar education with his three immediate collaborators. Riviello Bazán's Chief of Staff served as a cadet commander at the Heroico Colegio Militar when General Riviello was assistant director in 1970. Like Arévalo Gardoqui, Riviello Bazán also staffed many of his top posts with officers who were members of the early generations graduating from the Colegio de Defensa Nacional. This added still another locus of educational socialization and recruitment for the officer corps. In just six years, Bazán doubled the representatives of this school to half of his collaborators, a dramatic and remarkable increase that suggests its accepted importance as the fast track to top leadership in the armed forces.

As the prevalence of the Escuela Superior de Guerra and the Colegio de Defensa Nacional in the educational credentialing process among top officers has increased, the importance of the Heroico Colegio Militar has gradually declined. Nevertheless, ties to fellow cadets and instructors continue to be important. During the tenure of General Enrique Cervantes Aguirre as secretary of national defense (1994–2000), his two assistant secretaries had strong ties to fellow cadets. At least fourteen officers in his administration were students at the Heroico Colegio Militar when his assistant secretary served as a cadet commander from 1956 to 1957. Seven other officers were classmates of his second assistant secretary in the 1951–1954 generation. The Colegio de Defensa Nacional continued to increase its overall presence (60 percent were graduates) and importance as a networking educational locale. Ten of Cervantes' collaborators and one of his assistance secretaries were members of the first graduating class.

Of all the secretaries of national defense in recent years, General Vega García, who took the post in 2000, is the one who has most used his own ties to fellow cadets from the Heroico Colegio Militar. The primary reason for this is that General Vega García, unlike most of his predecessors, does not differ as sharply in age from his closest collaborators. As suggested earlier, national defense secretaries tend to be older than most of their collaborators, making it almost impossible for them to have attended the Heroico Colegio Militar at the same time. In General Vega's case, however, his chief of staff is a graduate of the 1960 class, as are six other appointees. An assistant secretary and seven other collaborators represent the two classes, 1959 and 1961, with which he most strongly overlapped.

Cadet friendship at the Heroico Colegio Militar has consequences for personnel decisions later in an officer's career. Equally important, such ties may have policy implications. Michael Dziedzic cites a significant instance. General Félix Galván, secretary of national defense from 1976 to 1982, appointed General Pérez Mejia as director of the Escuela Superior de Guerra during his administration. Their friendship went back to their days at the Heroico Colegio Militar, and Pérez Mejia used that friendship to obtain special funds to construct a new Escuela Superior de Guerra building.[82]

The armed forces created several other significant military specialty schools in the 1910s and 1920s. The most notable were the Escuela Constitucionalista Médico Militar (it later dropped the Constitucionalista), established on January 1, 1917 (actual classes in March of that year), and the Escuela Militar de Transmisiones, which opened its doors in 1925.[83] The medical school is one of the most important in Mexico, graduating military physicians who practice at the Central Military Hospital in Mexico City, among other institutions. In 1973, it admitted women. Recently, the school has been graduating approximately fifty physicians a year.

For many years, the graduating classes were numbered in the twenties and thirties. Due to small class size, these students often developed intimate friendships with both fellow students and faculty. Furthermore, as the school's historian points out, because of class size, they came to know many of their companions in ten other overlapping classes. For example, the 1936 graduates overlapped with the 1931–35 classes and the 1937–1941 classes.[84] Because of the school's prestige, its graduates have easy access to lateral transfers into the civilian medical community. More important from a recruitment perspective, these military officers have more interlocks, both familial and professional, with politicians, often including Mexico's most influential political families.

At the same time that the Escuela Superior de Guerra was established in 1932, the Secretariat of War and Navy created an intermediate training program ranking above the Heroico Colegio Militar but not equivalent to the Escuela Superior de Guerra. Called applied schools, they were established for officers of the rank of captain who were about to be promoted to major. In 1935, the Secretariat of War and Navy required all infantry officers below the rank of colonel to take an examination; those who failed were placed on a mandatory list for the schools.[85] In recent years attendance in specialty courses at these schools have become required for advancement. However, an examination of officers who have completed the curriculum in higher combat arms (one of many applied courses), reveals that it has little importance in officer recruitment and advancement compared to the Heroico Colegio Militar and the Escuela Superior de Guerra.

Nevertheless, officers who had not graduated from the Escuela Superior de Guerra would not advance in their careers without applied training. Some officers take these courses before being chosen for the Escuela Superior de Guerra. Officers who have completed the applied course but who did not attend an advanced school, tended to be regular line officers. From 1955 to 1982, 37 generations of 959 lieutenant colonels and colonels plus 109 junior officers, completed the Higher Arms Course under the auspices of the Escuela Superior de Guerra.[86]

Two schools are noteworthy among the more recently established applied schools. The first is Air Tactics, created in 1993 to train officers for leading commando groups and small tactical air units.[87] The second is the Center for Army Air Force Studies' advanced course in information analysis. This course teaches officers methods for producing better intelligence. The course covers national intelligence system doctrines, secretariat of national defense research methodology, general political analysis, Mexico's political system, major political actors, and the media.[88]

Among influential naval officers, the Escuela Naval Militar and the Heroica Escuela Naval Militar in the port of Veracruz has an influence that is equal to the Heroico Colegio Militar's impact on the army. The school's history extends back to 1825. The original Escuela Naval Militar was established April 21, 1897. It added the Heroica in 1949 in memory of the cadets who fought against the North American invasion of Veracruz in 1914.[89] In addition to training officers to command and providing them with technical naval skills, the navy defines the academy's goals as including: "inculcating the highest levels of honor, loyalty, honesty, discipline and duty as the supreme values of a navy professional."[90]

What distinguishes the navy from the army and air force is its comparatively small size and, therefore, the small size of its cadet classes. Not a single class between 1924 and 1965 (when 96 percent of the officers in our sample graduated) exceeded 50 graduates, and many in the 1930s and 1940s consisted of fewer than 30 students.[91] Consequently, not only was each class closely linked to each other, similar to the graduates of the Escuela Médico Militar, but graduates of one class were also likely to know many cadets from younger and older overlapping classes. Currently, the Escuela Naval Militar program is twelve semesters over six years. The first three years are a preparatory program to train students in physics and mathematics. An examination of the class lists also illustrates that more than one generation from the same family is represented among its graduates, and similar to the Heroico Colegio Militar, numerous siblings, in some cases as many as three, have graduated from this institution. Its directors, in a pattern similar to that of officers who directed the Heroico Colegio Militar, have gone on to hold top posts in the fleet and on the naval staff.

Because of small classes, a significant percentage of graduates from any given class (similar to what can be found among the classes at the Escuela Superior de Guerra), reaches the rank of admiral. For example, the class of 1942 produced two secretaries of the navy: Ricardo Cházaro Lara (1976–1982) and Miguel A. Gómez Ortega (1982–1988), as well as the assistant secretary under Cházaro and the oficial mayor under Gómez Ortega. Gómez Ortega recruited two other appointees from his own class. Cházaro recruited his oficial mayor and another collaborator from the following class. The class of 1947, which consisted of only 30 graduates, counted among its cadets one secretary of the navy, three oficial mayores, and three department heads. That pattern has not change among more recent classes. The 1956 class of 26 cadets produced another secretary of navy during the Zedillo administration and an oficial mayor, plus three department heads.[92]

Educating the Officer Corps 171

It is also important to note that for a brief period during World War II, the Escuela Náutica Mercante of Mazatlán, on the Pacific coast, was converted on June 12, 1941, to the Escuela Naval Militar del Pacífico, and the Escuela Naval Militar became the Escuela Naval Militar del Golfo. Those students in the merchant marine program who were members of the 1938–1941 class were given the option of completing a fifth year of training, which would make them eligible to become regular naval officers. Of the thirty-two members of the first eligible class, five chose to become naval officers. To increase the output of naval officers during the war, this program continued until January 1, 1948.[93]

Surprisingly, in seven years time this school produced a number of highly successful officers, including Admiral Luis C. Ruano Angulo (secretary of the navy, 1990–1994), the assistant secretary of navy from 1988–1994, and the assistant secretary of navy from 1982-1988. Each of these graduates recruited fellow cadets to their administration, including seven other high-ranking officers from this school. Recent naval cadets have made good use of technology to maintain their future ties. The 1990–1995 class created its own website in order to maintain contact with each other, calling itself the "Generation of Change."[94] Five other post-1976 classes have similar sites.

The impact of the two army and navy military academies on socialization and career patterns has been illustrated extensively. There is no question that the role of these military academies has been crucial in determining many of the features of Mexico's civil-military relationship, even when compared with other significant variables identified in Mexico or other societal settings. The extent of these consequences will be analyzed in the conclusion of the following chapter, after exploring the complementary effects of higher military education in Mexico's war colleges with that offered in the United States.

CHAPTER EIGHT

Higher and Global Officer Education

Education, the primary source of professionalization, is a controversial variable in the civil-military relationship. Students of the Latin American military have argued that higher war colleges have buttressed, rather than discouraged the military from intervening in civilian affairs. Elsewhere in Latin America, well into a period of democratization, one leading scholar concluded that "neither modernization nor professionalization have resolved the problem of military intervention in politics."[1] Important arguments have been put forward to explain why war colleges might reinforce or have little impact on interventionist tendencies. As war colleges expanded their curriculum to include political, economic, and social topics, they allegedly encouraged graduates to view themselves as competent to handle governmental responsibilities.[2] Second, increasing the contact with civilians as fellow students and teachers produced important linkages with politically ambitious civilians who shared similar ideological predispositions. Third, the war college culture may be crucial to establishing the principle of subordination to higher command within the military and, ultimately, to the civilian president. Fourth, it has been alleged that extended military training abroad affects the officer corps' values and behavior, including its subordination to civil authority. Fifth, one cannot understand the composition of the officer corps' leadership without understanding who is accepted and who graduates from the army and naval war colleges. Military college graduates provide the vast majority of individuals in the top ranks of both services. Sixth, war colleges have replaced initial military academies as a locus for recruitment among top ranks. Therefore, a complete sociology of the officer corps is possible only if one understand who teaches as these institutions and when each officer graduated.

The role of the Heroico Colegio Militar has been altered gradually since the founding of the Escuela Superior de Guerra, Mexico's first war college. General Joaquín Amaro, the single-most-important figure in professionalization, organized the Escuela Superior de Guerra in 1932 while serving as the first director of military education.[3] Succinctly, its purpose was to train company and field grade officers for battalion or high command and staff duties, and to develop and disseminate tactical and strategic doctrine.[4] The individual given the responsibility for actually setting up the program and designing the curriculum was Major Luis Alamillo Flores, who was sent on a study mission to United States military schools.[5] Prior to his mission, Alamillo Flores spent three years at the Higher Naval College in Paris, where he earned a staff and command diploma in 1931. He also studied at the Sorbonne and the Engineering School of Versailles.[6] Before the founding of the Escuela Superior de Guerra any officer desirous of advanced military training studied in France. Tomas Sánchez Hernández, who followed Alamillo Flores as the Escuela Superior de Guerra's second director in 1934, trained at the Higher War College in Paris and at the Fontainebleau artillery school.

Officer Formation at the Escuela Superior de Guerra

The original Escuela Superior de Guerra staff of nine instructors included one civilian and officers from the rank of captain through colonel. Three of the original instructors had studied in France, and all of these three later directed the Escuela Superior de Guerra; two also directed the Heroico Colegio Militar.[7] The Escuela Superior de Guerra program attracted the cream of the officer corps as both instructors and students. The program was particularly attractive for officers interested in teaching the technical fields of artillery, engineering, communications, and the like. According to the Secretariat of War and Navy, of seventy-eight applicants, five senior and twenty-six junior officers were accepted in the first class.[8]

The Escuela Superior de Guerra acquired immediate prestige in the military community. Joaquín Amaro enhanced its image by publicly labeling its students as a "real elite."[9] Graduating from the Escuela Superior de Guerra gradually took on greater importance for officers wishing to obtain the rank of general. The school's standing within the Mexican officer corps parallels an attitude expressed in 1949 about the Brazilian Higher War College; attendance there became "added insurance for upward mobility."[10] Students of other Latin American militaries have suggested that higher military education in and of itself altered military officers' level of confidence when in the company of better-educated civilians.[11]

The benefits of attending the Escuela Superior de Guerra are several. A graduate, identified by the acronym DEM (Diplomado de Estado Mayor) after his rank, receives an additional salary increase which continues throughout his active duty years. More important than this financial consideration is the enhanced potential for promotion: "It is generally recognized within military circles that without a diploma from the Superior War College, the highest rank an officer can hope to achieve is Lt. Colonel. On the other hand, most graduates are practically guaranteed the rank of Colonel, and many eventually become general officers."[12] In reality, this statement is generally but not entirely true. Small numbers of officers have consistently reached three star rank without passing through the Escuela Superior de Guerra, even within the traditional military occupational specialties in Mexico. Furthermore, numerous officers from other occupational specialties (who are not allowed to attend the Escuela Superior de Guerra) reach two star rank. Personal ties with superior officers who typically have those credentials, make these exceptions possible.

The number of higher-ranking army and air force officers with diplomas from the Escuela Superior de Guerra has risen steadily over time. A complete picture is available from promotion records (Table 8-1). The consistently upward pattern from 1958 to 2002 is apparent although the most significant changes occur in the late 1970s and 1980s. It is also important to note that, by 1990, all but one colonel in the major army fields of infantry and mechanized cavalry were Escuela Superior de Guerra graduates.[13]

In the 1980s, analysts argued that department heads and zone commanders, reserved only for brigade and division ranks, were required to graduate from the Escuela Superior de Guerra.[14]

Table 8.1 Colonels Promoted to General Who Graduated from the Escuela Superior de Guerra

Year	Percentage with the Diplomado de Estado Mayor (DEM)
1958	33
1964	37
1970	49
1976	51
1981	59
1990	67
2002	74

Note: All of the officers promoted to division and brigade general in 2002 were Escuela Superior de Guerra graduates, as were all the brigadier generals in the traditional military occupational specialties.

Again, this is not actually the case. Among field commanders the figures are even less comprehensive than for national defense staff. For example, in 1983, of the fifteen garrison commanders, a third did not have DEMs. Among zone commanders, the most important field position, 17 percent lacked this education in 1987. The most influential post in command of troops in Mexico is the regional commander. Among all the regional commanders from 1982 to 2003, only five officers were not graduates. In 2003, twenty-eight percent of the department heads at the Secretariat of National Defense were not DEMs, including the directors of military justice, social security, war materiel, engineers, communications, health, and information technology; none of these were in the traditional combat arms fields. The percentage of DEMs among garrison, zone and regional commanders has increased since the 1990s. Only 13 percent of garrison commanders, 5 percent of zone commanders, and no regional commanders were missing the coveted diploma in 2003.

Graduating from the Escuela Superior de Guerra is not a prerequisite to reach the rank of brigadier general; nearly 40 percent of army officers who reach this rank have not obtained a diploma. It is also clear that, even in the 2000s, it is still possible to reach the rank of brigade general and to hold top defense posts without being an Escuela Superior de Guerra graduate, but it would be nearly impossible to do so in the traditional combat arms specializations. By 2003, over 90 percent of brigade generals and 97 percent of division generals in the combat arms areas were graduates.[15]

It was not until 1982 that a diploma from the Escuela Superior de Guerra became the equivalent of a college degree. Despite formal certification as a licenciatura (a professional degree), an Escuela Superior de Guerra diploma still carries less prestige than its civilian equivalent.[16] Technically, this should be the case since it is only a three year program with a narrow curriculum; the typical civilian degree in Mexico consists of a five year program. Nevertheless, among officers themselves, the DEM is considered a crucial credential for advancement.

The Escuela Superior de Guerra came into legal existence on January 18, 1929. The school did not open its doors until April 15, 1932. Its articles of formation were precise about the original curriculum and instruction. The mission was simply "to impart to the officers and commanders of the Army military knowledge of a higher quality, enabling them to exercise higher command."[17] The curriculum was offered over a three year time span. The articles of formation also made clear that instructors were to be military officers exclusively. Current regulations allow civilians who have taught for two years and have graduate education to teach; few have. Interestingly, Article 12 stated that the curriculum was designed to promote ample initiative on the part of the student officers. Contrary to Article 12, observers and graduates of the Escuela Superior de Guerra have always characterized the instruction there as a program stressing rote memorization.

Its purpose, according to one analyst, was "to prepare combat officers for command staff duties and officers of the supporting services for technical staff duties. In a separate two year course, air officers were trained for corresponding assignments."[18] Two other important changes occurred. First, the Escuela Superior de Guerra opened a special one-year course in higher war studies to both selected civilians and officers of the rank of lieutenant colonel and above.[19] This could have produced significant implications for the socialization and recruitment of military officers. For example, commandants of the Brazilian Higher War College, believing the aim of their school was to train those who would influence government, graduated 599 officers, 224 businessmen, 200 civil servants, and 107 professionals by 1966. Thirty-nine of these graduates were politicians.[20] In practice, the Mexican experience has been quite different. Although civilians were to be given selected access to military schools, no evidence in the graduation records or information about the educational backgrounds of leading politicians suggests that any civilians attended the Escuela Superior de Guerra. The primary source of diversity among Escuela Superior de Guerra personnel is not civilian students but military officers from other countries, including the United States.[21]

The Escuela Superior de Guerra has not promoted officer contacts with influential civilians. Its primary means of influencing officer attitudes about social and political issues, and possible interest in political activities, is curriculum content and values. The values emphasized have been critical to officer socialization. Some commentators hold that changes in content have contributed to shifting officer interests.

In the 1970s the Escuela Superior de Guerra introduced greater diversity in curriculum and staffing, adding many new courses and inviting distinguished lecturers from the academic, political, and business worlds. In 1973 a course in military and humanities juridical investigation was offered to further high-level commanders' understanding of "National Doctrines."[22] However, according to reports by visiting military officers, most military doctrine, at least through the 1990s, was not integrated into their system but based on out-of-date U.S. Army manuals.[23]

Interestingly, it is only the third year of the curriculum that is critical to the political formation of the officer. Only 6 percent of the first-year courses and 5 percent of the second-year courses focus on general strategy or other sociopolitical subjects. The first two years reinforce discipline and group behavior but distance officers from nonpolitical studies.[24] In the 1990s, officers in the second year of the program agreed with this assessment.[25] However, members of the third-year class, who have been well-screened at the Escuela Superior de Guerra, are exposed to an entirely different emphasis. Course content devoted to strategy and related subjects rises to 30 percent. Civilian lecturers existed, but were rare. The graduating class as a whole produced a study of a sociopolitical problem, actually traveling to a field location.

In the late 1990s, the style and content of the teaching underwent a significant change. According to one source, the most interesting situation was the addition of a guest speaker program, emulating a long-standing component of the prestigious Colegio de Defensa Nacional.[26] The source reported that this program "took off his last year at the Escuela Superior de Guerra. . . . there are rumors that the director was replaced because he brought in too many PAN (National Action Party) speakers. Vicente Fox was scheduled to deliver a presentation and was cancelled one day prior to the presentation." In the classroom, the officer reported that respected instructors were openly suggesting that the students vote for PAN in the 2000 presidential election. "Some of my peers told me that the PRI had had their chance for the last 50 years and now it was time for someone new. Some of the more radical officers said a revolution was necessary. I must say there was no widespread support for Cárdenas."[27]

The potential impact of the Escuela Superior de Guerra is affected by the percentage of active duty officers who actually pass through its classrooms. Officers who enter the Escuela Superior de Guerra are graduates of other military academies, usually the Heroico Colegio Militar. Student officers are required to have had two years of experience commanding troops, but few have held actual command positions. Over the years, class size has been quite limited, both in terms of who is accepted and, equally important, who graduates. In the 1947 class, for example, twenty-four officers began the program but only nineteen graduated. In the 1960s and 1970s, average class size was twenty-four; in the early to mid-1980s, it averaged thirty-four. Ackroyd estimates that, in the 1980s, only 7 percent of the officer corps were Escuela Superior de Guerra graduates.[28] At that time, these were the only officers who had received some exposure to political and social issues in the classroom. The 1989 entering class, scheduled to graduate in 1992, began with eighty-one officers; one year later only forty-one were still enrolled, and some of those would drop out by the end of the year. The graduating class of 1990 consisted of 37 Mexican officers, including two naval and two air force officers, plus six foreign officers, including a representative from the United States.[29] In the mid-1990s, total enrollment in the three-year program was 143; in 2001, it had risen to 174.[30]

The percentage of Escuela Superior de Guerra graduates in the entire officer corps is small but their presence in the higher ranks and top defense posts is overwhelming. For example, if we take the 1956 graduating class as representative of the halfway point for most of the generals in our sample and examine their careers, we find that of seventeen lieutenants, captains, and majors (including the air college), fourteen were known to have reached the rank of brigadier general or higher (eight made two or three star rank), and two, the rank of colonel.[31] This means that an Escuela Superior de Guerra diploma is extremely useful to career advancement. Over three-quarters of the Escuela Superior de Guerra graduates will reach that rank. This pattern is repeated in earlier and later classes.

If we examine generals in important defense posts it is clear how important the Escuela Superior de Guerra experience has been for military decision makers. Of officers whose full educational backgrounds are known and who enrolled in the Escuela Superior de Guerra rather than a legal or medical program, the figures are remarkable. In the Fox administration, every top appointee graduated from the Escuela Superior de Guerra. In the previous administration, all but one key officer (a combat engineer) were alums. In the 1980s, they accounted for over 90 percent of the top appointees in the Secretariat of National Defense and, even as early as the 1970–1976 administration, 85 percent were graduates.

The patterns found at the Escuela Superior de Guerra are duplicated at the Navy's equivalent higher war college, the Centro de Estudios Superiores Navales. The navy created this institution in 1970 to train naval officers in a wide array of specialties, awarding them the military equivalent of a civilian MA degree. Between 1970 and 2001, 3,200 officers have passed through its classrooms. The variety of specializations and the numbers of officers graduating from them is worth noting. The program variety and class sizes are in contrast to a narrower curriculum and smaller class sizes at the Escuela Superior de Guerra. The programs at the Centro de Estudios Superiores Navales and numbers graduated are:

- Higher command and national security (246)
- Staff and command (600), naval command (131)
- Communications (1299)
- Communications and information technology (83)
- Information technology (122)
- Naval logistics (120)
- Communications for marines (44)
- Human resources (14)
- English (398) and other foreign languages (143).[32]

The Navy's staff and command program consists of three different courses. In the 2001 graduating class there were 89 graduates, 38 in naval command, 34 in staff and command, and 12 in high command and national security. Seventy-nine of these officers were naval personnel, including one admiral, 42 captains (colonels), and 36 other officers. The class also included representatives from the secretariats of foreign relations, government, social development, Petróleos Mexicanos (the government petroleum company), as well as foreign officers.[33]

According to the Navy's education regulations, every graduate of the Heroica Escuela Naval Militar promoted to Corvette Captain must complete the naval command course. It is designed to train junior officers in the principles and doctrines of the art of war and apply that knowledge in command of field units. This specific requirement explains why so many officers are enrolled in the course. On the other hand, the staff and command course, one similar to the Escuela Superior de Guerra course, is highly selective. It is designed for naval officers who have reached the rank of Captain or higher, or comparable foreign officers. This course is designed for officers who eventually will hold top staff positions. For example, the first class had 14 officers who graduated in 1971. This class produced two oficiales mayores, two chiefs of staff, and three assistant secretaries of the navy.[34]

The Centro de Estudios Superiores Navales offers a third course. It is billed as the navy's highest level course covering higher command and national security. It is comparable to the Colegio de Defensa Nacional's course in national security, and was initiated in 1982, the same year the Colegio de Defensa Nacional produced its first graduating class. These classes typically average 10–15 senior officers. Five of the first ten graduates were known to have held top positions in the late 1980s and 1990s. The first civilians appeared in the 1989–1990 class. This course enrolls rear admirals and captains, as well as invited civilians from government agencies represented in the national security sub-cabinet. These latter two courses, because they are highly selective, produce small, intimate classes.

A comparable survey to that of army graduates can be constructed for top naval officers serving in recent administrations. Because two naval secretaries served during this period, a listing of top leaders from the 1988–1994 period offers an opportunity to analyze a fairly large group. The importance of both the Heroico Escuela Naval Militar, as we suggested earlier, and the Centro de Estudios Superiores Navales is apparent. What is unique about the naval war college experience, however, is that naval officers can attend any of the three command schools, as well as the shorter courses mentioned above. At least eight of the officers who served in top posts from 1988 to 1994 held two MA's from this institution. Furthermore, an even larger group of officers (eleven individuals) returned to the program for a Ph.D.

The importance of these two figures are that officers generate increased possibilities of contact with one another because they attend the Centro de Estudios Superiores Navales during multiple periods of time. This is an opportunity which army and air force officers do not share. In the case of this administration alone, sixteen admirals (a third of the total) attended this school two or more times. It allows officers from different generations to make contact with each other. The same can be said for the Colegio de Defensa Nacional, where army, navy and air force officers of different generations meet. These figures also indicate the higher levels of education found among naval officers as compared to army officers, suggesting the importance which navy leadership has given to military education. These figures do not include the numerous MA's earned abroad, primarily at United States war colleges.

An American officer who attended the Escuela Superior de Guerra in the 1990s believed that the unstated goal of the program "is for the student to pay his 'dues' which leads to the enjoyment of a lifelong career as a special class of officer who will receive faster promotion and a lot more pay. This represents an oligarchy over the Mexican army and exercises almost complete power over all those who are not graduates regardless of rank."[35] Another officer reported that the Escuela Superior de Guerra diplomas were so prestigious that he had witnessed graduates of lower rank giving orders to a non-graduate of higher rank. This officer claimed that graduates share little respect for non-graduates.[36] It is also apparent that many graduates express little respect for their air force and naval peers. An American officer in the program found that air force officers who used to be in the regular Escuela Superior de Guerra were not respected, and the one naval officer in his class labeled himself "a foreigner." These attitudes suggest a potential for inter-service rivalries and conflict.[37]

Because attrition rates for the three-year program at the Escuela Superior de Guerra are rather substantial, it is helpful to know what type of officer persists. For example, approximately 59 percent of the 1982 graduating class dropped out by the third year. Another American officer, who attended the Escuela Superior de Guerra in the 1990s, noted that only 60 percent of the starting class actually graduates.[38] According to Daniel Mora, the officer who makes it through the program is one who is "willing to totally subordinate himself to the system, and . . . is an individual who knows what rewards the system has to offer."[39] Mora also believes that the officers sure to make it through are sons, or family friends, of generals. Of the officers completing the first year in the 1989 entering class, seven of the remaining forty were the sons of generals.[40] In the United States, children of military officers also demonstrate lower attrition rates.[41]

An examination of the generals in our sample reveals some support for this statement in Mexico. Nearly a third of all generals in our sample had fathers in the military; however, among generals who were Escuela Superior de Guerra graduates, the figure was substantially higher: nearly half. If Mora is correct (he limited his description to graduates with ties to high-ranking officers), it is an important indication of how the officer corps at the highest levels becomes more self-selecting. William S. Ackroyd also believes that the Escuela Superior de Guerra filters out officers from the lowest socioeconomic backgrounds.[42] However, an analysis of background data of generals on the basis of graduation from the Heroico Colegio Militar only versus the Heroico Colegio Militar and Escuela Superior de Guerra combined reveals that 90 percent of their graduates were middle and/or upper class, compared with 85 percent from such backgrounds who did not attend the Escuela Superior de Guerra.

The military and political content of the Escuela Superior de Guerra curriculum is important to providing a complete picture of the future general officer, but the impact of the program on officer discipline is even more significant. Even the founding philosophy of the Escuela Superior de Guerra, as laid out in Article 13 of its articles of its formation, implies that the staff are to serve as behavior models for the students.[43] Over the last twenty years, graduates of the program have made the following observations:

> There is no question that the most significant contribution made by the Escuela Superior de Guerra to the education of the officer corps is to enhance obedience to authority and self-discipline. Comparisons can be drawn with the political leadership. Nowhere do Mexican politicians formally learn that they must subordinate their views and their behavior to their superiors. Many observers note the self-discipline and silence maintained by the past PRI political leadership in times of personal and systemic crises. To be successful in the Mexican political system, an individual takes the blame for the benefit of the established institutions. It can be argued that the informally learned, self disciplined behavior demanded by the political establishment is a value shared with military officers who receive it from the Escuela Superior de Guerra.[44]

Despite the intensity and prevalence of this socialization process, an officer in the program in the late 1990s reported that his fellow students viewed this complete subordination at the Escuela Superior de Guerra as unnecessary, but realize that the only way they can change the system is to acquiesce to the system's requirements until such a time as they are in a position to make changes.[45] U.S. officers who have attended the Escuela Superior de Guerra provide an insightful, cohesive view of the experience. They suggest that the officer who becomes "part of the system" meets three conditions: "First, the dominant value would be the individual's willingness to subordinate himself totally to those in authority over him. Coupled with this would be the expectation that submission will be rewarded and independence will be severely punished. Finally, the officer's primary motivation would be to secure the rewards that the system has to offer."[46]

How is subordinate behavior instilled in these officers? According to observers, many instructors teach in an arrogant style. One officer-observer who attended the Escuela Superior de Guerra in the early 1980s reported that the instructors often "strutted onto the platform much like peacocks."[47] The instructor conveys to the class that he alone is the supreme authority. Students who offer differing or contradictory opinions are criticized or belittled in front of their classmates. Students are not encouraged to take the initiative intellectually. Students are not evaluated on their subject matter knowledge but on their willingness to subordinate themselves to authority, that is, to the instructors. One officer described the experience of a student who refused to drink with an instructor: he had not failed any examinations up to that point but promptly failed the next seven. The instructor, with the support of six colleagues, washed the student out of the program.[48] Classes since 1958 have reported an even higher level of instructor harassment that is intended to "wash out all but the truly loyal."[49]

The personal influence of instructors is overwhelming. A class soon learns that the members must make sacrifices as a group to ensure their instructors have a positive attitude toward them as a group. Dziedzic provided an example of students in one class trying to decide how much of their instructors' meals they could pay for on a training exercise. Their discussion was not about whether the class should offer something but, rather, how much.[50]

Such a climate leads to another unprofessional characteristic. Group work and cheating on examinations or individual projects are the norm rather than the exception. One officer describes their class work as follows: "The assignments are done by other officers or NCOs who are paid to have a paper ready—all the papers turned in are the same. It is physically impossible to do the assignment, so they are forced to participate in this fraud."[51] This pattern had not changed as of the last decade. Another officer noted:

> Students are forced to memorize incredible quantities of text to negotiate the over 120 examinations the student takes during the academic year. The students know they cannot do this, which leads to a cheating culture.

The testing process becomes a vicious circle with the instructor's job to make the tests impossible and the student's job to find any means to pass the test. This led one instructor to acknowledge that the job of the student is to cheat and the instructors to discover the student cheating.[52]

Student officers at the Escuela Superior de Guerra do not consider this to be unethical but simply a means of surviving.[53] Instructors share the same attitude. According to Article 129 of the internal Escuela Superior de Guerra code, such behavior is strictly forbidden.[54] In addition to the cheating culture, this pattern reinforces rote memorization in the extreme while drastically lowering the quality of learning. As one officer reported, "They waste most of their time. For example, they spent time learning what a page was. This is an example of the stupidity of the learning process."[55] Such silly classroom antics explain why civilian professionals do not equate an Escuela Superior de Guerra graduate with university graduates in the civilian world.

Many students who drop out of the Escuela Superior de Guerra program are those who refuse to subordinate themselves to the instructors, or who find some of the norms unacceptable. Others leave because they have not completed their studies and are failing academically. As one Escuela Superior de Guerra instructor observed: "Those who do not conform to the way of thinking–those who want to rebel–are weeded out."[56] The consequence of this emphasis is to produce an officer who obeys orders without question and without regard to the order's legality. As one officer of a recent Escuela Superior de Guerra class described it, "Our classmates are, for the most part, articulate, intelligent, and professional in their own minds; the system is grinding them down *to complete obedient servants incapable of making a decision while at the same time co-opting them with financial rewards*" [emphasis added].[57]

The program also does not encourage a military culture in which relatively high ranking officers take the initiative in making recommendations, nor are they directly involved in the decision-making process. Because a hallmark of the Mexican military culture is subordination to civilian authority, a concept repeated constantly in armed forces literature, the implication is that officers will remain loyal to the president. On the other hand, there is a weakness in this arrangement. If the supreme military commander were to deviate from presidential authority, he might be able to control his subordinates, given their unquestioning acceptance of the hierarchical structure.[58]

The likelihood of such behavior happening increased in recent years as the attitudes of younger officers toward civil authority appeared to have grown critical following the 1988 election. One source argued that many officers in the army claimed that large numbers of their colleagues could outperform their civilian counterparts in cabinet level agencies. Recent

Escuela Superior de Guerra classes give the impression that they are not strongly loyal to the political leaders and, when asked in class to rank the most important object of their loyalty, they ranked army above country. The formal oath taken by Escuela Superior de Guerra graduates, expressed in the December 1987 Escuela Superior de Guerra regulations, states that a staff officer's loyalty, honesty, dedication, and other qualities redound to the benefit of the armed forces first and the country second.[59]

Apparently, leaders of the institution, and perhaps the secretariat of national defense, learned of these critical attitudes toward civilians among the late 1980s graduating classes. The typical class in the 1980s consisted of 8 majors, 25 first captains, and 12 second captains. After 1988, in response to this perception, the class accepted for the 1989–1992 generation, "became the first since the 1940s to include large numbers of lieutenants, on the assumption that they were more easily socialized than somewhat older officers. Members of this class indicated that harassment increased, intended to weed out all but the truly loyal."[60]

The Escuela Superior de Guerra experience, translated into personal contact, becomes significant to recruitment and career advancement. It is not surprising, given the almost combat like antagonism and survival rate of the officers who complete the program, that this experience, for the elite of Mexico's office corps, replaces the Heroico Colegio Militar in importance. In this connection, a Mexican officer recalled:

> At the Heroico Colegio Militar a bond developed among the members of my class and this has been maintained during our early years of commissioned service. It lost its importance, however, when I became a War College graduate. My War College classmates became more important to me. My War College bond replaces the Heroico Colegio Militar bond. I haven't forgotten my Heroico Colegio Militar friends, but they are not as important as my War College friends. Having graduated from the War College we now have an advantage over non-graduates. It is like being a member of an exclusive fraternity. The personal relations that are created serve to keep us informed of what is happening within the military, help us to obtain personal favors, favorable future assignments, and it will serve to help us in future advancements.[61]

The same type of personal relationships are generated among Mexican politicians at the National University and, more recently, at prestigious private universities. Half of all influential politicians in the last thirty years formed such ties at college.[62] As with military officers, as educational credentials increased, graduate programs became significant. However, a difference exists between the officers' Escuela Superior de Guerra experience and the politicians' graduate school training. Nearly all high-ranking officers pass through only one program; politicians not only attend more than one institution but increasingly attend school abroad. To Mexican politicians, being a member of an exclusive fraternity frequently means having a master's or doctorate degree from Harvard, Yale, MIT, or Stanford. Such shared out-of-the-country experiences—just like an earlier generation's shared experience at one national university—not only brings individual politicians closer together and helps to develop the close bonds of trust essential to political equipos but is given special recognition by older mentors with similar credentials.

These personal connections in the military, perhaps like personal connections in political life, have produced many promotions and assignments which are not deserved. The impact of this characteristic in the armed forces is different from that in politics. General Garfías argues that when such results occur in the military, they are more unjust than similar circumstances among leading politicians. The reason for this is that the armed forces are so much smaller that practices which violate meritorious promotions damage respect for institutional structures and the military hierarchy.[63] A second point worth noting in making the comparison with politicians is that within the military command structure, unlike the higher civilian bureaucracy, officers are extremely restricted in their capabilities to appoint staff. The officer corps, through its extreme emphasis on centralizing decision-making in the hands of the secretary of national defense and a handful of collaborators, has made it structurally difficult for an officer to create his own *equipo* or group, thus substituting institutional loyalty for personal loyalty to a specific officer.[64]

Teaching at the Escuela Superior de Guerra enhances the personal contacts of an officer by associating him with a select group of colleagues who as students are likely to make field grade, and with a smaller group of instructors who also increased their opportunities for advancement.[65] For example, four of Enrique Cervantes Aguirre's collaborators taught with him at the Escuela Superior de Guerra. Five officers in the 1982–1988 administration taught together at the same time as the chief of staff. The importance of teaching at the Escuela Superior de Guerra, both in terms of career prestige and contacts, can also be demonstrated through an analysis of Escuela Superior de Guerra directors from 1932 to 2003. Of the twenty-eight directors, thirteen are known to have risen to top positions after their tenure, among them two assistant secretaries, two chiefs of staff, three oficiales mayores, three department heads, and three zone commanders, and two were chiefs of staff prior to their appointments.

The same patterns can be found among instructors and directors of the Centro de Estudios Superiores Navales, the naval equivalent of the Escuela

Superior de Guerra. It is viewed as a prestigious stepping stone to higher positions. One of its directors went on to become secretary of the navy, another assistant secretary, and two others, chief of staff. Given its small classes, any administrator would have close contact with staff and students alike.

Colegio de Defensa Nacional

For a Mexican military officer today, the culmination of educational professionalization occurs at the Colegio de Defensa Nacional. The school was opened in September 1981 in the old Colegio Militar in Popotla, Federal District. General Félix Galván provided the initiative for the Colegio de Defensa Nacional after expressing concern that his top military collaborators were typically uninformed about broader social, economic, and political issues. He assigned five officers, under the leadership of General Vinicio Santoyo Fería, to design and implement the curriculum.[66]

The Colegio de Defensa Nacional curriculum focuses on providing skills in national defense strategy formulation, force development, international affairs, economics, and politics to a select group of senior colonels and generals or naval captains and admirals who are marked for service in the highest military posts.[67] It is divided into five sections: politics, economics, international affairs, society, and national security. A lieutenant colonel is in charge of each subject area. The first class of twenty-nine army, navy and air force officers graduated in 1982. Officer students were required to hold the rank of colonel or its equivalent. This first graduating class was particularly distinguished; 21 officers reached division rank and 4 became full admirals. The remaining 4 were brigade and brigadier generals.[68] A former director of the Colegio de Defensa Nacional recalled that politicians were extremely worried and upset about the establishment of this program. Obviously, they were concerned that the Secretariat of National Defense was trying to train people to replace them in power.[69]

By the time an officer reaches the Colegio de Defensa Nacional, his career pattern is determined. Consequently, the Colegio de Defensa Nacional does not perform the same type recruitment function possible through the Heroico Colegio Militar and the Escuela Superior de Guerra or their naval equivalent institutions. It nevertheless brings together officers who would not otherwise have crossed paths at either the Heroico Colegio Militar or the Escuela Superior de Guerra. The Colegio de Defensa Nacional can accomplish this more effectively because of its small class size, a feature it has maintained for all of its years in existence. Its class size in recent years include: 1999, 27 (ten generals, one admiral, eight colonels, one navy captain, seven civilians); 2000, 24 (three were women and three were civilians);

2001, 28; and 2002, 33 (eight civilians).[70] As of 2003, 54 civilians had attended this institution, including six women. The agencies represented among those graduates included foreign relations, government, social development, treasury, public education, and communications and transportation. For example, among the generals reaching top posts as early as the 1982–1988 administration, six were members of the first graduating class, including General Santoyo Feria himself. Eight other officers graduated from the second, third, and fourth classes. Two of the officers had attended the Heroico Colegio Militar together in the 1950s, but none graduated from the Escuela Superior de Guerra at the same time. The Colegio de Defensa Nacional served to bring together a new group of officers rather than only reinforcing the previous contacts of just two officers.

In 1988, after less than eight years of operation, the importance of the Colegio de Defensa Nacional can be seen in its remarkable presence in the backgrounds of the most influential generals. Of the ninety-three top staff officers at the National Defense Secretariat, 46 graduated with M.A. degrees in national security from the Colegio de Defensa Nacional. The majority of zone commanders in 1990 passed through its classes, too. By 2004, 60 percent of the top officers in the secretariat of national defense were alumni. Some five hundred officers and civilians have graduated since its founding, and nearly all division generals are alumni. Graduates of advanced war colleges in South American countries are more influential nationally because they often end up in high political offices. This is the case with alumni of the Brazilian Escola Superior de Guerra, after which the Colegio de Defensa Nacional is patterned.[71] Of course, this is not the case in Mexico.

Directors of the Colegio de Defensa Nacional also have achieved prestigious career posts within the military. Vinicio Santoyo Fería, who served as first head from 1981 to 1982, quickly joined the 1982–1988 administration as chief of staff after completing the Colegio de Defensa Nacional course simultaneously with his directorship. Similarly, General Salgado Cordero became chief of staff from 1988 to 1994, immediately following his directorship of the Colegio de Defensa Nacional. General Ruiz y Esquivel became oficial mayor of the secretariat of national defense in the 1994–2000 administration. It's most distinguished director career wise is Division General Gerardo Clemente Vega García, who became the secretary of national defense under President Fox in 2000. Interestingly, since he became secretary of national defense, younger officers credit him with opening the door more widely to higher professional studies.

The Colegio de Defensa Nacional experience produces important implications for the training and orientation of the general staff. For the first time in recent history, Mexican leaders began to think through the formulation of an overarching national security policy.[72] The content of national security themes is considered elsewhere. What is most important here is the exposure of generals to a heavy dose of political topics and civilian instructors. This brings the Peruvian experience to mind.[73] The implication, according to scholars, is that increased exposure to political and social literature (which increased dramatically before a military coup) is linked to an increased interest in the officer corps in political matters, including intervention in political affairs. There is absolutely no evidence of such a link in Mexico with this or any other military academy program.

The Colegio de Defensa Nacional curriculum evolved in fits and starts and without a clear mission. According to General Vega García, a former director, several explanations apply: "One of the difficulties with the evolution of the Colegio de Defensa Nacional is the fact that it had eight directors since 1981 [between 1981 and 1988]. There was no direction in the program because of the lack of continuity in the leadership. In the early years of the program, the various directors thought of national security as solely a military topic. This was unfortunate because this excluded the importance of these other areas I mentioned earlier. But since 1988, I would define all aspects of Mexican society and the state as part of national security, including war strategy, state theory, and world leadership."[74]

Vega García, who directed the program from 1988 to 1992, defined its mission as including the following goals: "What we are essentially doing at this institution is preparing officers to understand the political, social, economic and other characteristics of our society, and not to replace civilians in power. This has never been our goal, and never will be the goal of this institution. We are not trying to train people so that they have the capacity to govern. This is not the purpose. We are trying to train people so that they have the capacity to do their jobs more effectively and to understand what is happening in the civilian world. Since 1988 we have included civilians in this program in order to broaden their approach as well as our approach. And of course, we have included naval and air force officers throughout the history of the curriculum."[75]

The college "has fostered one of the most systematic and serious analyses on security. Probably, this process was influenced by the constant presence of Mexican lecturers of different political leanings."[76] One source noted that, during a single year in the 1980s, the Colegio de Defensa Nacional devoted thirty-nine conferences to national and international situations, thirteen to national policy, ten to national security, fifteen to administration of the respective secretariats, and twelve to high-level staff studies—and those were only a portion of the overall offerings.[77]

The Colegio de Defensa Nacional also has played an unusual role in providing cohesion within the army. One of the serious deficiencies identified in the 1995 *Army and Air Force Development Program* were divisions within the army stemming from favoritism toward certain military occupational specialties. One division general offered the following insight about its selection of students:

The Colegio de Defensa Nacional tries to focus on the whole armed services without giving any special emphasis to any single one of the services, and to act as a group, which is reflected in turning in a single document as representative of a generation's (graduating class) thinking. Most of the graduates leave here with this broader mentality, rather than representing their own particular service.[78] Such collaboration among army, air force and navy officers has produced significant policy consequences. According to General Vega García, who attended the Colegio de Defensa Nacional, the fact that he shared a common experience with Admiral Marco Antonio Perot González, the Secretary of Navy, who graduated from the Colegio two years earlier, produced a closer relationship with the Admiral, who he has known for years, affecting positively the relationship between their respective services since they both took office in 2000.[79]

The Colegio also is the one military institution which provides army officers direct linkages to civilian students, most of whom are mid-level careerists in agencies sharing national security interests. Potentially, this was one of the most important changes in military education because, for the first time, civilians received an education in a military academy. This pattern has existed in other South American war colleges for many years. The eighth generation, the class of 1989–1990, was the first to include civilian students. The 1989–1990 class consisted of 26 military (including two from the navy and three from the air force), consisting of 10 generals, 14 colonels, one navy captain, one rear admiral, and two civilians. All of the military graduates became or already were generals and admirals.[80]

The first two civilians allowed into the program were from the secretariat of foreign relations and the programming and budgeting secretariat. In the 1990–1991 entering class three civilians joined the program, two from foreign relations and one from programming and budgeting.[81] Instructors who have taught at the Colegio de Defensa Nacional believe that the civilian students are treated equally and as respectfully as are the officers, and are viewed as professionals. Officers viewed these fresh linkages between civilians and the officer corps in a variety of ways. One view was that it would demonstrate to prominent civilians that "high-ranking officers in the military are not as ignorant as the civilians perceive them to be."[82] Another view is that it will also have positive consequences by providing civilians with an opportunity for understanding the Colegio de Defensa Nacional and its program.[83]

The inclusion of civilians does not suggest that it necessarily brings them closer to the officer corps' views and attitudes. One recent graduate believes that the backgrounds of the two groups are so distinct that it explains their differences. He suggested that civilian politicians and military officers sometimes are using different meanings for the same word, implying a different vocabulary. More importantly, he noticed a significant difference in their respective conceptual views. He found the officer corps formulates their ideas along a continuum of military policy, followed by strategy, and then tactics. Civilian politicians, on the other hand, approach it from strategy first, then policy, followed by tactics.[84]

The type of civilians invited to serve as lecturers at the Colegio de Defensa Nacional are intellectuals or professors respected in their fields. One of the striking characteristics of the program is that even individuals known to have direct connections with Central American guerrillas were asked to address the students; instructors report no automatic prejudice against contrary ideological views. Not only do officers read their published works, but they listen closely to their lectures and ask questions. In fact, one instructor reports that the officers in charge of the politics curriculum believe their course on student movements and mobilization is extremely important.[85] The Colegio de Defensa Nacional does maintain a policy of not inviting speakers who are actively involved in electoral politics.

The key factor in choosing a regular civilian instructor—as distinct from a guest lecturer—was the degree to which the military trusted the individual. Three criteria appeared to apply. A person's position might favor his inclusion in the program; for example, a cabinet secretary is interested in having material from his agency represented in the curriculum. The second criteria, trust, is typically determined by a personal relationship: kinship or professional ties. For example, one instructor, who began teaching there in 1983, shortly after the program began, was invited through a friend who directed the National Institute of Public Administration and had several military officers in a MA program.[86] Another instructor was chosen because he, too, had a connection with the military. His grandfather, who was a revolutionary officer, served as an aide on the staffs of General Alvaro Obregón and General Plutarco Elias Calles. Several other instructors believed that having a personal tie to the military, either social or through kinship, was crucial in their invitation to teach there. The third criteria is professional or intellectual merit. The reliance on special ties to the military appears to have declined significantly in recent years. Students report that their teachers have no special ties to the military and that civilian advisers for the curriculum are fairly permanent.

The ambience at the Colegio de Defensa Nacional is substantially different from that at the Heroico Colegio Militar and the Escuela Superior de Guerra. Despite the fact that the students are colonels and generals, they exhibit great respect for the civilian instructors and conduct themselves with dignity. Like students at the Escuela Superior de Guerra, they do not typically engage in intellectual debate in the classroom, despite prompting from some civilian instructors. Some instructors report that individual officers approach them during breaks for spirited give-and-take. The typical format is an hour of instruction, followed by a ten minute coffee break, followed by another hour of instruction. Considerable intellectual exchange also occurs between guest instructors and the lieutenant colonels in charge of the courses.

Increasingly, the majority of Colegio de Defensa Nacional lecturers are civilians, including some foreigners (for example, most of the prominent foreign military attaches speak to their classes), and a seminar format is used. The bibliography includes numerous sources from Latin America and the United States. The instructors who diagnose the general social, economic and political context are largely civilians. These lecturers include division heads, assistant secretaries, and cabinet secretaries. For example, the entire cabinet spoke to the 1989–1990 class during the course.[87] The caliber of the instructor was on par with that of the prestigious Colegio de México or the Autonomous Technological Institute of Mexico.

What is equally important to note is that the increase in civilian lecturers, regular or guest, has been accompanied by an increase in the percentage of civilian students. As noted above, in the 2002 graduating class, nearly a fourth were civilians. As instructors suggest, the officers who participate in the program, including the section chiefs, have excellent social relationships with civilians, eating meals with them regularly and going out for drinks. These social relationships are reported to be crucial to ties between the officer corps and civilian government officials as both move up the ladder in their respective institutions. General Vega García, Fox's secretary of national defense, considers increasing the number of civilian students an important priority of his administration. He believes that the officer corps was originally skeptical about including civilian students, but that it has made "an important contribution to increasing knowledge about the military in the civilian world since much of their information is inaccurate or incomplete."[88] The National Defense Secretariat also has been making use of political analyses by Mexican and foreign authors, including translated books, my own included.[89] Aguayo reported that, after 2000, it began inviting "qualified academics who were awkward for the old regime."[90] Thus, the Colegio de Defensa Nacional introduces a new linkage between civilian and

Higher and Global Officer Education

military leaders. Indeed, one leading analyst believes that the increased contact between military officials and academics from the civilian world, a program in which the Colegio took the lead, contributed to shortening the conflict in Chiapas.[91] It is not sufficiently broad to substitute for the political-military officer's role in years past, but it has potential significant positive consequences for the relationship in the twenty-first century.

Globalizing Officer Attitudes

The socializing role of professional education, whether it applies to the officer corps or any other leadership group in Mexico, cannot be understood unless one considers the impact of educational experiences abroad. In fact, no other force has exercised such an impact on leadership ideas and strategies as foreign education. Foreign education can be viewed as a decisive benchmark separating most older and younger generations among Mexican elites. These influences have the potential for affecting civil-military relations. Mexico has always been susceptible to these influences; distinguished Mexicans have traveled abroad to study since the post-revolutionary era. What has changed since the 1970s is the proportion of Mexican leadership studying abroad and the location of their studies. With the exception of Catholic bishops, the officer corps has kept pace with all other leadership groups in the level of their training abroad. What is most unique about the Mexican military experience is that, among all leadership groups in the last three decades, they are the most likely to have studied in the United States. Among all elites born before 1945 who studied abroad, only 35 percent did so in the United States. But among those born after World War II, 50 percent spent time north of the border. Among younger Mexican leaders, seven out of ten studied abroad.

Since the 1920s, selected officers have studied abroad after attending Mexican military academies. During the early post-revolutionary years, some officers studied in France. The roots of such training can be found in the revolutionary years, especially among officers who became the core of the future army and air force. Of the generals who were born between 1880 and 1890 and who remained on active duty after 1940, only 11 percent trained abroad—in equal numbers in Europe and the United States. The figure increased in the next generation to 18 percent but the geographic distribution remained the same.

The United States, although an enemy of Mexico in the nineteenth century, gradually superceded Europe as the most popular location for foreign military training. The post-revolutionary group of officers, as in so many other instances, set a benchmark figure for training abroad: Thirty-six percent left

Mexico for training, and 85 percent of them went to the United States. The next generation, those born between 1910 and 1920, traveled in even larger numbers. Nearly 50 percent of this generation received foreign training, all but 2 percent took it in the United States. The United States continued to dominate the foreign training of generals in command positions into the 1990s and 2000s. Fully 42 percent of the generals in our sample of top officers trained abroad, 38 percent in the United States, 3 percent in Europe, and 1 percent elsewhere.

The same pattern can be found among naval officers, but their training abroad is more extensive than among army officers. Similar to air force officers, they have maintained stronger ties to other countries and to naval programs in the United States. Even those officers born in the 1930s or earlier exceeded the percentage of recent army officers who have studied abroad. Sixty-one percent received training abroad, 53 percent in the United States. Among younger naval officers born in the 1930s and 1940s, 70 percent have studied abroad, half in the United States and half in Europe and Latin America.

The above figures suggest that U.S. military training programs are only behind the Heroico Colegio Militar, the Escuela Superior de Guerra, the Colegio de Defensa Nacional, the Escuela Naval Militar, and the Centro de Estudios Superiores Navales in the formation of the highest ranking Mexican officers. Over all, Mexican officers have received precious little training abroad.[92] An examination of the National Defense Secretariat *Memorias* confirms this assertion. Around 5 percent of all officers in the 1950s and 1960s studied abroad.[93] The reason for this pattern, according to officers educated abroad during that period, is that the secretariat never expressed a coherent policy regarding foreign studies; officers had to compete for scarce fellowships on their own initiative.

For all officers trained abroad, the United States has played a crucial role. Of the 546 Mexican soldiers who received advanced training between 1950 and 1968, 306 (55 percent) studied in the United States between 1964 and 1968, the formative years of the Mexican military educational system's modernization.[94] They took courses in two broad subject areas: the establishing of military schools and counter-insurgency warfare. This pattern was repeated between 1971 and 1976.[95]

What is significant, however, is that a much greater percentage of high-ranking officers, those who reached the rank of general, were sent abroad. Between 1978 and 1998, 4,173 Mexican soldiers trained abroad. What is remarkable about this figure is that 61 percent of these individuals did so during the first four years of the Zedillo administration, reflecting the dramatic increase in emphasis on professionalization, illustrated by advance foreign training.⁹⁶ Air force officers who, like their naval peers, tend to study abroad more frequently and in the United States specifically, were extremely well-represented during those same years. Fifty colonels or above, 1,138 other officers, and 165 enlisted men studied in the United States during that four year period. Nearly twice as many air force as army personnel have studied in the United States under President Fox, despite the fact that the air force accounts for only a small percentage of the total army/air force personnel. The emphasis on such educational experiences continued into the Fox administration. In 2001 alone, 1,363 members of the Mexican armed forces were enrolled in courses in the United States.⁹⁷ General Vega García, Fox's secretary of national defense, has made advanced studies abroad one of his priorities. Importantly, however, Mexican leadership is choosing these courses more carefully and concentrating on administrative skills in staff and command courses, rather than focusing on combat training.⁹⁸ Mexico is much better represented than the rest of the region. According to Sam Fitch, a leading expert on the Latin American military, only 0.39 percent received training from 1969–1971 and 0.16 percent from 1987–1989. In the 1990s, the United States was training approximately 2,000 Latin American military yearly.⁹⁹

A relationship exists between the type of training high-ranking officers receive, and whether or not they proceed abroad. While nearly a fourth of all generals born before 1940 did not graduate from the Heroico Colegio Militar or its equivalent, that was the case for only 1 percent of those sent abroad. The same pattern can be found among Escuela Superior de Guerra graduates, but not nearly so exaggerated. Interestingly, in terms of career experiences, a much higher percentage of officers who were section heads, four times as many, end up studying abroad, suggesting a preference for officers with more extensive staff compared to field experience.

There is substantial evidence to suggest the importance of foreign training and career success. Not only do over half of all top generals have such experience compared with only 5 percent of all officers, but certain military occupational specialties have received an unusual amount of foreign influence in their training. Not surprisingly, technical military occupational specialties (MOS's) are the most well represented among foreign-trained generals. Within the National Defense Secretariat, 59 percent of the pilots have received U.S. training, the most of any group, followed closely by the medical corps, with 54 percent.¹⁰⁰ Even higher figures exist for foreign training in all countries. In contrast, the infantry, the backbone of the army, has sent only one-fifth of its top officers to the United States. These figures are significantly higher among younger officers. This might be explained by the fact that, for some time, soldiers scoring the highest on various tests during basic training at the Heroico Colegio Militar were channeled into the more technical specialties. Because an officer needs a language capability and competes through examination for selection for foreign training, it is only logical that the more able officers would be over-represented in such specialties.

The Mexican military considers foreign training important for technical reasons and as a significant credential for leadership. By 2002–2003, 1,910 officers from all services were studying abroad.[101] In the past, however, most officers did not believe that foreign training was advantageous to their career but was useful to them only personally. In fact, it can be argued that training abroad was assigned as a financial reward, rather than providing special expertise. According to knowledgeable sources, before the 1980s the idea of sending officers abroad was not part of a preconceived educational program. Rather, it was a response to opportunities made available by foreign countries and the desire of the Secretariat of National Defense to maintain good relations with their armed forces. Despite empirical evidence to the contrary, in the past officers received the impression that the secretary of national defense discouraged foreign training.

Since the early 1980s sending officers abroad has been part of the military's larger educational goal. Between 1965 and 2003, 5,871 members of the military studied outside the country.[102] Such training is not a substitute for graduating from the Escuela Superior de Guerra. Advanced military education in Mexico remains a prerequisite to command. Officers chosen for such training are also chosen in larger numbers for foreign training. This is illustrated by figures demonstrating that, of the army generals who had studied only in Mexico, 38 percent were Escuela Superior de Guerra graduates; of those who had studied abroad, 51 percent had obtained the coveted DEM. Figures are even higher among recent generations of generals selected to study in the United States; over 90 percent of the officers born after 1940 who took courses in the United States were Escuela Superior de Guerra graduates and an equal percentage also had completed the Colegio de Defensa Nacional program. A similar pattern can be found among naval officers.

Officers higher in the hierarchy have studied in the United States. An example of this can be clearly seen in data provided by the Department of Spanish at the U.S. Military Academy, West Point, which has maintained an exchange program with the Mexican army since 1947.[103] Of the 16 officers about whom we can find information and who served on the exchange during the first thirty years of the program, during which time they could have risen to senior ranks, at least twelve reached two or three star rank, two became assistant secretary of national defense, and one became oficial mayor of national defense.

The United States military school and program best represented among older, top army officers in Mexico (based on the numbers who completed the program) is Ft. Leavenworth's Staff and Command School, an extensive 40 week course. Forty-two Mexican officers have graduated from this school since the first officer completed the course in 1956. A third of these program graduates have reached three star rank.[104] All but one of the Mexican officers who studied at Ft. Leavenworth were also Escuela Superior de Guerra graduates. Similar to the West Point visiting instructors, they have also gone on to highly successful careers. This is a flagship course taken by United States officers on their way to higher command.

The other institution which is well represented in the educational backgrounds of elite army officers and top naval commanders across all recent generations, is the Inter-American Defense College. This program was established in 1962 by the Inter-American Defense Board, located at Ft. McNair, Washington, D.C. It is similar in scope to the NATO Defense College in Rome, and can be accurately described as a truly inter-American institution. It offers material at a war college level and its faculty is employed by the Board, not by the United States Department of Defense.[105] Its curriculum includes labor organizations, social security, human communications, education, religion, housing, and health in the Western hemisphere. Guest speakers from United States colleges and the government give frequent lectures. The officers work in small groups in the afternoon, focusing on various problems. As a part of the course, each student writes a research thesis and presents it to their classmates.[106] Since 1962, with a few exceptions, an army colonel and navy commander have been enrolled each year.

The secretary and assistant secretary of the navy from 1982 to1988 graduated in the class of 1964 and 1965 respectively, included in their administration a high percentage of fellow Inter-American Defense College graduates. These men included their oficial mayor, chief of staff, director general of the navy, president of the laws and rules commission, inspector general and four other department heads. This suggests that the top four officials in the navy highly valued this training in their leading administrators. No other educational program, army or navy, comes close to that level of representation. Three assistant secretaries of national defense and another secretary of the navy are alumni. One hundred and two Mexicans have enrolled in this course since its inception.[107] Beginning with the 1996–1997 class, a representative of the Mexican foreign service has attended the college, creating a significant potential networking tie between future civilian and military leaders, duplicating the pattern found at the Colegio de Defensa Nacional.

Ironically, one of the most potentially influential sources for networking among civilians with an interest in military affairs, as well as with representatives of the officer corps, is the Center for Hemispheric Defense Studies, also located at Ft. McNair. It was founded in 1997 to educate civilians for positions in the defense establishments of Latin American countries.[108] Mexicans in attendance at seminars instituted since 1998 include members of congress, congressional staff, academic specialists on the armed forces, journalists, human rights leaders, and representatives of the armed forces.

Until 1984, a greater number of Mexican officers attended the School of the Americas at Ft. Benning, Georgia or Ft. Gulick, Panama Canal Zone. From 1940 to 2002, 320 members of the Mexican armed forces studied at Ft. Gulick, and 513 at Ft. Benning. The vast majority of Mexican officers who have studied at the School of the Americas, however, have taken short, specialty courses, most of which are several weeks in length. Data from the United States Department of Defense for 1997–1998, and 1998–1999, illustrate the distribution of Mexican personnel in such courses. In recent years, the School of the Americas offers only two courses longer than ten weeks. These are its command and general staff course, patterned after the same course at Ft. Leavenworth. It is 40 weeks in length and taught in Spanish. Typically, two Mexican officers are enrolled in this class. The school also offers a 4-month advanced combat arms course. Again, only several Mexican officers are enrolled in this class during a given year.[109]

Mexican officers have studied at numerous other United States military colleges. For example, a number of naval officers have graduated from the U.S. Naval War College in Newport, Rhode Island. Three Mexican navy secretaries are graduates of that institution. From 1978 to 1998, fifteen officers from the rank of Lt. Colonel to Lt. General have graduated from the U.S. Army War College in Carlisle, Pennsylvania, although only one has reached division general rank or held a top national defense post.[110] Many air force officers have attended courses at major U.S. air force bases, including programs at Randolph and Lackland Air Force bases in Texas, and Nellis Air Force base in Nevada. Seven out of ten top air force officers born after 1930 either studied extensively in the United States or served in the attaché office in Washington, D.C. Air force officers are distinguished from the army and navy peers by the number of times they have been sent to the United States and in the diversity of locations where they have trained.

In 2003, sixty-six officers were studying abroad, 56 percent of them with the U.S. army or air force. Most officers received advanced training with foreign militaries. The most important sources of that training, after the United States, is Latin America. Interestingly, the most influential country is Colombia, where five officers are receiving training, followed by Argentina and Chile. It is likely that the increased presence in Colombia is a reflection of Mexico's leadership wanting some members of their officer corps to have first-hand experience with the extensive problems Colombia faces with guerrilla warfare and drug-trafficking.

The fundamental issue foreign training raises for understanding the Mexican armed forces and civil-military relations, is the impact foreign training has on the formation of the officer corps, and the attitudes of the officer corps toward their role in society and their relationship with political leaders. This has been a controversial subject among Latin American officers trained in the United States.[111] The School of the Americas has generated intense controversy for decades because some of its Latin American graduates participated in notorious human rights violations. Critics of the School of the Americas assert that the U.S. training was responsible for those abuses.[112] When the Department of Defense investigated these charges, it discovered that the Southern Command and the School had used improper materials in training Latin American officers from 1982 to 1991. The improper materials included some passages "which appeared to condone or could have been interpreted to condone practices such as execution of guerrillas, extortion, physical abuse, coercion, and false imprisonment. The Department of Defense has removed all such texts and passages."[113] It does include a specific political bias as part of its mission: to promote democratic values and, since 1990, respect for human rights. Human rights materials have been incorporated in every course since 1990.[114] In recent years critics have focused on the argument that graduation from the program conveys prestige and power to those officers upon returning to their home institutions.[115]

In spite of the extensive experience shared by many top Mexican officers in the United States, it is doubtful that those experiences resulted in a cohesive, measurable influence on Mexican military policy or civil-military relations. The empirical evidence on this issue is ambiguous and sparse.[116]

Convincing arguments exist which temper possible influences from training experiences abroad. First, most of the courses taken by Mexican officers are short in duration, 1–2 weeks, and technical in nature, allowing for little interaction with United States instructors. Second, officers who graduated from courses taught in the Panama Canal Zone, the case until 1984, received their instruction in Spanish and in a Latin American setting. These two conditions discourage the impact of new ideas from a different cultural and professional perspective.[117] Third, the existing pre-conditions in Mexico ran counter to United States social and political ideas, and brief periods of training, especially in the case of mature adults, are not likely to displace existing beliefs about the role of the military in society or its relationship to the civilian population.[118] However, individual instructors, both inside and outside the classroom, can reinforce perceptions that encourage specific attitudes and behavior.

A RAND Corporation evaluation of the effectiveness of international military training in the United States, the most comprehensive evaluation of actual socializing consequences, concludes that such training has "almost no influence over . . . civil-military relations," and exerts only marginal influence, positive or negative, on the officer's home nation's development.[119]

Despite the explanations which diminish these socializing experiences from abroad, and the difficulty in identifying qualitatively what has been taught in the last four decades, careful analysts of these training programs suggest several possible results. These influences may well have significant professional and political consequences but, because they are not direct, they are easily overlooked.

The greatest impact of United States training on these officers may well be the legitimacy of exploring and discussing opposing views. Learning strategies used in U.S. military academies are totally new to Mexican officers. The ability of these officers to openly explore alternative ways to solve operational and strategic problems is completely counter to the rote memorization we have described at the Heroico Colegio Militar and the Escuela Superior de Guerra.[120]

Until 1995, no evidence of such an approach existed at Mexican military academies below the Colegio de Defensa Nacional level, yet the Colegio's own approach might well be the product of officer experiences in the United States. It is worth noting that the national defense secretary who created this school served as assistant military attaché in Washington, D.C. and lectured frequently at the Inter-American Defense College.[121] The Inter-American Defense College shares many similarities in its approach with Mexico's Colegio de Defensa Nacional.

Because the Colegio de Defensa Nacional produces the cream of the crop among recent officers reaching general rank, it legitimizes methodological approaches and curricular orientations previously ignored in Mexican military academies. As suggested earlier, strong evidence exists of significant changes occurring at the Escuela Superior de Guerra since the publication of an internal national defense document in the summer of 1995. This document specifically criticized severe failures in domestic military education and called for increased training in the United States. Recent directors at the Escuela Superior de Guerra have begun to emulate the Colegio de Defensa Nacional approach, bringing distinguished civilian speakers, including nationally prominent politicians, to lecture to the student officers. These presentations sometimes raise serious criticisms about civilian leadership among these officers, and may, in turn, encourage potential criticisms of civil-military relations.

The second potential source of influence is through personal contact with U.S. military personnel as students or instructors in these training programs, or with foreign military attaches in their countries. These contacts provide "myriad opportunities for the U.S. to communicate its policy preferences and its view of local politics."[122] In the 1950s and 1960s, the years most Mexican officers studied abroad, the dominant U.S. ideological message was opposition to local and global communism, consistent with the Mexican military's own perception of communism as anti-national, anti-Catholic, anti-Western, and anti-military. In the 1980s and 1990s, the U.S. concentrated on the strategy of low intensity conflicts, focusing on domestic threats to national security including drug trafficking, terrorism, and guerrillas, and on the need to win the "hearts and minds" of the non-combatant population. This was a new and important argument for promoting democracy and respect for human rights.[123]

Third, the requirement to speak English in order for Mexican officers to come to the United States is an indirect means through which educational participants expose themselves to external intellectual influences going well beyond strictly military topics. Officers whose second language becomes English open the door to literature unavailable in Spanish.[124] A revealing example of this is my own earlier book on the Mexican military which, for political reasons, was never published in Mexico. National defense headquarters widely circulated an unpublished version throughout the general staff.[125]

There is little question that selected Mexican officers are affected by their experiences in the United States. It is evident that they have carried back some intellectual currents which slowly filter down through the armed forces. Those influences appear strongest in domestic educational programs, primarily at the Colegio de Defensa Nacional.

As the larger political context in Mexico became increasingly open, these influences have reinforced the methodological shift favoring pluralism, paralleling that trend in the body politic.[126] This shift is part of the broader influence of globalization, which incorporates international attitudes about civilian political culture. Such international conceptualizations, including ideological conflicts, are often viewed by professional Latin American officers as threats to military nationalism and national values.[127] Expressed differently, in the Mexican context, the army is trying "to combine its traditional anti-Americanism with the necessities of change originating from the globalization process."[128]

Attitudes toward civil-military relations largely remain determined by professional training at home. Attitudes toward some non-military tasks, such as using the military to fight organized crime and carry out the war against drugs, can be attributed to international influences,[129] but not necessarily to ideas originally learned from educational experiences abroad. Instead, those policy choices have likely been reinforced in selected courses taken by Mexican officers abroad.

The Changing Role of Professional Education

Military education has played a multifaceted role within the Mexican officer corps. The Heroico Colegio Militar and the Escuela Superior de Guerra have exercised a critical influence in officer formation. The discipline and subordination to authority essential to Mexican civil-military relations have been learned through a militarily-controlled socialization process. The extreme level of subordination not only sets Mexico apart from most other militaries but is among the most important variables in explaining the civil-military relationship.

The two schools unquestionably play a critical role in internal recruitment and career success in all recent administrations. The Escuela Superior de Guerra has superseded the Heroico Colegio Militar in this capacity and like similar civilian schools, relationships are formed among instructors and students, as well as within both groups. On the other hand, the Heroico Colegio Militar, Escuela Superior de Guerra and, to a lesser extent, the Colegio de Defensa Nacional have ensured the educational separation between civilian and military groups. The Colegio de Defensa Nacional's recent decision to allow a select number of civilian public figures into the classroom, and its heavy use of civilian instructors—many also from the public sector—mirrored in the navy by the Centro de Estudios Superiores Navales, establishes a narrow but important bridge between Mexican politicians and the officer corps. This pattern is being reinforced abroad in seminars offered by the Center for Hemispheric Defense Studies in Washington, D.C. These recent linkages have already contributed to changing views within the officer corps—especially among the navy brass since 2000—and are likely to exert even greater influence as these channels mature and the actors reach influential positions in the civilian and military leadership.

Events in Chiapas in 1994 produced a series of consequences which have led to changes in the structure and curriculum of the military's advanced educational system. The increasing reliance on civilians as instructors, and the incorporation of civilians in the Colegio de Defensa Nacional program, is in response to the *Army and Air Force Development Program*, which came out a year after the Zapatista uprising. One of the curricular changes which can be directly linked to the events in Chiapas is an increased emphasis on information technology as a skill and a strategy in coping with internal and external security threats. As I have argued elsewhere, their "experience with Zapatistas, who mastered the internet to battle the military in the minds of public opinion, rather than tactically on the ground, made a deep impression on the high command. As President Zedillo reported in his 1997 State of the Union, the military educational system began offering an entirely new computer engineering degree."[130] More importantly, the military incorporated information technology into their strategies.

The military academies are viewed within the military as crucial to their formation, and leadership positions as desirable posts in their climb up the officer ladder. We have noted the importance of directorships and teaching at the three major army/air force and the two counterpart naval academies. The reverence for the most notable instructors, or those who have contributed significantly to the evolution of the military educational system, is no better reflected than in the career of General Antonio Ramírez Barrera. He received a eulogy and a detailed obituary in the official armed forces magazine unlike any other officer during the last three decades. The article goes on to discuss his impact on numerous generations of officers.[131]

Finally, the curricula in these institutions have typically stressed military rather than broader social, economic, and political subjects. Changes in the Escuela Superior de Guerra since the 1970s and, more important, the structure of the Colegio de Defensa Nacional introduced these larger concerns into officer training, thereby increasing the potential for the military's greater knowledge of, interest in, and inclination for politics. There is no indication whatsoever that, as civilians make a beachhead in the military educational system as students and lecturers, and the curriculum has shifted to broader, non-traditional military topics, these changes have compromised the armed forces subordination to civilian leadership. Instead, it has contributed, along with other policy decisions, to decreasing somewhat the suspicions between civilian and military officials. The changes are making officers more sophisticated about complex political and social issues. In the larger democratic setting, the increased contacts deep within the military educational system and the broader shared preparation are essential to establishing stronger levels of trust. In order to learn to operate more comfortably in an open pluralistic political process, the officer corps needs to witness the behavior of its civilian peers and establish trustworthy personal links in the national security community. This has begun to happen nationally and internationally through military education.

CHAPTER NINE

Reaching the Top

The military promotion process can shed considerable light on civil-military relations. In terms of the framework we outlined in the first chapter, three essential components influence this relationship. First, individuals who rise to two and three star rank and provide the top leadership within the armed forces, reflect the credentials and behavior prior leadership values. To understand more clearly who composes that leadership, it is essential to understand their collective characteristics and attitudes. Second, the process by which such individuals rise in rank, as distinct from the characteristics which are favored by the process, are equally revealing. How they are viewed inside the military affects the cohesiveness of each branch of service, as well as their relationship to each other. Third, the involvement of outside actors and political institutions, including the president and congress, may play a significant and influential role on the caliber of the relationship between civilians and the armed forces and the military's respect for civilian leadership.

One of the most interesting aspects of military compared with civilian leadership is how one climbs the decision-making ladder. The least well-known aspects of the Mexican military officer are the qualities or experiences that encourage rapid promotion, upward career mobility, and appointment to a significant command. In many other Latin American countries, the existence of alternating parties in power, of civil-military political alliances, and of a strong political opposition in the Senate creates an environment conducive to greater civilian involvement in the promotion process. Since 2000, Mexico has been, for the first time, characterized by a political setting which makes similar influences on civil-military relations possible.

In the Mexican case, scholars have argued that the "absence of civilian interference in the internal matters of the military, such as promotion, discipline, and assignments may help explain the noninterventionist attitude on the part of the military."[1] Analysts had no data to test this interpretation, but it is well worth introducing because some detailed, empirical data now exist to test its validity for Mexico.

In contrast to Mexican civilian leaders, who depend almost exclusively on personal ties, military leaders appear to arrive at the top through a rather structured process in combination with personal ties. In the civilian world, young politicians, such as Presidents Zedillo and Salinas, can reach cabinet-level positions in a relatively short time. It would take a military officer an additional decade or more to obtain an equivalent position. For example, an army officer cannot become a military zone commander until he attains the rank of brigade general. As of 2005, two-star rank in the army requires at least thirty five years of service at the date of promotion. This means such an officer would generally be in his early fifties.[2] A state governor, perhaps the most analogous political position in the civilian world, could be in his thirties, depending on the minimum-age stipulation in a state's constitution. Moreover, a young civilian governor might have only five years of relevant experience, whereas a brigade general, as a consequence of a structured promotion process, will have five times as much.

Presidential Promotion Policies and Civilian Intervention

The Mexican government, in line with President Cárdenas's larger professionalization drive, introduced the first important military promotion criteria in the post-revolutionary era. Specifically, infantry officers who failed to pass a comprehensive examination in military science after 1936 were given the option of retirement or assignment to a remedial training center. Age-in-grade limits were imposed in an effort to eliminate untrainable officers who were blocking an educated generation's promotion opportunities. Lyle McAlister believes that the two norms—retraining and age in grade—were observed in the cases of lower- and medium-rank officers, but many revolutionary officers, through political influence or sentimental appeals, avoided these restrictions.[3] The instances of many older revolutionary officers who held positions long after 1946 support his interpretation.

The same year that Cárdenas introduced restrictions on older officers, younger officers were required to pass a Military Studies Committee examination for promotion.[4] Still, National Defense Secretariat records illustrate continued excessive numbers of officers, generals specifically. In 1920, when the army numbered 100,047 officers and troops, only 10 division and 20 brigade generals were on active duty, but so were 600 brigadiers. By 1930, after three important military rebellions (1923, 1927, and 1929) during which the government promoted loyal generals and exiled, executed, or retired rebelling generals, the highest ranks included 31 division and 128 brigade generals, but only 267 brigadiers. The government had reduced the total number of officers from 630 to 426, but it had also reduced the total forces to 72,556, so the percentage remained about the same. By 1951, at the end of Alemán's administration, the total strength of the army was only 50,409, but the senior officer corps had grown by 32 percent, equaling its highest post-revolutionary strength of 627 generals thirty years earlier. Moreover, the number of three-star generals expanded from 31 in 1930 to 83 in 1951, and brigade generals from 128 to 217, tremendous proportional increases.[5] Compared with the U.S. Army, Mexico's officer corps is swollen. In 1964, before the Vietnam buildup, the U.S. Army was comprised 864,000 enlisted men and 41,000 officers, for an-officer-to-troops ratio roughly 1:21.1. The number of American generals was 497 (.0005 percent of the troops), fewer than the number of active duty Mexican generals in 1951.[6] By 2004, generals and officers were still disproportionately over-represented comparatively, but the ratio of generals to all other personnel had declined significantly from one percent in the 1950s to two-hundredths of a percent under President Fox. The percentage of all officers to troops has basically remained static since the 1920s.

Miguel Alemán, the president who did the most to reduce military influence in politics in mid-century, did not use the promotion process to reduce the ratio of officers to troops. Instead, he tarnished his reputation among the officer corps by politicizing the promotion process.[7] The Alemán administration's military policies generated considerable resentment among the institution's established leaders and, in effect, failed to maintain the balance that had ensured the gradual depoliticization of the institution. In bypassing the aging revolutionary generals, effectively forcing the retirement of many, and promoting and appointing professionally trained young officers to key military posts, including the presidential chief of staff, Alemán alienated many of the military leaders who had been critical to professionalization efforts. Because of the allegedly arbitrary process in selecting new military leaders, newly promoted young officers who occupied many top command and administrative posts were disparagingly called *los generales de dedo*. Consequently, by the early 1950s, Alemán's policies threatened to renew the military's politization.[8]

Military sources note that the president's behavior, while unquestionably scandalous, more typically applied to his civilian friends, not to large numbers of career officers. The record bears out this interpretation. The fact is, most of the officers Alemán appointed as his top field commanders were experienced combat veterans born in the 1890s, a decade prior to his own generation. These men included three former chiefs of staff, and such officers as Joaquín Amaro, former national defense minister, and, most important, *the* senior division general on active duty; and Matías Ramos Santos, former assistant secretary of national defense and field commander from the 1920s through 1946. Among his field commanders, Alemán also included such notable transition officers as Adrian Castrejón and Bonifacio Salinas Leal, the youngest brigadier in the Mexican army in 1929. Both of these men rejected their revolutionary ranks and attended the newly reconstituted Colegio Militar.

At the level of the Secretariat of National Defense, Alemán appointed as secretary, Gilberto R. Limón. Limón had been director of military education under Cárdenas, director of the Colegio Militar under Avila Camacho, and assistant secretary of national defense in 1945. His three assistant secretaries were political-military officers. All were revolutionary veterans. Alemán's department heads were similar in background; most were brigade generals.

A year-by-year examination of Alemán's promotions reflects a similar pattern. During his administration, many senior officers were promoted to division rank. However, he also promoted six junior officers, members of the first generation of professionally trained men from the Heroico Colegio Militar. Most of their early-1920s classmates did not obtain important staff posts or zone commands until the 1960s and 1970s. Of the six officers, Alemán appointed three to important staff positions.

How, then, did Alemán acquire such a negative reputation? It must not be forgotten that Alemán radicalized Mexican civil-military relations when he came into office, extraordinarily decreasing military political office-holding. His abuse of the promotion process focused on staff bureaucracy, not line commands, especially presidential and specialized staff positions. The image the Alemán administration conveyed is the result of numerous notable cases, not an-across-the-board pattern. The cases were highlighted by the fact that his presidential chief of staff, General Piña, was exceptionally visible. The president's arrogant abuse of the promotion laws, and the awarding of general ranks to civilians, assured a negative image among the officer corps.

Senate promotion records tell the story of General Piña. On September 4, 1947, the upper house approved his promotion (recommended January 16) to the rank of colonel in the infantry. Two years later, without proper time in grade, the Senate approved his promotion to brigadier general. In 1952, as part of the regular September promotions, three months before leaving office, Alemán recommended him for two-star rank. However, instead of the Alemán-dominated Senate National Defense Committee, a committee dominated by career officers and revolution veterans examined the nominee's credentials.[9]

The committee members considered Piña's case not as an individual promotion but as representative of Alemán's violations. Citing army regulations requiring five years in rank before promotion to general, they declared that in the past such nominations had demonstrated obvious favoritism. They also noted that the president had sent out a circular suggesting that time in rank was not a prerequisite for promotion.[10] Admiral Otal Briseño urged the committee to recommend rejection to the full Senate because the army was "saturated with generals" and other officers, and that it would be disastrous to disregard regulations.[11]

When the committee made its recommendation to the Senate on November 7, 1953, heated debate ensued, one of the few such occasions. The general promotion policy received a thorough airing, as did the probable effect of the Senate's refusing to go along with the president. One prominent civilian senator, Aquiles Elorduy, a friend and professor of Alemán's, settled the matter: "I am a friend of Mister Piña Soria, but I never vote for friendship, I vote with the law. If this nomination is irregular, then it should be refused. That is all I ask." The vote was 50 to 1 against approval, and 51 to 0 against another recommendation for a promotion to colonel for the same reasons.[12]

Presidential intervention in the promotion process, especially actions contravening internal military requirements, too easily politicizes the military, even in a one-party-dominant system. An indicator of the Mexican military's politization in regard to the rank of general is the disparity in the time required for individual junior officers to attain that rank. A means of testing the universal application of promotion criteria is to analyze the length of time an officer requires to reach the rank of colonel, the key stepping-stone to the rank of brigadier general and higher. Three important patterns can be discerned.

The first pattern is that regular military officers have required, on average, about twenty-five years to reach the rank of colonel. Individuals serving after 1946 who rose to the rank of colonel in less than twenty years did so as veterans of the Revolution whose promotion rates were not regulated. This is why more than four-fifths of such officers were born before 1900. The second pattern is the considerable regularity of promotions for the majority of officers reaching the rank of general over a long period of time. Whether an officer was born in the first, second, or third decade of the twentieth century, he generally required twenty-five to thirty years to reach the rank of colonel. (The 2003 law now requires a minimum of 27 years.) The third pattern is that, for officers born since 1930, a radical change of time in grade occurs in order to make colonel. Officers born prior to 1930 required, on average, five or more years to make the grade of colonel than did approximately nine in ten of those born after 1930.

The promotion records of the generals in our sample suggests that modern military officers, even those reaching the rank of general, are promoted with considerable regularity. This pattern is so consistent that it becomes fairly easy to predict their promotion dates to brigadier general. In the past, analysts have stressed the promotion system's irregularity.[13] I argue that the most important finding of these data is the consistency in the promotion pattern among those who have been most successful in the officer corps. Unlike civilian leadership patterns, where people in their thirties can vault to top posts, no significant variations in time in rank exist among general officers.[14]

President López Mateos made the first concerted effort to reduce promotions to both colonel and general beginning in 1958. In fact, the rate of promotion drops nearly in half for both ranks. From 1958 to 1970 the rate of promotions to both ranks remained rather stable and significantly lower than previous levels. Under Echeverría an extraordinary upsurge in promotions occurred from an annual average of only thirty-nine promotions to general by his predecessor to eighty-three yearly. This is more than double the previous rate.[15] Echeverría also significantly increased the rate of promotions to colonel. This increased for both himself and his immediate successor the pool of officers eligible for the rank of general. No president from 1940 through 1994 comes close to Echeverría's promotion rates for both ranks. Surprisingly, López Portillo returned the pattern of promotions to a level comparable to that of Echeverría's predecessors; he averaged 45 generals and 56 colonels per year during his administration.

Table 9.1 Promotions to Colonel and General in the Mexican Army and Air Force, 1939–2003

Year	Colonel	General	Administration
1939	31	22	Cárdenas
1941	63	77	Avila Camacho
1946	74	72	
1947	50	87	Alemán
1948	75	64	
1949	53	101	

Table 9.1 Promotions to Colonel and General in the Mexican Army and Air Force, 1939–2003 *(Continued)*

Year	Colonel	General	Administration
1950	–	–	
1951	103	87	
1952	48	40	
1953	81	59	Ruiz Cortines
1954	108	51	
1955	19	83	
1956	81	70	
1957	75	112	
1958	13	30	
1959	49	28	López Mateos
1960	66	51	
1961	22	23	
1962	34	19	
1963	18	25	
1964	43	44	
1965	34	33	Díaz Ordaz
1966	24	11	
1967	49	36	
1968	52	65	
1969	58	43	
1970	43	47	
1971	65	91	Echeverría
1972	65	97	
1973	64	67	
1974	66	61	
1975	86	88	
1976	76	96	
1977	74	53	López Portillo
1978	61	55	
1979	61	48	*(Continued)*

Table 9.1 Promotions to Colonel and General in the Mexican Army and Air Force, 1939–2003 *(Continued)*

Year	Colonel	General	Administration
1980	66	52	
1981	41	26	
1982	34	44	
1983	53	52	De la Madrid
1984	60	46	
1985	80	64	
1986	96	79	
1987	74	62	
1988	72	71	
1989	64	45	Salinas
1990	78	63	
1991	95	61	
1992	100	70	
1993	105	60	
1994	113	104	
1995	83	81	Zedillo
1996	104	82	
1997	99	89	
1998	105	98	
1999	130	101	
2000	114	88	
2001	77	37	Fox
2002	88	53	
2003	6	78	

Note: All regular promotions occur November 20. Because the president takes office December 1, it is his predecessor who promotes the officers in the inaugural year of a presidential term. These numbers, where possible, attempt to include all promotions during the entire year. Figures for promotions vary among governmental sources. The most significant sources of data are the presidency, the secretariat of national defense, the official army/air force magazine, and senate records. When discrepancies arose, I have used the higher figure, in part to assure that both regular and irregular promotions are included.

In the past decade, the typical promotion process has followed a standard timetable. Upon graduation from the Heroico Colegio Militar, an officer serves two years as a second lieutenant and then three years as a first lieutenant. To be eligible for the rank of lieutenant colonel, an officer needs at least fourteen years on active duty (in the future he will require 23 years). Next he must pass a compuiter-graded academic examination.[16] Before reaching the rank of major, the typical army officer on track for general will have been selected to complete the three year program at the Escuela Superior de Guerra. Promotion to colonel is essential for reaching senior officer rank. At this juncture in an officer's career, military politics begin to play a more important role. At times in the 1970s, younger officers denounced higher-rank promotions as based on compadrazco (friendship).[17] The opinion of the secretary of national defense becomes decisive because it is the secretary who decides who will obtain these slots.[18] The president does not intervene in the process below the rank of colonel, in theory or practice.[19]

In the 1970s Franklin Margiotta interviewed Mexican officers. He found they were proud of the apparent fairness of merit-based promotions. Margiotta believed that the typical promotion pattern was eight years (including Heroico Colegio Militar time) for second captain, eleven years for first captain, fourteen years for major, eighteen years for lieutenant colonel, and twenty-two years for colonel.[20] To become a three-star general would require approximately thirty-five to forty years on active duty.[21] These figures square with the extensive promotion records I have examined for Mexican generals and for all officers. These findings and the official promotion figures are important because they suggest that the time a general requires to reach the rank of lieutenant colonel tends to be very similar to that of an officer who would retire at that rank.

It is no longer the case that most officers believe the promotion process to be fair and meritorious beyond the rank of lieutenant colonel. Obviously, some dissatisfaction with the process extends back to at least the time of the Alemán administration. As suggested above, reaction to Alemán's tampering concerns the issue of civilian interference in the most sacred component of military affairs, the internal promotion process. However, since Alemán's time, no other president has abused his authority in this way.

By the 1980s, complaints began to emerge that were focused on abuses by military authorities, notably the secretary of national defense. In the mid-1990s, complaints about the unfairness of the process spilled into the public arena. According to an army chat site on the internet, officers refer to some allegedly unfairly promoted figures as "paper generals." This is a term which is used in the army to allude to those generals whose career trajectories were based on favoritism by individual secretaries of national defense or lengthy service in the presidential military staff. This particular site notes the examples of Arturo Cardona Marino, Salinas's chief of staff (1988–1994), and Roberto Miranda Sánchez, who held the same post under Zedillo (1994–2000). The site claims both were promoted to division general without ever having commanded regular troops.[22]

The internal promotion process has become a policy issue of some importance. This issue started with the efforts by the Party of the Democratic Revolution to force congress to address this and other concerns inside the armed forces. In 2002, they identified a significant number of reforms to be incorporated in a proposed Promotion and Compensation Law for the Army and Air Force. Their report suggested the following problems related to promotions:

- The armed forces should function under a rigorous hierarchy based on strict discipline, and that this requirement is associated directly with the way in which promotions are awarded.
- Past behavior and control by internal groups has generated an institutionally detrimental situation and an increasing lack of confidence in the rotation of assignments inside the army.
- Preoccupation with the promotion process itself is associated with the level of discretion in awarding promotions and compensation.
- The Senate Committee on National Defense and the Permanent Committee of Congress has shown little care in ratifying military promotions and has, instead, converted it into a simple pro forma process.
- The proposed changes are necessary given the need for internal democratization in light of recent external, democratic reforms.[23]

Importantly, the Party of the Democratic Revolution made specific recommendations to rectify these internal problems. Under Article 2 of the original promotion regulations, the special committee recommended that the phrase "colonels and lt. colonels in conformance with applicable legal requirements" be added to the statement giving the president the power to promote generals. With this change of wording, the president would ultimately control the promotions of these two lower ranks, too. Furthermore, the Party of the Democratic Revolution recommend that the "secretary of national defense, with the agreement of the President, should authorize the promotions of majors, first captains, second captains, lieutenants and second lieutenants in conformance with appropriate laws," thus giving the president the authority to oversee these promotions as well. Under Article 29, which describes the president's authority over promotions to colonel and all three ranks of general, they would add the phrase "based on time served, length in rank, professional ability, good conduct, good health and physical ability, *to be judged by a board made up of the department heads of military justice, health, the chief of staff, and the director of the service or arms from which the person originates"* (emphasis added).[24]

They further specify that, to be promoted to lt. colonel or colonel, time of service should be at least 19 and 23 years respectively, including 4 years in the preceding rank. The professional aptitude of lt. colonels should be determined from at least one year in command of either an active unit of the service arm to which the officer belongs or an educational unit. The rest of the time in grade must be spent on military activities in their specialty. A colonel's ability should be associated with completing the Colegio de Defensa Nacional course, and year in command under the same conditions as a lt. colonel, and the rest of his time in grade in his specialty. For brigadier and group generals, or brigade and wing generals, time of service should be 28 and 32 years respectively, including five years in rank. A brigadier general also would be required to have commanded an active unit, similar to the two preceding ranks.[25]

These complaints addressed above were exacerbated by the creation of small groups of military officers who were closely identified with individual secretaries of national defense. According to General Luis Garfias, these so-called "mafias" were created under General Félix Galván (1976–1982) and General Juan Arévalo Gardoqui (1982–1988). Both used their authority to promote personal favorites, rather than relying strictly on meritorious performance and time in grade qualifications.[26] In an interview, Garfias called these groups "the third floor military," referring to the fact that it is the third floor where the staff and the secretary of national defense have their offices.[27]

Some specific examples of personnel abuses have recently come to light. Generals Enrique Cervantes Aguirre, Rodolfo Reta Trigos, and Francisco Quirós Hermosillo were considered to be intimate members of Félix Galván's group, who are allegedly known within the army as "the Pitufos," or the "Gnomes." All three served as adjutants when Galván was private secretary to General García Barragán when he was secretary of national defense (1965–1969). When Galván became secretary in 1976, he promoted his three friends rapidly. He made Quirós Hermosillo the youngest division general in the Mexican army. He promoted Cervantes Aguirre who, of course, became secretary of national defense in 1994. And, he promoted Reta Trigos through all three ranks of general, from brigadier to division general, in just four years.[28] By contrast, Cervantes Aguirre's predecessor, General Riviello Bazán, spent nine years in those same ranks.[29] As General Garfias notes, individuals who are given irregular early promotions are then on active duty as three star generals for up to twenty years.[30] According to one source, Cervantes Aguirre continued a similar tradition during his six years as secretary of national defense. Cervantes Aguirre promoted 60–70 percent of the division generals on active duty in 2000.[31]

The internal conflicts over promotion process abuses affected the appointment of the secretary of national defense. The machinations surrounding that selection process has spilled over into the general promotion process after the selected general takes office. The succession which has received the most attention in published sources—and generated the most severe internal conflicts in recent history—is the 1988 appointment of General Riviello Bazán. Initially, Riviello Bazán was not the favored candidate. In fact, he ranked in last place among the contenders.[32] The then secretary of national defense, General Arévalo Gardoqui, was trying to ensure his own favorites succeed him and actually removed Riviello Bazán as Inspector General of the Army/Air Force and made him the military attaché to Madrid.[33] As one analyst described the situation, "General Riviello Bazán was infantry, and it seemed that the selection was between generals Enrique Cervantes Aguirre and Rodolfo Reta Trigos. But because they were young, promoted quickly by Félix Galván above many others, and since they were typical examples of favoritism, there was a tremendous resentment and lack of acceptance. At the last minute, because of this, General Riviello Bazán was chosen."[34]

Because of the way in which Arévalo Gardoqui had treated Riviello Bazán prior to the 1988 designation, he in turn, according to sources, set out to punish those closest to Arévalo Gardoqui, including General José Francisco Gallardo, Arévalo Gardoqui's protégé, and at one time, the youngest brigadier general in the Mexican army. According to Gallardo, Riviello Bazán called together Arévalo Gardoqui's group and humiliated them. He left many "en la banca." Others who were willing to kiss up to him were promoted. Gallardo refused, saying he wasn't loyal to persons but to institutions when Riviello Bazán told him he should be as loyal to him as he was to Arévalo Gardoqui.[35]

The rank of colonel is the crucial milestone on the road to becoming a general. At this rank, prior to 2003, the secretary of national defense, with input from the official mayor, the chief of staff, and the inspector general, recommended officers to be promoted to the president, although the secretary of national defense has the last word. The president in turn basically signs off on those recommendations, as well as similar recommendations for promotions to general, and passes them along to the Senate. In addition, promotion to colonel technically requires time in service to be considered. The unstated requirements include being visible, being in the good graces of generals who are on friendly terms with the secretary of national defense, being recognized as a team player, and being considered wholly subordinate to the system.[36] For promotion to general, again prior to 2003, the same criteria apply, except that no minimum years in service are necessary, only time in grade between promotions.[37]

Positioning oneself within a bureaucracy is part of the promotion game. In this sense, the military is no different from any other organization or government agency. But in Mexico, top staff positions (including that of the secretary of national defense and secretary of the navy), are held by career military only and it appears that only military officers influence the promotion process. Even given qualities that tend to protect the military from civilian influences, there are two means through which civilian politicians might interfere with an officer's climb up the leadership ladder.

The most important potential source of civilian influence, as the well-documented abuses of Miguel Alemán imply, is the presidency. A president can intervene in three possible ways. First, in extreme circumstances, he can circumvent the organic law of the military, contravening actual regulations by promoting people who do not meet minimal requirements. This has been true of some national defense secretaries. Second, the president can promote people who even though they meet formal requirements may not be the most deserving. Because this has to do with subjective judgment and may not be widely practiced, it would be difficult to detect during any six-year period. The results of such promotions are likely to be balanced out by a different chief executive's prejudices, or those of a national defense secretary, in successive administrations. Third, it is quite possible that a president can employ his promotion authority to reduce or increase the size of the officer corps in response to his own feelings of political security and legitimacy.

Promotion records, as suggested above, reveal that, since Alemán, no president has abused his authority to contravene promotion laws for personal or political reasons. Presidents have indicated to the author that they typically accept the Secretary of National Defense's recommendations concerning the promotion lists. Similarly, presidents usually choose from a short list of generals recommended by the incumbent secretary for their own secretary of national defense.[38] In fact, Senate records show no similar cases from 1953 until 1999, when the PRI used its majority on the Permanent Committee (when congress was not in session) to promote general Domiro García Reyes, the officer in charge of security for assassinated president candidate Luis Donaldo Colosio. The PRD strongly opposed García Reyes' promotion.[39] The second form of influence does occur; it is a natural part of any agency's politics.

The third form of presidential interference can be measured explicitly. It can be reasonably hypothesized that the president used military promotions above the rank of lieutenant colonel to assure greater loyalty among the officer corps. It is only natural that a president would like to see promotions to the rank of general go to the steadfastly faithful officers, and key staff assignments and zone commands to generals in whom he has personal confidence.[40] There is absolutely no evidence during recent administrations that presidents exercised such influence on these promotions.

Presidential neutrality in this process can be explained by the fact that the loyalty of the armed forces to civilian authority has become a given in the Mexican polity over the years. As the military's professional leadership has become increasingly separate from that of civilian politicians, individual presidents have not had to concern themselves with whether or not the armed forces are loyal to them personally, nor are presidents likely to be personally acquainted with many high-ranking officers. As Miguel de la Madrid suggested, "In Mexico, the army is really a treasure for our society. We have a group, unlike many other countries, especially in Latin America, which is extremely respectful of civilian authority, and has behaved in an extremely disciplined manner."[41]

Presidents know more officers than do most politicians, because they meet many zone commanders during giras (working trips), and they meet them after being elected president or during the campaign, typically not before. Consequently, only in times of relative political instability, or when the president perceives the situation to be extremely unstable, would it be necessary for him to skew the promotion process for the sake of loyalty. The technique was used in 1877 by Porfirio Díaz, who after his risky but successful rebellion against the government under the Plan of Tuxtepec, promoted many of his collaborators to general. In the twentieth century, after his successful coup d'etat, Victoriano Huerta promoted nearly every state governor whose fealty was unquestionable to the next highest general rank, many of them to division general.[42] A similar method to ensure military loyalty was used in the 1920s after successive military rebellions against the government failed (1923, 1927 and 1929).

The legitimacy of the individual leader as well as the system itself, could be described as tenuous in the cases cited above. Table 9-1 presents several interesting patterns of possible presidential influence in the promotion process that have occurred since 1946. The data can be examined from two perspectives. First, the year witnessing the largest combined number of promotions of generals and colonels within each administration, or the greatest increase in a given year, might suggest something about the president's state of mind. Second, a comparative analysis of each administration's promotion records could be revealing. Using the first approach, from 1946 through 2000, seven years stand out: 1951, 1957, 1960, 1968, 1976, 1986, and 1994. Of these, three or possibly four are politically significant.

Promotions for 1951, 1957 and 1986 do not appear to be politically connected. The other years, however, especially 1960, 1968, 1976, and 1994, closely correspond to important political events. In 1959 a major railroad strike occurred and the army was called out to break it. In 1960, President López Mateos increased promotions to general by nearly 66 percent over 1959. He then returned to the modest rate that characterized his first year in office. The 1968 promotions are related to the events of Tlatelolco Plaza and the loyalty displayed by the military in the tumultuous aftermath of that event. President Díaz Ordaz, who maintained a consistently low pattern of promotions from 1965 through 1967, suddenly increased the combined promotions to colonel and general; the highest numbers were among generals. He continued a higher rate of promotion for the remainder of his administration. The year 1976 is the only important promotion cycle that occurred during the last year of a presidential administration between 1946 to 1994. Typically, the end of a presidential term is characterized by a decline or continuity in promotions, not an increase.

The second perspective, looking at an administration as a whole in addition to the specific year of 1976, provides numerous insights into the Echeverría years. Two important characteristics of Echeverría's attitudes toward the military are evident in the promotion data. First, he consistently promoted more officers than any president since Miguel Alemán. This suggests that something important was going on during his entire tenure in office. Second, although 1976 is his highest year, the other years are not all that different. The *Revista de Ejército y Fuerza Aérea* proudly announced that in 1971 the president had promoted more officers than any predecessor since the 1956 promotion law went into effect, a fact borne out by the data.[43] Typically, the official magazine does not discuss promotions, so the announcement was meant to make the officer corps aware that the president was instituting a significant change in policy and officers could count on more promotions than before. Figures jibe with the decrease of time in rank for promotion to colonel among officers born after 1930 (those eligible for that rank about the time Echeverría came into office).

Observers have suggested that from 1971 to 1976 hundreds of generals and intermediate and low ranking officers were discharged from the army to make way for younger men.[44] The precise number of retired officers cannot be ascertained from public records, but the number of new generals can be ascertained. What is remarkable is that Echeverría used his promotion powers to replace all of the retired officers. He averaged 83 promotions to general per year, for a total of 500 generals during his administration. The data also show that he more than doubled the number of such promotions compared to the previous administration, which averaged 39 generals a year under Díaz Ordaz, and returned to a comparable level under his successor, Lopéz Portillo, of 45 a year.

Some observers believe Echeverría's unusual rate of promotions was an attempt to alter the officer corps's composition. An equally convincing argument can be made that he acted in response to what he perceived as threats to both himself and his administration. During his first year as president he was confronted by right-wing dissidents in his own administration, the involvement of military representatives in the para-military Halcones's student persecution, and the extensive anti-guerrilla warfare campaign in Guerrero using sizeable numbers of troops and officers between 1974 and 1975. Echeverría believed his own position and that of his administration was in considerable political danger.[45] These elements, combined with a general increase in urban terrorism and guerrilla activity, the repercussions from his ill-conceived land reform in northwest Mexico, and the serious economic malaise of the devaluation *of the Mexican peso* in 1976 sustained this perception throughout his six years in office.[46]

There is a danger associated with a president using the promotion process to reward military loyalty during a political crisis. It creates an expectation in the military of a payback for its allegiance to civil authorities.[47] Allegiance is something learned over a long period, both within the military socialization and professionalization process and in the political culture in general; it is not something engendered through a system of personalized, presidential rewards. If abused by future presidents, such manipulations of the promotion cycle could lead to dangerous repercussions within the officer corps. Fortunately, this has not been the case among presidents. However, this did turn out to be true of some national defense secretaries, producing the repercussions cited above.

Neither López Portillo nor Miguel de la Madrid intervened in the promotion process. The secretary of national defense provided the president with the service record of each officer to be promoted to colonel or general. Among the lists of eligible officers, on the basis of time in grade, the secretary of national defense makes his own recommendations. On occasion the president challenges a recommendation of the secretary, suggesting that an officer on the eligible list appeared more deserving of promotion than others on the list. On rare occasions the president might ask that an officer be held over until the next promotion cycle if he thought the officer was not yet deserving of a promotion.[48] President López Portillo described the process to the author:

> There are two factors which affect promotion, the most important of which is the person's merits, and time in grade and rank. There's also a

third factor, which involves personal connections, individual evaluations, or just plain luck, but this factor is largely an exceptional influence in the process. The secretary of national defense comes with an overall plan of promotion, and presents all of the service records. . . . I don't remember specifically denying any recommendations made by the secretary of national defense. I found them very reasonable and well supported. The secretary of national defense always brings the records with him, and I go over each one.[49]

Miguel de la Madrid did not increase the promotion rates among generals at a rate substantially different from that of his predecessor. He did, however, increase the promotion rate of colonels to the highest level since 1946, exceeding Echeverría's rate. Among the years of his administration, 1986 stands out for its notable level of promotions (96 colonels and 79 generals respectively). De la Madrid, as has been noted in our brief historical description of administration highpoints in the civil-military relationship, began in earnest the Mexican military's participation in the anti-drug war. This mission demanded thousands of troops and placed a strain on officers available for traditional assignments. The upsurge of promotions in 1986 may be attributed to the armed forces performance, especially that of the navy, in rescue operations in the aftermath of the September 1985 earthquake. But the most likely political explanation, if indeed one is responsible, is the highly contested state election in the northern state of Chihuahua in the summer of 1986. The controversy over this election led to a full page ad placed by northern Catholic bishops and leading intellectuals, demanding the end of election fraud. The bishops, for the first time since the 1920s, publicly threatened to shut down masses (church services) if the government did not rectify the situation. Their open involvement in electoral politics led to changes in the electoral law and sparked the beginning of the democratization movement among clergy and cultural elites.[50]

Throughout his administration, President Salinas continued an increasing level of promotions at both ranks. These actions reflected the overall growth of the armed forces and the expanded roles his administration assigned to the military. Like De la Madrid, Salinas dramatically increased the number of colonels promoted each year, reaching an average number of 93 per year, the highest thus far. Not surprisingly, after the Zapatista uprising in January, 1994 (during the last year of his administration), he increased promotions significantly. This was the highest combined level of promotions among colonels and generals since 1957 and the highest rate of promotions to colonel since 1946. The destabilizing consequences of the Zapatista uprising was followed, just two months later, by the assassination of the government's presidential candidate, Luis Donaldo Colosio. The assassination was "an unprecedented event in recent Mexican politics, [and it] began to initiate some doubts about both their personal economic future and their governmental institutions."[51]

The increase in promotions begun by de la Madrid was accelerated under Salinas and continued under Zedillo. Indeed, Zedillo is responsible for the largest number of colonels and generals promoted during a single administration. His yearly averages were 106 and 90 respectively (an increase of 13 percent and 20 percent respectively), a truly significant increase. In 1999 alone, he promoted the largest group of colonels since the 1950s. During the same period, Zedillo increased the total strength of the army and air force by 12 percent. His cycle of promotions exacerbated the problem of a top-heavy officer corps, making President Fox's and particularly General Vega García's task of reducing their numbers, all that more challenging.

The president and possibly other civilian authorities can become involved in the internal machinery of the military through another mechanism. If for some reason an officer believes he has been abused by the system, he may seek recourse through judicial or executive authority. In the 1990s a case came to light in the editorial pages of *Proceso*. Frigate Captain (equivalent to lieutenant colonel) Jesús Armando Lara Preciado explained that a presidential sanction, issued for his role in a naval collision, had removed him from the promotion process between 1972 and 1974. He completed the sanction, but naval authorities turned it into an indefinite punishment by refusing to hear his appeals. He turned to the federal courts, which ordered the navy to reinstate him in the promotion cycles. The navy ignored the order, and on three occasions Captain Lara presented a petition of "abuse of authority" against Admiral Miguel N. Gómez Ortega, the navy secretary. The navy retired Lara on April 1, 1987 for reaching the age limit of his rank.[52]

Captain Lara's resort to judicial authorities and his later appeal to the legislative branch of government did not prompt civilian intervention into the military's internal affairs, even though his case had unquestioned merit under federal law. His treatment illustrates the unwillingness of civilian authorities to intervene, even when the military acted illegally against a presidential order and a court decree. This case suggests—as do civilian attitudes toward military moonlighting—that such matters are left in the hands of the military.

Lara's case foreshadowed a more complex case involving General José Francisco Gallardo, who published an article proposing a military ombudsman to handle internal human rights cases within the armed forces.[53] He allegedly embarrassed the top brass because his essay implied that a number of disputes similar to Lara's existed within the military. All required arbitration or negotiation but were being suppressed by senior commanders. Gallardo was court-martialed in 1994 on a series of unrelated charges involving the misuse of military funds.[54] As suggested above, Gallardo ran afoul of internal politics between national defense secretaries. In October of 1996, the Inter-American Committee of Human Rights, after investigating his arrest and imprisonment on other charges, requested that he be released immediately.[55]

Formal Variables in the Promotion Process

In spite of significant informal factors which can influence the outcome of an officer's upward mobility, the promotion rates between ranks have become fairly regularized. However, a small percentage of officers achieved the rank of colonel at a faster than usual rate, thus making them eligible to become generals earlier than their peers. A number of variables that might potentially affect the rate of promotion, and the factors that senior officers in charge of promotion value are worth examining, These include level of military training, combat experience, service specialty, previous posts, and political and personal ties.

The impact of education on upward mobility in the officer corps is limited. It has been asserted that a crucial credential to further promotion and entrance into the armed elite is a diploma from the Escuela Superior de Guerra and, more recently, graduation from the Colegio de Defensa Nacional plus a teaching stint on one of the military school's staff. Those qualifications were more important in determining officers eligible for promotion to the rank of general than the actual pace at which all officers reached such a rank.

Among more recent generals who are Escuela Superior de Guerra graduates, a slightly higher correlation exists between those receiving their promotion before twenty-five years of service and those taking more than twenty-five years. This is largely due to the speed up of the military's promotion process and its regularization between the mid-1950s and the present. The time period is critical; it is a period during which graduation from the Escuela Superior de Guerra became a more important factor for successful advancement to general rank.[56] For example, in the regular November 1960 promotions, none of the newly promoted division generals were graduates, but 25 percent of the promotions to two star general were. Ten years later, 100 percent of the officers promoted to brigade general were graduates. In 1972, all of the new division generals were alumni. In 1981, among infantry officers only, 30 and 29 percent of First Captains and Majors promoted to the next rank were Escuela Superior de Guerra graduates. Among Lt. Colonels, the figure jumped dramatically to 79 percent. Among the newly promoted generals, 60 percent of the brigadier and 100 percent of the brigade and division generals had received their diploma.[57] Its importance is reinforced by the data for all active duty generals in the army and air force in 2003. These figures demonstrate that, as the rank increases, so does the prevalence of the diploma. Among division generals, the figure is 97 percent, among brigade generals it is 80 percent, and for brigadier generals, 60 percent.[58] The figures for brigade and division generals are significantly higher because officers in the non-combat arms can only be promoted to two star rank and, therefore officers from most of the other service specializations (such as health and military justice) are never assigned to the Escuela Superior de Guerra. Thus, if we compare only those specializations which are actually permitted to obtain active duty division rank who have graduated from the Escuela Superior de Guerra, the figures would be 92 percent among brigade and 74 percent among brigadier generals in 2003.[59]

For the younger generations, some of whom are obtaining the rank of colonel after only 20 years, most who achieve division general in the army are also graduates of the Colegio de Defensa Nacional. Having this diploma, however, is typical whether or not an officer is on a somewhat faster track.

A slightly more significant variable in the rapidity of promotions, one that sets apart many officers pursuing successful careers as generals, is technical training abroad, primarily in the United States. Nineteen percent more officers in the fast track than officers in the typical promotion cycle have been educated abroad.

As is true for most armies, conflict does more to increase the overall promotion rate than any other variable. Generals in the U.S. Army believe the key to advancement is serving as a combat commander.[60] In Mexico this was doubly so because the roots of the post-Revolution army were the unorganized guerrilla forces and the popularly recruited Constitutional Army. Furthermore, political leaders, many of whom were veterans of the Revolution and had pursued careers within the armed forces, stressed their revolutionary origin in politics. Symbolically, combat experience always received high visibility in the careers of Mexico's secretaries of national defense. Initially all were veterans of the 1910 Revolution. Juan Arévalo Gardoqui, appointed national defense secretary in 1982, was the first secretary without combat experience. This was the case for Salinas's, Zedillo's, and Fox's appointees. The last officer from the Revolution to serve on active duty was Division General Juan José Gastelum Salcido; he was assistant secretary of national defense from 1964 to 1970.[61]

The irregular promotion process of revolutionary officers speeded up their overall rise to the rank of general. Of the officers who reached colonel in fewer than fifteen years, who were still serving in top military assignments after 1946, all but one were combat veterans. Of officers promoted to colonel in fifteen to twenty years, more than 60 percent were combat veterans, all except one from the Revolution. As twenty years of service becomes more common among younger generations (born after 1940) of officers promoted to colonel, the percentage of those with combat experience declines significantly, although younger officers have fought against the Popular Revolutionary Forces, and some briefly against the Zapatistas. In the two promotion tracks that account for 75 percent of all officers, few fought in the Revolution, or for that matter, in combat situations in the 1920s and 1930s.

Analysts overemphasized the importance of combat to the promotion process long after it became passé. They attributed more importance to the symbolism of the secretary of national defense's combat experience and insufficient attention to the rank of general. By the 1920s' generation combat as a shared experience among generals had disappeared altogether.

In part, these data explain why combat has not been essential to rapid promotion in the armed forces, at least since 1946. Combat is a significant experience that not only develops a shared set of values but also creates a sense of trust and loyalty among those who served together.[62] Few combat experiences were shared by civilian and military leaders because fewer than one in twenty civilian politicians after 1940 had witnessed combat. Examples of these relationships can be found throughout all generations of military leadership. However, once combat experience is no longer the norm, its significance for promotion per se, and rapid promotion specifically, dissipates. In fact, the percentage of officers with combat experience of any kind in the faster of the two institutionalized promotion tracks is actually smaller than in the slower track. Combat, after the Revolution, never functioned as a significant variable in determining rapid promotion to general.

In the early 1970s military involvement in anti-guerrilla operations replaced traditional combat in the Mexican armed forces. Anti-guerrilla warfare could be seen as a modern measure of a Mexican officer's combat experience. Since the late 1970s, but especially during the 1980s, anti-drug campaigns came much closer in scope and intensity to actual combat experience of an older generation of officers than did the suppression of the guerrilla movements.[63] As I pointed out earlier, over 400 soldiers have died since anti-drug missions began in 1976. Under the Zedillo and Fox administrations, the army has taken on a increasing number of anti-crime and anti-drug tasks. In the 1990s, the number of troops and officers engaged in anti-guerrilla activities rose markedly. Actual combat experience against the Zapatistas was brief and limited, but army patrols and junior officers, are confronted daily with attacks by members of the Popular Revolutionary Army. During the last decade, this has become the greatest source of traditional combat experience.

Little empirical research has been done on the Mexican military generally, but no analysis whatsoever has been published on the individual military occupational specialties within the army or on the differences between the army, air force, and navy. In reality, air force officers can be treated as a military occupational specialty within the army because the department of the air force is under the secretary of national defense and much of the professional education is handled within army technical and staff schools.

If the generals in our sample are categorized as to specialty—infantry, artillery, mechanized cavalry, engineering, medicine, administration, communications, and air—the following pattern of promotion to colonel emerges. Formally, the army itself is divided into five major categories: infantry, artillery, mechanized cavalry, armored, and engineers. If we discard the two pre-1900's promotion tracks, 39 percent of the generals were in the faster of the two remaining tracks. A correlation exists between specialty and fast promotion. Interestingly, air force officers are promoted much faster than their peers in other specialties; exactly two-thirds reached the rank of colonel in fewer than twenty-five years, a rate almost twice that for all other categories.[64] Following in importance are artillery officers; more than half of these officers were promoted in the faster track. In contrast, infantry officers, who make up the bulk of the army and the officer corps, are promoted in the fast track only a fourth of the time, the slowest rate except for communications officers. All communications officers take the slower promotion track. It is also interesting that naval admirals also reach the rank of captain (naval rank equivalent to colonel) in the faster track as compared with their army peers.

There are two explanations of military specialization influence on the promotion record. One involves the specialty's representation at the highest ranks, a variable that does not affect air force and naval promotions comparatively. Do those officers who affect the promotion process favor individuals from their own specialties? Numerous sources within the military have suggested that national defense secretaries are strongly biased in favor of their own specialties. The other factor influencing promotion based on speciality is level of professionalization within the specialty or service.

The first explanation can be tested by analyzing top staff officers at the Secretariat of National Defense. Until 2003, the secretariat did not make public the precise distribution of military occupational specialties. On the basis of Heroico Colegio Militar graduates, an accurate idea of the initial distributions can be obtained. The graduating class of 1969, which reached colonel by the mid-1990s, was distributed as follows: 55 percent infantry, 18 percent mechanized cavalry, 9 percent artillery, 12 percent engineering, and 12 percent administration.[65] Among the Escuela Superior de Guerra class of 1979–1982 (the raw material for most future high ranking officers in the combat arms and the group which provided the colonels and brigadier generals in the 1990s), 58 percent were infantry; 28 percent, mechanized cavalry; 8 percent, artillery; and 6 percent, engineers. These figures suggest a certain consistency in the proportion of infantry who received the appropriate credentials for promotion beyond Lt. Colonel. It also suggests that engineers and, to a greater extent, administration specialists are at a significant disadvantage among their peers. As suggested above, administration specialists have not been assigned to the Escuela Superior de Guerra.

The actual distribution of occupational specialties among all officers as of 2003 is quite different from the figures drawn from these academy classes. In reality, the five traditional occupational categories account for only 48 percent of all officers. The figures are 25 percent infantry, 11 percent administration, 5 percent mechanized cavalry, 4 percent engineers, and 3 percent artillery. However, to obtain a more accurate picture among officers reaching general rank compared with all officers, we can extrapolate percentages among the five categories as follows: 42 percent infantry; 19 percent cavalry (mechanized cavalry and armor); 7 percent engineers (combat and communication); 6 percent artillery, and 3 percent administration. It is easy to see that certain specialties are strongly over-represented among officers reaching the rank of general, suggesting that the other specialties and administration are significantly under-represented.

Are the accusations against national defense secretaries of over-representing their own specialties borne out by the data? This is a significant policy question because officers believe it creates intense dissatisfaction with the officer corps and propagates an environment conducive to wide fluctuations in specialties represented in each administration. If we analyze the occupational backgrounds among General Vega García's appointees (2000–2006), it is true that he over-represented infantry (his own specialization) among his top three collaborators. Of the four individuals holding those influential staff posts through 2004, three were from infantry. Among those appointees to all top staff and command posts, 64 percent were infantry, 29 percent mechanized cavalry, 5 percent were artillery, and 2 percent engineers. While it is true that among Vega García's few most prominent collaborators it might appear infantry was over-represented, the actual distribution reflects fairly reasonably the percentages of officers graduating in those occupations from the Escuela Superior de Guerra. What is equally apparent, on the other hand, is that officers representing engineering and administration, who also are not fairly represented at the Escuela Superior de Guerra, are woefully underrepresented among influential officers.

Enrique Cervantes Aguirre, national defense secretary under Zedillo, was frequently accused of favoritism, including over-representing his own occupational specialty, artillery. Again, like Vega García, Cervantes Aguirre definitely gave preference to his own specialty among the four individuals who held his top staff posts; two were from artillery. Among his top appointees, his collaborators were distributed as follows: 44 percent from infantry, 32 percent from mechanized cavalry, 16 percent from artillery, 5 percent from administration, and 3 percent from engineering. Unlike Vega García, Cervantes Aguirre did over-represent his own specialty; they are represented in top posts at a rate nearly three times their percentage among the officer corps generally and twice that of Escuela Superior de Guerra graduates. Cervantes Aguirre slightly under-represented infantry and seriously over-represented the cavalry. Like Vega García, Cervantes Aguirre counted few engineers and administration backgrounds among his collaborators.

Finally, if we explore General Riviello Bazán's administration (1988–1994), do we encounter similar biases? Like Vega García, Riviello Bazán was a member of the largest specialty, infantry. Among his top three staff appointees, two were infantry. Among all of his collaborators, 39 percent were infantry, 23 percent were mechanized cavalry, 19 percent were artillery, 8 percent were engineers, 6 percent administration, 2 percent communications, 1 percent law, and 1 percent medical corps. Riviello Bazán strongly under-represented infantry, and again doubled or tripled the percentage of artillery and cavalry officers when compared to the number who, on a random basis, should have risen to these posts. Riviello Bazán did make greater use of administration specialists than other recent secretaries of national defense. What is important to note, however, is that he under-represented his own specialty. While he showed favoritism toward artillery and mechanized cavalry officers, it was not because of his own occupational background.

Artillery as a specialization within the army has been over-represented in the top posts at the Secretariat of National Defense from 1982 to 2000.[66] Why? As I have demonstrated, it is not determined by the military occupational specialty of the secretary and his immediate subordinates, because no national defense secretary from 1946 to 1994 has come from artillery. A possible explanation is level of professionalization as measured by advanced training and education. Generals with the highest level of education are from artillery.[67] This complements an earlier point: the most intellectually capable cadets were channeled into artillery. Ninety percent of generals with an artillery specialty have graduated from the Escuela Superior de Guerra and/or the Colegio de Defensa Nacional. Among those same generals born since 1930, only three do not have an MA from the Colegio de Defensa Nacional. Other highly educated specialties (compared with the average general) are naval engineering and the air force, with 77 percent and 73 percent graduating from one or both of those institutions or its naval equivalent. Artillery was considered the most technical of traditional military fields, thus requiring a higher level of education for success in it.

Another way of examining a specialty's professionalization is through officers who teach. As we found earlier, the academies are significant to recruitment, especially at the top. If we exclude the small technical specialties (i.e., medicine and communications) where teaching is almost a necessity, the specialties with the highest percentage of experienced instructors are the navy, air force, and army artillery.

Naval officers who reach the rank of admiral differ from their army peers because they are better educated and their teaching experience rate is extraordinarily high. Nine out of ten naval officers teach during their career. This can be explained, in part, by the nature of the sample: the vast majority of naval officers are younger than the generals. Navy personnel are also more likely to have been educated abroad, a variable that we found to have had some importance in fast-track promotions. More than two-thirds of naval officers studied outside Mexico; only a little more than a third of all general officers did so. Two-thirds of all admirals had served abroad as attachés; only a fifth of top generals had done so. Three times as many admirals as their army counterparts had served in the United States. None of the naval officers were mustangs which, in terms of promotion time, would slow down their overall promotion rates.

Air force officers, in spite of having much closer historic ties to the army, share certain similarities with navy officers, similarities which might be associated with faster promotion rates. They have a much stronger teaching record. Approximately four-fifths of air force generals have taught at the air college, the Heroico Colegio Militar, or at applied schools. Like their naval colleagues, they have studied abroad in larger numbers, more so than any other major specialty or service. Further, they have studied in the United States at rates higher than army officers.

The Mexican military is like any large organization; certain assignments within it lead to greater chances for advancement. Positions other than teaching also bear on the careers of generals. McAlister mentions only one: service with the presidential staff.[68] These troops and officers are under direct presidential command and they are responsible for protecting the president from not only external threats but also, historically, disloyal military forces. The presidential staff functions as the president's own intelligence, administrative, and security agency. Currently the troops assigned to this duty are commanded by a presidential chief of staff. The present presidential staff consists of a brigade, composed of 5 battalions (3 infantry, 1 special forces, and 1 artillery).

Sergio Aguayo explains why officers on their way up the promotion ladder might want to serve in these units: "With its abundant economic resources and its political authority and influence, the Presidential Military Staff wove over many years a complicated and powerful network of military who occupied strategic positions in the PRIista nervous system. Personnel recommended by the Presidential Military Staff were in charge of security and logistics for secretaries of state, governors, and para-state agencies."[69]

It is true that a number of officers have commanded the presidential guard, but doing so does not carry the weight of other types of positions in the careers of successful officers. For example, among the top national defense leaders in recent years, General Antonio Riviello Bazán, secretary of national defense 1988–1994, served with a commando group in 1953, and his official mayor, General Raúl Juárez Carreño, served in the 2nd Infantry Battalion in 1959 and then as a group commander from 1982 to 1985. Since 1994, no other top four staff officers in the secretariat of national defense have served in a presidential guard unit at any rank. However, all recent chiefs of the presidential military staff have gone on to become division generals, Mexico's highest active duty rank.

Service within the presidential staff has produced a decided influence on the careers of a select number of officers. Assignment to presidential units, especially when repeated, is an introduction to a much more politically colored career. The presidential staff plays a central role in planning the president's daily schedule and in his protection. It combines staff functions with functions like those performed by the U.S. Secret Service. These functions originally bolstered the military's prestige.

These functions also give a group of officers direct access to the president's activities. Junior officers serving on the presidential staff typically end up in higher positions there. The most important of these positions, is presidential chief of staff, the most influential political liaison between the president and the armed forces, particularly the army and air force. One observer commented, "It is really fair to say that the presidential chief of staff is the equivalent of a cabinet minister without portfolio."[70]

It is interesting to look at the careers of the five most recent presidential chiefs of staff; Generals Miguel Angel Godínez Bravo (1976–1982), Carlos

Humberto Bermúdez Dávila (1982–1988), Arturo Cardona Marino (1988–1994), Roberto Miranda Sánchez (1994–2000), and José Tamayo Casillas (2000–2006). The first three were assistant chiefs of staff immediately prior to their appointments, and the last two were assistant chiefs of operations, having served as directors of security and logistics in the campaigns of the presidents who appointed them. Each also served in other positions on the presidential staff and, equally important, three were executive officers or commanders of troops in the presidential guard. No other top military careers in the past two decades followed such a consistent pattern as the careers of presidential chiefs of staff.

These extensive careers within the confines of the presidential staff have contributed importantly to tensions between the regular army and the presidential staff, tensions which have escalated considerably in recent years and became part of a public discussion in the 1990s. These tensions stem from the perception that the officers who serve on the presidential staff are "politicized," and that their career tracks benefit from their close contacts with the president and leading members of his cabinet.[71] Officers from this unit accompany the president on every official working trip. Presidential staff officers, because of their political duties, think of themselves as an elite unit within the military and, to some fellow officers, are viewed as operating outside the orthodox, regular army units. Most of the presidential staff officers hold the same junior positions as any regular army officer, but it is apparent that the presidential chief of staff typically spends many years inside this same unit and a long period as an officer in presidential guard battalions.[72]

As noted previously, new information about the role of the presidential military staff in the 1968 massacre of students in Tlatelolco Plaza in Mexico City clearly demonstrates the secretariat of national defense's lack of control over the presidential staff.[73] According to the recently published papers of general Marcelino García Barragán (the then secretary of national defense) President Gustavo Díaz Ordaz's chief of staff, Colonel Luis Gutiérrez Oropeza, secretly positioned ten sharpshooters, officers dressed in civilian clothes, in the apartment buildings surrounding the plaza. They were responsible for instigating the bloody confrontation between regular army troops and students.[74] The secretary of national defense had no prior knowledge of the existence of these men or their assignment.[75] They reported directly to Colonel Gutiérrez Oropeza who, in turn, reported directly to the president.[76]

These abuses have led reformers, including military officers, to argue that special groups such as the presidential staff should be modified and no longer have some of the special privileges alluded to above. The ability of personnel to remain within the presidential units for decades encourages these individuals to lose sight of what the army is in reality. Furthermore, proponents of change advocate that individual officers should not be body guards or aides to politicians.[77]

One of the key plum positions that appeared in the fast track promotions of naval officers is prior service as an attaché. The post is considered prestigious, not only because it positively affects one's career but also because of the perquisites it entails. The perquisites include higher pay, allowances, and travel.[78] The attaché assignment is seen as a deserved reward.[79] The most important of these posts is as an assistant or full military attaché in the United States. Such an assignment is nearly as integral to the career of a secretary of national defense as the ambassadorship to the United States is to careers in the Foreign Relations Secretariat. Altogether, the number of military posts is limited. During the 1940s, 1950s, and 1960s, typically six or seven positions were available: Mexican embassies in the United States, Canada, France, and generally several South and Central American countries.[80] Naval attaché positions were somewhat different, depending on the country's importance to Mexico's navy.

Among leading generals, only 22 percent have been attachés. Yet, examination of the three post-revolution promotion tracks reveals the post's prominence in the faster track to general rank. Even the faster-track officers who reached the rank of colonel in fifteen to twenty years in the 1920s and 1930s, and who remained in top positions after 1946, were attachés half the time. Moreover, an even larger percentage have been assistant attachés or have been members of the attaché staffs. The two more recent promotion tracks illustrate the difference. In the slower track, only 16 percent of the generals have been attachés, fewer than all generals combined, and only one in five has served in the United States or Canada. Among the colonels promoted to general in less than twenty-five years, however, 45 percent served in these posts and a third of them spent time in the United States and Canada. It is also the case that a disproportionate number of naval and air force officers served in the United States and Canada compared to all generals. In fact, the last two secretaries of the navy, Admiral José Ramón Lorenzo Franco (1994–2000) and Admiral Antonio Perot González (2000–2006), were attachés. Lorenzo Franco was assistant naval attaché in Washington, D.C., naval attaché to France, and at the time of his appointment as secretary, was serving as the naval attaché to England.

The importance of the United States in the service careers of Mexican officers is understandable because of shared technical and tactical influence. On the other hand, given our earlier discussion of Mexican distrust toward the United States, officers conveying a strong pro-United States attitude are likely to suffer in the promotion process.[81] The top air force officers, similar to their naval counterparts, are more likely to have spent time in the United

States, either in extensive training programs or in the attaché section of the embassy. In the Fox administration, the director of the air force, the chief of staff, and the operations assistant chief of staff, all served as attachés or assistant attachés in Washington, D.C. Among the youngest generation of top generals in the army, those born after 1940, many have served as attachés, including General Vega García, the secretary of national defense in 2000, and some of those same officers served in the United States, including Vega García's first chief of staff.[82]

An additional career distinction arises in the disparity between staff and line officers. Most graduates of the Escuela Superior de Guerra are initially assigned to a military zone headquarters in the field, but most return to the national defense staff headquarters within six to twelve months.[83] Service on the national defense staff, as noted earlier, is extremely useful to advancement. It is not, however, statistically related to the rapidity with which an officer reaches the rank of general but, rather, is an experience shared by most recent general officers, which typically affects their appointments to specific posts, especially the most influential staff positions. Still, the distinction between staff and line officers is worth examining.

During the twentieth century, professionalization in Mexico increased the presence of the staff officer, at least in the top ranks. By 1926, General Joaquín Amaro, the man responsible for the initial thrust of military professionalization, established the Ministry of War general staff.[84] The general staff's existence provided an impetus to the increasing importance of staff relative to line officers. This can be seen in a sharp alteration of emphasis in career backgrounds from the pre-1900 to post-1900 generations of generals. By the 1900s generation, half or more of the officers reaching the rank of general were primarily staff officers.

Among all the generals in our sample, slightly over half (53 percent) can be categorized as line officers. Stephen Wager argues that line officers, especially younger men who serve as battalion or mechanized cavalry squadron commanders, will be promoted at a faster rate.[85] Command assignments may lead to faster promotions for some Mexican officers but, overall, staff positions appear to be more advantageous. Excluding medical and legal officers, only 40 percent of all generals in our sample could be classified as staff, but some 59 percent of fast-track generals followed staff careers, compared with 49 percent of slower-track generals. Data from the 1940s generation clearly suggest staff careers are more significant as a trend among higher command in the late 1990s and 2000s as a means of accelerated promotion.

An informal means of promotion, one that might possibly be the most influential but the most difficult to ascertain, is personal contact within and outside the military. Some analysts, those who believe that presidential influence is important to career advancement within the military, have suggested that ties to or connections with the incoming president are critical to acquiring top positions during a particular administration.[86] Recent presidents have denied this, attributing such networking influence to the national defense secretaries.[87] Indeed, one officer who served on a presidential staff for many years and became very close to that president was not promoted. He did not have the "right attitude," asked too many questions, and was not unquestioningly subordinate to his superiors.

As chapter 7 explains, military recruitment shares many characteristics with recruitment in the civilian political world. Indeed, the most common recruitment element is the mentor-disciple relationship, a characteristic found in other elite communities.[88] The military version is "pyramidal cliques, with a senior officer acting as an unofficial leader and father figure. More frequently, though, the word which is associated with the formation of such quasi father-son relations is *palanca*, or crowbar, and the relationship is more analogous to that of a godfather and godson."[89] The mentor-disciple relationship builds loyalty between junior and senior officers and moderates potential generational splits. Personal ties within the military are so complex and hidden from public view that they cannot be evaluated in terms of their impact on the promotion process, other than to say they are without question crucial.

Stephen Wager believes military kinship ties are critical to an officer's success. He concluded: "[A cadet will] often marry a woman from a military family after he graduates and becomes an officer. Or it is quite common for an officer to marry into a fellow officer's family or that of his wife. This is quite significant when one considers the personalistic nature of the Mexican armed forces as well as its generally small size."[90] Some notable examples of officers with military relatives are the previous two secretaries of defense. General Riviello Bazán is the son and stepbrother of generals; his predecessor, Juan Arévalo Gardoqui, is the son of a three-star general. The vast majority of influential navy officers, including the most recent vice admirals and admirals, are the children of civilians and many of them are from modest socio-economic backgrounds. Among generals whose parents' occupations are known, one-third have a career military father, a figure higher than those applying for entrance into the officer corps as cadets. On the other hand, no substantial difference exists between officers on the slow and faster track based on an officer having a father in the military.

At the Apex of the Officer Corps

The most prestigious positions in the army and their air force and navy equivalents are, in descending order of importance, the secretary of national defense, the assistant secretary of national defense, and oficial mayor at the very top. These are followed by chief of staff, regional commander, department head (for example, director general of infantry), zone commander, and the head of the presidential staff.[91] How do these two- and three-star generals in the inner circle differ from their peers? Their characteristics are meaningful because they exercise decision-making authority within the military establishment. As is also evident in the U.S. Army, selection board members (generals who promote other officers to the rank of general) tap people like themselves and thereby determine the future composition of the officer corps. Since the navy and army have created new promotion procedures since 2000 that involve promotions committees, these individuals have acquired greater influence.

Two types of top officers can be compared: the staff officer, represented by secretaries, assistant secretaries, and department heads; and the troop commander, represented by the zone commander. Most top staff officers are likely to end up as department heads in their military occupational specialties (such as director general of cavalry, artillery, communications, etc.) or in some cases, in more than one of these occupationally-oriented national defense or naval posts. Such an assignment is important because of its prestige at the apex of the military structure and—as is true of most high-level bureaucratic positions—department heads normally determine which senior officers are awarded subordinate staff jobs.[92]

An analysis of the career backgrounds and origins of department heads makes clear that numerous variables are unimportant in an officer's rise to that post. Among those variables are geographic origin, social class, and father's profession. What seems to be far more relevant is the career path an officer traveled. The department head's career focuses more heavily on the same experiences that help all officers rise above the rank of colonel. In other words, the department head's career is a more precise prototype of what it takes to become—and even more so in the future—a two or three star officer.

Staff positions are the most conspicuous feature of the department head's career. Even in leadership positions over combat units, a department head is 25 percent more likely than generals in the aggregate to have served as executive officer to a zone commander. Interestingly, however, despite the importance and prestige of zone commanders, holding a top troop command is not a significant career step toward achieving a departmental headship, although it is becoming more common. The other staff position of importance, suggestive of the value high command places on a grasp of foreign military tactics and weaponry (and on enjoying the perks of a plum assignment), is the post of military attaché. Of the more than 120 officers in our sample of generals who were attachés, 80 percent became department heads. General Vega García, secretary of national defense under Fox, served as the attaché to the Soviet Union before becoming director general of military education in 1998. One in three department heads, compared with only 20 percent of all top generals, served abroad. That figure increases among recent generations of department heads in the 1990s and 2000s. A larger percentage of these staff officers were trained abroad as well.

Interestingly, one of the most significant variables in top staff backgrounds is teaching. Teaching is increasingly relevant to an officer's career because generals who have helped younger men rise to the rank of general have themselves been teachers in much larger percentages than generals overall. Nearly three-quarters of department heads, versus only half of all generals, were instructors, most at the Escuela Superior de Guerra, the Heroico Colegio Militar, and, more recently, at the Colegio de Defensa Nacional. The same is true among navel department heads, most of whom have taught at the Heroico Escuela Naval Militar and the Centro de Estudios Superiores Navales.

Perhaps most interesting of all, a general's military training appears to be helpful in reaching top staff posts. The most over-represented specialties, at rates of more than three times their proportions among all generals, were artillery, engineers, and communications. In the U.S. Army, according to Mylander, men of ambition avoid the support branches, which include engineers; these branches account for 59 percent of the total officer corps but only 30 percent of the generals.[93]

Even as an elite position among generals, the departmental headship is an opportunity open to a sizeable percentage of generals. Few, however, will reach assistant secretary and secretary of national defense or navy. These posts are so politically sensitive that considerations other than military take precedence in the selection process. Analysis of this even more elite group of generals reveals considerable differences between them and department heads.

Assistant secretaries, based on a sample of fifty-three cases, had certain similarities to department heads. They, too, tended to have staff backgrounds and to have held some of the same career posts, notably as executive officers and attachés. Further, service on the general staff had become increasingly useful; it was almost a prerequisite for reaching an assistant secretary post. Two-thirds of all assistant secretaries could claim general staff experience, compared with two-fifths of all generals. By the 1920–1929 generation, 83 percent of all assistant secretaries had prior general staff assignments in their respective ministries.

Two features set the assistant secretary apart. The political nature of the appointment is reflected in the fact that assistant secretaries, relative to all other generals, have much stronger personal and familial ties to political and military leaders. More than half of all assistant secretaries had such ties, more than half again as many as the typical general. However, this pattern is not found among assistant secretaries in the last two administrations. Likewise, one-third of the assistant secretaries, but only one-sixth of all generals, had held elective political office, suggesting the value of political contacts through careers in politics among older officers who reached that post. Within the military, the command position requiring considerable political skill, somewhat analogous to a governorship in the civilian world, is that of zone commander. It is not an absolute prerequisite to becoming an assistant secretary, but having been a zone commander was much more typical of an assistant secretary than of a department head or all other generals.

By far the most interesting variable in elite officer backgrounds, one repeated among the national defense secretaries, is the importance of combat. I suggested earlier that, symbolically, combat experience has traditionally been emphasized in the officer corps prior to the 1970s. Nearly two-thirds of the assistant secretaries were combat veterans at a time when only 40 percent of all generals counted combat experience in their careers. More intriguing, and a point I raised many years ago, is that a disproportionate percentage of assistant secretaries were at one time political-military opponents of the government.[94]

Two formal requirements apply to the secretary of national defense: the individual must be a three-star (division) general and of Mexican parentage. The latter is an indication of the importance of nationalism to the most sensitive political posts.[95] Many other characteristics of the assistant secretaries can be found among the national defense and naval secretaries, including the importance of relatives in high military or political positions (true of 60 percent of secretaries compared to only half of all generals);[96] service as attachés, zone commanders, and department heads; political office-holding, elective and appointive; and having been in combat (56 percent in the Revolution, 8 percent in post-revolution battles and revolts through 1939, and 3 percent in World War II). Two-thirds of the secretaries experienced combat compared with only 30 percent of the generals in the aggregate.

The bureaucracy of the Mexican military's command structure is located in the capital city, centered in the Secretariat of National Defense and, to a lesser extent, naval headquarters. Representing the army on the state level is the military zone. The present zone system was established in 1924.[97] Today, it is composed of 12 military regions and forty-five zones. There also exist 19 smaller garrisons.[98] Each region, which is composed of various military zones and garrisons, is at the apex of the command structure. The purpose of regional commands, in response to post-1995 reforms, is to increase the autonomy of the regional and zone commanders over operations, logistics, administration, finance, and training based on the individual commanders' perception of local problems.

The navy currently maintains ten bases on the east and west coasts. There are also six naval regions encompassing these bases, the equivalent of army regions.[99] The air force, administered by a department under the secretary of national defense, is divided into eighteen bases and three regions, commanded by one and two stars and division generals respectively.[100] New zones or regions may be added at will by the president in his role of supreme commander.[101]

By law an officer must be a brigade or division general to command a zone.[102] But in recent years, in response to reforms designed to assign tasks based on a hierarchy of responsibilities, regional commands are exclusively the purview of three star generals, and zone commands two star generals. By the 1960s, the president was said to be selecting zone commanders at the suggestion of the secretary of national defense.[103] Earlier, especially as late as the 1930s, it was more likely to be the president himself who independently made the selection. This was logical, given the need for presidents to assure the military's loyalty. More recently, it has been suggested that the secretary of national defense generates a pool of eligible officers, from which the president chooses.[104] Presidents have personally confirmed this to be the case. As they have suggested, they rarely know any zone commanders or potential zone commanders personally and, therefore, defer to the secretary's recommendations. It is the secretary of national defense who makes regional and zone command appointments during the presidential term.

The zone commander, in charge of a well-armed body of troops, has been rotated rather regularly. This does not imply that a new president automatically replaces all zone commanders, but the initial period of an administration is likely to be the time of greatest turnover. In a typical first year, about a third of the zone commanders are replaced. Examination of the career histories of 140 zone commanders shows an average tenure of 2.4 years. There have been some notable exceptions, even in recent years. The longest continuous commands I encountered in national defense records are that of Division General Félix Ireta Viveros (who commanded the 21st zone in Michoacán from 1954 to 1970, spanning three full presidential administrations) and that of Modesto A. Guinart López (who commanded the 26th zone in Veracruz from 1959 to 1972). Division General Victor Manuel Ruiz Pérez is perhaps a more significant case since he commanded Mexico's most influential zone, that containing the Federal District, for the entire de la Madrid administration (1982–1988). The most recent case is that of Division

General José A. García Elizalde, who commanded the 3rd Region, which included extensive drug-trafficking areas, from 1989 to 1995.

Historically, the zone commander played a conspicuous political role in the expansion of central power and served as a counterbalance to the influence of the state governor. In the 1940s and 1950s, commanders sometimes substituted for governors when the latter resigned or were forced from office by central authorities.[105] The close association between governors and zone commanders is borne out by our data. Among the generals in this study, 12 percent had been governors at some point, but among the generals who were zone commanders, nearly twice that figure, 25 percent, served as governors. By the 1930s generation, no officers became governors. Zone commanders are in direct communication through their own military network with the national defense secretary and provide alternate sources of national security intelligence. In the case of Chiapas in the early 1990s, civilian authorities ignored such military intelligence.[106]

The intertwining of political with military responsibilities and its potential impact on the broader scope of civil-military relations goes far beyond the fact that zone commanders often became governors. If we examine the notion of zone commanders' political experience by age, a clear pattern becomes apparent. Zone commanders who fought in the Revolution dominated zone assignments in the 1940s and 1950s, a period when political office-holding by military officers was the norm. A decline occurs in each succeeding generation, but a marked difference occurs between pre- and post-revolutionary zone commanders, and among the post-1910 generation of zone commanders. Zone commanders with national political experience born from 1910 to 1919 proportionately drop precipitously from three-quarters to one-quarter. Compared with all other large groups of generals, zone commanders shared the highest levels of political experience: about two fifths of zone commanders held such offices in contrast to only one-fifth of other generals. These figures also suggest, as do those for secretaries and assistant secretaries, the more influential the military post, the more likely the officer will have acquired political skills, at least until the 1980s when direct political experience disappears from an officer's credentials.

Zone commanders share important qualities with their peers who have risen to top staff positions. Like their most successful peers, they have taught in large numbers at the military academies. Similarly, they have served abroad as attachés twice as frequently as their fellow officers. What really stands out among recent appointees, however, is the dominance of Escuela Superior de Guerra graduates among the army and air-force commanders. In 2003, all of the air force regional and base commanders were recipients of air war school diplomas. Among army commanders, all regional commanders had graduated from the Escuela Superior de Guerra. Among the 44 two star generals in charge of military zones, 93 percent were alums, and 80 percent of garrison commanders were graduates. These figures suggest that, even among top troop commanders, the higher one rises, the more likely they are to hold that credential.[107] These percentages are only likely to increase, based on the promotion lists in 2003. A study of these lists shows that all division generals in the army and air force, who would hold regional commands, are graduates of the Escuela Superior de Guerra, as are all brigade generals in the traditional army and the air force specialties, with the exception of one officer in administration. All of the brigadier generals in both the army and air force also graduated with War College diplomas.[108]

Zone commanders, like secretaries and assistant secretaries, more typically have been combat veterans; this is not surprising because such veterans acquired the practical skills that kept troops loyal to the government and defeated rebel commanders. The importance of those skills continued into the 1940s, 1950s, and 1960s, which explains why nearly 60 percent of all zone commanders were combat veterans, compared with 20 percent of all generals. Such experiences have now disappeared but, as I argued, combat in the form of anti-drug campaigns is likely to appear more frequently among future zone commanders' backgrounds, more so than among their staff counterparts. Finally, the minority of officers coming from lower socioeconomic strata have a much stronger chance of becoming zone commanders than high ranking staff officers. The qualities demanded of the zone commander seem to attract the self-made officer in much greater numbers than do other posts held by generals.

Consequences of Promotion on Civil-Military Relations

Our analysis of the promotion process demonstrates conclusively that the military has developed a largely autonomous system. Promotions are fairly consistent over time and, more important, civilian interference is negligible, even on the part of recent presidents. In the introduction we hypothesized that a possible explanation for discouraging military intervention in civilian affairs is to keep politicians out of the promotion process and limit the politization of promotions. There is no question that Mexico generally accomplished this task, aided structurally and significantly prior to 2000 by a one-party-dominant system.

The promotion process, on the other hand, has been unsuccessful in ameliorating tensions within the armed forces. As we have seen, the problems associated with the promotion process became a focal point in the army/air force internal reform proposals of 1995. Internal dissension, when it reaches significant levels, generates the potential for adverse consequences on civil-military relations. Dissatisfied officers who have not received the promotions and/or posts they believe they deserve become more susceptible to other complaints about the institution, including its role in society. I am not suggesting that the issues associated with the promotion process in recent years have destabilized the armed forces as an institution, but it has weakened it and heightened the possibilities of other potential conflicts within and outside the military.

The most significant issue impacting on civil-military relations associated with promotion processes in Mexico is the well-recognized glut of top-ranked officers. There is no disagreement that it is excessive in all three services. The data from the army alone clearly illustrate this. In 2003, the army had 501 active duty generals, including 32 division generals, among 188,000 personnel. The rate of promotion between the ranks, based on this data, is the following: captain to major 75.9 percent; major to lieutenant colonel, 60.5 percent; lieutenant colonel to colonel, 50.7 percent; colonel to brigadier general, 42.4 percent; brigadier to brigade general, 50.3 percent; and brigade to division general, 20.4 percent.[109] The consequence of this excess is that top ranking officers are performing the duties of significantly lower ranking officers. In 2004, the formal military structure indicates that colonels should command actual units, with lieutenant colonels acting as their executive officers. Majors should be section chiefs and captains company commanders. One and two star generals were only supposed to serve as executive officers and zone commanders respectively, and division generals, regional commanders.[110]

The army has made little headway on this issue. The navy, on the other hand, responded to all of the criticisms in the army/air force internal documents, and to public criticism, too. Fox's secretary of the navy, Admiral Marco Antonio Peyrot González, announced that they had 247 active duty admirals, openly admitted that the secretariat itself was too large, and stated that too many individuals were serving in unnecessary administrative posts. To solve this problem, he suggested that the navy should assign some of these officers to other agencies in state governments whose geographic boundaries include coastlines and reduce the number of department heads from 18 to 5.[111]

An examination of the navy website, and its new organizational chart, demonstrates that they have implemented these drastic changes. Admiral Peyrot González reduced the number of admirals by 40 percent, announcing that 100 admirals would be retired immediately.[112] The secretary also indicated that he would ask the appropriate admirals to retire voluntarily if no post was assigned to them or wait without an assignment until one became vacant. Only ten full admirals now remain in the navy, and they are in command of the naval regions and the departments. Because of the number of forced retirements, the navy sought out state and federal agencies interested in recruiting former military personnel with knowledge about security issues to ease the impact of those draconian personnel changes. Simultaneously, the navy also increased pensions to make actual retirement financially feasible.[113] Finally, they awarded the retired admirals active duty pay until they reached the mandatory retirement age.[114]

Most significantly, the navy wrote an entirely new organic law, passed by congress, which included among its most striking changes a Council of Admirals in charge of the promotion process. The council recommends qualified individuals for promotion from captain through full admiral. It also is responsible for recommending naval policy and strategy.[115] One of the primary purposes of the new law was to generate an organizational process to establish naval assignments commensurate with an individual's rank.[116] Members of the council include the secretary of the navy, the assistant secretary, the oficial mayor, the inspector general, the chief of staff, the commander of the Pacific forces, and the commander of the Gulf forces. All officers from the rank of captain through full admiral will receive the same salary according to their rank, rather than different salaries based on the specific assignment, thus eliminating favoritism in assigning well-reimbursed posts.[117]

The ability of the naval brass to make these dramatic alterations to the officer corps is even more remarkable given the fact that Fox's navy secretary personally required promotion to full admiral in order to be nominated for the post and was, therefore, junior to all other full admirals in 2000. Fox's secretary of national defense, General Vega García, is equally junior. He was promoted to division general in January 2000, making him the most junior of three star army generals. Vega García, as of 2004, had not yet reformed the army's organic law but, in October 2003, he did introduce a new army/air force promotions and commendations law.[118] This law is similar to the navy law insofar as it sets up, for the first time, an evaluation committee to recommend promotions to the highest ranks.[119] In his testimony before congress in 2004, General Vega García noted that the new promotions law had solved most of the problems associated with that process and that the secretary of national defense had been effectively removed from influencing promotions.[120] He has, in the 2001 and 2002, kept promotions to general to one of the lowest levels in recent history. In fact, in the 2001 promotions, only 37 individuals were given general ranks, two at the division level, nine at the brigade, and twenty-one at the brigadier rank.[121] Although we have no basis for prior comparisons because the army only released this data in 2003, in 2002 they considered 246 and 355 colonels for promotion to general or to

Reaching the Top   243

the next highest rank of general. Only 53 (9 percent) were actually promoted. A total of 747 lieutenant colonels were considered for promotion; Only 88 (11 percent) were promoted to colonel. On the other hand, his predecessor, in his last two years, promoted 187 officers to general rank, one of the largest groups ever promoted.

General Vega García also recognized repeated complaints about inadequate compensation for officers and implemented a retroactive pay increase as of July 1, 2001. Under the new pay scale, a division general would receive 161,150 pesos monthly (approximately $16,000), a brigade general 132,598 pesos ($13,000), and a brigadier 99,246 pesos ($9,900). In 2003, actual monthly pay for these three ranks before taxes and minus benefits were 174,078, 134,885, and 99,356 pesos respectively. An officer holding one of the top four positions, as well as department heads and unit commands, would earn more. These figures conform to pay scales in all federal departments.[122] Retirement pay, however, remains woefully inadequate; it stands at 15,000 pesos, 14,000 pesos, and 13,000 pesos respectively for the three highest army ranks.[123]

A second significant source of potential conflict between the armed forces and civilian political leadership may emerge from within the armed forces through inter- and intra-service rivalries. Such rivalries, which are well known in other Latin American countries (i.e., Chile), have led to political interventions and specific service partisan identifications with political parties. Intra-service rivalries relate to preferences or perceived preferences given to military occupational specialties, or to significant political differences which emerge between enlisted ranks and the officer corps. Mexico's armed forces do not suffer from the latter problem but, at least within the army, military occupational specialties, the position of the members of the presidential military staff, and the recipients of Escuela Superior de Guerra diplomas, all pose special problems which have generated substantial tensions within this service. One observer with access to inside information suggests that General Riviello Bazán was selected as the secretary of national defense in 1988 to avoid further splits within the ranks.[124]

As our data clearly shows, there has been favoritism in the promotion process, which some secretaries of national defense exaggerated. Over the long term, although certain specialties appear to be favored among the higher ranks, they are not necessarily associated with the national defense secretary's own occupational specialty. The perception of abuse is stronger than the actual level of incidence. On the other hand, the abuses may be more accurate when measured by more qualitative measures. For example, officers may be assigned to the most lucrative positions rather than to the most significant or appropriate posts for their abilities.

The inter-service rivalry between the navy and the army/air force introduces the greatest potential of any form of rivalry for influencing military behavior in the civilian arena. President José López Portillo considered unifying the armed forces into one agency to reduce the potential for such conflicts.[125] This unification concept was raised again before Fox took office. Civilian commentators proposed a civilian national defense secretary, similar to the arrangement in the United States. Miguel de la Madrid admitted that there were intra-service problems with favoritism toward some specialties, but perceived no major problems between the two services.[126] According to insiders, the overwhelming source of tension between the navy and the army is their difference in size. Because it is the larger service, the army received the bulk of the financial resources and the media attention.[127] This perception is borne out by the fact that, since Salinas's administration (1988–1994), the secretariat of national defense has grown 35 percent while the navy grew only 25 percent.[128] This pattern, however, is a natural result of the increased missions and responsibilities assigned to the army and not the result of civilian favoritism toward one service versus another.

The most likely source of tension between the two services, however, will not come from typical patterns found in other services and countries, but from the differences which are emerging as a result of the radical changes within the navy since 2000 compared to only modest alterations in the army mid-way through the Fox administration. Members of congress and journalists are likely to focus on the changes, and the revamped naval organic law, which suggest a whole new level of comprehensive professionalization within the navy compared to the army. The army's reputation in the civilian world is likely to suffer in comparison and the potential exists for a more independent congress to took more favorably on a navy which has put its house in order on many controversial issues when compared to an army which continues to drag its feet on the issue of reforms.

CHAPTER TEN

Challenges to Civil-Military Relations in the 21st Century

Civil-military relations in Mexico prior to 2000 have piqued the interest of analysts for two principle reasons. The first, and the most theoretically grounded, was identifying the path Mexico used to withdraw the military from politics. In performing this task, this nation has shared some similarities with other countries, while simultaneously generating characteristics which are peculiarly unique to Mexico. Second, and seemingly contradictory, has been the constant concern among analysts and leaders regarding the loyalty of the armed forces to civilian politicians, and the likelihood that the armed forces might intervene in civilian political affairs. This book addresses both of those issues in some detail. Since the 1990s, and especially since Vicente Fox was inaugurated as president in December 2000, the crucial issue is how has an electoral democracy altered the civil-military relationship? How has the military responded to the beginnings of democratic consolidation in the twenty-first century? Are the armed forces dragging their institutional feet? Or, will they transform their institutional culture to conform to the changing structural relationships and internal rules of behavior characteristic of democratic systems in the throes of dynamic change? Finally, are the qualities of the armed forces described in the preceding pages continuing after 2000? Or, has the presence of Mr. Fox, a new party in the executive branch with a plurality (2000-2003) in the legislative branch, affected their behavior?

From the 1960s through the 1990s, one point on which most Mexican political analysts agreed was that the military's future political role was more likely to increase than decrease. This view suggests that, in the continuum of civil-military relations, the military already had reached its lowest point of political influence. Logically, other than remaining static, the military could only embark on a more activist course, thereby reversing a long-term trend of military withdrawal from politics. The reverse argument can be found in many Latin American countries where the military reached the apex of its political influence in the 1970s and 1980s.[1] Great care should be taken in accepting this argument because some confusion exists between the fundamental issue of military subordination to civilian leadership and military intervention, defined by both its old and new missions in society.

Implicitly, analysts have equated an expansion of the military's role with greater political influence and greater political influence with a decline in respect for civil authority. Clearly, these are not mutually exclusive. Focusing on changing tasks does reveal valuable insights into the armed forces and the civil-military relationship. In the end, however, the crucial question is not the tasks themselves nor who performs them, but who decides on what those tasks are and who is assigned to them. In spite of "lack of support for democracies [which is not the case in the Mexican armed forces], military role expansion is still civilian initiated, and therefore, does not pose a threat to civilian control."[2] This argument is central to the modified equilibrium model we have used to frame our analysis.

Recent literature on Latin America argues that democratic systems of civil-military relations must be consciously constructed due to the lack of a historical foundation for such a model.[3] I would argue that the democratic transformation is crucial to both civilian and military institutions. In the past, the crucial role and strength of the Institutional Revolutionary Party and its antecedents in Mexico influenced the balance in civil-military affairs. Today, the performance of civilian democratic institutions may well be the most important variable in civil-military relations in Mexico and elsewhere in the region.[4] Thus, the behavior and strength of civilian institutions after 2000 is the first theme which deserves consideration in our analysis of the current relationship. Presently, the high level of confidence which the citizenry expresses for the armed forces contrasts with the low level of confidence it expresses in governmental institutions and political parties. This does not mean that the typical Mexican wants the military to intervene. Rather they have greater satisfaction with the outcome of duties performed by the armed forces compared to those performed by most civil and political institutions.

During the last decade in Latin America, observers argued that the typical member of the officer corps shared a unique view of democratic politics. As Fitch notes, "most Latin American officers have a decidedly bi-polar view, where politics—the clash of competing views and competing interests, the mobilization of support and opposition—is the rather distasteful side of

Challenges to Civil-Military Relations in the 21st Century 247

democracy."[5] Mexico, on the other hand, has shifted gradually from a semi-authoritarian to a semi-democratic to a more fully democratic model, and done so without radical transformations in political behavior or performance. No evidence exists for the Mexican officer corps sharing the view Fitch describes among other Latin American militaries. Some scholars believe the armed forces' support for democracy has little to do with ideological preferences. These scholars feel that military support for democracy stems from the practical advantages democracy offers to groups of officers in maintaining or obtaining control within the armed forces.[6]

The degree to which the armed forces continues its isolation from civilian actors within the democratic setting raises a second theme which will impact strongly on the civil-military relationship in this decade. The military has not encouraged the free flow of ideas. Nor has the military fostered natural exchanges—social or otherwise—between the officer corps and the civilian leadership, at least not up through 2000. The dilemma is that, if one accepts the shared responsibilities between civilians and the officer corps inherent in our model as a more accurate representation of what contemporary civil-military relations should be, and indeed are, then congruence between civil and military leadership would require significant changes in the typical traditional Mexican pattern. At the same time, such changes might be seen as expanding the military's political role rather than modifying and solidifying civilian supremacy. The secretary of national defense under President Fox has made it abundantly clear in his public comments that the advent of democracy only reinforces the military's loyalty. On Army Day in February 2002, the secretary remarked:

> His [President Fox] democratic election as president of the republic does not permit us to question anything and motivates us to complete with loyalty as we have always done, in spite of the winds which blow more strongly every day.... The Army in its behavior and action is by law subject without discussion to civil authority. Our Army is part of the change and progress our Supreme Commander has pushed. This change in no way is a personal or a group matter, it comes from the state, and the Congress of the Union is the competent organ to determine our organization and functions. Mexico can count on its soldiers in any circumstances, and this is important. This is our promise and is our strength.[7]

In 2004, General Vega García began taking a more outspoken posture toward government policies and, more importantly, toward the failure of the civilian leadership to address Mexico's pressing economic and social issues. His first step in the arena of public policy referred only to a minor issue, but it included implied criticism that the judicial system was not handing down sufficient penalties against drug traffickers detained by the Mexican army, allowing them to return after short periods of imprisonment to their criminal activities.[8] On February 19, 2005, the secretary of national defense, for the first time in the last five decades, issued a much stronger criticism of civil government during Army Day celebrations at the Heroico Colegio Militar. The audience included President Fox and other leading political figures. The secretary forcefully expressed his view that it was urgent for all political groups to negotiate policy differences for the betterment of the nation, otherwise the country's future would be in danger. He also noted that the armed forces would fully support such conciliatory methods and that such a strategy was essential for the country's national interests.[9] Four months later, on June 30, General Vega García not only called for conciliation among politicians but also asked the political leadership to pardon the military for past human rights abuses. This controversial appeal was supported by PRI leadership, since it was its members and former presidents who would bear responsibilities for these acts.[10]

The national defense secretary's posture appears to reflect the pattern that, as the legislative branch takes a more pro activist interest in military affairs, the armed forces takes a more open interest in government decision-making. The implications of the recent theoretical literature on civil-military relations, as well as elements from the modified equilibrium model, suggest a more balanced exchange between civilian and military personnel, the participants from both groups agree on the political rules of the game. The public statements cited above may suggest the beginnings of a newly defined relationship. Within the armed forces, General Vega García's public statements have produced numerous reactions. Among younger officers, he is credited with making it acceptable to speak more openly about national defense affairs.

Vicente Fox's selection of his national defense and navy secretaries suggests certain similarities with his predecessors. The process itself, however, produced some important contrasts with past selections. The appointees have qualities different from their predecessors, qualities which introduce potential implications for the larger civil-military relationship. Fox, like other Mexican presidents, maintained little contact with the armed forces or with high-ranking generals. In selecting his national defense secretary, he considered 16–18 generals, a large percentage of the pool of active duty division generals. What distinguishes Fox from his predecessors in considering names from this pool is that he has said he included President Zedillo and Zedillo's national defense secretary, General Cervantes Aguirre, in making his decision.[11]

Several important explanations have been offered for his selecting General Vega García as his secretary of national defense. First, Fox wanted to make sure his secretary of national defense had no hidden skeletons involving human rights violations. He believed Vega García was an excellent choice in this respect because his career had followed the educational administration tract.[12] Second, Vega García did not know Fox, but he did have personal contact with Fox's national security adviser, Adolfo Aguilar Zinzer. Third, all of the leading generals and regional commanders had dined together during the campaign with Francisco Labastida, the PRI candidate. Vega García was the only individual who declined the invitation.[13] Fourth, only Vega García, and General Delfino M. Palmerin Cordero, the other leading contender for the position, actually met Fox before he took office.[14] Finally, Vega García was viewed as an excellent choice to facilitate interaction and exchanges between the armed forces and civilians. Other analysts characterized him as an individual who was disposed to listening and tolerant of differences of opinion. The analysts believed that he was the most likely of any officer from his generation to have the skills needed to reasonably modify relations between the army and society.[15] He also was predisposed to complete any reevaluation of the army using civilian scrutiny and participation.[16]

When compared to his predecessors, Vega García's selection also is unique because of his credentials. Vega García, as noted above, held several major educational positions. This distinction, however, is exaggerated by Mexican analysts. A careful exploration of his career reveals numerous command positions, including serving as a battalion commander in Yucatán and Tabasco, as a zone commander in Chihuahua and Quintana Roo, and as a regional commander of the most strategically important and sensitive post, the 1st military region, which encompasses the Federal District.

The most risky characteristic of Vega García's credentials was the fact that he was the division general with the least seniority. This prompted 15 senior division generals, of the 30 on active duty (including five who were promoted November 20, 2000) to meet with Fox and his national security adviser several days before the cabinet was to be announced. They wanted to oppose Vega García's nomination. Allegedly, they were opposed to Vega García on the grounds that his promotion was only a year old, that he did not have troop command experience, and that his association with General Cervantes Aguirre, the incumbent national defense secretary, could possibly be interpreted as continuing Cervantes Aguirre's line.[17] Just a month before the designation, Vega García's name was not even included among the leading candidates. Vega García's lack of seniority (he ranked twenty-fourth among senior officers) is all the more remarkable considering that Fox's new secretary of navy, Admiral Peyrot González, and many of his immediate collaborators, had to be promoted to full admiral in order to fill their posts.[18]

As Latin American countries enter a period of democratization, "the nature of military leadership slowly will evolve as the officer corps discovers someone who can negotiate effectively with, rather than confront and attempt to bully, civilian authorities."[19] While the later part of this statement has never characterized Mexico's military relationship with civilian authorities, the argument that an effective negotiator, someone with political skills, is appropriate to the Mexican case. What has happened in Mexico at this point in time is that the civilian leadership, in the person of President Fox— not the officer corps—has picked just such an individual. If Vega García is successful in his tenure from both the officer corps' and civilian leadership's points of view, then both are more likely to coincide in their choice in 2006.

The implication of the isolation argument is that state leadership is divided along civil-military lines. Mexico's civilian leadership, at least until 2000, has been composed of individuals who were largely homogeneous. They were urban, middle class, and highly educated professional politicians. This had the "net result of reducing the level of hostility and conflict" within various agencies.[20] Fox introduced a significantly more heterogeneous group of politicians, including individuals from gubernatorial and congressional backgrounds, from the business community, and from international agencies. These changes, and the increased autonomy and influence of the legislative branch and governors, have significant consequences for a more diverse civilian leadership.[21]

In the past, in order to professionalize itself, to remove civilian or political influences from the military, Mexico's armed forces became increasingly hermetic and inwardly focused. One officer concluded that the military had pursued a purposeful policy: "Really, they don't want us to talk to anyone in order to make comparisons of our life and civilian life. In fact, of all the armies I can think of worldwide, I can't think of any military where this separation is more exaggerated. We have been purposely isolated in our development from civilians."[22] Modifications in Mexican society, especially since 1988, made it more apparent that the military, however many barriers it threw up against external "civilian" intervention, has been increasingly influenced by the values, attitudes, and expectations of civilian life. This influence is illustrated by the dramatic changes in their higher military academies, both in terms of the presence of civilian students and in the increased role civilian instructors, including politicians, play in imparting information and interpretations about major social, economic and political issues.

In the past, the presence of large numbers of military officers in civilian political offices, and large numbers of experienced politicians in top career military posts, lubricated channels of communication. Not only were these sets of leaders similar in background and experience but they expanded the breadth of personal ties between civil and military bureaucracies. The steady decline and essential elimination of the political-military officer removed this significant linkage and its many beneficial consequences for Mexican civil-military relations. New ties and bridges will have to be forged through freshly established relationships between representatives of the armed forces and members of the legislative and executive branches. These new relationships will emerge from democratic consolidation. This squares with a characteristic of our model, that the relationship is dynamic, and that neither actor should be isolated from the other.

A third characteristic which might impact on civil-military relations in the context of a modified equilibrium model, is the potential for conflict within a service branch or between branches. Mexico has moderated this tendency somewhat by providing a more unified service structure in terms of command, creating only two services, army and navy.[23] Under President López Portillo, the executive branch considered a proposal to unite the armed forces into one cabinet agency. López Portillo, after serious consideration, rejected the proposal.[24] After Fox's victory, critics again pushed this idea, including the appointment of a civilian national defense minister, but there is no evidence he or his staff gave it serious consideration. In his 2004 testimony before congress, General Vega García was asked if the armed forces was ready for a joint command or civilian leadership. He responded negatively to both questions.[25] Analysts argue that a civilian in charge of the armed forces would eliminate a significant barrier in civil-military relations because it would encourage the proliferation of civilian public officials specializing in military affairs.[26] Bland considers this lack of expertise as one of the fundamental weaknesses in civil-military relations.[27] This weakness continues to persist in the Mexican case.

Among the services, only the navy and the army function as independent executive branch agencies in Mexico. The air force is structurally integrated into the National Defense Secretariat, and is subordinate to that agency's leadership. In fact, it is only about one-twenty-fourth (7,480 personnel) the size of the army.[28] For many years, as indicated previously, most air force officers were trained with army cadets at the Heroico Colegio Militar, and later, when the Air College replaced it, at the Escuela Superior de Guerra. Today air force personnel attend the Heroico Colegio Militar for a short period of basic training before transferring to the Air College. The air force staff course at the Escuela Superior de Guerra is separate, and lasts only two years. According to officers who have attended the Escuela Superior de Guerra, air force and naval officers are not given equal respect by their army peers.[29] The marines do not even have departmental status but are incorporated directly into the navy.

Some evidence is beginning to come to light about inter-service rivalries between the army and navy. In 1981, during the pre-election fervor leading up to the designation of a government party presidential candidate, an important disagreement between the two became public. At issue were whether a military officer should run for the presidency and differences concerning national security plans. The Constitution does not bar the candidacy of a career officer, but the naval secretary publicly stated that a military candidate was inappropriate because plenty of well-qualified civilians were available. The national defense secretary, in contrast, noted some good army candidates were available, and said there was no reason to automatically exclude them just because they were career officers.[30] The two continued to disagree repeatedly and vocally on this and other issues.

Factionalism within the military has been identified in the literature as a feature which could open the door for civilian alliances and consequently involvement in internal military affairs. In turn that could have significant consequences for military subordination to civilian leadership. Mid-way through the Fox administration, some significant structural changes have been set in motion which increasingly distinguish the navy from the army. The navy has completely revised its internal governance and structure. It made the decision to reduce its bureaucratic apparatus and make its administrative structure more compact and efficient.[31] As I indicated earlier, the changes were introduced by a new generation of the youngest admirals, and are incorporated into the Navy Organic Law. For example, Article 25 of that law posits that a Council of Admirals should advise the secretary on policy and strategy, who in turn would execute their recommendations, that it should designate assignments above the rank of frigate captain (lieutenant colonel), that promotions should be in the hands of a committee of captains and admirals, and that the navy secretary should participate in the formulation of national security plans.[32]

The Army has not yet revised its organic law, although it has abrogated a number of outdated statues which went into effect between 1932 and 1976.[33] In 2002, the army revised Article 49 of its code to include changes in the Department of Social Communications, the agency in charge of the secretariat's public relations. Under the revisions, the department was directed to analyze information published in the media and the effects of its own information on media commentary.[34] In October 2003, as described in the previous chapter, the army created a Promotions Committee, similar in composition to the navy's. More importantly, beginning in June 2003, as part of the federal government's transparency laws, it began for the first time (as did the navy) to answer direct questions about the military, including providing previously unavailable statistics about numerous aspects of army/

air force life. The secretariat of national defense also made available on its website information about awards to private contractors, including names and amounts, prompting the media to criticize it for awarding six large contracts to Constructora y Edificadora Comalcalco, a company owned by the son of a retired division general.[35]

The fact that the navy has taken the lead on this and other radical internal structural changes, including a drastic reduction in the top ranks of the officer corps, is likely to make it more attractive to civilian politicians in both the executive and the legislative branches. Neither branch of government has as yet shown any favoritism toward the navy in reaction to these changes, but the army runs the risk of damaging its own image among political elites if these differences become well known. This is not yet the case in Mexico or abroad.

At this moment it is more likely that internal differences will produce more ramifications on civil-military relations than inter-service rivalries. The appearance of the internal army document in 1995 (referred to earlier) brought the serious level of dissension within the military out into the open. The most dramatic issue influencing internal divisions emerged during the succession process in 2000 resulting from President Fox's appointment of a new secretary of national defense. The media alleged that a group of 80 retired officers, most of whom were division generals, proposed General Miguel Angel Godínez, the former Chief of the Presidential Staff under President López Portillo, commander of the 31st Military Zone in Chiapas during the Zapatista uprising, and a congressman representing PRI from 1997 to 2000. According to sources in the army, this was purely a rumor. Nevertheless, the fact that it was reported in the media suggests the degree to which many senior officers, active and retired, were upset with the designation of a relatively junior officer, a move that ignored a fundamental principle of the armed forces rank structure, seniority and time in grade.[36]

Some structural changes did occur after the publication of this document during the Zedillo administration. All of the changes responded to strong criticisms and they included the following. The secretariat of national defense implemented a plan to decentralize training and place it in the hands of regional commanders, who in turn could respond to local conditions and situations. This criticism implied that the document's authors believed decision-making in the army to be over-centralized, a view expressed to the author by many individual officers.[37]

The army organized mobile Special Forces units in each region. Analyst Benítez Manaut, prior to 2000, called the creation of a special forces company in the army's First Corps the most revolutionary change in structure in the armed forces. The purpose of this change was to provide such mobile units for each region, a goal which was completed by 1996. The army added a Rapid Response Force in 1997, and mobile units to their military police and parachute brigades.[38] The army also created two schools for Special Forces training; the officer and instructor school was established formally in April, 2001, after Fox became president.[39] The army also restructured the general military educational plan and its educational system, and began requiring a preparatory certificate before enrolling in the Heroico Colegio Militar.[40]

The armed forces must also cope with externally-focused issues. In order for the military to become more integrated with its civilian counterparts, it will have to alter how it is perceived by both society and its own officers. When Fox became president, he said publicly that he wanted to "humanize" the armed forces, thus recognizing the existence of a gap in public perception.[41] The changes in democratic political influences taking place internationally are affecting the military and its relationship with society. As the armed forces have taken on non-traditional missions, especially in countries like Mexico, the boundaries between the military and society have become more obscure.[42] Both citizens and the officer corps have to wrestle with the acceptability of these missions, which are often related to internally-focused national security issues.[43]

Vicente Fox has highlighted three issues which impact the civil-military relationship in his administration: the violation of human rights, a major campaign theme; the role of the military in drug trafficking, which he initially wanted to terminate before taking over the presidency, and instead, made them a more effective tool in this mission; and the use of the military in international peacekeeping, a dramatic shift in the armed forces' mission and in Mexico's foreign policy posture.[44]

In redefining and reformulating civil-military relations, the democratic setting is both a goad to a modified relationship and, at the same time, a possible source of obstacles to maintaining civilian supremacy. The major weakness of the modified equilibrium model, as applied to the Mexican and Latin American case, is that it assumes a priori, since it originates from analyses of democratic, post-industrial societies, that civil institutions are strong and legitimate. In the Mexican case, this was true for the pre-democratic model for many years, and explains why Mexico, unlike the rest of Latin America, has been able to maintain civilian supremacy since 1929. But in shifting to the democratic model in the 1990s, although it fulfills numerous other characteristics of the modified equilibrium model's description of civil-military relations, the strength and legitimacy of Mexican democracy remains untested. The condition of the civil institutions themselves is the most vulnerable quality. This ambivalence is borne out by a 2004 United Nations survey of Latin America, in which 44 percent agreed that democracy cannot solve their country's problems, and that 55 percent would support an authoritarian government if it would resolve their economic problems.[45]

The modified equilibrium model offers another characteristic which fits smoothly with a consolidating and consolidated democracy, the concept of friendly adversaries. As suggested in the introduction, this presumes that the adversaries disagree with one another at times yet pursue their priorities using democratic "rules of the game."[46] Mexico is now deeply into a transition to a more pluralistic model. But Mexican society's appreciation for democratic principles may be tenuous. For example, after 2000, voters whose candidate won the presidency were more likely to view Mexico as a democracy than those who supported the losing party. In other words, if their candidate lost, it affected how Mexicans viewed the actual existence of democratic processes. Not all Mexicans have accepted democratic norms. The most difficult concept to accept is tolerance toward opposition.

The concept of friendly adversaries not only affects the way politics is conducted but also encourages various individuals to function as spokespersons for particular interests. One of the peculiarities of the military, one shared across societal boundaries, is the military's inability in developing countries to bargain politically. According to one analyst, the military finds it difficult to adjust to political bargaining because its socialization process takes place in a closed educational and training environment.[47] Mexico is no exception. This exclusivity typically encourages institutional secrecy and isolation. Naturally, the competitiveness of the Mexican political system since 1997 has created structural conditions favorable to breaking down some of these barriers. Indeed, Mexican officers report that all leading political parties are showing increased interest in military affairs. This is reflected in the fact that, in 2004, it was not only members of the National Defense Committee who addressed questions to the secretariat of national defense when he appeared before that body. Other members of congress also had questions.

Isolation enhances non-bargaining behavior, but is not likely the most important variable in determining it. First, lack of adversarial respect affects all political actors, civilian and military alike. The difference is that military actors elsewhere, unaccustomed to operating in the context of democratic give-and-take, often resort to force, finding it an acceptable rule of the game. Instead, Mexican national defense and navy secretaries have represented military interests to the executive branch. They have negotiated within the confines of a narrow and well-established agenda, one which presupposed limited budget expenditures, an established tradition in civil-military affairs.

Equally important, acceptance of opposing viewpoints rarely exists among leadership groups in isolation from the beliefs of the populace;

rather, it is a by-product of the general citizen culture. This is why the socialization of ordinary Mexicans establishes a foundation from which the military academies can build their own formative values. Second, the political system can be structured in such a way that interest articulation, as it is usually understood in the United States, is atypical. Prior to 1997, open interest articulation was inhibited by the fact that the legislative branch played little, if any, role in decision making in Mexico. The level of electoral competition and representation since 1997 redirected a emphasis on bargaining or brokering skills. It became readily apparent during the first five years of the Fox administration that neither his cabinet, nor congressional representatives, displayed these skills, resulting in voter cynicism with the democratic process.

The concept of representing one's interests before congress has only just begun to take on importance in the political system. The armed forces are far behind other groups, notably NGO's, in presenting their case to congress.[48] Occasionally, when a political issue involves veterans' benefits, some evidence of associational support from retired military officers is apparent.[49] Generally speaking, however, the military procurement process is a silent one, closed to outsiders. These decisions, prior to the 1990s, were made in the executive branch, not congress. For example, when Mexico made the decision to purchase F-5 fighter planes from the United States, it was evident that no efforts were made to mobilize supporters in the outer realm of policy-making, including interest groups or opposition members of Congress.[50]

The increasingly important role of the legislative branch in policy-making is a third theme altering the traditional pre-democratic civil-military pattern entrenched in the executive branch. First, by law, it is congress which is responsible for overseeing what goes on in all government agencies. Given its increasing desire to perform oversight functions, the secretaries of navy and national defense have had to respond to congress differently from their predecessors. Mexico's traditional lack of congressional oversight is typical of most Latin American countries.[51]

According to critics, in spite of the fact that the opposition parties controlled the Chamber of Deputies in the fifty-seventh Congress (1997–2000), they never modified or even discussed the three proposed armed forces budgets presented by the executive branch.[52] PRD representatives did demand an explanation for the Secretariat of National Defense's excess expenditures of $2,000 million pesos in 1999.[53] The best the fifty-seventh Congress could do was to request the oficial mayor of both military secretariats to appear before their committee to explain the budget, the first time someone at this level had made such a presentation.[54] In the Senate, the secretary of the National Defense Committee publicly stated that the military was obliged to inform the committee of its activities.⁵⁵ When he discovered that the expenditures were increasing, he complained that "there is a total secretiveness from the Secretary of National Defense and from the National Defense Committee presided by a general who most helps his institution."⁵⁶ The National Action Party delegation specifically requested budget information from the Navy and the National Defense secretariats, saying that the data made available to them was too general.⁵⁷

These and other patterns found within the military impact significantly on civil-military relations and led for the first time a political party, the PRD, to publicly criticize the Mexican army in 1999. The PRD's major criticisms are revealing in what they suggest about civilian politicians' views of the armed forces at the end of the century. Among their most significant points are:

- Abuses in the presidential military staff should be curbed.
- Key presidential budget staff on the armed forces should be controlled by the Controller General.
- Presidential military aides should be replaced by civilian aides.
- Personnel files used in the promotion process are superficial.
- Persons to be promoted are friends protected by various interests creating "enormous injustice and deep demoralization within army ranks."
- The Heroico Colegio Militar and other schools are not adequate to train officers, and it, and other military academies should be reorganized to graduate college level students.
- The future Secretariat of National Defense should combine all the services.
- The army/air force should revise the promotion regulations so that assignments and personnel correspond.⁵⁸

As I have indicated, some of these criticisms have actually been addressed since 2000. But the structural change in the Mexican political system with the greatest potential for changing the process of civil-military relations is congress's newly assertive role. In September 2000, representatives of the newly elected Congress stated they would end the privilege of the armed forces' secretaries in typically avoiding direct appearances before Congress.⁵⁹ General Vega García became only the second secretary of national defense to address the deputies directly in the legislative palace, and his counterpart in the navy was the first.⁶⁰ Previously, deputies had usually met with the secretaries in private, and at a site chosen by the secretaries.⁶¹ In 2002, 36 deputies attended a session with the secretary of national defense, and most of them asked questions, all of which were answered. By the fall of 2004, Vega García had appeared before the deputies four times.

During his 2004 appearance, several deputies asked that the press be allowed to witness the session.[62] Members of the national defense committee visited national defense headquarters, the department of military education, the Army/Air Force University, the Heroico Colegio Militar, the Escuela Superior de Guerra, and the Colegio de Defensa Nacional that same year.[63] General Vega García himself characterized his budget discussions with congress as more detailed and open, and his contact with both senators and deputies as more frequent.[64]

The Mexican senate also asserted its oversight role more aggressively after 2000. In December, 2000, two weeks after Fox's inauguration, the National Defense Committee held a working meeting to discuss the promotion process and review all of the proposed promotion requests from the president and the secretary of national defense. Individuals up for promotion can now expect to get requests for more information. The Navy Committee held two meetings with the secretary of navy, who presented the navy's plan for the following years, including the radical restructuring and the proposed candidates for promotion.[65] More interestingly, the Senate engaged in a debate over what in the United States would be a highly controversial issue, military base closings.[66]

The situation between the armed forces and congress can also be explained by the characteristics found in the relationship between the Mexican executive branch and the armed forces. This relationship, as is true of the legislative patterns, is highlighted by budget issues, which largely are tied to increases in size and equipment. Under the 1994–2000 administration, the armed forces increased only 9.7 percent, the smallest increase in decades, and as of 2003, Fox had expanded the military by only 1.7 percent.[67] Historically, relative to its Latin American counterparts, it has been under-equipped in regard to modern weaponry and support vehicles. Nevertheless, expenditures for equipment have been so niggardly since the 1940s that even the most complacent military officers are disgruntled. Analysts suggest that the military budget "is recognized as insufficient for the completion of its mission repeatedly and publicly, but the high command also recognizes publicly the need for revenues to cover other demands such as education and public health."[68] General Vega García, in his published writings, has given equal emphasis to social and economic development as a crucial component of national security.[69]

The relationship between the civilian decision-makers in programming and budgeting and the Secretariat of National Defense reveals some important aspects of civil-military relations in general. These have affected the current relationship with both the executive and legislative branches. A former budget secretary described the way military funding decisions are made (his account was corroborated by several other former secretaries in interview sessions):

> Let me explain how the funding is allocated. In the first place, there are two types of accounts; current accounts and investments. The first type of account, the current account, includes payments that are provided for salaries and basic clothing and equipment. Increases in the current account occur through two basic channels. The first increase, which one might call a "natural" increase, is through wages. The second increase, which is more important, is the increase in the number of military units. *What you need to understand is that in this second type of increase, because of our lack of information and expertise on military matters, it is extremely difficult for us to evaluate if such increases are actually needed.*
>
> I will say, by and large, that both types of requests, even in the case where they ask for an additional battalion, are typically reasonable and modest. They don't ask for a new unit every year. In my experience, I found them to be reasonable in their requests for current account expenditures. However; automatically, when you have an increase in a battalion, there will be an increase in the investment side. In other words, you have to authorize increases in equipment, housing, and a variety of other costs associated with maintaining a new battalion.
>
> Now, let's examine the investment side as opposed to the current account. The investment side has three channels. First, new investment that is automatically derived from the establishment of a new unit or battalion. Second, and the easiest to judge, is the maintenance and repair of existing equipment. These two areas are reasonable to determine because we have some basis in past experience for determining their cost. The third channel, however, is the one involving new equipment over and above equipment that is only being replaced. It is in this category, the new equipment category, which the decisions are entirely in their hands. That is to say, *they are the ones that request the new investment.* It is really very easy to evaluate the first two types of requests, but the third category is very difficult. As I said before, you have a basis for the first two. However, I again would emphasize that the actual expenditures are very low. We give that figure to them in a lump sum. That is the one category that we do provide the money in a lump sum.
>
> In my time there was a department that handled the Secretariats of National Defense, Navy, and Government. In other words, these were people within programming and budgeting who helped me evaluate the requests of those three secretariats. But, even those individuals who were more well informed than the average official in my agency were really not able to adequately judge new acquisitions.[70]

This careful explanation suggests two points. First, the amount of money requested is small. No one in government disputes this conclusion. Multiple presidents have made similar statements. López Portillo was emphatic about this point, noting that "the military never had put any pressure on me as president or when I was budget secretary to expand their budget. It is always the president who takes the initiative, not the secretary of national defense. They never had asked for an increase in salaries in my personal experience. I initiated this myself for my own reasons, not because they put any pressure on me."[71] President de la Madrid echoed these sentiments, indicating that when he served as budget secretary he would give the national defense secretary a general figure. The national defense secretary then would come back to him with a report on the distribution of funds in each category and a rationale for those amounts. He always found their requests to be reasonable and extremely modest, and that they never exaggerated their expenses.[72] Because it is perceived by presidents and their finance secretaries as reasonable, the military's budget request is usually approved.

Second, it is clear that in the budgetary context, as elsewhere in the relationship, civilians are essentially ignorant about the military and its needs. The two points an interrelated. Regarding budgetary matters, a wall between the two groups persists because there is no economic pressure for the civilians involved to learn more about the military. The military's allocations are such a small part of the overall budget that civilian politicians generally, and budgeting officials specifically, have little incentive to strengthen relations with the military. This general lack of interest among politicians is transferred to the citizenry in general. In an editorial published during the congressional elections of 2003, General Garfías Magaña complained about the total lack of interest in military affairs during the campaign.[73]

Despite evidence that budget matters have not become a subject of controversy in civil-military relations, unlike other Latin American countries, Mexican military budgets are a serious issue among the officer corps when it comes to salaries and to pensions. The military's budget as a percentage of Gross Domestic Product has remained stable at the 0.50 to 0.60 percentage since the first year of the Zedillo administration.[74] As a percentage of the government expenditures, however, figures began to move from the 2 percent level at the beginning of the 1990s, where it had been for many years, to 5 percent by the first year of the Zedillo administration.[75] But during the remainder of his administration, it declined in real terms because of a decline in overall government expenditures. As a result of the new transparency rules, the military budget became much more open to scrutiny, in terms of expenditures, after 2003, when both the secretariats of navy and national defense published budget links on their websites. These budget figures break down expenditures by numerous categories, including regional and zone commands.[76]

Despite added spending on personnel and new weaponry, regardless of whether it appears in the military budget, the total outlay for the military is low relative to needs. Much of its regular funding goes into educational and social services. One of the most persistent and controversial issues in the armed forces, on which there is universal agreement within the institution, is the uncompetitive pay and retirement benefits. Presidents have recognized the severe inequalities between civilian and military pay.[77] The base pay of a division general with 45 years of service in 1998 was only three times what a private made.[78] In 2004, a retired division general was receiving the paltry amount of $10.50 pesos daily. In contrast, a retired supreme court justice was receiving $3,800 pesos daily.[79]

The retirement situation is worse. An active duty major receives more pay than a retired division general. Military officers were shocked when President Fox, for the first time in history, vetoed the armed forces social security bill on April 2, 2003. The veoted legislation attempted to correct some of the more serious disparities. According to many officers, the pay and retirement situation has bred significant levels of resentment and distrust among officers of all ranks. Midway through the Fox administration, however, the monthly salary (prior to taxes) of the general ranks rose to 174,078, 134,885, and 99,356 pesos respectively for a three star, two star and one star general, reflecting a significant increase from previous pay scales. In US dollars, those figures would approximate $17,400, $13,500, and $9,900 in 2003.

Perhaps the single-most important alteration in civil-military relations in the last two decades is the changing role of the armed forces in the decision-making process, specifically in policy arenas related to national security. National security policy has unquestionably been characterized in Mexico as fluid and evolving since the 1980s. What is most significant about the evolution of national security policy for civil-military relations is its redefinition, and the military's expanded role in performing some of those redefined missions. In the early 1980s the officer corps, believing the state needed its assistance, sought an expanded role. The move presaged a trend toward military expansion into areas that were previously the responsibility of civilian agencies. The new roles were primarily related to controlling drug trafficking. By the 1990s, they also were dealing with the consequences of widespread criminal activity, only some of which was drug related. Critics viewed these new missions as the militarization of Mexican society.

The drug war began in earnest under President Zedillo, when the secretariat of national defense issued the Azteca directive, establishing a permanent military campaign against drug-trafficking.[80] Zedillo expanded the military's law enforcement powers by modifying the constitution and criminal codes.

Generals were put in charge of the Federal Judicial Police, the National Institute to Combat Drugs, and the Center for the Planning of Drug Control (CENDRO). CENDRO has expanded its role well beyond drug control; it now has a role in a wide range of federal crimes.[81] Perhaps most importantly, from a decision-making perspective, the military has increased its control of the Center for National Security and Investigation, the government's intelligence agency. At the state level, military personnel occupied two thirds of the top law enforcement posts by 1998.[82] Since the end of the Salinas administration, after nearly fifty years of declining expenditures, national security spending increased nearly three-fold between 1986 and 1995.

After taking office, Fox realized the magnitude of the drug problem and decided to not only maintain the armed forces' national security posture on drug trafficking but also expand it in other ways. In terms of policy making itself, Fox has encouraged officials from all the services to participate in inter-institutional efforts to establish federal public security policies, similar to the way inter-agency groups operate in the United States. This pattern is being repeated at the state level.[83] The secretariat of national defense staff sections 2 and 7, the staff in charge of army intelligence and military operations respectively, have taken over responsibility for investigating drug cartels' leadership structures and apprehending their leaders. Furthermore, Fox has directly involved the special forces battalions in supporting regional commanders' "high-impact" operations.[84]

Structurally, Fox introduced two notable institutional changes in Mexico. First, he created a new cabinet level agency of Public Security and Justice Services.[85] His administration also expanded the Federal Preventative Police by 25 percent in 2001–2002.[86] The second, and most influential change, one which has significantly affected the military's performance of these crime-related missions, is the increased level of collaboration between the Attorney General's office and the secretariat of national defense. This was brought about by Fox's surprise appointment of a career military officer as his first attorney general.[87] In 2003, 202 members of the armed forces were assigned to the attorney general.[88] This collaboration has altered the pattern of civil-military relations in general and established a positive relationship in what has been a traditionally antagonistic relationship in previous administrations. This new linkage between federal civil and military leaders serves as a linchpin in the relationship and as a precedent for improved relations generally at the federal agency level.

The armed forces presented their newly defined tasks in three National Defense Plans. The first of these, DN-I, focuses on the military's self-identified tasks for improved modernization and professionalization. The second,

DN-II, is the most controversial of the three plans. It covers all national security missions, including activities in military zones and regional structures and intelligence. The third plan focuses on humanitarian aid missions. The army has taken up challenges under all three plans. But in order to carry out the numerous tasks in the expanded national security missions, they may well be taking a detour on their path toward modernization and professionalization. The new path could lead to less efficiency in performing traditionally civilian tasks or, perhaps, to more overt politization.[89] In spite of these real dangers, it has performed some of these national security tasks more effectively than under Fox's predecessor, and as yet, has not allowed itself to become politicized by civilian factions or political parties.

Under Fox, the navy has pursued a similar set of missions. Importantly, it defines national security, which it views as a fundamental naval responsibility, as guaranteeing security and peace in order to consolidate democratic advances and social and economic development.[90] More importantly, in the navy's pioneering new organic law, national security receives greater priority as the primary naval function compared to the traditional view setting forth external defense.[91] It elucidates the navy's position further, clearly placing drug trafficking, organized crime, and terrorism as primary threats to the integrity of society, the population, and Mexico's infrastructure. It calls on the civilian leadership to define just solutions for these problems.[92]

Analysts and military officers alike have been accurate in their assessment that such national security missions would expose the officer corps to higher levels of corruption. Between 1995 and 2000, nearly 150 officers were tried for crimes linked to drug trafficking. In the Navy, between 1993 and 2003, 7 officers were tried for similar crimes, including 3 captains (colonels). In the first three years of the Fox administration, only 12 individuals have been arrested for crimes related to drug trafficking.[93]

The Fox administration, however, has tried numerous officers, among them top-ranked individuals, for drug-related crimes committed prior to his administration. In 2001, the army convicted the former drug czar, General Jesús Gutiérrez Rebollo, for illicit enrichment, among other charges.[94] A council of war convicted General Ricardo Martínez Perea and two other officers of protecting gulf cartel members. They planned to charge 10 other ex-military from the 21st mechanized cavalry regiment for the same crimes.[95]

The other national security issue confronting recent administrations has been the rise of guerrilla movements since the Ejército Zapatista de Liberación Nacional made its presence known in January 1994. Fox, however, has not considered the Zapatistas to be a national security threat. As his national security adviser argued, "On the contrary, it is the Zapatistas and their supporters who have been threatened, who have lost the most people since 1994. It is their communities that have been in danger. . . . War was not declared against us but against a regime that is now over and done with."[96]

Fox has not had any more success than his predecessors in negotiating a final solution with the Zapatistas. But the army's view, expressed by General Vega García, reflects a similar posture to that of the president's first national security adviser, that the strategy favored by the armed forces is dialogue because, as he has noted in his own national security writings, eradicating poverty is the first step in eliminating insurgencies.[97] General Vega García views the task of national security as a civil and military policy issue, with humanistic components, constructed on a societal consensus.[98] However, he does view the Revolutionary People's Army (ERP), which is committed to violent tactics, as a major national security threat.

The increasing emphasis on national security missions has not only altered the role of the military in the decision-making process but, since the 1970s, has highlighted a controversial issue involving the armed forces: human rights violations. The armed forces human rights record is significant for civil-military relations within the larger setting because it impinges on military subordination to civilian leadership. Human rights abuses are not confined to the issue of military violations, but equally important in the context of civil-military affairs and civilian supremacy within a democratic setting, the accountability of officers and troops to legal punishment. Human rights are central to the issue of military autonomy from civilian oversight and control and, until quite recently, the military has enforced its autonomy from civilian interference on this matter.

National and international human rights organizations state the problem succinctly. Even after Fox took office, soldiers who committed abuses in the line of duty were legally accountable to military authorities, but neither they nor the military court system were accountable to civilians. This arrangement resulted in human rights violations going unpunished.[99] Specifically, the Military Code of Justice grants the military courts jurisdiction over military personnel accused of civilian crimes when such crimes are committed as part of military service.[100] The Military Code of Justice also permits the military to punish soldiers for not following an order, without taking into consideration whether or not it was unconstitutional or violated a civil law.[101]

The military heritage and practice of human rights abuses is not confined to Mexico. The military's relation to the administration of justice will be a dominant theme in the coming decade in Latin American civil-military relations. This is partly the case because of ongoing efforts to reduce levels of military immunity and to extend jurisdiction of civilian courts into military affairs.[102] The increased presence of the Mexican armed forces in anti-drug trafficking missions and anti-crime tasks generally, has contributed to the increased number of violations.[103] The Organization of American States Inter-American Commission on Human Rights, at the end of the Zedillo administration, urged the government to reform the legislation on the national system of public security to restrict the military to an external defense role against outside attackers in conformance with international law, a position that neither Mexico nor any other Latin American military is likely to take in the foreseeable future.[104]

The armed forces human rights record involves two sets of actors. The group which has received the most attention is civilians who have been abused by the military, whether they were students, suspected guerrillas, family members and friends of guerrillas, or alleged drug traffickers. Unfortunately, the armed forces has a long history of abuses, including its own severe dirty war against leftists in the early 1970s. General José F. Gallardo, who investigated the disappearance of 12 students who passed through his command as a junior officer in 1970, discovered they had been injected with a horse anesthetic and thrown out of a plane over Lake Chapala, Jalisco.[105] Army human rights abuses, including summary executions, were documented in the Zapatista uprising, as have cases involving persecuted members or alleged members of the Popular Revolutionary Army in Oaxaca in the late 1990s.[106] President Fox has allowed investigations into earlier human rights violations from this period, but investigators have discovered that crucial orders and papers are missing from the National Archives, including records from the Secretariat of Government, the Secretariat of National Defense, and the Federal Security Directorate.[107] The Secretariat of National Defense also dragged its feet in cooperating with government prosecutors investigating the death of human rights leader Digna Ochoa.[108]

The army's abuse of civilians is part of a larger problem endemic to the criminal justice system in Mexico. Torture and forced confessions are a common practice in Mexico. These practices contribute to, and are a product of, societal attitudes toward alleged criminals. Citizens were asked in a 1993 survey if a group of soldiers decided to kill a drug trafficker they had just arrested, do you believe those soldiers should be punished for this crime? Mexicans gave the following answers: 13.4 percent said definitely yes; 29.3 percent, yes; 18.8 percent, depends; 15.7 percent, no; 9.3 percent, definitely no; 11.8 percent, don't know; and 1.7 percent, no answer. Citizen expectations about how alleged criminals are to be treated need to change fundamentally in order to reinforce human rights friendly standards in the justice system.

Independent human rights organizations in Mexico present statistics indicating that the military and the police are typically among those groups cited for the highest number of human rights violations.[109] International organizations present well-documented examples of fabrication of evidence and torture by the military in the late 1990s.[110] These organizations believe that the use of military personnel to conduct counter-narcotics operations and counter-insurgency missions, allowing them direct access to the civilian population, exacerbate the likelihood of such violations.[111]

The armed forces also have committed abuses against its own personnel; the victims are not protected by civilian authorities. The notable cases in recent years received national and international media attention. The case of General José Francisco Gallardo is instructive. Gallardo, the youngest brigadier general of his generation, attended a special breakfast for Vicente Fox on September 8, 1993. During the meal, he spoke about military human rights abuses and the need for a military ombudsman. He gave Fox a copy of his dissertation on the topic. The editor of the magazine Forum asked if he could publish what Gallardo had written.[112] Shortly after this article appeared in print, the army arrested him. Gallardo was arrested for "spreading negative ideas about the Mexican military, with the object of dishonoring, offending, and discrediting the military in the eyes of the public."[113] The army prosecuted Gallardo on a series of unrelated charges involving the misuse of military funds. He was court-martialed, convicted of these charges, and imprisoned.[114] Despite repeatedly pleas by the Inter-American Organization of Human Rights first to the Zedillo administration and then to Fox, Gallardo remained in prison until February 8, 2002, when president Fox granted him a release but not a pardon.[115]

The second case, which occurred in December, 1998 and involved even more broadly the internal problems of human rights in the military, was a group protest, consisting of several dozen enlisted personnel and junior officers led by Lt. Colonel Hildegardo Bacilio Gómez, a medical corps officer. Calling themselves the Patriotic Command to Raise the Consciousness of the People, they presented an odd mixture of confused demands. The central complaint voiced by its members was that armed forces personnel should "receive the same rights as ordinary citizens and that the military court system be reformed along the lines of civilian courts to stop corruption and the imprisonment of innocent soldiers."[116]

Bacilio Gómez's complaints generated much greater publicity than Gallardo's case because he led fifty soldiers in a public protest march down the Paseo de la Reforma, the main thoroughfare in downtown Mexico City, which included members of congress from the Democratic Revolutionary Party, the only political party which had taken an interest in military affairs.[117] The Army was unprepared for such a demonstration.[118] Because of the significant media coverage, the army had to respond to some of these public complaints. Surprisingly, the oficial mayor of the secretary of national defense, General Fausto M. Zamorano Esparza, admitted to reporters that "we know that many of his complaints have some truth to them."[119] The president of the congressional committee on national defense, a longtime PRI member and division general, Ramón Mota Sánchez, blamed the PRD for manipulating the discontent to create fissures within the armed forces, claiming that "we know that for the Marxists the number one enemy in order to obtain power is the army."[120]

The commotion Bacilio Gómez created within the army and in the public arena eventually prompted the Mexican senate, in April of 1999, to request information on the situation of military human rights and individual guarantees within the armed forces.[121] Bacilio Gómez, who went into hiding, was eventually arrested, tried, and imprisoned in the 3rd Military Region for a year. President Fox removed him from jail. Since his release, he has not made any statements. As of 2005, this protest has not led to any reforms in the internal military justice system. In 2001, Anthony Pereira concluded that, in spite of its "history of civilian supremacy over the military and its different mode of democratic transition, Mexico shares with Brazil and Chile a highly insulated military justice system that at present seems impervious to democratic reform."[122]

The notable national and international attention given to human rights abuses inside and outside the military has produced some changes within the armed forces. The army began giving human rights serious attention beginning in 1999 when, for the first time, they devoted the entire July issue in the official *Revista de Ejército y Fuerza Aérea* to that topic. A significant and continuous change in emphasis on human rights can be detected in the magazine since January, 2001.[123]

The navy, in its new *Manual for Naval Personnel*, includes the history and a detailed description of human rights issues, noting that President Fox's National Development Plan 2001–2006 establishes a new vision of Mexico in relation to the protection and defense of human rights as incorporated in the Mexican Constitution.[124] According to statistics made available by the secretariat of national defense, thousands of officers and enlisted men have attended courses and conferences on human rights. The numbers exceeded 7,000 personnel in 2002 alone. These figures did not include numerous conferences given by representatives of state human rights commissions.[125] General Vega García reintroduced a significant legal inconsistency in military law, however, when he suggested in 2002 that military personnel would be subject to criminal punishment if they rely on presidential orders to commit illegal acts, when the same consequences are not clearly delineated for acts committed under military orders.[126]

In the last year of the Zedillo administration, the Mexican government set a precedent regarding military violations of human rights by paying 100,000 pesos, awarding student scholarships, and providing medical attention to the family of a Tarahumara Indian tortured and murdered by an army captain. In addition, the captain was sentenced to 30 years in prison. Human rights observers believed this to be a significant example of reversing the existing pattern of impunity for human rights violations committed by members of the armed forces.[127]

This individual case received attention largely from the human rights community. Of much greater significance was the trial of influential high-ranking officers for their role in the torture and disappearance of citizens during the 1970s dirty war. Two generals were convicted of murdering 143 people at a military base in Acapulco and later dumping their bodies from a plane into the Pacific Ocean.[128] Sergio Aguayo, a leading human rights figure, noted that the military, not civilians, were the first to try and convict individuals for these notorious abuses. He believed this judgment will have an enormous impact inside the armed forces and demonstrate that General Vega García's reformist tendencies on this issue are continuing. Vega García himself considers their internal efforts on human rights training to be one of the most significant changes during his administration.[129] However, General Vega García, as suggested earlier, is not requesting continued civilian investigation of crimes committed in the past. Instead, the message being sent is that the army is capable of reforming itself and recognizes its responsibilities.[130]

The other policy-making sphere in which military involvement is likely to impact on civil-military relations is foreign affairs. The military's role in bilateral relations with the United States has been minimal, if not nonexistent. Since the mid-1980s cooperation between the two militaries became more extensive. In spite of their cooperation, the Mexican army steadfastly rejected any relationship with the Panama-based U.S. Southern Command (now Miami). Any security assistance programs the U.S. oversaw from Mexico City operated out of a small defense attaché's office in the American embassy (the Mexican government would not allow the Americans to run the usual "military group" out of the national defense secretariat).[131] During the Zedillo administration (1994–2000), the secretary of national defense helped foster "interaction and cooperation with the United States to a greater extent than had been present in the past."[132] In spite of his efforts and a growing level of cooperation, at the end of 1999 the United States and Mexico suspended their cooperation on the exchange of military equipment after Mexico refused to participate in joint naval operations in the pursuit of narcotics traffickers.[133] The United States provided Mexico with $264,912,000 in military aid from 1990 to 2000.[134]

Some evidence exists of greater military participation than normal in foreign affairs. Beginning in 1980, as a result of Mexico's Central American policy, the Secretariat of National Defense increased and reassigned its personnel in the region, providing alternative military intelligence.[135] But in the 1990s, as the Zapatista uprising in Chiapas makes clear, civilian leadership ignored military intelligence on potential guerrilla activity, allowing the uprising to occur unchallenged. The armed forces never played a crucial role in determining foreign policy in the region, but it did exercise a larger voice on some issues, such as southern immigration.[136]

Three issues directly involving the military have replaced the foreign policy concerns of the 1980s. Each one has a potential for altering the military's voice in the general decision-making process, and therefore on established patterns of civil-military relations. The first of these is the armed forces drug enforcement mission. The pursuit of that mission, which the United States strongly encouraged, involves some cooperation between the armed forces and American federal agencies.[137] Recently, the United States has increased its pressure on the national defense staff, especially special operations, to focus on terrorism threats.[138] The armed forces also has become increasingly involved in border disputes with the U.S. Border Patrol. They even fired on an agent on the American side of the border in Ajo, Arizona in May 2002. Since 1996, there have been more than 118 incursions across the U.S. border, 61 by the Mexican military.[139]

The second issue is border security, which also is linked to drug trafficking and illegal immigration. These concerns have been highlighted since the September 11, 2001 terrorist attacks. Institutionally, the United States created a Northern Command, responsible for cooperation in coordinating military affairs and security with Canada and Mexico.[140] In spite of his friendship with Colin Powell, General Vega García indicated that Mexico would not join this command in the immediate future, maintaining the armed forces traditional posture of independence from all foreign militaries.[141] Nevertheless, in comparison with previous administrations, the secretary of national defense has increased military contact with the United States and, as of early 2004, General Vega García had traveled to the United States on three occasions, including a visit with Defense Secretary Donald Rumsfeld. Vega García characterized their contacts as "more frequent and at a higher level."[142]

The most interesting shift in the armed forces posture linked to foreign policy is the military's role in humanitarian or international missions. In August, 1990, President Salinas offered to send troops as part of a multilateral force under United Nations command after Iraq invaded Kuwait. Mexico had never previously offered to participate in an international force in a combat situation. The president came in for severe criticism from intellectuals and opposition parties, although the officer corps said nothing publicly.[143] The military pressured the president to withdraw this offer on January 3, 1991.[144] In 1996, under President Zedillo, Mexico began sending troops abroad for humanitarian missions, although doing so violates the constitution. It did so ten times between 1996 and January 2001.[145] In undertaking those missions, the army pursued a new level of international cooperation, and, as one analyst correctly argues, demonstrated an increased ability to respond to domestic problems in Mexico through its experience and flexibility in practicing international rapid response strategies.[146] Despite performing these new tasks, the officer corps expressed serious reservations about this mission.[147]

The Mexican navy has participated in these missions but, unlike the army, has also involved itself in international war games exercises. In December 2001, the secretary of navy, Admiral Antonio Peyrot González, announced that the navy would participate in multi-national war games, and that presidential approval was sufficient. The PRI congressional delegation opposed this decision on the grounds that it lacked congressional approval.[148] The following year, once again the navy secretary announced that the fleet would participate in multinational exercises without Senate authorization.[149] In response, the Senate naval committee announced it would request the Supreme Court to clarify this question under Article 76, which authorizes the Senate to approve any foreign troops in Mexico or any Mexican troops stationed abroad.[150] The Senate, in September 2002, introduced a reform to Article 76, Section 3, of the Constitution.[151]

All of these changes in military behavior, including its relations with the United States, have occurred within the larger context of closer economic cooperation between Mexico and the United States as part of the North American Free Trade Agreement. Monica Serrano argued that:

> To the extent that NAFTA has increased the strategic importance of Mexico for the United States, it has already unleashed a regional security dynamic likely to affect the tasks and roles performed by the armed forces. NAFTA's implications for civil-military relations in Mexico cuts both ways. On the one hand, under NAFTA the U.S. government could exert pressure on Mexico to modify its understanding of national security and to incorporate an external dimension, possibly bringing instability to the civil-military pact. On the other, NAFTA could provide the Mexican government with an external platform to regulate civil-military relations and to reinforce civilian supremacy.[152]

Serrano's forecast of possible influences have been correct. In the aftermath of September 11, 2001, it appeared that the United States was not successful in persuading Mexico to redefine its security concerns or strategy. In actuality, the national defense staff has made such a shift, and officers report that the special operations staff takes pride in the fact that they are equipped to oversee both anti-drug and terrorism threats to national security. Broadly speaking, NAFTA has been most effective in encouraging media attention from the North, therefore reinforcing attention from human rights groups (which preceded the agreement by many years), and modifying issues and behavior which have affected the civil-military relationship in the past.

Conclusions

The model we have used to analyze Mexican civil-military relations posits seven important characteristics. As these conclusions demonstrate, the current relationship squarely meets five of the conditions set forth in the model. These conditions include agreement on the rules of the political game and the processes used for their interactions, civilian political actors making the primary decisions about military missions, civilian control is superior but responsibility is shared among civilian and military officials, civilians outside of the military are ultimately in control, and that Mexico, similar to other societies, has generated its own specific features. The two remaining characteristics in our model are only partially fulfilled. First, various actors are not fully in agreement on the norms of behavior. This is most clearly illustrated in the armed forces' relations with the media and outsiders generally. Second, the civil-military relationship is dynamic, but the army still remains isolated from society and from civilian actors. It is less isolated today than just several years ago, nevertheless, it remains overly protective of its identity and activities.

In general terms, what has been the military's role in the decision-making process in the last several decades, and has the military increased its influence significantly since Fox took office? The available evidence reaffirms that the military through the 1990s exercised a limited role in the decision making process. Historically, in highly selective political decisions, several of which introduced tremendous consequences, the military did not ask to be involved but was brought into the decision-making process in crises situations. This is illustrated by the events of 1968 (discussed in detail in a previous chapter), by the crisis within the Echeverría administration in 1971, and by the Zapatista rebellion in January 1994.[153] These examples, which are exceptional, nevertheless share a common characteristic and illustrate the degree to which the armed forces has been kept out of the process on the front end.

Civilian treatment of military input into the decision-making process is dangerous for several reasons. First, the military, when appropriate, needs to offer its own interpretation of a situation and the repercussions for the armed forces and society from its institutional perspective. Second, to omit the military from the informational chain clearly affects the outcome of a decision. Decisions are made on the basis of information, inadequate or otherwise. This deficiency applied specifically and notably to the Zapatista situation. Third, waiting until a situation is at a critical stage to bring the military into the decision-making process risks, as the Zapatista rebellion illustrates, having the military make its own decisions. In this case, the civilian leadership created a destabilizing political mess and exacerbated the existing situation. The president had to step in and restrain the armed forces in the face of national and international criticism.

Mexican political leaders boast certain advantages in maintaining a position of supremacy in civil-military relations. The advantages work against expanded military decision making. Civilian political leadership skills differ radically from military leadership skills, especially in connection with mass appeals. In contrast to military personnel who have few negotiating skills, politicians are socialized early into the techniques and process of negotiation, These skills have become even more highly valued in a democratic, pluralistic political setting.[154] Of course, the lack of such skills has not deterred the military from entering into the decision-making process nor from intervening directly in political affairs in the past. Mexico's civilian leadership, however, acquired a special advantage in this regard because it did not have to contend with a serious opposition party until the 1990s. Throughout that period, there was no political party which could compete for the military's loyalty.

Culturally, another way of exploring why military personnel facilitate civilian politicians in maintaining their supremacy is that the officer corps never has been encouraged to develop verbal skills useful in the larger political world. This pattern, however, is being altered in the Colegio de Defensa Nacional, where officers learn give and take from the behavior of their civilian counterparts. They also gain similar skills when training abroad in the extensive staff and command courses. There they witness American officers avidly questioning various lecturers.

Civilian leaders make effective use of another informal, but more positive, quality in their relationship with the officer corps. Politicians, from presidents on down, have always been careful to publicly praise the military for its loyalty and service to the republic. President Fox is no exception to this pattern and all of his public pronouncements to and about the military have been positive and generous. The armed forces has not altered their level of loyalty by any degree since Fox became president, thus further cementing the depth of their loyalty to Mexican political institutions and not to partisan organizations or leaders.

An informal limitation on military influence severely tested in the process of democratic transformation is the level of consensus civilian leaders maintain on the military's role. The Democratic Revolutionary Party did initially raise the possibility that, for the first time in more than thirty years, an important group of political leaders might request the military's support of constitutional and legislative protections. Such a request would force the military to choose between loyalty to the state and loyalty to the law. That possibility never came to pass; instead, some retired officers joined the PRD or advised it on civil-military matters.[155] The PRD became an assertive voice after 1997. It favored pro-active congressional oversight and greater access to information but has not sought to use military allies in any partisan manner. Some analysts believe that a possible informal political alliance may be emerging between the armed forces and the PRI over the issue of human rights abuses committed during the "dirty war." PRI and the armed forces are opposed to bringing up past abuses. In contrast, both the PAN and PRD have supported investigations into these historic events.[156]

The most important cultural pattern explaining military subordination to civil authority in any society is the intensity with which the citizenry itself is committed to civilian supremacy. This set of beliefs is overwhelmingly critical.[157] As one analyst notes, "Latin American civil-military relations can never replicate North America and Western Europe because Latin American civilians have never rejected the military's use for the promotion of partisan political goals."[158] Mexicans, however, do not fit that more typical Latin American pattern. Public opinion survey data presented previously indicate a relatively strong societal consensus against military intervention.

Since the 1990s, and even more so under Fox, the army has been used to identify and capture leading drug traffickers. The success of the army in effecting these arrests under Fox has become a hallmark of his anti-crime measures and suggests, in part, why ordinary Mexicans give such high marks to the first attorney general, a brigadier general, and to the secretary of national defense. The broader significance of this, however, is that citizens have now accepted the military mission as normal or, at worst, necessary.

The informal inhibitions imposed by civilian and presidential leadership are integrated into the Mexican political model. Formally, however, presidential authority over the military is extensive. Specifically, presidential powers include naming the secretary of national defense, assistant secretary, oficial mayor, inspector general, controller general, attorney general of military justice, and the president and judges of the supreme military court; the presidential chief of staff; zone commanders; unit and special commanders; and all department heads at the National Defense Secretariat.[159] The Organic Law of the Navy, revised in 2002, corresponds roughly to army statutes.[160]

Legal statutes are a significant step in establishing the boundaries of civil-military relations because they reflect the cultural norms of society. A constitution and organic law are hollow documents in the absence of strong political institutions which can enforce those regulations. Of all the possible formal components of the Mexican model that impact on civil-military relations, this is perhaps most important, reinforcing civilian society's ideology relative to civil-military relations.

Today, there is no question that civilians unquestionably control decision making, and that the relationship favors civilian actors. Nevertheless, two spheres of influence remain open to the military. Civilian decision makers still do not determine the military's internal budget allocations. Second, politicians basically have not inserted themselves in the military's promotion process since the 1950s. Presidents have, on occasion, altered the pace of senior officer promotions but have not promoted ineligible officers out of turn. The Navy reformed its own internal promotion process, eliminating defects and professionalizing it, and the army followed suit two years later. There exists greater civilian oversight of this internal military process, but both parties appear to have agreed that military leadership is largely responsible for these decisions.

As Mexico begins the difficult task of consolidating its democracy and faces the many obstacles pluralism introduces to governance, how will the changes affect civil-military affairs and, in return, what impact does the armed forces have on that consolidation process? All the variables identified as working hypotheses in the introduction have been shown to have exerted an influential role on Mexican civil-military relations. But, in the first decade of the twenty-first century, several of these characteristics seem more likely than others to produce changes in the relationship or to exert a greater influence on established patterns. Broadly speaking, in the same way that Mexicans have shifted their views and attitudes to support a more democratic political model, their underlying views toward military subordination to civil authority are equally important in sustaining the balance in the relationship. These views are fundamental because the officer corps is, in the end, a product of the larger society, and therefore the views it holds toward civilian control are largely determined and reinforced by the whole of society.

The officer corps has instilled the ethic of subordination to civil authority through extensive socialization in military academies. Professionalization, of course, has been a variable in the general literature on civil-military relations. But professionalization defined as instilling a strong sense of subordination to authority generally, and subordination to civil authority specifically, is critical to the relationship in Mexico. What is shifting in the socialization process, and in the institutional structure in the armed forces, is a focus on the extreme degree of hierarchy and subordination to higher command. The military has to achieve a new balance between a more democratic culture within the military while maintaining hierarchical control.

What is not changing within the socialization process is military subordination to civilian authority. That feature remains a bedrock principle of Mexico's officer corps. There is a division within the armed forces as to the degree to which the military should "democratize" internally. This is a fundamental issue for the current relationship because, in the long run, it would be unhealthy and threatening to maintain a state institution built on a fundamentally authoritarian culture generating authoritarian leaders in the midst of a democratic society. It would create a danger within the heart of a democratic society to maintain such an institution. Such issues as the military's human rights record toward civilians and its own personnel illustrate the need for the military to open itself up to scrutiny and, more importantly, to fundamentally alter its own attitudes on these issues so that its institutional behavior is in alignment with societal institutional behavior.

Compared to all other institutions, the Mexican armed forces maintained a unique degree of autonomy from state control and intervention. As we have seen, this level of autonomy was particularly noteworthy on such issues as promotion, budget, and criminal accountability. Mexico's new-found pluralism and the makeup of congress, has led to multiple political parties in the legislative branch and the legislative leadership as a whole to demand stronger oversight and control over the armed forces. Since changes are afoot in the areas of budget decision-making, approval of promotions, and impunity for human rights abuses, the officer corps will have to learn to accept and function under more pervasive civilian interference.

Finally, internal military factionalism within the respective services is more widespread than meets the eye. Since the mid-1990s, many of the issues, most of which are internal to the military (including pay, retirement, promotion, professionalization, etc.), have led to internal documents and severe criticisms. Since 2000, the navy has responded to these internal conflicts in a comprehensive and decided fashion. The army, by far the most influential institution, has taken much smaller steps to address these concerns.

There is no general desire on the part of the military to involve itself in political matters or to ally itself with any political party or faction in a partisan manner.[161] Today, the greatest danger to destabilizing the relationship is to turn the unresolved internal conflicts within the army and air force into partisan civilian political issues. Given the fledgling nature of Mexico's democracy, it should maintain pressure on the national defense secretary to make these alterations, but not to make them directly, which would threaten the careful balance between oversight and internal intervention and increase the danger of introducing partisan conflicts within military institutions.[162]

Other analysts have focused on the expanded and different missions the armed forces have been asked to carry out in the last decade or so, suggesting that the breadth and nature of these tasks is a significant danger to civil-military relations and military subordination. In performing these national security tasks, the military has increased its role in the policy process. These newly-defined missions are acceptable as long as they meet certain conditions, including the capabilities of civilian organizations to fulfill such functions and the development of civilian alternatives in the future.[163] The military has long deserved to be involved not just in the execution of civilian-made policies, but in their formulation. Only one fundamental issue is at stake here. Does an expanded role for the military alter civilian control over the military? This is the underlying premise of our model of civil-military relations. While there may be a potential for that to occur, as critics are often quick to point out, no evidence exists in the Mexican case to support any such change. Indeed, quite the opposite. Civilian control is actually on the increase, as evidenced by the changing patterns in congressional oversight even while the military has been asked to perform an increasingly broad array of tasks.

The greatest test of the civil-military relationship today does not stem from the military's behavior, nor the changing patterns of legislative-executive relations, but from the ability of a democratic political model to function effectively and solve Mexican problems. Citizens and elites alike continue to favor a democratic model, but their support is based directly on the performance of this political system. If Mexico cannot overcome its underlying economic conditions, democracy in Mexico, as elsewhere in the region, will come under heavy fire. Such a political situation, in the extreme, will create severe stress on the established features of civil-military relations.

Notes

Preface

1. Roderic Ai Camp, *Generals in the Palacio, the Military in Modern Mexico* (New York: Oxford University Press, 1992).
2. For reasons of length, most of the detailed data presented in tables, acquired through the initiation in 2003 of Mexico's transparency law, have been omitted. The more than 60 tables are available in the Spanish edition of this work forthcoming by Planeta, 2006.
3. Claude E. Welch, Jr., *A Farewell to Arms? Military Disengagement from Politics in Africa and Latin America* (Boulder, Colo.: Westview Press, 1987), 10.
4. David Pion-Berlin, *Civil-Military Relations in Latin America, New Analytical Perspectives* (Chapel Hill: University of North Carolina Press, 2001), 1–35, one of the most imaginative of such works, is such an example.
5. Frank D. McCann, "Brazilian Army Officers Biography Project," Unpublished paper, Latin American Studies Association, Miami, December 1989, 4.
6. Roderic Ai Camp, *Mexico's Mandarins, Crafting a Power Elite for the 21st Century* (Berkeley, Calif.: University of California Press, 2002), 21.
7. Any references to detailed statistics about the officer corps, unless otherwise indicated, come from the author's own data sources, described in the Collective Biographical Data appendix.
8. Bruce W. Farcau, *The Transition to Democracy in Latin America: The Role of the Military* (Westport, Conn.: Praeger, 1996), 3.
9. David Ronfeldt, "The Mexican Army and Political Order since 1940" (Santa Monica, Calif.: Rand Corporation, 1973), 7.
10. Kate Doyle, "The Blind Man and the Elephant, Reporting on the Mexican Military," Americas Program, Inter-hemispheric Resource Center, Washington, D.C., May 2004, 1.
11. Zhiyong Lan, "China," in *The Political Role of the Military, An International Handbook*, eds. Constantine Danopoulos and Cynthia Watson (Westport, Conn.: Greenwood Press, 1996), 57.

Chapter One Civil-Military Relations in a Democratic Mexico

1. See Peter D. Feaver, "The Civil-Military Problematique: Huntington, Janowitz, and the Question of Civilian Control," *Armed Forces and Society*, Vol. 23 (Winter 1996), 149–178.

2. Sam C. Sarkesian, "Military Professionalism and Civil-Military Relations in the West," *International Political Science Review* Vol. 2, no. 3 (1981): 290.

3. Douglas L. Bland, "A Unified Theory of Civil-Military Relations," *Armed Forces and Society*, Vol. 26 (Fall 1999), 9.

4. One recent proposal is Rebecca Schiff's theory of concordance, which "sees a high level of integration between the military and other parts of society as one of several types of civil-military relationship." See "Civil-Military Relations Reconsidered: A Theory of Concordance," *Armed Forces and Society*, Vol. 22 (Fall 1995), 7, and Richard W. Wells' useful rebuttal, "The Theory of Concordance in Civil-Military Relations: A Commentary," *Armed Forces and Society*, Vol. 23 (Winter 1996), 269–275.

5. Sam C. Sarkesian, "Military Professionalism and Civil-Military Relations in the West," 291.

6. Richard H. Kohn, "How Democracies Control the Military," *Journal of Democracy*, Vol. 8 (no. 4 1997), 152.

7. Douglas L. Bland, "A Unified Theory of Civil-Military Relations," 12–13.

8. S. E. Finer, *The Man on Horseback: the Role of the Military in Politics* (Boulder, Colo.: Westview Press, 1988), 180.

9. It is worth noting that Guzmán's father, a federal army colonel, died fighting against the Maderistas in Chihuahua.

10. Talukder Maniruzzaman, *Military Withdrawal from Politics: A Comparative Study* (Cambridge, U.K.: Ballinger, 1987), 212.

11. Brian Loveman and Tom Davies, eds. *The Politics of Antipolitics: The Military in Latin America* (Wilmington, Del.: Scholarly Resources, 1997), 369.

12. Robert D. Putnam, "Toward Explaining Military Intervention in Latin American Politics," *World Politics* 20, no. 1 (1967): 106.

13. Orlando Pérez explores this issue broadly for Central America. "New Missions or Old Mandates: The Transformation of Civil-Military Relations in Post-Authoritarian Central America," Unpublished paper, Latin American Studies Association, Miami, March 2000.

14. Roderic Ai Camp, *The Making of a Government, Political Leaders in Modern Mexico* (Tucson, Ariz.: University of Arizona Press, 1984), 134–135.

15. Linda Stevenson and Mitchell Seligson, "Fading Memories of the Revolution, Is Stability Eroding in Mexico?," in *Polling for Democracy, Public Opinion and Political Liberalization in Mexico*, ed. Roderic Ai Camp (Wilmington, Del.: Scholarly Resources, 1996), 71–72.

16. Orlando Pérez is attempting to explore this in general terms. "New Missions or Old Mandates."

17. See his discussion of Argentina and Ecuador in *The Armed Forces and Democracy in Latin America* (Baltimore, Md.: Johns Hopkins University Press, 1998), 84–86.

18. Paul Gronke and Peter D. Feaver, "Uncertain Confidence: Civilian and Military Attitudes about Civil-Military Relations," in *Soldiers and Civilians: The Civil-Military Gap and American National Security*, eds. Peter D. Feaver and Richard H. Kohn (Cambridge, Mass.: MIT Press, 2001), 129–161.

19. Roderic Ai Camp, ed., *Citizen Views of Democracy in Latin America* (Pittsburgh, Penn.: University of Pittsburgh Press, 2001).
20. Alfred Stepan, *Rethinking Military Politics: Brazil and the Southern Cone* (Princeton, NJ: Princeton University Press, 1988), 138.
21. Finer, *The Man on Horseback*, 306.
22. Maniruzzaman, *Military Withdrawal from Politics*, 211.
23. C. Wright Mills, *The Power Elite* (New York: Oxford University Press, 1959), 283.
24. Camp, *Mexico's Mandarins*.
25. Donald F. Harrison, "United States-Mexican Military Collaboration During World War II" (Ph.D. dissertation, Georgetown University, 1976), 206.
26. One prominent officer, Division General Luis Garfias Magaña, argued that the social class of the military was the most important variable in determining Mexico's civil-military relationship. As he bluntly put it, they value security—or food in their stomachs—more than the risk of participating in politics. Personal interview, Mexico City, August 24, 1990.
27. Gordon C. Schloming, "Civil-Military Relations in Mexico, 1910–1940: A Case Study" (Ph.D. dissertation, Columbia University, 1974), 317–318.
28. Roderic Ai Camp, "The Education and Training of the Mexican Officer Corps," in *Forging the Sword, Selecting, Educating and Training Cadets and Junior Officers in the Modern World*, Vol. 5, Military History Symposium Series, USAF Academy (Chicago: Imprint Publications, 1998), 340.
29. Thomas Bruneau and Jeanne Giraldo, "Domestic Roles of the Colombian Armed Forces: Implications for Civil-Military Relations," Unpublished paper, Latin American Studies Association, Dallas, Texas, March 2003, 14.
30. John Fishel, "The Organizational Component of Civil-Military Relations in Latin America: The Role of the Ministry of Defense," Unpublished paper, Latin American Studies Association, Miami, Florida, March 2000, 2.
31. Schloming, "Civil-Military Relations in Mexico," 318.
32. Samuel P. Huntington, *Political Order in Changing Societies* (New Haven, Conn.: Yale University Press, 1968), 198.
33. Sharly Cross, "Cuba," in *The Political Role of the Military, An International Handbook*, eds. Constantine Danopoulos and Cynthia Watson (Westport, Conn.: Greenwood Press, 1996), 75.
34. Samuel P. Huntington, *The Soldier and the State: The Theory and Politics of Civil-Military Relations* (Cambridge, Mass.: Harvard University Press, 1964), 81–82.
35. Douglas L. Bland, "What do Officers Need to Know about Civil-Military Relations?," Unpublished paper, Latin American Studies Association, Washington, D.C., March 2000, 5.
36. See the recent testimony of General Gerardo Clemente Vega García and detailed deputies' questions in Mexico's Chamber of Deputies, October 13, 2004. I am indebted to Raúl Benitez Manaut for bringing this document to my attention.
37. Finer, *The Man on Horseback*, 23.
38. Stephen J. Wager and Donald E. Schulz, *The Awakening: The Zapatista Revolt and its Implications for Civil-Military Relations and the Future of Mexico* (Carlisle, Penn.: U.S. Army War College, 1994), 19.
39. Huntington, *The Soldier and the State*, 83–84.
40. Richard Betts has argued that United States officers rank control over their internal organization quite highly. See his *Soldiers, Statesmen, and the Cold War Crises* (New York: Columbia University Press, 1991), 6–12.

41. William S. Ackroyd, "The Military in Mexican Politics: The Impact of Professionalization, Civilian Behavior, and the Revolution," Unpublished paper, Pacific Coast Council of Latin Americanists, San Diego, October 1982, 13.
42. Frederick M. Nunn, "On the Role of the Military in Twentieth-Century Latin America: The Mexican Case," in *The Modern Mexican Military: A Reassessment*, ed. David Ronfeldt (La Jolla, Calif.: Center for U.S.-Mexican Studies, University of California, San Diego, 1984), 45.
43. Lieuwen, *Mexican Militarism*, 149.
44. Welch, *Farewell to Arms?*, 20–21, 28.
45. Judith Goldstein and Robert Keohane, *Ideas and Foreign Policy: Beliefs, Institutions, and Political Change* (Ithaca, N.Y.: Cornell University Press, 1993), 20.
46. Franklin D. Margiotta, "Civilian Control and the Mexican Military: Changing Patterns of Political Influence," in *Civilian Control of the Military: Theories and Cases from Developing Countries*, ed. Claude E. Welch, Jr. (Albany, N.Y.: State University of New York Press, 1976), 253.
47. Franklin D. Margiotta, "The Mexican Military: A Case Study in Non-intervention" (M.A. thesis, Georgetown University, 1968), 165.
48. Ying-Mao Kau, *The People's Liberation Army and China's Nation Building* (White Plains, N.Y.: International Arts and Sciences Press, 1973), xiv.
49. Claude E. Welch, Jr., "Civilian Control of the Military: Myth and Reality," in *Civilian Control of the Military, Theory and Cases from Developing Countries*, ed. Welch (Albany, N.Y.: State University of New York Press, 1976), 22.
50. Amos Perlmutter, "The Military and Politics in Modern Times: A Decade Later," *Journal of Strategic Studies*, Vol. 9 (March 1986): 5.
51. Raúl Benítez-Manaut, "Mexico and the New Challenges of Hemispheric Security," Latin American Program, Woodrow Wilson International Center for Scholars, Washington, D.C., 2004.
52. Harold Trinkunas, "Militarizing the State: Implications for Democracy in Venezuela," Unpublished paper, Latin American Studies Association, Dallas, Texas, March 2003.
53. Farcau, *The Transition to Democracy in Latin America: The Role of the Military*, 4.
54. Roderic Ai Camp, ed., *Citizen Views of Democracy in Latin America*.
55. See Roderic Ai Camp *Militarizing Mexico, Where is the Officer Corps Going?* Policy Paper on the Americas (Washington, D.C.: CSIS, 1999).
56. Many of these issues are addressed by Juan Rial in his "Armies and Civil Society in Latin America," in Larry Diamond and Marc F. Plattner, *Civil-Military Relations and Democracy* (Baltimore, Md.: John Hopkins University Press, 1996), 47–65.
57. For a broad discussion of internal vs. external variables, see Michael C. Desch, "Threat Environments and Military Missions," in *Civil-Military Relations and Democracy*, eds. Larry Diamond and Marc F. Plattner (Baltimore, Md.: Johns Hopkins University Press, 1996), 12–29.
58. Mark J. Ruhl, "Changing Civil-Military Relations in Latin America," *Latin American Research Review* 33, no. 3 (1998), 258.
59. For example, I recall interviewing a prominent division general in the mid-1990s, shortly after the Zapatista uprising, who unequivocally maintained that it was a communist-sponsored event, contrary to all intelligence reports.
60. J. Sam Fitch, *The Armed Forces and Democracy in Latin America* (Baltimore, Md.: John Hopkins University Press, 1998), 88.

Chapter Two   Civil-Military Relations in Historical Context

1. Talukder Maniruzzaman, *Military Withdrawal from Politics: A Comparative Study* (Cambridge, Mass.: Ballinger, 1987), 212 ff.

2. David Pion-Berlin suggests that the institutional literature may provide useful insights for comparative analysis of civil-military relations. See his *Civil-Military Relations in Latin America, New Analytical Perspectives* (Chapel Hill, N.C.: University of North Carolina Press, 2001).

3. Roderic Ai Camp, *Political Recruitment Across Two Centuries, Mexico, 1884–1991* (Austin, Tex.: University of Texas Press, 1995), 62.

4. Lorenzo Meyer "Continuidades e innovaciones en la vida política mexicana del siglo xx, el antiguo y el nuevo régimen," *Foro Internacional* 16 (July–September, 1975): 37–63.

5. Roderic A. Camp, "Civilian Supremacy in Mexico, the Case of a Post-Revolutionary Military," in *Military Intervention and Withdrawal*, ed. Constantine P. Danopoulous (London: Routledge, 1991), 3.

6. Gordon C. Schloming, "Civil-Military Relations in Mexico, 1910–1940: A Case Study" (Ph.D. dissertation, Columbia University, 1974), 321.

7. Camp, "Civilian Supremacy in Mexico," 5.

8. See Roderic A. Camp, *The Making of a Government: Political Leaders in Modern Mexico* (Tucson, Ariz.: University of Arizona Press, 1984), 40ff.

9. Edwin Licuwen, *Mexican Militarism* (Albuquerque, N.M.: University of New Mexico Press, 1968), 71.

10. Ibid., 69.

11. Schloming, "Civil-Military Relations in Mexico," 225.

12. Ibid., 232–233.

13. Ibid., 241.

14. Lieuwen, *Mexican Militarism*, 110.

15. Phyllis Greene Walker, "The Modern Mexican Military: Political Influence and Institutional Interests in the 1980s" (M.A. thesis, American University, 1987), 4.

16. Schloming, "Civil-Military Relations in Mexico," 257.

17. Ibid., 289.

18. Donald F. Harrison, "United States-Mexican Military Collaboration During World War II" (Ph.D. dissertation, Georgetown University, 1976), 206.

19. Schloming, "Civil-Military Relations in Mexico," 297–298.

20. José Luis Piñeyro, "The Mexican Army and the State: Historical and Political Perspective," *Revue Internationale de Sociologie* 14 (April–August, 1978): 120.

21. Many top officers in our study were beneficiaries of this program. Officers recruited through this program held influential positions in the secretariat of national defense as late as 1983.

22. Schloming, "Civil-Military Relations in Mexico," 297.

23. Walker, "The Modern Mexican Military," 21.

24. Schloming, "Civil-Military Relations in Mexico," 340.

25. Piñeyro, "The Mexican Army and the State," 121.

26. Jorge Alberto Lozoya documented these doubts. See his *El ejército mexicano (1911–1965)* (Mexico: El Colegio de México, 1970), 60.

27. Luis Javier Garrido, based on an interview with General Alfonso Corona del Rosal, in his *El partido de la revolución institucionalizada, la formación del nuevo estado en México (1918–1945)* (Mexico: Siglo XXI, 1982), 243.

28. Lieuwen, *Mexican Militarism*, 124.
29. Lozoya, *El ejército mexicano*, 61.
30. Ibid., 61.
31. John Bailey and Leopoldo Gómcz, "The PRI and Liberalization in Mexico" (Unpublished paper, Georgetown University, October 1989), 11.
32. Lozoya, *El Ejército mexicano*, 59–60.
33. Garrido, *El partido de la revolución institucionalizada*, 245.
34. Schloming, "Civil-Military Relations in Mexico," 243–244, 336.
35. Lieuwen, *Mexican Militarism*, 135.
36. See Albert L. Michaels, "The Mexican Election of 1940." *Special Studies No. 5*, Council on International Studies, Buffalo, State University of New York, 1971.
37. Virginia Prewctt, "The Mexican Army," *Foreign Affairs* 19 (April 1941): 615.
38. Piñeyro, "The Mexican Army and the State," 121.
39. Lozoya, *El ejército mexicano*, 64.
40. Arturo Sánchez Gutiérrez, "Los militares en al década de los cincuentas," *Revista Mexicana de Sociología*, 50, no. 3 (Julio–Septiembre, 1988), 273.
41. See Lázaro Cárdenas, *Apuntes*, Vol. 2 (Mexico: UNAM, 1972–1974), 365.
42. Lieuwen, *Mexican Militarism*, 143; Walker, "The Modern Mexican Military," 25. Although not negating Avila Camacho's determination to pare down the military's influence, budget reductions could be made while actually increasing military expenditures. This was made possible by the sizeable military aid Mexico accepted from the United States during the war years.
43. Sánchez Gutiérrez even argues that Cárdenas's appointment as secretary of national defense, along with the appointments of Abelardo Rodríguez, Francisco Mújica, and Joaquín Amaro as regional or zone commanders, effectively eliminated the major division between revolutionary generals. "Los militares en la década de los cincuentas," 276.
44. Guillermo Boils, *Los militares y la política en México, 1915–1974* (Mexico: El Caballito, 1975), 76.
45. Elisa Servín, *Ruptura y oposición, el movimiento henriquista, 1945–1954* (Mexico: Cal y Arena, 2001), 44.
46. Camp, "Civilian Supremacy in Mexico," 8–9.
47. See Roderic A. Camp, "Education and Political Recruitment in Mexico: The Alemán Generation," *Journal of Inter-American Studies and World Affairs* 18 (August 1976): 295–321, and *Mexico's Leaders, Their Education and Recruitment* (Tucson, Ariz.: University of Arizona Press, 1980), 107ff.; and Peter H. Smith, *Labyrinths of Power: Political Recruitment in Twentieth Century Mexico* (Princeton, N.J.: Princeton University Press, 1979), 250.
48. See Lozoya, *El ejército mexicano*, 69, and Piñeyro, "The Mexican Army and the State," 122, for their views on Alemán's contributions.
49. Personal correspondence from Division General Luis Garfias Magaña, n.d., 1992.
50. See note 56 below for my interview with Miguel Alemán. For Sergio Aguayo's interpretation, see his excellent *La charola, una historia de los servicios de inteligencia en México* (Mexico: Grijalbo, 2001), 63.
51. I am indebted to Division General Luis Garfias Magaña for this background on the presidential guard. Personal correspondence to the author, n.d., 1992.
52. Elisa Servín, *Ruptura y oposición*, 114.
53. Luis Rubio and Roberto Newell, *Mexico's Dilemma: The Political Origins of Economic Crisis* (Boulder, Colo.: Westview Press, 1984), 82–83.

54. Ibid., 63.
55. Boils, *Los militares y la política en México*, 79.
56. Alemán's extreme need for loyalty from the military may have been in part the result of his own personal experiences. Because his father had been killed by the very government Alemán ultimately led, he would naturally harbor some suspicions against the military in general and individual officers specifically. The military had nearly killed Alemán in 1929 (when his father was in revolt) and he had been saved only by a safe conduct from a general and friend of his father who had remained with forces loyal to the government. Personal interview with Miguel Alemán, Mexico City, October 27, 1976.
57. Lyle N. McAlister, *The Military in Latin American Socio-political Evolution: Four Case Studies* (Washington, D.C.: Center for Research in Social Systems, 1970), 208.
58. Walker, "The Modern Mexican Military," 28.
59. Ibid., 29.
60. José Luis Piñeyro, "The Mexican Army and the State," 125–127.
61. Boils, *Los militares y la política en México*, 82.
62. Julio García Scherer and Carlos Monsiváis, *Parte de guerra, Tlatelolco 1968* (Mexico: Aguilar, 1999), 40. The legal justification for this, which derives from section 14, article 73, of the Constitution of 1917, authorizes the president, as commander in chief of the armed forces, to use the military, when necessary, to maintain internal order.
63. Ibid., 41. Had the commander, General José Hernández Toledo, not been wounded in the initial gunfire, it is possible that the troops, given operation orders, might not have fired into the crowd. Apparently, his second-in-command, Lt. Col. Edmar Euroza Delgado, ordered the troops to return fire. In addition to their commander, 8 soldiers were wounded and one was killed. Seven additional soldiers in the reserve battalion also were wounded.
64. Michael J. Dziedzic, "The Essence of Decision in a Hegemonic Regime: The Case of Mexico's Acquisition of a Supersonic Fighter" (Ph.D. dissertation, University of Texas, Austin, 1986), 113.
65. Michael J. Dziedzic, "Mexico's Converging Challenges; Problems, Prospects, and Implications" (Unpublished manuscript, U.S. Air Force Academy, April 21, 1989), 9.
66. George Phillip, *The Presidency in Mexican Politics* (New York: St. Martin's, 1992), 56.
67. "Colonel Luis Gutiérrez Oropeza met with Gustavo Díaz Ordaz the day before he took office and Gustavo Díaz Ordaz allegedly told him: Colonel, if in the performance of your duties you have to violate the constitution, don't ask me because I, as president, never will authorize you to violate it; *but if you are dealing with Mexico's security or my life or that of my family, colonel, violate it....*" See Sergio Aguayo, *1968, los archivos de la violencia* (Mexico: Grijalbo, 1998), 41.
68. Sergio Aguayo Quezada, "La acusación del general," *Diario de Yucatán,* July 1, 1999, www.diariodeyucatan.com.mx.
69. Miguel Granados Chapa, "Plaza Pública," June 29, 1999, *Diario de Yucatán.* www.diariodeyucatan.com.mx. This is confirmed by a declassified U.S. Defense Intelligence Agency report, "General Officers in Disfavor with Secretary of Defense," National Security Archives, www.gwu.edu/~nsarchiv.
70. Scherer García and Monsiváis, *Parte de guerra*, 43, based on papers left by General Barragán. Also see Sam Dillon, "General Illuminates '68 Massacre in Mexico," *New York Times,* June 29, 1999, nytimes.com.
71. Sergio Aguayo, *La charola*, 135ff.

72. Carlos Ramírez, "Indicador Político," *El Debate*, February 20, 1998, np.
73. Scherer García and Monsiváis, *Parte de Guerra*, 38, 43–44.
74. Ibid., 41.
75. Sergio Aguayo, "La acusación del general."
76. Defense Intelligence Agency, "General Officers in Disfavor." Both men were relieved of their commands.
77. Personal interview with Division General Gerardo Clemente Vega Garcia, Secretary of National Defense, Mexico City, February 26, 2004.
78. However, he did tell close friends that "the army never had any interest in taking power in Mexico and was completely loyal to the President in 1968. His version was that the military did not decide on the repression of the students, but followed the President's orders." Personal interview with José Rogelio Alvarez, Mexico City, August 17, 1990.
79. Williams S. Ackroyd, "Descendants of the Revolution: Civil-Military Relations in Mexico" (Ph.D. dissertation, University of Arizona, 1988), 254, based on interviews with Mexican officers in 1982–1983.
80. The Heroico Colegio Militar does not list a 1968 graduating class in its official memoria. Instead, it has a class graduating January 1, 1967 (the traditional graduation date), a class graduating November 1, 1967 (which would be the 1968 class), and then a class graduating September 1, 1969. See *Memoria gráfico del cincuentenario de la reapertura del Heroico Colegio Militar* (Mexico: HCM, 1970), 498ff.
81. Personal interview, Mexico City, 1990. The officer surmised that many young cadets, given their popular social roots, would have been upset at the level of repression against students and bystanders, thus explaining their removal.
82. Edward J. Williams, "The Evolution of the Mexican Military and Its Implications for Civil-Military Relations," in *Mexico's Political Stability: the Next Five Years*, ed. Roderic A. Camp (Boulder, Colo.: Westview Press, 1986), 156.
83. Alden M. Cunningham, "Mexico's National Security in the 1980s–1990s," in *The Modern Mexican Military: A Reassessment*, ed. David Ronfeldt (La Jolla, Calif.: Center for United States Mexican Studies, University of California, San Diego, 1984), 169; Edward J. Williams, "The Mexican Military and Foreign Policy: The Evolution of Influence," in *The Modern Mexican Military: A Reassessment*, ed. David Ronfeldt (La Jolla, Calif.: Center for United States-Mexican Studies, University of California, San Diego, 1984), 186.
84. Wager, "The Mexican Military," 25.
85. Piñeyro, "The Mexican Army and the State," 134. Interestingly, the careers of the officers who led the various units involved in interactions with the students from September 18 through October 27 were not adversely affected; several of them reached three star rank, and held important assignments in following administrations.
86. Personal interview, Mexico City, 1992.
87. Neil Harvey, *The Chiapas Rebellion, The Struggle for Land and Democracy* (Durham, N.C.: Duke University Press, 1999), 124–125.
88. Guillermo Boils, "Los militares en México (1965–1985)," *Revista Mexicana de Sociología* 47 (January–February, 1985); 175.
89. Piñeyro, "The Mexican Army and the State," 135.
90. Dziedzic, "Mexico's Converging Challenges," 8.
91. Personal interview, Mexico City, 1991.
92. *Revista de Ejército y Fuerza Aérea*, October 1974, 79.
93. Williams, "The Mexican Military and Foreign Policy," 9.

94. *Diario de Yucatán*, June 9, 2003, www.sureste.com.mx. Col. Díaz Escobar was promoted to Brigade General before the end of the Echeverría administration and commanded the 34th military zone during the last year Echeverría held office.
95. Smith, *Labyrinths of Power*, 295.
96. Dziedzic, "The Essence of Decision in a Hegemonic Regime," 323.
97. Gloria Fuentes, *Ejército mexicano* (Mexico: Grijalbo, 1983), 309; personal interview with President José López Portillo, Mexico City, 1991.
98. A career officer close to the president also believes that he increased economic benefits to the military because of stories he heard from his father about military life. Personal interview, Mexico City, August, 1990.
99. José Luis Piñeyro, "The Modernization of the Mexican Armed Forces," in *Democracy under Siege: New Military Power in Latin America*, ed. Augusto Varas (Westport, Conn.: Greenwood Press, 1989), 115.
100. Personal interview, Mexico City, 1991. Otto Granados Roldán, "Regreso a las armas?" in *El desafío mexicano*, ed. Francisco de Alba, et al. (Mexico: Ediciones Océano, 1982), 127.
101. Christopher Dickey, "Modernization Could Lead Mexican Military into Polities," *Washington Post*, September 23, 1982, 29A.
102. Fuentes, *El ejército mexicano*, 306.
103. Brian Latell, *Mexico at the Crossroads: The Many Crises of the Political System* (Stanford, Calif.: Hoover Institution, 1986), 29.
104. Richard B. Craig, "Mexican Narcotics Traffic: Binational Security Implications," in *The Latin American Narcotics Trade and U.S. National Security*, ed. Donald J. Mabry (Westport, Conn.: Greenwood Press, 1989), 35.
105. *National Development Plan* (Mexico: Ministry of Planning and Budget, 1983), 19.
106. Caesar Sereseres, "The Mexican Military Looks South," in *The Modern Mexican Military: A Reassessment*, ed. David Ronfeldt (La Jolla: Center for U.S.-Mexican Studies, University of California, San Diego, 1984), 212.
107. Jorge G. Castañeda, "Mexico at the Brink," *Foreign Affairs* 64 (Winter 1985–1986): 293.
108. *Diario de Yucatán*, March 8, 2003, www.diariodeyucatan.com.mx.
109. Salinas also used the military to arrest a labor leader for alleged corruption. According to a military source, the army substituted for the police because the government feared that the civilian police authorities might actually kill him in making the arrest. Personal interview, August 20, 1990.
110. Larry Rohter, "Use of Troops a Cause of Concern in Mexico," *New York Times*, November 5, 1989, A8.
111. Lorenzo Moyer, "Ejército y Cananeas del futuro," *Excélsior*, September 6, 1989, 12A.
112. As specified in Article 3 of the Army's revised organic law, September 1, 1992. See *Diario Oficial*, September 1, 1992, 1–21.
113. Between January 1994 and December 1996, the army lost 13 enlisted personnel, and four officers, including one colonel. www.sedena.gob.mx, transparency request, folio 22012004, January 2004.
114. As Human Rights Watch reported, those abuses included extra-judicial executions and torture and no one was held accountable. See *Implausible Deniability, State Responsibility for Rural Violence in Mexico* (New York: Human Rights Watch, 1997), 89.
115. This is fully documented in newly released classified information from the Defense Intelligence Agency available on the National Security Archive website

(Mexico project) at George Washington University. I am indebted to Kate Doyle, director of the Mexico project, for sending me the documents.

116. Andres Oppenheimer, "Mexican Army Chaffs at Salinas' Actions," *Miami Herald*, n.d., 1994, 1A.

117. Stephen J. Wager and Donald E. Schulz, *The Awakening: The Zapatista Revolt and its Implications for Civil-Military Relations and the Future of Mexico* (Carlisle, Penn.: U.S. Army War College, 1994), 20.

118. Base on a conversation with a reporter from the *New York Times* who attended the press conference; Ibid., 14.

119. José Luis Piñeyro, "Chiapas: la seguridad nacional y la corta guerra," Unpublished paper, Latin American Studies Association, Washington, D.C., September 1995, 11.

120. José Luis Piñeyro, "Gobernabilidad democrática y fuerzas armadas en México con Fox," Unpublished paper, Latin American Studies Association, Washington, D.C., September 2001, 13.

121. The document is entitled *Mexican Army and Air Force Development.* See Roderic Ai Camp, *Militarizing Mexico, Where Is the Officer Corps Going?* (Washington, D.C.: CSIS, 1999).

122. Sallie Hughes, "The Pen and the Sword: Mexican Mass Media Coverage of the Armed Forces, 1986–1996," Unpublished paper, Tulane University, 1999.

123. Stephen J. Wager and Donald E. Schulze, *The Awakening*, 17.

124. *Diario Oficial*, November 21, 1994, 8.

125. Raúl Benitez Manaut, "Chiapas: Policies or War," Unpublished paper, Inter-American Council, Washington, D.C., September 1998, 11.

126. Ibid., 11.

Chapter Three   The Sociology of Civil-Military Relations

1. J. Samuel Fitch, "The Armed Forces and Society in South America: How Similar? How Different?," Paper presented at the 6th Annual Research and Education in Defense and Security Studies, Santiago, Chile, October 2003.

2. Theodore Newcomb, "Persistence and Regression of Changed Attitudes: Long-Range Studies," in Jack Dennis, ed., *Socialization to Politics* (New York: Wiley, 1973), 422.

3. Allen H. Barton, "Background, Attitudes and Activities of American Elites," in *Studies of the Structure of National Elites*, 1, ed. Gwen Moore (Greenwich, Conn.: JAI, 1985), 201.

4. George J. Szablowski, "Governing and Competing Elites in Poland," *Governance*, 6, no. 3 (July 1993), 354.

5. Roderic Ai Camp, *The Making of a Government: Political Leaders in Modern Mexico* (Tucson, Ariz.: University of Arizona Press, 1984), 1.

6. See my "Age as a Variable in Political Recruitment," *Political Recruitment Across Two Centuries, Mexico, 1884–1991* (Austin, Tex.: University of Texas Press, 1995), 37–57.

7. Roderic Ai Camp, "Province Versus the Center, Democratizing Mexico's Political Culture," in *Assessing Democracy in Latin America: A Tribute to Russell H. Fitzgibbon*, ed. Philip Kelly (Boulder, Colo.: Westview Press, 1998), 76–92.

8. José Luis Piñeyro, "The Mexican Army and the State: Historical and Political Perspective," *Revue Internationale de Sociologie* 14 (April–August 1978): 154.

9. Gavin Kennedy, *The Military in the Third World* (New York: Scribner's, 1974), 129.

10. Actually, it was his successor, General Manuel Avila Camacho, who implemented the law; he retired 550 officers during the first year of his administration, 1941. See Talukder Maniruzzaman, *Military Withdrawal from Politics: A Comparative Study* (Cambridge, Mass.: Ballinger, 1987), 97.

11. In practice, it often was ignored as far as time in grade requirements for promotion to the next rank. In the Fox administration, it has been raised as an issue because many officers are serving in the attorney general's office, including the first attorney general, thus delaying their promotions to higher ranks. See Sigrid Artz, "La militarización de la Procuraduría General de la República: riesgos para la democracia mexicana," USMEX 2003-04 Working Paper Series, UCSD, 2004, 21–22.

12. Phyllis Greene Walker, "The Modern Mexican Military: Political Influence and Institutional Interests in the 1980s" (M.A. thesis, American University, 1987), 29.

13. Mexico, Dirección Técnica de Organización, *Directorio del gobierno federal, 1951,* 182–83; *Directorio del gobierno federal, 1956,* 201.

14. Elisa Servín, *Ruptura y oposición, el movimiento henriquista, 1945–1954* (Mexico: Cal y Arena, 2001).

15. Ibid., 40.

16. Edwin Lieuwen, *Mexican Militarism, the Political Rise and Fall of the Revolutionary Army, 1910–1940* (Albuquerque, N.M.: University of New Mexico Press, 1968), 122.

17. Lyle N. McAlister, *The Military in Latin American Socio-political Evolution: Four Case Studies* (Washington, D.C.: Center for Research in Social Systems, 1970), 241.

18. Roderic Ai Camp, "Mexican Military Leadership in Statistical Perspective Since the 1930s," in *Statistical Abstract of Latin America,* vol. 20, eds. J. W. Wilkie and Peter Reich (Los Angeles: Latin American Center, University of California, Los Angeles, 1980), 604.

19. Roderic Ai Camp, "The Political Technocrat in Mexico and the Survival of the Political System," *Latin American Research Review* 20, no. 1 (1985): 112.

20. Personal interview with a general, United States, 1984.

21. Mexican Military Biography Data Set.

22. See my "Mexican Attitudes toward Democracy and Vicente Fox's Victory in 2000," in *Mexico's Pivotal Democratic Elections, Campaign Effects and the Presidential Race of 2000,* eds. Chappell Lawson and Jorge Dominguez (Palo Alto, Calif.: Stanford University Press, 2003), 25–41.

23. Edward J. Williams, "The Resurgent North and Contemporary Mexican Regionalism," *Mexican Studies* 6 (Summer 1990): 299–323.

24. Roderic Ai Camp, *Political Recruitment across Two Centuries,* 167.

25. *Diccionario biográfico del gobierno mexicano* (Mexico: Presidencia de la República, 1989), 955.

26. The Secretariat of National Defense does not maintain statistics on the residential origins of the officer corps, but it does have yearly statistics of all enrollments in the air force and army by state. From 1998 to 2003, those states or entities with the highest enlistments are Veracruz which accounts for nearly a fifth of the birthplaces among these service personnel, the Federal District at between 10–13 percent, followed by Oaxaca and México, at 8–11 percent. Thus four states account for nearly half of all enlistments, soldiers and officers alike. www.sedena.gob.mx., transparency request, folio 0000700031603, October 15, 2003.

27. Personal communication from J. Samuel Fitch, March 10, 2004, and his "The Armed Forces and Society in South American."

28. Lieuwen, *Mexican Militarism,* 120.

29. Virginia Prewett, "The Mexican Army," *Foreign Affairs* 19 (April 1941): 614.
30. Comments by General Luis Garfias Magaña, Workshop on the Modern Mexican Military, Center for U.S.-Mexican Studies, University of California, San Diego, La Jolla, March 21, 1984.
31. "Editorial," *Revista de Ejército y Fuerza Aérea*, September 1955, 3; Raúl Díaz de León Durán, "Bienvenidos los sargentos primeros al H. Colegio Militar," *Revista de Ejército y Fuerza Aérea*, August 1955, 64–65; and S. Rangel Medina, "El nuevo curso de formación de oficiales en el H. Colegio Militar," *Revista de Ejército y Fuerza Aérea*, June 1955, 3–5.
32. Generals suggest that these men rarely rise beyond the rank of major because of their shortened Heroico Colegio Militar training and regular graduates' resentment against them. Personal interviews, Mexico City, 1990.
33. Personal interview, Mexico City, 1990.
34. See Collective Biographical Data.
35. Roderic Ai Camp, "Generals and Politicians in Mexico: A Preliminary Comparison," in *The Modern Mexican Military: A Reassessment*, ed. David Ronfeldt (La Jolla, Calif.: Center for U.S. Mexican Studies, University of California, San Diego, 1984), 141.
36. Roderic Ai Camp, *Crossing Swords, Religion and Politics in Mexico* (New York: Oxford University Press, 1997), 193.
37. Camp, "Generals and Politicians in Mexico," 141.
38. John J. Johnson, *The Military and Society in Latin America* (Stanford, Calif.: Stanford University Press, 1964), 172.
39. Personal communication from Division General Luis Garfias Magaña, December 15, 2003, author of an official history of the Mexican army.
40. Alan B. Spitzer, "The Historical Problem of Generations," *American Historical Review* 78 (December 1973): 1353–1385.
41. Luis González, *La ronda de generaciones* (Mexico City: SEP, 1984).
42. Daniel Cosío Villegas, *Memorias* (Mexico City: Joaquín Mortiz, 1976), 57.
43. Personal interview with General Gerardo Clemente Ricardo Vega García, Secretary of National Defense, Mexico City, February 26, 2004.
44. See the career of Edmundo Castro Villarreal as an example of this generation. *Diccionario biográfico del gobierno mexicano* (Mexico: Presidencia de la República, 1987), 87; *Revista de Ejército y Fuerza Aérea*, June 1976, 13.
45. Although a small group of air force officers served in the Philippines during World War II, and many held top command positions after 1945, the impact on their ideology is unknown. They are such a small group numerically that whatever influences they carried probably were limited within the armed services.
46. Camp, "Mexican Military Leadership in Statistical Perspective since the 1930s," 598.
47. Alden M, Cunningham, "Mexico's National Security in the 1980s–1990s," in *The Modern Mexican Military. A Reassessment*, ed. David Ronfeldt (La Jolla, Calif.: Center for U.S. Mexican Studies, University of California, San Diego, 1984), 172.
48. Frank D. McCann, "Brazilian Army Officers Biography Project," Unpublished paper, Latin American Studies Association, Miami, December 1989, 6; and his *Soldiers of the Pátria, A History of the Brazilian Army, 1889–1937* (Palo Alto, Calif.: Stanford University Press, 2004), 237.
49. José de Imaz, *Los Que Mandan* (Albano, N.Y.: State University of New York, 1970), 58.
50. Javier Romero, *Aspectos psicobiométricos y sociales de una muestra de la juventud mexicana* (Mexico: Dirección de Investigaciones Antropológicas, 1956), 47.
51. McCann, "Brazilian Army Officers Biography Project," 22.

52. Personal interview, Mexico City, 1990.
53. Personal interview, Mexico City, 1991. Half of the states were not represented at all.
54. Wager, "The Mexican Military," 8; McCann, "Brazilian Army Officers Biography Project," 5.
55. McAlister, *The Military in Latin American Socio-political Evolution*, 221.
56. Roderic Ai Camp, *Militarizing Mexico, Where Is the Officer Corps Going?* Policy Paper on the Americas (Washington, D.C.: CSIS, 1999), 7–8.
57. Ann L. Craig, *The First Agraristas, An Oral History of a Mexican Agrarian Reform Movement* (Berkeley, Calif.: University of California Press, 1983), 77.
58. Personal correspondence to the author, n.d., 1992.
59. Michael J. Dziedzic, "Civil-military Relations in Mexico: The Politics of Co-optation" (unpublished paper, University of Texas, Austin, 1983), 11. Stephen J. Wager, "Civic Action and the Mexican Military" (unpublished paper, Department of History, U.S. Military Academy, 1982), 7.
60. Survey of *Revista de Ejército y Fuerza Aérea*, 1943 to 2003.
61. Roderic Ai Camp, *Crossing Swords*, 147–148, 181.
62. *Diccionario biográfico del gobierno mexicano*, 1989, 955.
63. George Kourvetaris and Betty Debratz, *Social Origins and Political Orientations of Officer Corps in a World Perspective* (Denver, Colo.: Graduate School of International Studies, University of Denver, 1973), 11.
64. Morris Janowitz, *The Military in the Development of New Nations* (Chicago: University of Chicago Press, 1964), 58.
65. See, for example, his conclusions in *The Professional Soldier* (Glencoe, Ill.: Free Press, 1960), 86.
66. Ibid., 58.
67. Personal interviews, Mexico City, 1990.
68. See his "The Middle-Class Military Coup Revisited," in *Armies and Politics in Latin America*, ed. Abraham Lowenthal (New York: Holmes and Meier, 1976), 49–86.
69. Marion Levy, Jr., "Armed Forces Organizations," in *The Military and Modernization*, ed. Henry Bienen (Chicago: Aldine-Atherton, 1971), 63.
70. Kourvetaris and Debratz, *Social Origins and Political Orientations of Officer Corps in a World Perspective*, 78.
71. Gordon C. Schloming, "Civil-Military Relations in Mexico, 1910–1940: A Case Study" (Ph.D. dissertation, Columbia University, 1974), 317.
72. José Luis Piñeyro, "The Modernization of the Mexican Armed Forces," in *Democracy under Siege, New Military Power in Latin America*, ed. Augusto Varas (Westport, Conn.: Greenwood Press, 1989), 127.
73. Janowitz, *The Military in the Development of New Nations*, 56.
74. Frederick M. Nunn. "On the Role of the Military in Twentieth-Century Latin America: The Mexican Case," in *The Modern Mexican Military. A Reassessment*, ed. David Ronfeldt (La Jolla, Calif.: Center for U.S.-Mexican Studies, University of California, San Diego, 1984), 41.
75. Rafael Segovia, *La politización del niño mexicano* (Mexico: El Colegio de México, 1975), 68.
76. Roderic Ai Camp, ed., *Citizen Views of Democracy in Latin America* (Pittsburgh, Penn.: University of Pittsburgh Press, 2000).
77. José Enrique Miguens, "The New Latin American Military Coup," in *Militarism in Developing Countries*, ed. Kenneth Fidel (New Brunswick, N.J.: Transaction, 1975), 99–123.
78. Personal interview, Mexico City, 1990.

79. A typical officer would reach two-star rank around the age of 55, therefore all of the generals in our sample were born before 1950. Unfortunately, the armed forces does not maintain collective data on the socio-economic background of cadets' parents, so there is no way to foresee changing patterns in the backgrounds of younger officers.
80. James W. Wilkie and Paul D. Wilkins, "Quantifying the Class Structure of Mexico, 1895-1970," in *Statistical Abstract of Latin America*, vol. 21, eds. James W. Wilkie and Stephen Haber (Los Angeles: Latin American Center, University of California, Los Angeles, 1982), 585.
81. Roderic Ai Camp, *Mexico's Mandarins*, 82.
82. Oscar Hinojosa, "Cualquier régimen de gobierno, con apoyo popular, será respetado por el Ejército," *Proceso*, March 1982, 9.
83. William S. Ackroyd, "Descendants of the Revolution: Civil-Military Relations in Mexico" (Ph.D. dissertation, University of Arizona, 1988), 154-155.
84. Universal agreement among politicians and generals existed on this point. Personal interviews, Mexico City, 1989-1990.
85. Kourvetaris and Debratz, *Social Origins and Political Orientations of Officer Corps in a World Perspective*, 10.
86. William S. Ackroyd, "Civil-Military Relations in Mexico: A Study of Mexican Military Perceptions and Behavior" (Paper presented at the Rocky Mountain States Conference of Latin American Studies, Las Cruces, 1980), 15.
87. From comments provide to the author by two majors who graduated from the Escuela Superior de Guerra, February 2004.
88. Lieuwen, *Mexican Militarism*, 147.
89. McAlister, *The Military in Latin American Sociopolitical Evolution*, 222
90. Roderic Ai Camp, *Militarizing Mexico*, 8.
91. Nevertheless, in the 1950s and 1960s, top U.S. officers were well represented in the upper-middle classes. In Lloyd Warner's study of colonels to four-star generals in 1963, 13 percent of their fathers were in big business, 15 percent were professionals, 16 percent were in small business, and 12 percent were white collar. *The American Federal Executive. A Study of the Social and Personal Characteristics of the Civilian and Military Leaders of the United States* (New Haven, Conn.: Yale University Press, 1963). Among air force generals in a 1950 study, 30 percent were upper middle class, 62 percent, lower middle class, and 8 percent, upper lower class. R. F. Schloemer and G. E. Myers, "Making It at the Air Force Academy: Who Stays? Who Succeeds?" in *The Changing World of the American Military*, ed. Franklin D. Margiotta (Boulder, Colo.: Westview Press, 1978), 335.
92. Janowitz, *The Professional Soldier*, Frank McCann discovered that in Brazil cadets from middle-class families also increased, but officers from both upper- and lower-class families have decreased since World War II. See his "Brazilian Army Officers Biography Project," 13.
93. Charles H. Coates, "America's New Officer Corps," in *The American Military*, ed. Martin Oppenheimer (Chicago: Aldine, 1971), 50. Alfred Stepan found in Brazil that in the early 1960s 78 percent were from the middle class; 6 percent, upper class; and 9 percent, lower classes. *The Military in Politics, Changing Patterns in Brazil* (Princeton: Princeton University Press, 1971), 33.
94. Coates, "Americas New Officer Corps," 51.
95. Camp, "Mexican Military Leadership in Statistical Perspective," 599.
96. Piñeyro, "The Mexican Army and the State," 154-155.

97. Peter H. Smith, *Labyrinths of Power: Political Recruitment in Twentieth Century Mexico* (Princeton, N.J.: Princeton University Press, 1979), 95–96.
98. Camp, "Generals and Politicians in Mexico," 116.
99. Daniel Mora, "Profile of the Mexican Company Grade Officer" (Paper presented at the Rocky Mountain States Latin American Conference, Tucson, February 1984), 5.
100. Stepan, *The Military in Politics,* 33.
101. Camp, "Generals and Politicians in Mexico," 120.
102. Roderic Ai Camp, *Mexico's Mandarins,* 73.
103. Interestingly, even in a society like the United States, war can broaden the career military backgrounds of an officer corps. Among Air War College graduates shortly after Vietnam, the percentage of graduates whose fathers were career military declined to only 5 percent, indicating the impact of war on breaking down caste qualities. See Schloemer, "Making It at the Air Force Academy," 339.
104. Roderic Ai Camp, *Mexico's Mandarins,* 73.
105. Romero, *Aspectos psicobiométricos y sociales de una muestra de la juventud mexicana,* 49.
106. Wager, "Civic Action and the Mexican Military," 12.
107. Figures for all U.S. Air Force Academy graduates are somewhat similar. One in four officers had a father who was career military, and 2 percent had fathers and grandfathers with military backgrounds. See Schloemer, "Making It at the Air Force Academy," 338.
108. McCann, "Brazilian Army Officers Biography Project," 14, 16.
109. John F. Fitzgerald found that 25 percent of naval cadets at Annapolis were the children of career military fathers. See his article with Chance L. Cochran, "Who Goes to the United States Naval Academy?," in *The Changing World of the American Military,* ed. Franklin D. Margiotta (Boulder, Colo.: Westview Press, 1971), 362.
110. Schloemer, "Making It at the Air Force Academy," 338.
111. This is the tentative conclusion of J. Samuel Fitch, "The Armed Forces and Society in South America," 4.
112. Roderic Ai Camp, *Mexico's Mandarins,* 64.

Chapter Four   Military-Civilian Interlocks, the Politicized Officer

1. For the theoretical underpinnings of such an argument, see Ruth Spalding, "State Power and its Limits: Corporatism in Mexico," *Comparative Political Studies* 14 (July 1981): 139–61. For the broad transformation, see George Grayson's *Mexico, From Corporatism to Pluralism?* (New York: Harcourt Brace, 1998).
2. Franklin D. Margiotta, "The Mexican Military: A Case Study in Non-intervention" (M.A. thesis, Georgetown University, 1968).
3. Roderic Ai Camp, "Generals and Politicians in Mexico: A Preliminary Comparison," in *The Modern Mexican Military, A Reassessment,* ed. David Ronfeldt (La Jolla, Calif.: Center for U.S. Mexican Studies, University of California, San Diego, 1984), 148.
4. Although they did not share comparable training or levels of professionalization, career military officers, as used in this table, are individuals who spent at least 20 years on active duty and rose to the rank of lieutenant colonel or higher. Although many Mexicans between the 1850s and 1920s entered the military in response to political events associated with violence, many chose to make the national guard, the federal army, or the revolutionary army their profession.

5. "Experience and Leadership: The Role of Combat," in my *Political Recruitment across Two Centuries, Mexico, 1884–1991* (Austin, Tex.: University of Texas Press, 1995), 58–80. The theoretical arguments have been offered in Peter Loewenberg's classic work, *Decoding the Past: The Psychohistorical Approach* (New York: Knopf, 1983).

6. Harold D. Lasswell and Daniel Lerner, eds., *World Revolutionary Elites: Studies in Coercive Ideological Movements* (Cambridge, Mass.: MIT Press, 1965).

7. Calles was actually born in 1871, but because of his formative experience and background, he belongs to this significant political generation.

8. For the formation of this generation, see Héctor Aguilar Camin's *La frontera nomada: Sonora y la revolución mexicana* (Mexico: Siglo XXI, 1977).

9. Roderic Ai Camp, "Mexican Military Leadership in Statistical Perspective since the 1930s," in *Statistical Abstract of Latin America*, 20, eds. James W. Wilkie and Peter Reich (Los Angeles: Latin American Center Publications, University of California, Los Angeles, 1080), 602.

10. Personal letter from Eduardo Bustamante, Mexico City, December 16, 1975.

11. *Diccionario biográfico del gobierno mexicano* (Mexico: Presidencia de la República, 1989), 961.

12. Sigrid Arzt, "La militarización de la Procuraduría General de la República: riesgos para la democracia mexicana," USMEX 2003-04 Working Paper Series, UCSD, 2004, 11.

13. Volker G. Lehr, *Manual biográfico del Congreso de la Unión* (Mexico: UNAM, 1984).

14. *Washington Post*, September 23, 1982, 29A.

15. *Diccionario biográfico del gobierno mexicano* (Mexico: Presidencia de la República, 1987), 322.

16. *Diccionario biográfico del gobierno mexicano* (Mexico: Presidencia de la República, 1992); *Integrantes de la LV Legislatura* (Mexico: Senado de la República, 1992).

17. Letter from Marco Antonio Fernández Martínez, chief of staff to Senator Juan José Rodríguez Pratts, May 20, 2003.

18. He played an active role in demanding increased transparency within the armed forces budget process as well as increased accountability of the secretary of national defense to the committee. See Hugo Martínez McNaught, "Piden a Sedena rendir cuentas," *Reforma*, April 28, 1998.

19. See my *Entrepreneurs and Politics in Twentieth-Century Mexico* (New York: Oxford University Press, 1989), 113, 190.

20. Personal interview with César Sepúlveda, Mexico City, August 21, 1990.

21. Alicia Olivera de Bonfil and Eugenia Meyer, *Gustavo Baz y sus jucios como revolucionario, médico y político* (Mexico: INAH, 1971), 43–44.

22. Colegio Nacional, *Memorias* 8, no. 1 (1974): 265–267.

23. Salinas' military connections extended more deeply than his uncle's generation. His maternal grandfather, Eduardo de Gortari Zerecero, a graduate of the Colegio Militar, founded a Maderista club in Mexico City and was on the staff of General Cándido Aguilar, a major revolutionary figure, in Veracruz.

24. Lyle McAlister, *The Military in Latin American Socio-political Evolution*, 237.

25. Personal interview, Mexico City, August 24, 1990.

26. George Philip, *The Military in South American Politics* (London: Croom-Helm, 1985), 17.

27. Personal interview, Mexico City, August 23, 1990.

28. Personal interview with Carlos Tello, former secretary of planning and budgeting, Mexico City, 1990.

29. Thomas E. Weil, "The Armed Forces," *Area Handbook for Mexico* (Washington, D.C.: GPO, 1975), 368–369.
30. Personal interview with Carlos Tello, Washington, D.C., April 1984.
31. Personal interview with Gabriel Zaid, August 17, 1990.
32. Personal interview with General Gerardo Clemente Vega García, Mexico City, August 19, 1990.
33. See Ginger Thompson, "Mexican Army Protestor Goes Loudly into Hiding," *New York Times*, December 29, 1998.
34. Personal interview with a former military presidential aide, August 20, 1990.
35. Personal interview with Carlos Tello, Mexico City, August 24, 1990. Tello served as secretary of the presidency, among other cabinet-level posts.
36. Official biography, www.sedena.mx, 2003.
37. Personal interview with Carlos Tello, Mexico City, August 24, 1990.
38. Personal interview with Javier Oliva Posada, national security specialist and instructor at the Colegio de Defensa Nacional, August 19, 1990. Oliva Posada currently is the national security affairs adviser to PRI.
39. *Diario Oficial*, August 21, 1990, 34. According to Raimundo Riva Palacio, the law was changed so that these officers would be rotated back to Mexico regularly and not become, as a result of long foreign residence, less nationalistic. The secretary of national defense was the origin of this change, not the secretariat of foreign relations. The secretariat of foreign relations expressed no interest in exerting greater control over the attachés. Personal interview, Mexico City, February 13, 1991.
40. Ibid., December 26, 1986, 16.
41. José Luis Piñeyro. "Presencia, política militar nacional y en el Distrito Federal: Propuestas de análisis," in *Distrito Federal, gobierno y sociedad civil,* ed. Pablo González Casanova (Mexico: El Caballito, 1987). 64.
42. www.sedena.gob.mx, transparency request, folio 2003000055, June 2003.
43. William S. Ackroyd, "Descendants of the Revolution: Civil-Military Relations in Mexico" (Ph.D. dissertation, University of Arizona, 1988), 198–199.
44. www.presidencia.gob.mx, transparency request, Folio 0210000058303, November 14, 2003.
45. Based on 502 known sources of friendship among 398 power elites from 1970–2000 with a power elite member from a different group.
46. Roderic Ai Camp, *Mexico's Mandarins, Crafting a Power Elite for the Twenty-first Century* (Berkeley, Calif.: University of California Press, 2002), 13.
47. Ibid., 107.
48. Personal interview, Mexico City, August 1990.
49. Luis Herrera-Lasso and Guadalupe González G., "Balance y perspectiva en el uso del concepto de la seguridad nacional en el caso de México" (Unpublished paper, 1989), 29.
50. Miguel Basáñez, *La lucha por la hegemonia en México, 1968–80* (Mexico: Siglo XXI, 1981), 58.
51. See Michael A. Burdick, *For God and Fatherland: Religion and Politics in Argentina* (Albany, N.Y.: State University of New York Press, 1996), and Brian Smith, *The Church and Politics in Chile, Challenges to Modern Catholicism* (Princeton, N.J.: Princeton University Press, 1982).
52. Guillermo Boils, "Los militares en México (1965–1985)," *Revista Mexicana de Sociologia* 47 (January–February 1985): 182.
53. Roderic Ai Camp, *Mexico's Mandarins*, 107.

54. *Diccionario biográfico del gobierno mexicano* (1989), 961, 977, 985, 995.
55. Roderic Ai Camp, "Militarizing Mexico, Where Is the Officer Corps Going?" *Policy Paper on the Americas* (Washington, D.C., CSIS, 1999), 13-14.
56. Based on interviews with six instructors at the Colegio de Defensa Nacional, Mexico City, summers 1989, 1990.
57. Most classes number in the mid to high twenties. Based on data requested under the transparency law covering all graduates from the Colegio de Defensa Nacional since it graduated its first class in 1982. Personal interview with General Rafael de la Paz, director of the Colegio de Defensa Nacional, Mexico City, December 1998.
58. Personal interview with General Gerardo Clemente Vega García, Mexico City, August 19, 1990.
59. General Notholt Rosales is also the son-in-law of General Aureo L. Calles, the former assistant secretary of national defense. He served as chief of aides to President Adolfo Ruiz Cortines, a position which allowed him to establish numerous political contacts.
60. Occasionally, an uncommon contact through education occurs between two individuals which will impact on their careers. Such is the case of President José López Portillo, who attended primary and the National Preparatory School in Mexico City with General Miguel Mendoza Marquez, director of the Air Force, 1982-1988, and with General Juan Antonio de la Fuente Rodríguez, the assistant secretary of national defense during his administration, at the National Preparatory School.
61. Marion J. Levy, Jr, "Armed Forces Organization," in *The Military and Modernization*, ed. Henry Bienen (Chicago: Aldine-Atherton, 1971), 64.
62. This changed in 2000 with the appointment of General Vega García as secretary of national defense. Fox passed over all the senior division generals when he named Vega García, who had received his third star in January 2000 only 10 months before his selection, thus becoming the most junior division general. Even more surprising, the navy secretary had to be promoted to admiral in order to take his post. Roderic Ai Camp, "Civilian Supremacy in Mexico, the Case of a Post-Revolutionary Military," in *Military Intervention and Withdrawal*, ed. Constantine P. Danopoulous (London: Routledge, 1991), 20.
63. According to the media, he was fired for alleged nepotism (appointing his brother-in-law oficial mayor and his son private secretary), inexplicable wealth, and links to drug trafficking. See *El Nacional,* July 19, 1990, 5 and *Proceso,* July 23, 1990.
64. Evelyn P. Stevens. "Mexico's PRI: The Institutionalization of Corporatism?" in *Authoritarianism and Corporatism to Latin America*, ed. James Malloy (Pittsburgh, Penn.: University of Pittsburgh Press, 1977), 233.
65. Talukder Maniruzzaman, *Military Withdrawal from Politics: A Comparative Study* (Cambridge, Mass.: Ballinger, 1987), 97.
66. José Luis Piñeyro, *Ejército y sociedad en México: Pasado y presente* (Puebla: Universidad Autónomo de Puebla, 1985), 56.
67. Less than two weeks after taking office on December 10, 1940, Avila Camacho ordered this change in a communiqué to the Secretariat of National Defense. For details on the impact of his decision on the party, see Luis Javier Garrido's insightful, *El partido de la revolución institucionalizada* (Mexico: Siglo XXI, 1982), 303ff.
68. Roderic Ai Camp, *Entrepreneurs and Politics in Twentieth Century Mexico* (New York: Oxford University Press, 1989), 125.
69. For example, see Yemile Mizrahi, on the relationship with the Nacional Action Party, in her "A New Conservative Opposition in Mexico: the Politics of Entrepreneurs

in Chihuahua (1983–1992)," Ph.D. dissertation, University of California at Berkeley, 1994 and Matilde Luna, "Entrepreneurial Interests and Political Action in Mexico," in *The Challenges of Institutional Reform in Mexico*, ed. Riordan Roett (Boulder, Colo.: Lynne Rienner, 1995), 77–94.

70. *Revista del Ejército y Fuerza Aérea*, August 1975, 142; *Hispano Americano*, April 11, 1983, 6; *Excélsior*, March 30, 1983, 18.

71. "Autopostulado, Cuenca será gobernador," *Proceso*, December 25, 1976, 6–9; Elías Chávez, "El ejército, desprestigiado por gobernantes sin autoridad moral," *Proceso*, May 15, 1978, 18.

72. Its leaders have included Division General Jacinto B. Treviño, a revolutionary general, Juan Barragán Rodríguez, former chief of staff to President Venustiano Carranza, and Division General Antonio Gómez Velasco, chief of staff to several leading revolutionary generals and zone commander; and Admiral Antonio Vázquez del Mercado, former secretary of the Navy.

73. José Luis Piñeyro, "The Mexican Army and the State: Historical and Political Perspective," *Revue Internationale de Sociologie* 14 (April–August 1978), 127.

74. Margiotta, "The Mexican Military," 24.

75. Ackroyd, "Descendants of the Revolution," 200.

76. Camp, "Civilian Supremacy in Mexico," 17.

77. Lieuwen, *Mexican Militarism*, 98.

78. Personal letter from Manuel R. Palacios, Mexico City, February 1, 1973.

79. Edwin Lieuwen, "Depolitizacion of the Mexican Revolutionary Army, 1915–1940," in *The Modern Mexican Military, a Reassessment*, ed. David Ronfeldt (La Jolla, Calif.: Center for U.S.-Mexican Studies, University of California, San Diego, 1984), 60.

80. Elisa Servín, *Ruptura y oposición, el movimiento henriquista, 1945–1954* (Mexico: Cal y Arena, 2001), 46.

81. Ibid., 92–93.

82. *New York Times*, February 18, 1947, 15; Luis Medina, *Historia de la revolución mexicana, periodo 1940–1952, civilismo y modernización del autoritarismo*, no. 20 (Mexico: El Colegio de México, 1979), 97.

83. He served as Vice-president of the Constituent Assembly of the Party.

84. Olga Pellicer de Brody, "La oposición en México: El caso de henriquismo," in *Las crisis en el sistema político mexicano, 1928–1977*, Centro de Estudios Internacionales (Mexico: El Colegio de México, 1977), 36–37.

85. Servín, 192.

86. Ibid., note 54, 197.

87. A year earlier, he had written a letter to President Alemán suggesting that, if his personal friendship with General Henríquez Guzmán produced offensive consequences or misinterpretations, he would accept whatever decision the government might make about his assignment. It is clear from his career trajectory that he did not suffer personally, and that his reassignment responded to the symbolic importance of retaining a known personal friend of the general in one of the most visible and influential army posts. In November, 1951, he was promoted to Division General, and, in 1956, he commanded the 1st Military Zone, the most significant zone assignment. *Revista de Ejército y Fuerza Aérea*, June, 1976, 136.

88. Cristóbal Guzmán Cárdenas, *Mis Seis Años* (Mexico: n.d.).

89. "Mexico's 'New' PRI Looks Like Old," *Miami Herald*, October 1, 1990.

90. *Excélsior*, January 14, 1997.

91. *Proceso*, November 2, 1987, 9.

92. Véjar Vázquez never attended the Colegio Militar, nor had he received any military training. However, he joined the military justice system in 1925 with a commission as a colonel, two years after graduating from the National School of Law. He taught at the Colegio Militar, the Applied Military Academy, the Military Aviation School, and at the Escuela Superior de Guerra. He authored the Code of Military Justice. He rose to the rank of Brigade General and to the post of Military Attorney General. In 1944, he founded the National Independent Democratic Party. See Francisco R. Illescas and Juan Bartolo Hernández, *Escritores veracruzanos* (Veracruz, 1945), 603–04.

93. Oscar Hinojosa, "Con licencia o sin licencia, están en campaña," *Proceso*, May 2, 1988, 10.

94. Lieuwen, *Mexican Militarism*, 145.

95. In addition, officers were seeking out his expertise to confirm their legal right to take a leave and become politically involved.

96. *Hispano Americano*, November 18, 1974, 10; *Excélsior*, November 11, 1974, 20; *New York Times*, April 15, 1952, and April 18, 1952, 5.

97. Personal interview with Division General Luis Garfias Magaña, Mexico City, August 24, 1990.

98. www.csis.org., 2000; www.presidencia.gob.mx, 2003.

99. Personal interview with President José López Portillo, Mexico City, February 19, 1991.

100. Personal interview, Mexico City, August 20, 1990.

101. Edward J. Williams, "The Evolution of the Mexican Military and Its Implications for Civil-Military Relations," in *Mexico's Political Stability: The Next Five Years*, ed. Roderic Ai Camp (Boulder, Colo.: Westview Press, 1986), 154.

102. Jorge Luis Sierra, "El ejército en tiempos de Fox: continuidad con los planes zedillistas," www.proceso.com.mx. *Proceso*, August 18, 2002.

103. Oscar Hinojosa "Su veto demonstró que los militares no son homogeneamente gobiernistas," *Proceso*, August 8, 19.

104. *El Nacional*, March 13, 1990, 7. Earlier, a corporal had been charged with firing on a group of PRD sympathizers. In a rare news conference, General Antonio Riviello Bazán, the secretary of national defense, told reporters that the corporal had been turned over to civil authorities for prosecution. See Larry Rohter, "Use of Troops Cause of Concern in Mexico," *New York Times*, November 5, 1989, 8.

105. Herrera-Lasso and González, "Balance y perspectiva en el uso del concepto de la seguridad nacional con el caso de México," 30.

106. Ibid., 18.

107. The army and navy, as part of a formal enforcement of its non-partisan electoral posture, no longer allowed the Federal Electoral Institute to place polling booths in military zones in various states because they would restrict civilian access. See *Diario de Yucatán*, June 13, 2003, diariodeyucatan.com.mx.

Chapter Five   Civilian Missions: Redefining Civil-Military Relations?

1. Louis W. Goodman and Johanna Mendelson, "The Threat of New Missions: Latin American Militaries and the Drug War," in *The Military and Democracy in Latin America*, eds. Louis W. Goodman and Johanna Mendelson (Lexington: Lexington Books, 1990), 189–195.

2. Sigrid Arzt's "La militarización de la Procuraduría General de la República: Riesgos para la democracia mexicana," USMEX 2003-04 Working Paper Series, UCSD, 2004, defines militarization quite precisely.

3. David Pion-Berlin, "Military Autonomy and Emerging Democracies in South America," *Comparative Politics* 25, no. 1 (October 1992), 83–102, "Decision-Makers or Decision-Takers? Military Missions and Civilian Control in Democratic South America," *Armed Forces and Society* 26, no. 3 (Spring 2000), 413–436, and "A New Civil-Military Pragmatism in Latin America," www.resdal.org.ar/redes-03.

4. Personal interview, Mexico City, August 20, 1990.

5. Raúl Benítez Manaut, "Las fuerzas armadas mexicanas a fin del siglo," Unpublished paper, Latin American Studies Association, Miami, 2000, 10–12.

6. José Piñeyro, "The Modernization of the Mexican Armed Forces," in *Democracy Under Siege, New Military Power in Latin America*, ed. Augusto Varas (Westport, Conn.: Greenwood Press, 1989), 118–119.

7. Sigrid Arzt, "Combating Transnational Organized Crime in Mexico, Only an Illusion?" International Studies Association, Chicago, February 2001, 12–13.

8. Michael J. Dziedzic, "Civil-Military Relations in Mexico" (Unpublished paper, University of Texas, Austin, 1983), 12; and Stephen J. Wager, "Civic Action and the Mexican Military" (Unpublished paper, Department of History, United States Military Academy, West Point, 1982), 14.

9. J. Samuel Fitch, *The Armed Forces and Democracy in Latin America* (Baltimore, Md.: Johns Hopkins University Press, 1998), pp. 182–194.

10. *Constitution of the United Mexican States* (Washington, D.C.: Pan American Union, 1964), 59.

11. David F. Ronfeldt, "The Mexican Army and Political Order Since 1940," in *Armies and Politics in Latin America,* ed. Abraham F. Lowenthal (New York: Holmes and Meier, 1976), 293.

12. Lyle N. McAlister, *The Military in Latin American Sociopolitical Evolution: Four Case Studies* (Washington, D.C.: Center for Research in Social Systems, 1970), 209; Edwin Lieuwen, *Mexican Militarism, The Political Rise and Fall of the Revolutionary Army, 1910–1940* (Albuquerque, N.M.: University of New Mexico Press, 1968), 72.

13. Wager, "Civic Action and the Mexican Military," 19.

14. Karl M. Schmitt, "The Role of the Military in Contemporary Mexico," in *The Caribbean: Mexico Today,* ed. Curtis A. Wilgus (Gainesville, Fla.: University of Florida Press, 1964), 55.

15. Stephen J. Wager, "The Mexican Military, 1968–1978: A Decade of Change" (Unpublished paper, Stanford University, June 1979), 15.

16. Confidential Cable, U.S. Embassy, 1995Mexico10043, U.S. Department of State, May 11, 1995, National Security Archives, George Washington University, 2004.

17. Alden Cunningham, "Mexico's National Security in the 1980s–1990s," in *The Modern Mexican Military: A Reassessment,* ed. David Ronfeldt (La Jolla, Calif.: Center for U.S.-Mexican Studies, UCSD, 1984), 174.

18. Roderic Ai Camp, "The Military," in *Prospects for Mexico*, ed. George W. Grayson (Washington, D.C.: Foreign Service Institute, 1988), 87.

19. See Joe Foweraker and Ann L. Craig, eds. *Popular Movements and Political Change in Mexico* (Boulder, Calif.: Lynne Rienner, 1990).

20. Phyllis G. Walker, "The Modern Mexican Military: Political Influence and Institutional Interests in the 1980s" (Unpublished M.A. thesis, American University, 1987), 75.

21. Stanley E. Hilton, "The Brazilian Military: Changing Strategic Perceptions and the Question of Mission," *Armed Forces and Society* 13 (Spring 1987): 330, 346.

22. Paul Zagorski, "Flashpoint II: Internal Security," in *Democracy Versus National Security: Civil-Military Relations in Latin America* (Boulder, Colo.: Lynne Rienner, 1992); Jack Child, "Geopolitical Thinking in Latin America," in *The Military and Democracy: The Future of Civil-Military Relations in Latin America*, eds. Louis Goodman et al. (Lexington, Mass.: Lexington Books, 1990); Gabriel Marcella, "The Latin American Military, Low Intensity Conflict, and Democracy," *Journal of Inter-American Studies & World Affairs* 32 no. 1 (Spring 1990), 45–82; and David Pion-Berlin, "Latin American National Security Doctrines: Hard- and Soft-line Themes," *Armed Forces and Society* 15, no. 3 (1989): 411–428.

23. Levy, "Armed Forces Organization," 47.

24. Gabriel Marcella, "Latin America in the 1980's: The Strategic Environment and Inter-American Security" (Carlisle: Strategic Studies Institute, U.S. Army War College, 1981), 31.

25. Bruce M. Russet, "Political Perspectives of U.S. Military and Business Elites," *Armed Forces and Society* 1 (Fall 1974): 87.

26. Martin C. Needler, *Politics and Society in Mexico* (Albuquerque: University of New Mexico Press, 1967), 66, citing General Alfonso Corona del Rosal, *Moral militar y civilismo*, 2nd ed. (Mexico: Estado Mayor Presidencial, 1952).

27. Guillermo Boils, "Fuerzas armadas y armamentismo en México," *Nueva Política* 2 (April–September 1977): 357.

28. *El Nacional, Suplemento Especial,* October 27, 1990, 1.

29. The Department of Federal Security (DFS) allegedly was in league with the drug cartels and cooperated with the Central Intelligence Agency. It was disbanded in an attempt to root out corruption and repair Mexico's intelligence image. See William Brannigan, "With Friends Like These, Who Needs Enemies," *Washington Post,* National Weekly Edition, July 23–29, 1990, 31.

30. Sergio Aguayo, *La Charola, una historia de los servicios de inteligencia en México* (Mexico: Grijalbo, 2001), 66.

31. Heroico Colegio Militar, *Memoria gráfico del cincuentenario de la reapertura del Heroico Colegio Militar* (Mexico: 1970), 467.

32. Sergio Aguayo, *La Charola,* 67.

33. Arturo R. Blancas and Tomás L. Vidrio, *Indice biográfico de la XLIII Legislatura Federal* (Mexico, 1956), 88–89.

34. Personal letter from Sergio Aguayo, January 10, 2000.

35. Captain Pablo González Ruelas briefly held the post in 1985, before it was disbanded.

36. For the alleged corruption in the agency, see William Brannigan, "With Friends Like These, Who Needs Enemies?" *Washington Post,* National Weekly Edition, July 23–29, 1990, 31; *Los Angeles Times,* May 16, 1990.

37. Tim Weiner, "Mexico Indicts Former Chief of Secret Police," *New York Times,* March 30, 2003. In December, 2003, the Mexican authorities issued warrants for both Luis de la Barreda Moreno and Miguel Nazar Haro for the torture and disappearance of a Mexican activist in 1975. "Mexico Issues Warrants for 3 'Dirty War' Suspects," *Los Angeles Times,* December 10, 2003. Nazar Haro finally was arrested in 2004, charged with crimes committed during Mexico's dirty war. See Tim Weiner, "Mexico Seizes Official in 'Dirty War' Case of 70s," *New York Times,* February 20, 2004.

38. David Pion-Berlin and Craig Arceneaux, "Decision-Makers or Decision-Takers? Military Missions and Civilian Control in Democratic South America," *Armed Forces and Society*, Vol. 26 (Spring 2000), 433.
39. Olga Pellicer de Brody, "National Security Concerns in Mexico: Traditional Notions and New Preoccupations," in *U.S.-Mexico Relations, Economic and Social Aspects*, eds. Clark W. Reynolds and Carlos Tello (Stanford, Calif.: Stanford University Press, 1983), 187.
40. Ibid., 188.
41. Walker, "The Modern Mexican Military," 76.
42. www.sedena.gob.mx, transparency request, folio 0000700043903, November 2003.
43. *Diario Oficial*, December 7, 1988, 4.
44. Personal interview, Mexico City, February 13, 1991.
45. *Diario Oficial*, April 19, 2003.
46. www.sedena.gob.mx, transparency request, folio 0000700022203, November 2003.
47. *Diario de Yucatán*, June 15, 2003, www.sureste.com.mx.
48. *Manual de organización del gobierno federal, 1973* (Mexico: Secretaria de la Presidencia, 1973), 136.
49. Sergio Aguayo, *La Charola*, 301.
50. *Diccionario biográfico del gobierno mexicano* (Mexico: Presidencia de la República, 1989), 197.
51. *Diario de Yucatán*, October 7, 2002, www.sureste.com.mx.
52. *Diario de Yucatán*, August 8, 2001, www.sureste.com.mx. General Vega García believes that health, education, poverty, demographics, and civil society are critical to national security. In a recent conversation with General Vega Garcia, it is clear that he considers broad macro economic and social conditions as critical to Mexico's security and stability. He is well-versed in many of these issues, including the adverse impact China is having on jobs in Mexico. Personal interview, Mexico City, February 26, 2004.
53. Karl Schmitt, "The Role of the Military in Contemporary Mexico," 60.
54. Stephen J. Wager, "Civic Action and the Mexican Military" 7.
55. Michael J. Dziedzic, "Mexico's Converging Challenges: Problems, Prospects, and Implications" (Unpublished manuscript, U.S. Air Force Academy, April 21, 1989), 13, citing a report from Oaxaca, September 3, 1981.
56. Steve Wager, "The Mexican Military Approaches the 21st Century," in *Mexico Faces the 21st Century*, eds. Donald E. Schulze and Edward J. Williams (Westport, Conn.: Greenwood Press, 1995), 68.
57. Personal interview, Mexico City, August 1990.
58. Personal interview, Mexico City, August 1990.
59. For an excellent description and comparison between the EZLN and the ERP, see Gustavo Hirales Morán, "Radical Groups in Mexico Today," *Policy Papers on the Americas* (Washington, D.C.: CSIS, 2003).
60. Graham H. Turbiville, Jr., "Mexico's Other Insurgents," *Military Review* (June–July 1997), 81–89.
61. Immigration and Refugee Board, "Mexico: Armed Insurgent Groups," Ottawa, Canada, Research Directorate Documentation, May 1997, 16–18.
62. Graham H. Turbiville, Jr., "Mexico's Other Insurgents."
63. Personal interview, Washington, D.C., 2000.
64. Raúl Benítez Manaut, "México: la nueva dimensión de las Fuerzas Armadas en los años noventa," *Análisis Político*, no. 31 (May–August 1997), 59.

65. *Diario de Yucatán*, November 29, 1999, www.sureste.com.mx. New groups continue to emerge. The Comité Clandestino Revolucionario de los Pobres (CCRP) announced an attack in Guerrero. See *Diario de Yucatán*, August 19, 1999, www.sureste.com.mx.
66. www.sedena.gob.mx. transparency request, folio 0000700022203, October, 2003.
67. Louis Goodman and Johanna Mendelson, "The Threat of New Missions: Latin American Militaries and the Drug War," in *The Military and Democracy: The Future of Civil-Military Relations in Latin America*, eds. Louis Goodman, et al. (Lexington, Mass.: Lexington Books, 1990), 191.
68. Jeffrey S. Cole, "Militarism in Mexico: Civil-Military Relations in a Transforming Society" (Unpublished M.A. thesis, Naval Postgraduate School, Monterey, California, December 1997), 61.
69. Personal interview, Mexico City, 1990.
70. *Unomásuno*, December 2, 1988, III.
71. Luis Herrera-Lasso and Guadalupe González G. "Balance y perspectiva en el uso del concepto de la seguridad nacional en el caso de México" (Unpublished paper, 1989), 26.
72. Kate Doyle, "The Militarization of the Drug War in Mexico," *Current History*, February 1993, 88.
73. Douglas Farah and Dana Priest, "Mexico Drug Force is U.S. Bred," *Washington Post*, February 26, 1998, 1A. Mexico is the recipient of large amounts of financial assistance from the United States for military and police training, ranging from 16.6, 27.5, 51.7 and 26.8 million dollars in 2000, 2001, 2002, and 2003. See "Paint by Numbers, Trends in U.S. Military Programs with Latin America," WOLA, August 2003, 7.
74. Stefan John Wray, "The Drug War and Information Warfare in Mexico," M.A. thesis, University of Texas, Austin, August 1997, chapter 4, www.nyuedu/projects/wray/thesis.
75. *Diario Oficial*, September 5, 2000, 7.
76. Boils, "Los militares en México," 180.
77. www.sedena.com.gob., transparency request, October 7, 2003.
78. Wray, "The Drug War and Information Warfare in Mexico," chapter 3.
79. Camp, "The Military," 90.
80. Personal interviews, Mexico City, 1990.
81. Arzt, "Combating Transnational Organized Crime in Mexico," 12.
82. www.sedena.gob.mx, transparency request, folio 000700031503, October 15, 2003.
83. Personal interview with General Gerardo Clemente Vega García, Mexico City, February 26, 2004.
84. Their support stemmed from necessity, not desire. The secretary of the navy, Admiral José Lorenzo Franco, stated publicly that fighting narcotics shouldn't be its mission, but it has no choice. *Diario de Yucatán*, September 13, 2000, www.sureste.com.mx.
85. Roderic Ai Camp, "Militarizing Mexico: Where is the Officer Corps Going?" *Policy Paper on the Americas* (Washington, D.C.: CSIS, 1990). 13–14.
86. Personal interview, Mexico City, August 19, 1990. In a now declassified report from the United States embassy in 1995, they argue that counternarcotics has become the "preoccupying, permanent task of the Mexican military. Military counternarcotics efforts are centered almost exclusively on manual eradication. . . . It is a task which the army is said not to relish, both because of the connotations of degrading

manual labor which the task entails, and because involvement in counternarcotics always carries with it the risk of compromise by narcotraffickers." Confidential Cable, U.S. Embassy, 1995Mexico10043, U.S. Department of State, May 11, 1995, National Security Archives, George Washington University, 2004.

87. Benítez Manaut, "México: la nueva dimensión," 57

88. Max G. Manwaring, "Guerrillas, Narcotics, and Terrorism: Old Menaces in a New World," in *Beyond Praetorianism: the Latin American Military in Transition* (Miami, Fla.: North-South Center Press, 1996), 37–57.

89. He referred only to the ERP and other intense Marxist groups and specifically excluded the Zapatistas. Personal interview, February 26, 2004.

90. Donald Schulz, "Between a Rock and a Hard Place: the United States, Mexico and the Agony of National Security," (Carlisle, Penn.: Strategic Studies Institute, U.S. Army War College, 1997), 25.

91. Richard B. Craig, "Mexican Narcotics Traffic: Binational Security Implications," *Latin American Narcotics Trade and U.S. National Security*, ed. Donald J. Mabry (Westport, Conn.: Greenwood Press, 1989), 35.

92. Personal interview, Mexico City, August 1990.

93. Wesley A. Fryer, "Mexican Security," Unpublished paper, August 24, 1993, www.wtvi.com/wesley/mexican security.

94. Stanley A. Pimentel, "The Nexus of Organized Crime and Politics in Mexico," in *Organized Crime and Democratic Governability: Mexico and the United States-Mexican Borderlands*, eds. John Bailey and Roy Godson (Pittsburgh, Penn.: University of Pittsburgh Press, 2000), 49.

95. Arzt, "Combating Transnational Organized Crime in Mexico," 12.

96. Americas Watch, *Report on Mexico* (NewYork: Americas Watch, 1990), 17; *Los Angeles Times,* June 14, 1990, The most specific evidence ever presented against the military is the testimony of a former enlisted man, Zacarías Osorio Cruz, who testified to the Canadian Immigration Board that he took part in executions ordered by senior Mexican army and air force officers between 1977 and 1982, during which he lined up hooded and handcuffed prisoners on a military firing range near Mexico City and riddled their bodies with gunfire. See Americas Watch, *Report on Mexico*, 35–36. Other convincing evidence has recently been discovered in government archives and several of the military officers who committed those crimes are being brought to justice.

97. *Diario Oficial,* June 6, 1990, 3–4; August 1, 1990, 2–9.

98. Consejo Nacional de Derechos Humanos, recommendation 4–90, July 25, 1990, addressed to General Antonio Riviello Bazán; interview with Jorge Carpizo, director of the new commission, Mexico City, August 1990.

99. *El Nacional,* October 25, 1990, 13.

100. The Secretary of Navy claimed that under Salinas there were 14 known cases of ties to drug trafficking among officers, while under Zedillo, they had declined to 9. None of the 9 were admirals. See *Diario de Yucatán*, September 12, 2000, www.sureste.com.mx.

101. Based on my examination of the complete interrogation, exceeding 1,100 pages, there is no question that he was deeply involved with known traffickers, some of whom he socialized with, and whose go-betweens actually came to the 15th Zone headquarters in Jalisco. These ties were well established over several years. The real question is why Mexican military intelligence or the U.S. Drug Enforcement Agency were unaware of these blatant associations. For a version in English, see Sam Dillon, "Court Files Say Drug Baron Used Mexican Military," *New York Times*, May 23, 1998, www.nytimes.com.

102. Raúl Monge, "Tres años de claroscuros en la PGR," *Proceso*, December 12, 1999, www.proceso.com.mx.
103. Patrick O'Day, "The Mexican Army as Cartel," *Journal of Contemporary Criminal Justice* 17, no. 3 (August 2001), 280.
104. *Diario Oficial*, December 5, 1995.
105. Eric L. Olson, "The Evolving Role of Mexico's Military in Public Security and Antinarcotics Programs," *Briefing Series*, Washington Office on Latin America, May 1996, 4.
106. Angel Gustavo López-Montiel, "The Military, Political Power, and Police Relations in Mexico City," *Latin American Perspectives* 27, no. 2 (March 2000), 83.
107. Benítez, "Mexico," 59.
108. Olson, "The Evolving Role of the Mexican Military," 5; and Arzt, "Combating Transnational Organized Crime in Mexico," 11.
109. Graham H. Turbiville, Jr., "Enforcement and the Mexican Armed Forces: New Internal Security Missions Challenge the Military," *Low Intensity Conflict and Law Enforcement* 6, no. 2 (Autumn 1997), np.
110. *El Universal*, July 15, 1999.
111. Raúl Benítez Manaut, "México: doctrina, historia y relaciones cívico-militares del siglo xxi," *Las relaciones cívico-militares en el mundo iberoamericano*, ed. José A. Olmeda (Madrid: Instituto Universitario General Gutiérrez Mellado, 2003).
112. Raúl Benítez Manaut and Stephen J. Wager, "National Security and Armed Forces in Mexico: Challenges and Scenarios at the End of the Century," *Working Paper Series*, Latin American Program, Woodrow Wilson Center for International Scholars, Washington, D.C., October 1998, 34.
113. Mark Stevenson, "Long Out of Politics and Limelight," Associated Press, August 19, 2002.
114. Raúl Monge, "Los generales Acosta y Quirós, solo dos ramos de la narco-milicia," *Proceso*, September 3, 2000, www.proceso.com.mx.
115. Tim Weiner, "Mexico Convicts Two Generals on Drug Trafficking Charge," *New York Times*, November 2, 2002, www.nytimes.com.
116. "Aparente vínculo de generales con un capo," *Diario de Yucatán*, October 30, 2002, www.sureste.com.mx.
117. Roderic Ai Camp, "Mexico's Armed Forces, Marching to a Democratic Tune?" *The Dilemma of Mexican Politics in Transition*, ed. Kevin Middlebrook (London: Institute of Latin American Studies, University of London, 2004), 358.
118. Secretariat of National Defense official website, www.sedena.gob.mx, September 6, 1999.
119. *Diario de Yucatán*, February 11, 1999.
120. Boils, "Los militares en México," 180.
121. Walker, "The Modern Mexican Military," 112; Craig, "Mexican Narcotics Traffic," 35.
122. Reed Johnson, "Crackdown in Mexico Points to New Policy," *Los Angeles Times*, January 18, 2003, A3.
123. *La Jornada*, August 17, 2000, www.lajornada.com.mx.
124. These special units originated from Rapid Response Forces in 1986. They became GAFE's in 1990. They were consolidated into 10 units in 1995, and two additional units, assigned to military regions 11 and 12, were added for a total of 12. "La cara del ejército ante los nuevos retos," *Revista de Ejército y Fuerza Aérea*, August 2002, 3–4; and "Nacimiento de una nueva generación de combatientes: 'Fuerzas Especiales'," January 1999.

125. *Diario de Yucatán*, March 18, 2002, www.sureste.com.mx.
126. www.sedena.gob.mx, transparency request, June 23, 2003.
127. Ibid.
128. David Gaddis Smith, "Mexico's Military Coming Out of Shadows and Onto TV," *San Diego Union Tribune*, March 17, 2002.
129. Patrick O'Day, "The Mexican Army as Cartel," 288–289.
130. "Combate al narcotráfico," *Diario de Yucatán*, January 18, 2003.
131. *Diario de Yucatán*, February 4, 2002, www.sureste.com.mx.
132. Reed Johnson, "Crackdown in Mexico Points to New Policy," A3.
133. Tim Weiner, "Mexico's Image is Buffeted and Tarnished with Military Drug Arrests," *New York Times*, April 7, 2001.
134. www.sedena.gob.mx, transparency request, folio 0000700022203, October 15, 2003.
135. Pedro Zamora, "Sin soporte legal, presencia militar en el combate al narco," *Proceso*, April 29, 2002, www.proceso.com.mx.
136. Craig, "Mexican Narcotics Traffic," 31.
137. Chabat, "Seguridad nacional y narcotráfico," 108.
138. For a broad picture of U.S.-Mexico security concerns, see Raúl Benítez-Manaut, *Mexico and the New Challenges of Hemispheric Security*, Woodrow Wilson Center Reports on the Americas (Washington, D.C.: Woodrow Wilson Center for Scholars, 2004).
139. José Luis Piñeyro, "Gobernabilidad democrática y fuerzas armadas en México con Fox," Unpublished paper, Latin American Studies Association, Washington, D.C., September 2001, 11.
140. Sigrid Arzt, "La militarización de la Procuraduría General de la República: Riesgos para la democracia mexicana," 16.
141. O'Day, "The Mexican Army as Cartel," 280–281.
142. Turbiville, "Mexico's Evolving Security Posture."
143. Graham H. Turbiville, Jr., "Mexico's Multimission Force for Internal Security," *Military Review* (July–September 2000).
144. *Diario de Yucatán*, September 20, 1999. www.sureste.com.mx
145. *Diario de Yucatán*, June 25, 2002, www.sureste.com.mx.
146. *Diario de Yucatán*, December 17, 2000, www.sureste.com.mx.
147. *Revista de Ejército y Fuerza Aérea*, August 2002, 42.
148. In an extraordinary departure from previous military leadership, the secretary of navy appeared on a popular radio talk show, "Imágenes de la Política," with Guillermo Ortega in January 2004. During his appearance he discussed the role of the navy and armed forces in national security. He specifically discussed anti-terrorism missions and repeatedly reinforced the subordination of the military to civilian decision-makers. See Radio Imágen Informativa, January 23, 2004.
149. For an opposing view, that Mexico is becoming militarized, with implications for military subordination, see Laurie Freeman and Jorge Luis Sierra, "Mexico: The Militarization Trap," in *Drugs and Democracy in Latin America,* eds. Coletta Youngers and Eileen Rosin (Boulder, Colo.: Lynne Rienner, 2005), 263–302.

Chapter Six   Citizen and Military Views of Civil-Military Relations

1. A recent study argues that top American generals are connected to society politically, even though their institutional culture is conservative. See James J. Dowd's

fascinating interviews with 62 generals: "Connected to Society: The Political Beliefs of U.S. Army Generals," *Armed Forces and Society*, Vol. 27 (Spring 2001), 343–372.

2. Carina Perelli and Juan Rial, "Changing Military World Views: The Armed Forces of South America in the 1990s," in *Beyond Praetorianism, The Latin American Military in Transition* (Miami, Fla.: North-South Center Press, 1996), p. 71.

3. David Ronfeldt, *The Mexican Army and Political Order since 1940* (Santa Monica: Rand Corporation, 1973), citing Daniel Cosío Villegas, *Visión*, April 8, 1972, 8.

4. Martin Edmonds, *Armed Services and Society* (Leicester, U.K.: University Press, 1988), 38–41.

5. Sam C. Sarkesian, *Beyond the Battlefield: The New Military Professionalism* (New York: Pergamon Press, 1981), 13.

6. Frederick M. Nunn, "The South American Military and (Re)Democratization: Professional Thought and Self-Perception," *Journal of Inter-American Studies and World Affairs*, 37, no. 2 (Summer 1995), 1–56.

7. Lyle N. McAlister, *The Military in Latin American-Socio-political Evolution; Four Case Studies* (Washington, D.C.: Center for Research in Social Systems, 1970), 245.

8. Personal correspondence to the author from General Luis Garfias Magaña, n.d., 1992.

9. Roderic Ai Camp, "Militarizing Mexico, Where Is the Officer Corps Going?," *Policy Paper on the Americas* (Washington, D.C.: CSIS, 1999).

10. Personal communication from V.H. Michel, reporter, *Mileno*, Mexico City, November 31, 2004.

11. Guillermo Boils, "Los militares en México (1965–1985)," *Revista Mexicana de Sociología*, 47 (January–February 1985): 171.

12. Peter H. Smith, *Labyrinths of Power: Political Recruitment in Twentieth-Century Mexico* (Princeton, N.J.: Princeton University Press, 1979), 14.

13. Frederick M. Nunn, "On the Role of the Military in Twentieth-Century Latin America: The Mexican Case," in *The Modern Mexican Military: A Reassessment*, ed. David Ronfeldt (La Jolla: Center for U.S.-Mexican Studies, University of California, San Diego, 1984), 42.

14. Michael J. Dziedzic, "The Essence of Decision in a Hegemonic Regime: The Case of Mexico's Acquisition of a Supersonic Fighter" (Ph.D. dissertation, University of Texas, Austin, 1986), 28.

15. Roderic Ai Camp, *Mexico's Mandarin's, Crafting a Power Elite for the 21st Century* (Berkeley, Calif.: University of California Press, 2002), 108. Interestingly, a study which compared American students in pre-commissioning military programs with other seniors in undergraduate institutions found remarkably similar attitudes in the conceptualization of military professionalism. See Don M. Snider, Robert F. Priest, and Felisa Lewis, "The Civilian-Military Gap and Professional Military Education at the Precommissioning Level," *Armed Forces and Society*, Vol. 27 (Winter 2001), 249–272.

16. Serge Guimond, "Encounter and Metamorphosis: The Impact of Military Socialization on Professional Values," *Applied Psychology: An International Review*, 44, no. 3 (1995), 253, 269.

17. Edwin Lieuwen, *Mexican Militarism, the Political Rise and Fall of the Revolutionary Army, 1910–1940* (Albuquerque, N.M.: University of New Mexico Press, 1968), 93.

18. Luis G. Franco, *Glosa del periodo de gobierno del C. Gral. e Ing. Pascual Ortiz Rubio, 1930–32, 3 años de historia del ejército de México* (Mexico, 1946), 67.

19. McAlister, *The Military in Latin American Socio-political Evolution*, 230.

20. Interview with Mexican army officer, Mexico City, August 1990.
21. William S. Ackroyd, "Descendants of the Revolution: Civil-Military Relations in Mexico" (Ph.D. dissertation, University of Arizona, 1988), 112.
22. T.M. McCloy and W.H. Clover, "Value Formation at the Air Force Academy," in *The Military: More Than Just a Job?* eds. C.C. Moskos and F.R. Woods (Washington, D.C.: Pergamon, 1988), 135.
23. Gary L. Wamsley, "Contrasting Institutions of Air Force Socialization: Happenstance or Bellweather?," *American Journal of Sociology*, 78 (1972), 401.
24. J.G. Backman, L. Sigelman, and G. Diamond, "Self-Selection, Socialization and Distinctive Military Values: Attitudes of High School Seniors," *Armed Forces and Society*, 13 (1987), 182.
25. Serge Guimond, "Encounter and Metamorphosis: The Impact of Military Socialization on Professional Values," 270.
26. Ackroyd, "Descendants of the Revolution," 113.
27. Personal interview, Mexico City, August 24, 1990.
28. Personal interview, Mexico City, August 20, 1990. Another source cited a more pernicious example of a good friend, a division general, who was a zone commander in the 1970s. He took over a ranch during an anti-drug campaign. The then secretary of national defense allegedly ordered him to transfer the cattle from that ranch to his own. When the zone commander refused to carry out that order, his career ended. Personal interview, August 22, 1990.
29. Sergio Aguayo, *1968, los archivos de la violencia* (Mexico: Grijalbo, 1998), 217.
30. Roderic Ai Camp, *Militarizing Mexico*, 4–5.
31. Gilberto López y Rivas, "Subordination of the Mexican Military to the United States," *La Jornada*, November 9, 1999.
32. Roderic Ai Camp, "Mexico's Armed Forces, Marching to a Democratic Tune," in *The Dilemma of Mexican Politics in Transition*, ed. Kevin Middlebrook (London: Institute for Latin American Studies, 2004), 354.
33. *El Nacional*, January 28, 1990, 14.
34. "Imágen del Ejército," National Survey, August 13–17, 2004, Bimsa, 3.5 margin of error.
35. Personal interview with Gabriel Zaid, Mexico City, August 17, 1990.
36. "Testimony of General Gerardo Clemente Vega García before the 59th Session of Congress," October 13, 2004, p. 27.
37. For a discussion of loyalty in Mexican political culture, see my *Intellectuals and the State in Twentieth-Century Mexico* (Austin, Tex.: University of Texas Press, 1985), 18ff.
38. Roderic Ai Camp, "Civilian Supremacy in Mexico, the Case of a Post-Revolutionary Military," in *Military Intervention and Withdrawal*, ed. Constantine P. Danopoulous (London: Routledge, 1991), 13.
39. Personal interview with Luis Herrera, Mexico City, June 24, 1989. Significantly, three years later, under a new secretary of national defense, his classmate at the Colegio Militar, he was reappointed as commander of the same military zone.
40. Personal interview, Mexico City, August 1990.
41. Donald E. Schulz, "Between a Rock and a Hard Place: the United States, Mexico and the Agony of National Security" (Carlisle, Penn.: U.S. Army War College, 1997), 3.
42. Samuel P. Huntington, *The Soldier and the State: The Theory and Politics of Civil-Military Relations* (Cambridge, Mass.: Harvard University Press, 1964), 79.
43. Personal interview, Mexico City, August 15, 1990.

44. R.F. Schloemer and G.E. Myers, "Making It at the Air Force Academy: Who Stays Who Succeeds?," in *The Changing World of the American Military*, ed. Franklin D. Margiotta (Boulder, Colo.: Westview Press, 1978), 327.

45. Sarkesian, "An Empirical Reassessment of Military Professionalism," 46.

46. Gary Spencer, "Methodological Issues in the Study of Bureaucratic Elites," *Social Problems* 21 (Summer 1973): 92.

47. However, in a comparative study of businessmen and officers, Bruce Russet found that U.S. officers were not "markedly more conservative on other kinds of issues or in their basic human nature, as some observers would have us believe." The possibility does exist that businessmen are just as conservative as officers, thus revealing little about officers' values compared to society as a whole. "Political Perspectives of U.S. Military and Business Elites," *Armed Forces and Society* 1 (Fall 1974): 87.

48. Roderic Ai Camp, "Generals and Politicians in Mexico: A Preliminary Comparison," in *The Modern Mexican Military: A Reassessment*, ed. David Ronfeldt (La Jolla, Calif.: Center for U.S.-Mexican Studies, University of California, San Diego, 1984), 153.

49. McAlister, *The Military in Latin American Socio-political Evolution*, 235.

50. Phyllis Greene Walker, "The Modern Mexican Military: Political Influence and Institutional Interests in the 1980s" (M.A. thesis, American University, 1987), 88.

51. Sarkesian, "An Empirical Reassessment of Military Professionalism," 43.

52. Ackroyd, "Descendants of the Revolution," 124.

53. Guillermo Boils, *Los militares y la política en México, 1915–1974* (Mexico: El Caballito, 1975).

54. David Ronfeldt, "The Modern Mexican Military," in *Armies and Politics in Latin America*, eds. Abraham Lowenthal and J. Samuel Fitch (New York: Holmes and Meier, 1986), 234. But as Sarkesian has argued, it is necessary for the professional officer "to become more politically astute, knowledgeable, and sensitive to political imperatives of domestic and international societies." *Beyond the Battlefield*, 185.

55. José Luis Piñeyro, "La seguridad nacional con Salinas de Gortari," *Foro Internacional*, 34, no. 4 (October–December 1994): 758.

56. Edward J. Williams, "Mexico's Central American Policy: National Security Considerations," in *Rift and Revolution: the Central American Imbroglio*, ed. Howard J. Wiarda (Washington, D.C.: American Enterprise Institute, 1984), 303–328.

57. *Diario Oficial*, December 26, 1986, 2; and "Ley orgánica de la Armada de México," Comisión de Marina, Cámara de Diputados, November 27, 2002. The 1986 version of the army's organic law remains in effect as of 2003, with only slight modifications, the last of which was in January 1998.

58. Leon Padgett, *The Mexican Political System*, 97; Boils, "Los militares en México," 179.

59. Jorge Alberto Lozoya, *El ejército mexicano*, 3rd ed. (Mexico: El Colegio de México, 1984), 126.

60. Stephen D. Wesbrook, "Historical Notes," in *The Political Education of Soldiers*, eds. Morris Janowitz and Stephen D. Wesbrook (Beverly Hills, Calif.: Sage Publications), 275–276.

61. Monica Serrano, "The Armed Branch of the State: Civil Military Relations in Mexico," *Journal of Latin American Studies*, 27, no. 2 (1995): 426.

62. Sarkesian, *Beyond the Battlefield*, 124.

63. Personal interview with a Division General, Mexico City, August 24, 1990.

64. "Imagen del Ejército."

Notes

65. Personal correspondence from Isabelle Rousseau, October 13, 1993, based on an interview with one of the intellectuals. President Salinas' military aide, who had read a pirated copy in 1991, urged me to have it translated and published in Spanish in Mexico.
66. Personal interview with Javier Oliva, Mexico City, August 19, 1990.
67. Personal interviews, Mexico City, 1989 and 1990.
68. Enrique Aldúncin Abitia, *Los valores de los mexicanos, México: Entre la tradición y la modernidad* (Mexico: Fondo Cultura Banamex, 1986), 176.
69. Alberto Hernández Medina, et. al., *Como somos los mexicanos* (Mexico: Centro de Estudios Educativos, 1987), 110.
70. See www.gallup.com.ar, and Raúl Benítez Manaut, "Mexico: Doctrina, historia y relaciones cívico-militares a inicios del siglo xxi," in *Las relaciones cívico-militares en el mundo iberoamericano*, ed. José A. Olmeda (Madrid: Instituto Universitario General Gutiérrez Mellado, 2003).
71. "Imagen del Ejército."
72. John D. Blair, "Emerging Youth Attitudes and the Military," in *The Changing World of the American Military*, ed. Franklin D. Margiotta (Boulder, Colo.: Westview Press, 1973), 159.
73. Christopher Dickey, "Modernization Could Lead Mexican Military into Politics," *Washington Post*, September 23, 1982, 29A.
74. *Encuesta sobre el ejército y la fuerza aérea mexicanos* (Mexico: Secretaria de Defensa Nacional, 1993), based on a national sample of 1511 respondents, February 1993.
75. *Reforma*, December 2, 2002.
76. McAlister, *The Military in Latin American Socio-political Evolution*, 222.
77. Ibid., 221.
78. "Imagen del Ejército."
79. John J. Johnson, *The Military and Society in Latin America* (Stanford, Calif.: Stanford University Press, 1964), 171.
80. McAlister, *The Military in Latin American Socio-political Evolution*, 222.
81. Blair, "Emerging Youth Attitudes and the Military," 167.
82. I found only two exceptions from 1922 through 1970. However, both examples are clouded by the fact that one was the son and the other a grandson of prominent military officers.
83. The most notable example is that of Miguel Alemán. As a teenager, he wanted to pursue the same career as his father, a revolutionary general. His father was dead set against his son's interest and told him that "he didn't want him to become a military officer because it had no future." Instead, his father encouraged him to attend college and pursue a legal career. Personal interview, Mexico City, August 17, 1990.
84. Personal interview with Miguel Basáñez, Mexico City, August 15, 1990.
85. Personal interview, Mexico City, August 1990. A prominent intellectual, José Rogelio Alvarez, confirmed this view despite the fact that many of his secondary school classmates went into the military. "In reality, I have had few friends who were career military officers. I think that the social distinctions between the military and the civilian political and intellectual elite does make a difference in terms of the level of interchange between the two groups. In other words, I know a number of officers from some point in my life, but I don't have close social relations with them." Personal interview, Mexico City, August 17, 1990.
86. Roderic Ai Camp, "The Military," in *Prospects for Mexico*, ed. George Grayson (Washington, D.C.: Foreign Service Institute, 1988), 87.

87. One prominent reporter, Raimundo Riva Palacio, who specialized in national security issues and the military, regretfully blamed the press for not actively pursuing interesting and controversial stories involving the military. He cited the example of the resignation of the navy secretary under Salinas, noting that only *Proceso* actually investigated and pursued the story. Personal interview, February 13, 1991.

88. Sallie Hughes, "The Pen and the Sword: Mexican Mass Media Coverage of the Armed Forces, 1986-1996" (Unpublished paper, Tulane University, New Orleans, 1999), 24.

89. José Luis Piñeyro, "Las fuerzas armadas en la transición política de México," *Revista Mexicana de Sociología* 59, no. 1 (January–March 1997), 178.

90. Javier Ibarrola, "El ejército y la prensa: Dos poderes en busca de un vínculo," Center for Hemispheric Defense Studies, Washington, D.C., May 22-25, 2001, 8.

91. Gerardo Albarrán de Alba, "En el 94, la Sedena organizó su propia guerra de papel'," *Proceso*, March 19, 2000, www.proceso.com.mx.

92. Kevin O'Connell and Kevin McCarthy, *Stability and the Military in Mexico: An Assessment of the Military in a Changing Mexico* (Santa Monica, Calif.: RAND, May 1997), 35.

93. Walker, "Modern Mexican Military," 89-90.

94. Partido Revolucionario Institucional, *Encuesta Nacional*, April 1983.

95. The straightforward results of this and the 1983 poll, without cross-tabulations, have been published in Miguel Basáñez's *El pulso de los sexenios, 20 años de crisis en México* (Mexico: Siglo XXI, 1990), 238-240.

96. Roderic Ai Camp, *Crossing Swords, Politics and Religion in Mexico* (New York: Oxford University Press, 1997), 35-36.

97. However, the Catholic Church's own internal code bans priests from holding political office.

98. Roderic Ai Camp, "The Cross in the Polling Booth: Religion, Politics, and the Laity in Mexico," *Latin American Research Review*, Vol. 29, No. 3 (Winter 1994), 69-100.

99. "Imagen del Ejército."

100. *Diario Oficial*, December 26, 1986, 14.

101. Vicente Ernesto Pérez Mendoza, "The Role of the Armed Forces in the Mexican Economy in the 1980s" (M.A. thesis, Naval Postgraduate School, Monterey, California, June 1981), 21.

102. Roderic Ai Camp, "Militarizing Mexico, Where is the Officer Corps Going?," 13.

103. Franklin D. Margiotta, "Civilian Control and the Mexican Military: Changing Patterns of Political Influence," in *Civilian Control of the Military: Theories and Cases from Developing Countries*, ed. Claude E. Welch, Jr. (Albany, N.Y.: State University of New York Press, 1976), 221.

104. Rodney V. Jones and Steven A. Hildreth, *Emerging Powers: Defense and Security in the Third World* (New York: Praeger, 1986), 393.

105. Frederick Nunn, *Yesterdays Soldiers: European Military Professionalism in South America, 1890-1940* (Lincoln, Neb.: University of Nebraska Press, 1983).

106. Nunn, "On the Role of the Military in Twentieth-Century Latin America: The Mexican Case," 33.

107. Donald F. Harrison, "United States-Mexican Military Collaboration during World War II" (Ph.D. dissertation, Georgetown University, 1976), introduction.

108. Walker suggests that their relations were closest from this period until the 1980s, "The Modern Mexican Military," 23.

109. Williams, "The Mexican Military and Foreign Policy," 40.

110. Jones and Hildreth, *Emerging Powers*, 389.

111. Based on numerous conversations with former U.S. assistant military attaches, 1989–2003.
112. John A. Cope, "In Search of Convergence: U.S.-Mexican Military Relations into the Twenty-first Century," in *Strategy and Security in U.S.-Mexican Relations Beyond the Cold War* (La Jolla, Calif.: Center for U.S.-Mexican Studies, University of California, San Diego, 1996), 191.
113. José Luis Piñeyro, "The Mexican Army and the State: Historical and Political Perspectives," *Revue Internationale de Sociologie* 14 (April–August 1978): 134.
114. Cope, "In Search of Convergence: U.S.-Mexican Military Relations into the Twenty-first Century," 193.
115. Ibid., 194.
116. Ibid., 193.
117. Jennifer M. Taw, "The Effectiveness of Training International Military Students in Internal Defense and Development" (Santa Monica: RAND, 1993), 7, 15. An earlier study came to a similar conclusion. Ernest W. Lefever, "The Military Assistance Training Program," *Annals of the American Academy of Political and Social Science*, no. 424 (March 1976), 90.
118. John C. Dreier, *The Organization of American States and the Hemisphere Crisis* (Baltimore, Md.: Johns Hopkins University Press, 1962), 47. Jaime Torres Bodet, *La Victoria sin alas* (Mexico: Fondo de Cultura Económica, 1970), 293ff.
119. Edwin Lieuwen, "Depolitization of the Mexican Revolutionary Army, 1915–1940," in *The Modern Mexican Military: A Reassessment*, ed. David Ronfeldt (La Jolla, Calif.: Center for United States-Mexican Studies, University of California, San Diego, 1984), 61.
120. Personal correspondence from Al Leftwich, member of the U.S. delegation to the Inter-American Defense Board, Washington, D.C. 1993–1995, and the Joint Mexico-U.S. Defense Commission, Washington, D.C., March 25, 1997.
121. Ibid.
122. *El Nacional*, June 9, 1990, e.
123. Ibid.
124. Carlos Marín, "Inexplicablemente rico, Schleske omitió declarar sus residencias en Houston," *Proceso*, July 23, 1990, 8.
125. See José Ortiz Pinchetti, "Actividades de narcos de las que Schleske debio estar enterado," *Proceso*, August 3, 1990, 8–13.
126. *Washington Post*, August 15, 1989. However, the official records of zone command postings from the secretariat of national defense do not indicate an increased pace in new assignments.
127. Personal interview with President José López Portillo, Mexico City, February 19, 1991.

Chapter Seven   Educating the Officer Corps

1. Frederick M. Nunn, "On the Role of the Military in Twentieth-Century Latin America: The Mexican Case," in *The Modern Mexican Military: A Reassessment*, ed. David Ronfeldt (La Jolla, Calif.: Center for U.S.-Mexican Studies, University of California, San Diego, 1984), 34.
2. Edwin Lieuwen, *Mexican Militarism, the Political Rise and Fall of the Revolutionary Army, 1910–1940* (Albuquerque: University of New Mexico Press, 1968), 4.

3. Ibid.; William S. Ackroyd, "Descendants of the Revolution: Civil-Military-Relations in Mexico (Ph.D. dissertation University of Arizona, 1988), 71.

4. The original school was established October 11, 1823.

5. Gloria Fuentes, *El ejército mexicano* (Mexico: Grijalbo, 1983), 147.

6. *Memoria gráfica del cincuentenario de la reapertura del Heroico Colegio Militar* (Mexico: SHCP, 1970), 442; Valentín López González, *Los compañeros de Zapata* (Morelos, 1980), 63–64; and José López Escalera, *Diccionario biográfico y de historia de México* (Mexico: Editorial del Magistrado, 1964), 183.

7. Jacques van Doorn, *The Soldier and Social Change* (Beverly Hills, Calif.: Sage Publications, 1975), 75.

8. Interestingly, however, the navy has never required a preparatory certificate to enter this five year engineering program. That continues to be the case today even though an examination of naval officers reveals that nearly all did complete a preparatory program before entering the Heroica Escuela Naval.

9. www.lavevista.com.mx; www.semar.com.mx; www.csis.org.com, 2001.

10. www.sedena.com.mx. 1999.

11. *Hispano Americano*, September 24, 1984, 13.

12. *Tercer informe del gobierno, anexo*, September 1, 1997 (Mexico: Presidencia de la República, 1997).

13. Roderic Ai Camp, "Militarizing Mexico, Where Is the Officer Corps Going?," *Policy Paper on the Americas* (Washington, D.C.: CSIS, 1999). It is important to note that both the naval and army academies have numerous applications for the spaces available. For example, from 2001 to 2003, the Heroico Colegio Militar accepted only 16 percent of the applicants and the Military Aviation School only 11 percent. Between 2000 and 2003, the Heroica Escuela Naval Militar accepted 18 percent of its applicants. See www.sedena.gob.mx, transparency request, folio 12012004, January 27, 2004, and www.semar.gob.mx, unidad de enlace, 050UE/04, February 10, 2004. By 2001, nearly 30,000 individuals applied for admission to all the army and air force military schools. See www.sedena.gob.mx, transparency request 0000700022804, April 22, 2004.

14. *Diario Oficial*, December 29, 1975.

15. Wager, "The Mexican Military;" Fuentes, *El ejército mexicano*, 232. The functions were reallocated under the Director General of Military Education and the Rector of the Army/Air Force Defense University in 1996. "La educación militar," www.sedena.gob.mx. September 6, 1999.

16. Ibid., 116. For a complete list of these schools, see www.sedena.com.mx.

17. Roderic Ai Camp, "Militarizing Mexico, Where Is the Officer Corps Going?," *Policy Paper on the Americas* (Washington, D.C.: CSIS, 1999), 2.

18. Francisco Solís Peón, "El síndrome de Oxford," *El Nacional*, February 26, 2000, F.

19. William S. Ackroyd, "The Military in Mexican Politics: The Impact of Professionalism, Civilian Behavior, and the Revolution," *Pacific Coast Council of Latin American Studies Proceedings*, 12 (1985–1986), 101.

20. Roderic Ai Camp, "Generals and Politicians in Mexico: A Preliminary Comparison," in *The Modern Mexican Military: A Reassessment*, ed. David Ronfeldt (La Jolla, Calif.: Center for U.S.-Mexican Studies, University of California, San Diego, 1984), 120. Originally, air force officers who were on their way to higher command positions took a special air staff course at the Escuela Superior de Guerra, established in 1947. It began as a year-and-half-long program in February, 1948, but later became a two year program. It was suspended in 1953 after the fourth class graduated and

reestablished in 1965. Escuela Superior de Guerra, *Escuela Superior de Guerra* (Mexico: SDN, 1992), pp. 50–52.

21. J.G. Backman, L. Sigelman, and G. Diamond, "Self-Selection, Socialization and Distinctive Military Values: Attitudes of High School Seniors," *Armed Forces and Society* 13 (1987), 182.

22. T.M McCloy and W. H. Clover, "Value Formation at the Air Force Academy," in *The Military: More than Just a Job?* eds. C.C. Moskos and F.R. Wood (Washington, D.C.: Pergamon, 1988), 135.

23. Serge Guimond, "Encounter and Metamorphosis: The Impact of Military Socialization on Professional Values," *Applied Psychology: An International Review* 44, no. 3 (1995), 269.

24. Ted Goertzel and Acco Hengst, "The Military Socialization of University Students," *Social Problems* 19 (1971), 262.

25. See Elizabeth G. French and Raymond R. Ernest, "The Relationship Between Authoritarianism and Acceptance of Military Ideology," *Journal of Personality*, 24 (December 1955), 190.

26. Ackroyd, "Descendants of the Revolution," 87.

27. Air force cadets take basic training for 3–6 months at the Heroico Colegio Militar then complete the rest of their education at the air academy.

28. *Diario de Yucatán*, August 9, 2002; www.sedena.gob.mx, 2001.

29. Wager, "The Mexican Military," 15.

30. Javier Romero, *Aspectos psicobiométricos y sociales de un muestra de la juventud mexicana* (Mexico: Dirección de Investigaciones Antropológicas, 1956), 52. Many of the cadets entered the Heroico Colegio Militar as young as fifteen. This prevented them from completing an education beyond secondary before enrolling.

31. Presidencia de la República, Unidad de la Crónica Presidencial, archives.

32. On March 1, 1948, the Secretariat of National Defense initiated the Escuela Militar de Clases General Mariano Matamoros at Military Camp No. 1. By the following November first sergeants enrolled in infantry and cavalry courses could graduate as second lieutenants upon satisfactory completion of the program. The school was later moved to the military camp in Puebla, Puebla. The Heroico Colegio Militar continues to offer an intensive officer course in the combat specialties for first sergeants. If they complete the year long course successfully, they graduate as second lieutenants. Applicants must earn a certain score to occupy a place in the quota established each year. www.sedena.gob.mx, transparency request, May 19, 2004.

33. Fuentes, *El ejército mexicano*, 155.

34. McAlister, *The Military in Latin American Socio-Political Evolution*, 218.

35. Frank D. McCann, "Brazilian Army Officers Biography Project," Unpublished paper, Latin American Studies Association, Miami, December 1989, 6.

36. Thomas E. Weil, "The Armed Forces," in *Area Handbook for Mexico* (Washington, D.C.: GPO, 1975), 364.

37. Some of the military professional schools are even more selective. For example in 2004, 4 percent of pilot school and medical school applicants were actually accepted. www.sedena.gob.mx, transparency request 0000700075904, November 24, 2004.

38. This represents a significant increase since 1999, when it was offered at 20 locations. As of that year, half of all applications still took the exam at the Heroico Colegio Militar in the Federal District. See *Revista de Ejército*, August 1999, 25.

39. www.sedena.com.mx, 2003.

40. The Secretary of National Defense indicated that in 2004, of the 35 individuals who were 16 years old, and the 68 who were 17 years old, all were cadets. www.sedena.gob.mx, transparency request 0000700022704, May 1, 2004.
41. Ibid.
42. Camp, *Mexico's Leaders*, 94ff; and Roderic Ai Camp, *The Making of a Government: Political Leaders in Modern Mexico* (Tucson: University of Arizona Press, 1984), 48ff.
43. Ackroyd, "The Military in Mexican Politics," 12.
44. William S. Ackroyd, "The Military in Mexican Politics: The Impact of Professionalism, Civilian Behavior, and the Revolution," *Pacific Coast Council of Latin American Studies Proceedings*, 12 (1985–1986), 98.
45. Women were allowed in the armed forces for the first time in 1938, but only as students in the Military Nursing School. In 1958, they were permitted to rise no farther than the rank of First Captain. In 1976, they could be promoted as high as Lt. Colonel. In 1973, the Escuela Médico Militar open its doors to women. Three women completed the army parachute course in 1975, and since 1977, women have been allowed to complete a basic training course at the Heroico Colegio Militar. They complete the same basic course as men, and are allowed to attend service schools in administration, medical care, communications and physical education. In spite of these restrictions, 8 percent of the Mexican army is now staffed by women, primarily in administration, law and medicine. Of the 5,770 females, 440 are majors or higher in rank, and 2,189 are other officers. President Fox recognized publicly that the army needed women as well as men. Women can now be promoted to brigade general in several occupational specialties, and the first woman to reach the rank of brigadier general, a graduate of the nursing and dentistry schools, did so in 1994. General María Eugenia Gómez López, Mexico's first female general, completed the Applied Arms and Service Course from the Escuela Superior de Guerra. *Revista de Ejército y Fuerza Aérea*, October 1997, 52. *Diario de Yucatán*, September 3, 2003; www.sedena.gob.mx, transparency requests 0000700025903 and 0000700069704 October 22, 2004. In the navy, a female frigate captain (Second Captain) directed the department of public relations from 1991–1994.
46. Daniel Mora, "Profile of the Mexican Company Grade Officer" (Rocky Mountain States Latin American Conference, Tucson, February 1984), 5.
47. Frank D. McCann, "Brazilian Army Officers Biography Project" (Unpublished paper, Latin American Studies Association, Miami, December 1989), 15.
48. Mora, "Profile of the Mexican Company Grade Officer," 3.
49. Thomas E. Weil, "The Armed Forces," in *Area Handbook for Mexico* (Washington, D.C.: GPO, 1975), 363.
50. Luis G. Franco, *Glosa del periodo de gobierno del C. Gral. e Ing. Pascual Ortiz Rubio, 1930–32, 3 años de historia del ejército de México* (Mexico, 1946), 44; Virginia Prewitt, "The Mexican Army," *Foreign Affairs* 19 (April 1941): 613.
51. Ibid.
52. Roderic Ai Camp, "Mexico's Armed Forces, Marching to a Democratic Tune?," *The Dilemma of Mexican Politics in Transition*, ed. Kevin Middlebrook (London: Institute for Latin American Studies, 2004), 356.
53. Stephen J. Wager, "The Mexican Military" (unpublished paper, 1983), 9, much of which is incorporated into Robert Wesson's section on Mexico in his *The Latin American Military* (Westport: Greenwood Press, 1986), 9.
54. *Revista de Ejército y Fuerza Aérea*, April–June 1952, 38–57.
55. Weil, "The Armed Forces," 365.
56. Ackroyd, "Descendants of the Revolution," 118.

57. Roderic Ai Camp, *The Making of a Government, Political Leaders in Modern Mexico* (Tucson, Ariz.: University of Arizona Press, 1984), 70–71.
58. *Diario Oficial*, November 9, 1998.
59. Sanford M. Dornbusch, "The Military Academy as an Assimilating Institution," *Social Forces* 33 (May 1955), 316, 318. His study focuses on the U.S. Coast Guard Academy, which at the time was more comparable in size to the Heroico Colegio Militar.
60. Personal letter from a 1990 graduate, December 14, 2001.
61. Gary L. Wamsley, "Contrasting Institutions of Air Force Socialization: Happenstance or Bellweather?," *American Journal of Sociology*, 78 (1972), 401, 416.
62. J. P. Lovell, "The Professional Socialization of the West Point Cadet," in *The New Military: Changing Patterns of Organization*, ed. Morris Janowitz (New York: Russell Sage, 1964), 120.
63. Roderic Ai Camp, *The Making of a Government*, 125ff.
64. McAlister, *The Military in Latin American Socio-Political Evolution*, 231.
65. Personal interview, Mexico City, August 20, 1990.
66. Roderic Ai Camp, *Mexico's Mandarins, Crafting a Power Elite for the 21st Century* (Berkeley, Calif.: University of California Press, 2002), 29.
67. Ackroyd, "Descendants of the Revolution," 10.
68. Secret Report, Department of the Army, United States Army Intelligence and Security Command, *Army Country Profile–Mexico*, April 1993, National Security Archives, George Washington University, 2004.
69. Vicente Ernesto Pérez Mendoza, "The Role of the Armed Forces in the Mexican Economy in the 1980s" (M.A. thesis, Naval Postgraduate School, Monterey, California, June 1981), 21.
70. Kenneth Walker, "Political Socialization in Universities," in *Elites in Latin America*, eds. Seymour Martin Lipset and Aldo Solari (New York: Oxford University Press, 1967); Edgar Litt, "Civic Education, Community Norms, and Political Indoctrination," *American Sociological Review* 28 (1963): 69–75.
71. Roderic Ai Camp, *Mexico's Leaders, Their Education and Recruitment* (Tucson, Ariz.: University of Arizona Press, 1982).
72. Gary Spencer, "Methodological Issues in the Study of Bureaucratic Elites," *Social Problems* 21 (Summer 1973): 91. As one U.S. officer noted, until a decade ago, all graduates of U.S. military academies pursued combat arms specialties, whereas Reserve Officer Training Corps (ROTC) graduates were in combat support areas. Since most billets for generals are in combat arms, academy graduates acquired an advantage.
73. Camp, "Generals and Politicians," 126–127.
74. Roderic Ai Camp, *Mexico's Mandarins*, 47.
75. Ministro de Guerra y Marina, *Memoria* (Mexico: Imprenta Central, 1900), appendix.
76. Camp, "Generals and Politicians," 155.
77. Daniel Mora, "Profile of the Mexican Company Grade Officer," 6. This bond will be superceded by officers who continue on to the Escuela Superior de Guerra. Little fraternity from the Heroico Colegio Militar remains after an officer graduates from the Escuela Superior de Guerra.
78. Roderic Ai Camp, "The Educating and Training of the Mexican Officer Corps," in *Forging the Sword, Selecting, Educating, and Training Cadets and Junior Officers in the Modern World*, ed. Elliott V. Converse, Vol. 5, Military History Symposium Series of the United States Air Force Academy (Chicago: Imprint Publications, 1998), 336–346.

79. Boils, *Los militares y la política en México*, 108, 114.
80. Camp, *Mexico's Leaders*, 68.
81. C. Wright Mills, *The Power Elite* (New York: Oxford University Press, 1959), 295.
82. Michael J. Dziedzic, "The Essence of Decision in a Hegemonic Regime: The Case of Mexico's Acquisition of a Supersonic Fighter" (Ph.D. dissertation, University of Texas, Austin, 1986), 382. Ironically, this new building is not normally used for the Escuela Superior de Guerra, only for tests and overflow classes. It remains under the control of the Secretariat of National Defense.
83. www.sedena.gob.mx, 2003.
84. Jesús Lozoya Solís, *La Escuela Médico Militar de México* (Mexico, 1977), 104.
85. Boils, *Los militares y la política en México*, 110–111.
86. *Escuela Superior de Guerra, 1932–1982*, 52.
87. *Diario Oficial*, April 13, 1993.
88. Javier Ibarrola, "Fuerzas Armadas," *El Financiero*, October 11, 1995, 34.
89. The present campus was inaugurated on August 22, 1952 by President Miguel Alemán. The official name is Heroica Escuela Naval Militar. It is located in Antón Lizardo, Veracruz, about 32 kilometers from the port of Veracruz.
90. www.semar.gob.mx.herescna. June 26, 2003.
91. In April 2003, the secretary of navy, Marco Antonio Peyrot González, welcomed a new class of 136 cadets, suggesting that the size of the school has increased significantly in spite of the fact that graduation numbers are smaller due to attrition rates during the previous six years. *El País*, April 22, 2003.
92. Enrique Cárdenas Peña, *Educación Naval en México* Vol. 2 (Mexico: Secretaria de la Marina, 1967).
93. www.nauticamzt.edu.mx, June 25, 2003; Enrique Cárdenas Peña, *Educación Naval en México*, 99.
94. www.naval19095.com.

Chapter Eight   Higher and Global Officer Education

1. J. Samuel Fitch, *The Armed Forces and Democracy in Latin America* (Baltimore, Md.: Johns Hopkins University Press, 1998), 35.
2. See Alfred Stepan, "The New Professionalism of Internal Warfare and Military Role Expansion," in *Armies and Politics in Latin America,* eds. Abraham Lowenthal and J. Samuel Fitch (New York: Holmes and Meier, 1986), 134–150, and Luigi Einaudi, *The Peruvian Military: A Summary Political Analysis* (Santa Monica, Calif.: RAND, 1969).
3. See "la educación militar," www.sedena.gob.mx, September 6, 1999.
4. Lyle N. McAlister, *The Military in Latin American-Socio-political Evolution: Four Case Studies* (Washington, D.C.: Center for Research in Social Systems, 1970), 206.
5. Félix Galván López, *Escuela Superior de Guerra, 1932–1982* (Mexico: Secretaria de Defensa National, 1982), 38.
6. *Diccionario biográfico de México* (Monterrey: Editorial Revesa, 1968), 15; *Revista de Ejército y Fuerza Aérea*, September 1976, 133.
7. Luis G. Franco, *Glosa del periodo de gobierno del C. Gral. e Ing. Pascual Ortiz Rubio, 1930–32, 3 años de historia del ejército de México* (Mexico, 1946), 164.
8. Galván López, *Escuela Superior de Guerra*, 53.

9. Plutarco Elías Calles, "La Escuela Superior de Guerra y principios de doctrina para la organización del ejército de México," *Del México Actual*, no. 15 (Mexico: Secretaria de Relaciones Exteriores, 1934), 64.

10. Frank D. McCann, "Brazilian Army Officers Biography Project," Unpublished paper, Latin American Studies Association, Miami, December 1989, 9.

11. Christopher Brogan, "Military Higher Education and the Emergence of 'New Professionalism': Some Consequences for Civil-Military Relations in Latin America," *Army Quarterly and Defense Journal*, no. 112 (January 1982): 28.

12. Stephen Wager, "Civic Action and the Mexican Military" (Unpublished paper, Department of History, United States Military Academy at West Point, 1982) 18.

13. www.sedena.gob.mx, transparency request, folio 0000700046304, December 22, 2003.

14. Dolores Cordero, "El ejército mexicano," *Revista de Revistas*, September 12, 1973, 7; William S. Ackroyd, "Descendants of the Revolution: Civil-Military Relations in Mexico" (Ph.D. dissertation, University of Arizona, 1988), 119.

15. www.sedena.gob.mx, transparency request, folio 0000700046304, December 22, 2003.

16. Ibid., 171.

17. Luis G. Franco, *Glosa del periodo de gobierno del C. Gral. e Ing. Pascual Ortiz Rubio, 1930-32*, 65.

18. Thomas E. Weil, "The Armed Forces," in *Area Handbook for Mexico* (Washington, D.C.: GPO, 1975), 365.

19. As of 1987, when the Escuela Superior de Guerra's regulations were revised for the first time since 1960, the school offered four programs: "Higher Arms and Services" (six months), for majors and lieutenant colonels who are not graduates of the regular Escuela Superior de Guerra course (which has included female officers); "Staff and Command" (three years), the regular course; "Air Force Staff and Command" (two years); and "Higher War" (six months), to develop combined operations skills of the Escuela Superior de Guerra graduates. See Article 12, Secretaria de Defensa Nacional, *Reglamento de la Escuela Superior de Guerra* (Mexico: December 30, 1987).

20. Christopher Brogan, "Military Higher Education and the Emergence of 'New Professionalism': Some Consequences for Civil-Military Relations in Latin America," *Army Quarterly and Defense Journal*, no. 112 (January 1982): 23.

21. Cordero, "El ejército mexicano," 7.

22. José Luis Piñeyro, "The Mexican Army and the State: Historical and Political Perspective," *Revue Internationale de Sociologie* 14 (April–August 1978): 140.

23. Michael J. Dziedzic, "Civil-military Relations in Mexico: The Politics of Co-optation" (Unpublished paper, University of Texas, Austin, 1983), 25.

24. Ackroyd, "Descendants of the Revolution," 119.

25. Personal interviews, Mexico City, 1991.

26. Roderic Ai Camp, "Mexico's Armed Forces, Marching to a Democratic Tune?," in *The Dilemma of Mexican Politics in Transition*, ed. Kevin Middlebrook (London: Institute of Latin American Studies, University of London, 2004), 356.

27. Personal correspondence to the author, February 1999.

28. Ackroyd, "Descendants of the Revolution," 123.

29. *Revista de Ejército y Fuerza Aérea*, August, 1990, 68–69.

30. www.sedena.gob.mx, 2001; *Tercer informe del Presidente Zedillo* (Mexico: Presidencia de la República, 1997), 71. In the 1990s, 1,000 officers applied each year for admission. Of these, approximately 600 were allowed to take the test. Of those tested, 110

entered the first year class. Confidential Cable, U.S. Embassy, 1995, Mexico10043, U.S. Department of State, May 11, 1995, National Security Archives, George Washington University, 2004, 17.

31. *Escuela Superior de Guerra,* 1932–1982 (Mexico, 1982)
32. Press release, Secretariat of the Navy, July 14, 2001, www.semar.gob.mx.
33. Ibid.
34. Secretaria de Marina, *Centro de Estudios Superiores Navales, 1970–2000* (Mexico: Secretaria de Marina, 2000), 45.
35. Personal correspondence to the author, February 1999.
36. Personal interview, Mexico City, 1990.
37. Richard Kilroy Jr., "The Mexican Army Digs In" (Unpublished paper), 1991.
38. Personal letter to the author, February, 1999.
39. *Revista de Ejército y Fuerza Aérea,* February 1956, 29–30; Daniel Mora, "Profile of the Mexican Company Grade Officer" (Paper presented at the Rocky Mountain States Latin American Conference, Tucson, February 1984), 5.
40. Personal interviews, Mexico City, 1991.
41. For example, cadets at the Air Force Academy are from higher-income families, have conservative views, and are the children of career military officers. See R.F. Schloemer and G.E. Myers, "Making It at the Air Force Academy: Who Stays, Who Succeeds?," in *The Changing World of the American Military,* ed. Franklin D. Margiotta (Boulder, Colo.: Westview Press, 1978), 321–344. On the other hand, U.S. children from non-military families are in general much more familiar with military life than their Mexican peers.
42. Ackroyd, "Civil-Military Relations in Mexico," 15.
43. Franco, *Glosa del periodo de gobierno del C. Gral. e Ing. Pascual Ortiz Rubio,* 66.
44. Roderic Ai Camp, "Generals and Politicians in Mexico: A Preliminary Comparison," in *The Modern Mexican Military: A Reassessment,* ed. David Ronfeldt (La Jolla, Calif.: Center for U.S.-Mexican Studies, University of California, San Diego, 1984), 124.
45. Personal letter to the author, February 1999.
46. Michael J. Dziedzic, "Mexico's Converging Challenges; Problems, Prospects, and Implications" (Unpublished manuscript, U.S. Air Force Academy, April 21, 1989), 34. This has been attested to by officers interviewed.
47. Ibid., cited from an exchange officer school report, October 26, 1982.
48. Ibid., 36
49. Kilroy, "The Mexican Military Digs In," 4.
50. Ibid., 37.
51. Personal interview, Mexico City, 1990.
52. Personal correspondence, February 1999.
53. Dziedzic, "Civil-military Relations in Mexico," citing an exchange officer's school report, June 15, 1982.
54. See section 7, which states that resorting to copying or other fraudulent means will result in a grade of zero and suspension from the examination. Secretaria de Defensa Nacional, *Reglamento de la Escuela Superior de Guerra,* 28.
55. Personal interview, Mexico City, 1990.
56. Ibid., 36; Mora, "Profile of the Mexican Company Grade Officer," 10.
57. Personal letter to the author, 1990.
58. The degree to which a higher war college can bring a decline in respect for civil authority, a thesis originally argued by Alfred Stepan, has been severely critiqued, in

the Brazilian case, by John Markoff and Silvio Baretta, who found no such relationship. See their "Professional Ideology and Military Activism in Brazil; Critique of a Thesis of Alfred Stepan," *Comparative Politics* 17 (January 1985):183.

59. See Article 145, Secretariat of National Defense, *Reglamento de la Escuela Superior de Guerra*, 31.

60. Kilroy, "The Mexican Military Digs In," 2, 4. Several sources told Kilroy that as a result of the 1988 elections, many younger officers expressed sympathy for Cuauhtémoc Cárdenas, a tendency they apparently hoped to limit.

61. Mora, "Profile of the Mexican Company Grade Officer," 15.

62. Roderic Ai Camp, *Mexico's Mandarins, Crafting a Power Elite for the 21st Century* (Berkeley, Calif.: University of California Press, 2002), 64.

63. Personal correspondence to the author, n.d., 1992.

64. I am indebted to Javier Oliva, a national security adviser to the PRI and professor at UNAM, for suggesting this point. Personal interview, Mexico City, August 19, 1990.

65. Camp, "Generals and Politicians in Mexico."

66. Personal interview, Mexico City, 1990.

67. Wager, "Modernization of the Mexican Military," 12; Alden M. Cunningham, "Mexico's National Security in the 1980s–1990s," in *The Modern Mexican Military: A Reassessment*, ed. David Ronfeldt (La Jolla, Calif.: Center for U.S.-Mexican Studies, University of California, San Diego, 1984), 167.

68. www.sedena.gob.mx, transparency request, folio 0000700026103, October 6, 2003.

69. Personal interview with General Gerardo C. Vega García, Mexico City, August 19, 1990.

70. Luis Alegre, "Traza cambio política de seguridad," *Reforma*, August 18, 2002, www.reforma.com; *La Jornada*, August 17, 2000; *Revista de Ejército y Fuerza Aérea*, August 2002, 4; www.sedena.gob.mx, 2001.

71. Wilfred Bacchus, *Mission in Mufti* (Westport, Conn.: Greenwood Press, 1990), 36ff.

72. Edward J. Williams, "Mexico's Modern Military, Implications for the Region," *Caribbean Review* 10 (Fall 1981): 12.

73. Brogan, "Military Higher Education and the Emergence of 'New Professionalism'," 26. For an interesting description of curricular changes in Brazil's higher war college, see Stanley E. Hilton, "The Brazilian Military: Changing Strategic Perceptions and the Question of Mission," *Armed Forces and Society* 13 (Spring 1987): 330.

74. Personal interview, August 19, 1990.

75. Ibid.

76. Sergio Aguayo Quezada, "The Uses, Misuses, and Challenges of Mexican National Security: 1946–1990," in *Mexico, In Search of Security*, eds. Bruce M. Bagley and Sergio Aguayo Quezada (New Brunswick, N.J.: Transaction Publishers, 1993), 117.

77. Cunningham, "Mexico's National Security in the 1980s–1990s," 171.

78. Personal interview, Mexico City, 1990.

79. Personal interview with General Gerardo Clemente Vega García, Secretary of National Defense, Mexico City, February 26, 2004.

80. Personal interview, September 15, 1998. *Revista de Ejército y Fuerza Aérea*, August 1990, 58. The actual ranks they achieved as of 2003 were: 6 division, 13 brigade, and 5 brigadier generals, and one admiral and rear admiral. www.sedena.gob.mx., transparency request, folio 0000700026103, October 6, 2003.

81. Personal interview with Javier Oliva, an instructor in the program, August 19, 1990.
82. Personal interview with Division General Luis Garfías.
83. Personal interview, Mexico City, August 1990.
84. Personal interview, 1998.
85. Interview with the instructor in charge of the course, Mexico City, August 1990.
86. Personal interview with Luis Rubio, Mexico City, August 24, 1990.
87. Personal interview, 1998.
88. Personal interview with General Gerardo Clemente Vega García, Secretary of National Defense, Mexico City, February 26, 2004.
89. David Ronfeldt, "The Modern Mexican Military," in *Armies and Politics in Latin America*, eds. Abraham Lowenthal and J. Samuel Fitch (New York: Holmes and Meier, 1986), 232.
90. Sergio Aguayo, "La seguridad nacional," *Diario de Yucatán*, August 30, 2001.
91. José Piñeyro, "Chiapas: la seguridad nacional y la corta guerra" (Unpublished paper, Latin American Studies Association, Washington, D.C., September 1995), 14.
92. Edward J. Williams, "The Mexican Military and Foreign Policy: The Evolution of Influence," in *The Modern Mexican Military: A Reassessment*, ed. David Ronfeldt (La Jolla, Calif.: Center for U.S.-Mexican Studies, University of California, San Diego, 1984), 196.
93. Jorge Alberto Lozoya, *El ejército mexicano (1911-1965)* (Mexico: El Colegio de México, 1970), 126.
94. What has not occurred, with several rare recent exceptions, is the presence of United States instructors in Mexico. As of 2003, 31 members of the armed forces are being trained by foreign officers in Mexico, all of them from the United States. www.sedena.gob.mx, transparency request, folio 0000700024503, September 2003.
95. Piñeyro, "The Modernization of the Mexican Armed Forces," 116.
96. www.sedena.gob.mx, September 6, 1999.
97. Adam Isacson and Joy Olson, *Just the Facts 2001-2002* (Washington, D.C.: WOLA, November 2001), 5.
98. Personal interview with Division General Gerardo Clemente Vega García, Secretary of National Defense, Mexico City, February 26, 2004. For specific courses, and their location, see "Cursos realizados durante el año 2004, 2003, 2002," www.sedena.gob.mx./educacion/curext.
99. J. Samuel Fitch, "The Decline of US Military Influence in Latin America," *Journal of Inter-American Studies and World Affairs* (Summer 1993), 18-19.
100. The figures for the medical corps are particularly interesting given the fact that they must obtain their own positions abroad and are not financed by the Secretariat of National Defense.
101. *Diario de Yucatán*. November 9, 2002.
102. www.sedena.gob.mx, transparency request, June 25, 2003.
103. www.dean.usma.edu, September 3, 2003.
104. www.sedena.gob.mx, transparency request, folio 0000700033903, November 18, 2003; correspondence from the Secretary of National Defense, March 12, 2004.
105. Russell W. Ramsey, "U.S. Military Courses for Latin America Are a Low Budget Strategic Success," *North-South: The Magazine of the Americas,* 2 (February/March 1993), 39.
106. "Inter-American Defense College," *Military Review*, 50 (April 1970), 21-23.

107. I am indebted to Margaret Daly Hayes, director of the Center for Hemispheric Defense Studies, for this information, personal letter, May 22, 2003.
108. John T. Fishel, "The Organizational Component of Civil-Military Relations in Latin America: The Role of the Ministry of Defense," Unpublished paper, Latin American Studies Association, Miami, March 2000, 2.
109. "U.S. Army School of the Americas," *Military Review*, 50 (April 1970), 89.
110. Letter from the United States Army War College, December 1, 1997. Since 1988, one Mexican has been enrolled in the course yearly.
111. Material from the next three pages borrows liberally from my conclusions in *Mexico's Mandarins*, 194–197.
112. In reality, however, there is little empirical evidence to support a connection between the school's training and its graduates' behavior. As John A. Cope notes, 59,000 students have graduated from the school since its inception, and most of these attended 1–2 week technical courses, allowing for little instructor influence. Fewer than .5% were known to be guilty of misconduct. Such influences are difficult to prove, but it is equally difficult to identify actual cases of human rights violations, which are underreported. *International Military Education and Training: An Assessment* (Washington, D.C.: Institute for National Strategic Studies, 1995), 22.
113. Darrin Wood, "Mexico Practices What School of the Americas Teaches," *Covert Action Quarterly* (Winter 1996–1997), www.thirdworldtraveler.com.
114. John T. Fishel and Kimbra L. Fishel, "The Impact of an Educational Institution on Host Nation Militaries, the U.S. Army School of the Americas as An Effective Instrument of Policy or Merely a Scapegoat," Unpublished paper, Latin American Studies Association, Guadalajara, Mexico, April 1997, 4. Russell Ramsey, "Forty Years of Human Rights Training," *Journal of Low Intensity Conflict & Law Enforcement*, 4, No. 2 (Autumn, 1995), 254–270, and Russell W. Ramsey, "U.S. Strategy for Latin America," 78.
115. Cope, *International Military Education and Training*, 22
116. J. Samuel Fitch, "The Political Consequences of U.S. Military Aid to Latin America: Institutional and Individual Effects," *Armed Forces and Society*, 5, No. 3 (1979), 361.
117. Cope, *International Military Education and Training*, 23.
118. J. Samuel Fitch, "The Decline of U.S. Military Influence on Latin America," *Journal of Inter-American Studies and World Affairs*, 35 (Summer 1993), 22.
119. Jennifer M. Taw, "The Effectiveness of Training International Military Students in Internal Defense and Development" (Santa Monica, Calif.: RAND, 1993), 7, 15. A much earlier study by Ernest W. Lefever found little evidence one way or the other of US training influencing the armed forces' political role. "The Military Assistance Training Program," *Annals of the American Academy of Political and Social Science*, No. 424 (March 1976), 90.
120. John A. Cope, *International Military Education and Training*, 15.
121. General Félix Galván López.
122. J. Samuel Fitch, "The Decline of U.S. Military Influence in Latin America," 16.
123. Ibid., 24–26.
124. H. Amos, et al., *US Training of Foreign Military Personnel*, 1 (McLean: General Research Corporation, March 1979), 2.
125. Personal interview with a member of the presidential staff, Mexico City, July 17, 1992.

126. For example, the high command has insisted on learning American techniques from U.S. public affairs officers in order to present its own story to the Mexican public and to enhance its image in the media. Letter from Major Al Leftwich, March 25, 1997.
127. Frederick M. Nunn, "The South American Military and (Re) Democratization: Professional Thought and Self-Perception," *Journal of Inter-American Studies and World Affairs*, 37, no. 2 (Summer 1995), 27.
128. Erubiel Tirado, "Relación civil-militar en México: Hacia la reformulación de un nuevo pacto," Center for Hemispheric Defense Studies, Washington, D.C., May 2001, 11.
129. Sigrid Arzt, "The Shaping of Mexico's Civil-Military Relations under the Fox Administration in Light of the Law Enforcement Challenges," Unpublished paper, Latin American Studies Association, Washington, D.C., September 2001.
130. Camp, "Mexico's Armed Forces, Marching to a Different Tune?," 12.
131. Camp, *Mexico's Mandarins*, 144.

Chapter Nine   Reaching the Top

1. Roderic Ai Camp, "Generals and Politicians in Mexico: A Preliminary Comparison," in *The Modern Mexican Military: A Reassessment*, ed. David Ronfeldt (La Jolla, Calif.: Center for U.S. Mexican Studies, University of California, San Diego, 1984), 149.
2. "Ley de ascensos y recompenses del ejército y fuerza aeréa mexicanos," Article 32, *Diario Oficial*, October 30, 2003. Colonels require 27 years on active duty and brigadier generals 31 years active duty. These specific minimum requirements were not instituted until 2003.
3. Lyle N. McAlister, *The Military in Latin American Socio-political Evolution: Four Case Studies* (Washington, D.C.: Center for Research in Social Systems, 1970), 206.
4. Jorge Alberto Lozoya, *El Ejército mexicano* (1911–1965) (Mexico: El Colegio de México, 1970), 66.
5. Jesús de León Toral, et al., *El Ejército mexicano* (Mexico: Secretaria de Defensa Nacional, 1979), 486.
6. Charles H. Coates and Roland J. Pellegrin, *Military Sociology: A Study of American Military Institutions and Military Life* (University Park, Md.: Social Science Press, 1965), 137.
7. Even officers who were just starting their careers as lieutenants at the time remember his reputation. Personal interviews, Mexico City, 1989–1990.
8. Phyllis Greene Walker, "The Modern Mexican Military: Political Influence and Institutional Interests in the 1980s" (M.A. thesis, American University, 1987), 26–27.
9. Direción Técnica de Organización, *Directorio del gobierno federal*, vol. 1 (Mexico, 1951) 11, Direción Técnica de Organización, *Directorio del gobierno federal*, vol. 1 (Mexico, 1956), 10.
10. Senado, *Diario de los debates*, 1953, 5–6.
11. Ibid., 6.
12. Ibid., 7.
13. David Ronfeldt, "The Mexican Army and Political Order since 1940," in *Armies and Politics in Latin America*, ed. Abraham R. Lowenthal (New York: Holmes and Meier, 1976), 300.

14. Camp, "Generals and Politicians in Mexico," 131.
15. According to Secretariat of National Defense records, during his entire administration, Echeverría retired 108 generals (19 division, 36 brigade and 53 brigadier). www.sedena.gob.mx, transparency request, folio 000700033903.
16. Thomas E. Weil, "The Armed Forces," in *Area Handbook for Mexico* (Washington, D.C.: GPO, 1975), 367.
17. Gabriel Parra, "Inconformidad en el ejército con el sistema de ascensos," *Excélsior*, June 19, 1971, 1. This is the first published account I have encountered of military dissatisfaction with the promotion process.
18. Michael J. Dziedzic, "Civil-Military Relations in Mexico: The Politics of Co-optation" (Unpublished paper, University of Texas, Austin, 1983), 33.
19. Personal interview, Mexico City, 1990.
20. Franklin D. Margiotta, "Civilian Control and the Mexican Military: Changing Patterns of Political Influence," in *Civilian Control of the Military: Theories and Cases from Developing Countries*, ed. Claude E. Welch, Jr. (Albany, N.Y.: State University of New York Press, 1976), 232.
21. Gloria Fuentes, *El Ejército mexicano* (Mexico: Grijalbo, 1983), 222. These figures are somewhat similar to the number of years its takes to become a general in the U.S. Army. At the time Maureen Mylander completed her study of generals at the end of the Vietnam era, a brigadier general required twenty-six years; a major general, thirty years; and a lieutenant general, thirty-two years. *The Generals* (New York: Dial Press, 1974), 342.
22. Comment by Eugenio Domínguez Ruiz, January 26, 2002, at www.foros.gob.mx. In reality, Miranda Sánchez does not seem to have commanded any troops until he was appointed regional commander after 2000. Cardona Marino only briefly commanded the 36th Infantry Battalion in Minatitlán, Veracruz, in 1976, immediately before joining the presidential staff.
23. www.PRDleg.cddhcu.gob.mx.
24. Ibid.
25. Ibid.
26. Luis Garfias Magaña, "El ejército, en un profunda crisis," *Proceso*, archivo, www.proceso.com.
27. Juan Veledíaz, "El secreto revelo de los generales," *Revista Milenio*, no. 143 (June 2000), www.restamilenio.com.
28. *Revista de Ejército y Fuerza Aérea*, December 1994, 65, *Diario de Yucatán*, March 8, 2003, *El Financiero*, September 27, 1994, 53. Quirós Hermosillo reached division general at age 51, just 34 years after he enrolled as a cadet. Cervantes Aguirre was just six months older when he achieved that rank. Reta Trigos actually received his promotion to division general after only 33 years on active duty.
29. *Revista de Ejercito y Fuerza Aérea*, December 1988, 11–12.
30. Such a situation allows individuals who are allegedly corrupt, such as Quirós Hermosillo, to commit these violations as a senior officer over much greater periods of time. Personal letter from General Garfias Magaña, March 3, 2004.
31. Garfias, "El ejército, en una profunda crisis."
32. When Riviello Bazán was asked at a meeting of army generals in 1988 what he thought about being in last place on the list of aspirants for secretary of national defense. He more or less replied, "Yes, I am at the end of the list, but what if the President orders an about face." *Diario de Yucatán*, March 8, 3003.
33. *Diario de Yucatán*, March 8, 2003, www.sureste.com.

34. Velediaz, "El secreto revelo de los generales;" and Jorge L. Sierra, "Preparan la selección del próximo jefe castrense," *To2*, December 6, 2000, www.to2.com. Apparently, Riviello Bazán was the senior division general at that time, so his appointment in part was to assuage those senior officers who might have been passed over by less senior division generals. The navy has shared in this problem as well. Admiral José Lorenzo Franco, who was appointed secretary of the navy in 1994, was promoted over 14 vice admirals with more time in grade to full admiral on November 20, 1994, so as to be eligible for the post, just days before he took office. See Laura Quintero and Gonzalo Martré, *El desafío* (Mexico: Planeta, 1995).

35. *Diario de Yucatán*, March 8, 2003.

36. Daniel Mora, "Profile of the Mexican Company Grade Officer" (Unpublished paper, Rocky Mountain States Latin American Conference, Tucson, 1984), 16.

37. Stephen J. Wager, "The Mexican Military" (Unpublished paper, 1983), 21, parts of which appear in Robert Wesson, *The Latin American Military* (Westport, Conn.: Greenwood Press, 1986).

38. According to General Riviello Bazán, a secretary presents a list of 4–7 recommended officers to the president-elect. Ultimately, the president chooses the person he considers to "guarantee obedience, loyalty and discipline." Javier Ibarola, "La designación más difícil," *Revista Milenio*, no. 143 (June 2000), www.milenio.com.

39. *Diario de Yucatán*, February 24, 1999, www.sureste.com.

40. McAlister, *The Military in Latin American Socio-political Evolution*, 234.

41. Personal interview with President Miguel de la Madrid, Mexico City, August 23, 1990.

42. Camp, "Generals and Politicians in Mexico," 140.

43. November 1971, 37.

44. José Luis Piñeyro, "The Mexican Army: and the State: Historical and Political Perspective," *Revue Internationale de Sociologie* 14 (April–August 1978):150, citing *El Día*, February 29, 1976, 17.

45. For an interesting analysis of Echeverría's own perceptions of these and other destabilizing events, see George Philips, *The Presidency in Mexican Politics* (New York: St. Martin's, 1992), 65ff.

46. Camp, "Generals and Politicians in Mexico," 140–141.

47. Roderic Ai Camp, "Civilian Supremacy in Mexico: The Case of a Post-Revolutionary Military," in *Military Intervention and Withdrawal*, ed. Constantine P. Danopoulous (London: Routledge, 1991), 25.

48. Personal interview, Mexico City, 1990.

49. Personal interview with President José López Portillo, Mexico City, 1991.

50. Roderic Ai Camp, *Crossing Swords, Politics and Religion in Mexico* (New York: Oxford University Press, 1996), 64, for an analysis of the consequences of this conflict.

51. Roderic Ai Camp, *Politics in Mexico, The Democratic Transformation* (New York: Oxford University Press, 2003), 58.

52. Letter to the editor, *Proceso*, September 4, 1989, 62.

53. "El Caso Gallardo," *Proceso*, www.proceso.com.archivo.

54. Roderic Ai Camp, "Mexico's Armed Forces, Marching to a Democratic Tune?," in *The Dilemma of Mexican Politics in Transition*, ed. Kevin Middlebrook (London: Institute of Latin American Studies, University of London, 2004), 353–372.

55. "Plaza Dominical," *Diario de Yucatán*, February 10, 2002, www.sureste.com.mx.

56. The 1956 promotions law, the basis of all future legislation governing armed forces promotions, specifically required time in grade, time in service, and appropriate educational training (although no advanced training is specified) in Sections I, V, and VI of Article 7. See "Ley de ascensos y recompenses del ejército y fuerza aérea nacionales," *Diario Oficial,* January 7, 1956, 2–8.

57. *Revista de Ejército y Fuerza Aérea,* November 1981, 27.

58. www.sedena.gob.mx, transparency request, folio 0000700027503, October 2003.

59. www.sedena.gob.mx, transparency request, folio 0000700040304, December 22, 2003.

60. Mylander, *The Generals,* 63.

61. *Hispano Americano,* May 11, 1981, 11.

62. See my "The Mexican Revolution as a Socializing Agent: Mexican Political Leaders and Their Parents" (Unpublished paper, Rocky Mountain States Latin American Studies conference, Tucson, 1977).

63. Richard B. Craig, "Mexican Narcotics Traffic: Binational Security Implications," *The Latin American Narcotics Trade and U.S. National Security,* ed. Donald J. Mabry (Westport, Conn.: Greenwood Press, 1989), 35.

64. This appears to be true among Colegio de Defensa Nacional graduates as well. The air force graduates reach division general rank faster than their army counterparts.

65. *Memoria gráfica del cincuentenario de la reapertura del Heroico Colegio Militar* (Mexico: SHCP, 1970), 499–501.

66. The same distortion also appears to be true in Brazil. Frank McCann found that from 1891 to 1965, only 30 percent of Brazilian generals were infantry; 23 percent artillery, and 17 percent cavalry. See his "Brazilian Army Officers Biography Project" Unpublished paper, Latin American Studies Association, December 1989, Miami, 8.

67. Academic performance is a variable among U.S. generals, too. Mylander found that of the 233 West Point graduates among the army's 491 generals in 1973, half were in the top third of their class. *The Generals,* 330.

68. McAlister, *The Military in Latin American Socio-political Evolution,* 230.

69. Sergio Aguayo Quezada, *La charola, una historia de los servicios de inteligencia en México* (Mexico: Grijalbo, 2001), 72.

70. Personal interview, Mexico City, 1990.

71. I originally developed these arguments in my, "Mexico's Armed Forces, Marching to a Different Tune?"

72. Miguel A. Granados Chapa, in his regular column "Plaza Pública," and with considerable insight, discusses the career backgrounds of chiefs of staff extending back to the time of Miguel Alemán. Complete details on their careers can be found in Roderic Ai Camp, *Mexican Political Biographies, 1935–1993,* 3rd edit. (Austin, Tex.: University of Texas Press, 1995). He, too, believes the presidential military staff's silence on a number of issues has produced serious consequences. See for example *Diario de Yucatán,* July 1, 1999 and June 29, 1999, www.sureste.com.mx.

73. As Sergio Aguayo Quezada, an expert on Mexican national security and one of the few careful students of this subject recently remarked, the presidential military staff and guards are operationally controlled by the presidency, but are administratively responsible to the secretariat of national defense. The results "are permanent tensions between the EMP [Estado Mayor Presidencial] and Sedena [secretariat of national defense]." It is unlikely that such an incident would be repeated, but technically

the lines of command make possible such a scenario. See his discussion in *Diario de Yucatán*, July 1, 1999, www.sureste.com.

74. An English synopsis is provided by Sam Dillon, "General Illuminates '68 Massacre in Mexico," in the *New York Times*, June 29, 1999, www.nytimes.com.

75. The policy implications of this for the command hierarchy in the Mexican military, which is so stringent, is even more significant when one considers that Gutiérrez Oropeza, a lowly colonel at the time, was operating completely autonomously from the secretary of national defense. The image of the regular military suffered tremendously and the student massacre produced numerous consequences for the institution.

76. These details are nicely summarized in Pascal Beltrán del Río, "Ahora acusado, Gutiérrez Oropeza recibió el apapacho del sistema al que sirvió," *Proceso*, July 4, 1999, www.proceso.mx.com.

77. Luis Garfias Magaña, "Hacia un nuevo ejército para México," *Forum*, no. 67 (June 1998), 22.

78. Wager, "The Mexican Military," 25.

79. Personal interviews, Mexico City, 1990.

80. Secretaria de Defensa Nacional, *Memorias* (Mexico: SDN, 1948), 75, and *Memorias* (Mexico: SDN, 1965), 58.

81. Interview with a Mexican general, August 1973.

82. General Vega García attributes his experience as an attaché in Eastern Europe and the USSR as formative on his ideas about socialism and its influence on society. These experiences combined with the visions of his grandfather, a Spanish national who fought on the side of General Franco during the Spanish Civil War in the 1930s.

83. Mora, "Profile of the Mexican Company Grade Officer," 13.

84. Edwin Lieuwen, *Mexican Militarism: The Political Rise and Fall of the Revolutionary Army, 1910–1940* (Albuquerque, N.M.: University of New Mexico Press, 1968), 93.

85. Wager, "The Mexican Military," 23.

86. McAlister, *The Military in Latin American Socio-political Evolution*, 234.

87. Personal interview, Mexico City, 1990.

88. Camp, *Mexico's Mandarins*, 20–21.

89. William S. Ackroyd, "Descendants of the Revolution: Civil-Military Relations in Mexico" (Ph.D. dissertation., University of Arizona, 1988), 160.

90. Personal interview, Mexico City, 1990.

91. See www.semar.gob.mx/transparencia/sueldos and www.sedena.gob.mx/leytrans/remun, September 12, 2003.

92. Stephen J. Wager, "Modernization of the Mexican Military: Political and Strategic Implications" (Unpublished paper, Department of History, U.S. Military Academy, 1983), 24.

93. *The Generals*, 63. Morris Janowitz also notes that officers "believe that combat arms is the major route to upward mobility." *The Professional Soldier* (Glencoe, Ill.: Free Press, 1960), 147.

94. Roderic Ai Camp, "Mexican Military Leadership in Statistical Perspective since the 1930s," in *Statistical Abstract of Latin America*, vol. 20, eds. James W. Wilkie and Peter Reich (Los Angeles, Calif.: Latin American Center Publications, University of California, Los Angeles, 1980), 605.

95. *Diario Oficial*, December 26, 1986, 3.

96. Being a "military brat," however, did not aid a general or admiral in rising to the post of secretary. About one in three generals can claim a military father, the same as secretaries.

Notes

97. Virginia Prewett, "The Mexican Army," *Foreign Affairs* 19 (April 1941): 613.
98. www.sedena.gob.mx, August 13, 2003.
99. www.semar.gob.mx, August 13, 2003.
100. www.sedena.gob.mx, August 13, 2003.
101. *Diario Oficial*, January 14, 1985, 9.
102. See Article 36 of the organic military law, *Diario Oficial*, December 26, 1986, 4.
103. Jorge Alberto Lozoya, *El ejército mexicano (1911-1965)* (Mexico: El Colegio de México, 1970), 73.
104. Guillermo Boils, *Los militares y la política en México, 1915-1974* (Mexico: El Caballito, 1975), 112.
105. Lozoya, *El ejército mexicano*, 74.
106. Oscar Hinojosa, "Cualquier régimen de gobierno, con apoyo popular, será respetado por el Ejército," *Proceso*, March 1982, 8.
107. www.sedena.gob.mx, August 12, 2003.
108. www.sedena.gob.mx, communicado de prensa, November 19, 2003.
109. www.sedena.gob.mx, transparency request, folio 4084003, August 4, 2003
110. www.sedena.gob.mx, transparency request, folio 2003000053, June 30, 2003.
111. "El titular de marina da conocer de reestructuración," *Diario de Yucatán*, March 19, 2000.
112. "La Armada de México reducirá a 40% la cifra de almirantes en activo," *Diario de Yucatán*, December 29, 2000.
113. www.foros.gob.mx, January 26, 2002.
114. *Diario de Yucatán*, October 22, 2001.
115. Senado de México, *Diario de debates*, November 6, 2001, 8, 11.
116. "Los militares también afrontan una reforma," *Diario de Yucatán*, July 2, 2001.
117. *Diario de Yucatán*, October 22, 2001.
118. Jeffrey Weldon, "The Spring 2003 Term of the Mexican Congress," *CSIS Mexican Congressional Series* (Washington, D.C.: CSIS, 2003), 4.
119. "Ley de ascensos y recompenses del ejército y fuerza aeréa mexicanos," Article 33, *Diario Oficial*, October 30, 2003. In 2003, the officer corps received an increase of 1.8 percent in their base salary, and a 4 percent increase in their retirement funds. www.sedena.gob.mx, transparency request, February 12, 2004.
120. "Testimony of General Gerardo Clemente Vega García before the 59th Session of Congress," October 13, 2004, p. 37. As he bluntly put it, "There are no longer Generals who I can select..."
121. *Diario de Yucatán*, January 14, 2002.
122. www.sedena.gob.mx/leytrans/remun, September 12, 2003.
123. *Diario de Yucatán*, October 22, 2001.
124. Major Richard Kilroy Jr., "The Mexican Military Digs In," Unpublished paper, 1991, 4. Ironically, many officers believe that he only exacerbated the problems.
125. Personal interview with President José López Portillo, Mexico City, February 19, 1991.
126. Personal interview with President Miguel de la Madrid, Mexico City, August 23, 1990.
127. In 1995, the United Status embassy political section considered the relations between the navy and the army to have been cordial. See Confidential Cable, U.S. Embassy, 1995Mexico10043, U.S. Department of State, May 11, 1995, National Security Archives, George Washington University, 2004.

128. Jorge Luis Sierra, "El ejército en tiempos de Fox: continuidad con los planes zedillistas," *Proceso*, August 18, 2002, www.proceso,com.mx.

Chapter Ten Challenges to Civil-Military Relations in the 21st Century

1. J. Mark Ruhl, "Changing Civil-Military Relations in Latin America," *Latin American Research Review* 33, no. 3 (1998), 257. Recent literature suggests the power and prerogatives of the armed forces have declined in some Latin American countries.

2. David Pion-Berlin, "Between Regional Strength and Domestic Stress: A New Civil-Military Pragmatism in Latin America," Unpublished Paper, Latin American Studies Association, Dallas, Texas, March 2003, 17.

3. J. Sam Fitch, *The Armed Forces and Democracy in Latin America* (Baltimore, Md.: Johns Hopkins University Press, 1998), 34. Fitch did not specifically include Mexico in this statement.

4. Felipe Aguero, *Soldiers, Civilians, and Democracy: Post-Franco Spain in Comparative Perspective* (Baltimore, Md.: Johns Hopkins University Press, 1995).

5. J. Sam Fitch, "Bridging the Conceptual Gap: Latin American Military Views of Democracy, Politics, and Policy," Unpublished paper, Latin American Studies Association, Washington, D.C., September 2001, 14.

6. Bruce W. Farcau, *The Transition to Democracy in Latin America: The Role of the Military* (Westport, Conn.: Praeger, 1996), 4.

7. www.sedena.gob.mx, comunicado de prensa, February 2002.

8. Jorge A. Medellín and Javier Cabrera, "Sedena: Poder Judicial favorece delincuencia," *El Universal*, January 28, 2004, 1.

9. Jorge Zepeda Patterson, "Histórico discurso del general secretario, el ejército declara la alerta,: *Diario de Yucatán*," February 23, 2004, www.edicion.yucatan.com.mx.

10. See Lorenzo Meyer's insightful discusión, "El general, metido en nuestro laberinto," *Diario de Yucatán*, www.edicion.yucatan.mx., July 9, 2004. PRI party president Roberto Madrazo is cited in "Madrazo: Que se olvide la guerra sucia," *Diario de Yucatán*, July 9, 2004.

11. *Diario de Yucatán*, July 21, 2000. www.sureste.com.mx.

12. *Diario de Yucatán*, March 8, 2003. www.sureste.com.mx.

13. Jorge Luis Sierra, "El ejército en tiempos de Fox: continuidad con los planes zedillistas," *Proceso*, August 18, 2002, www.proceso.com.mx.

14. *Diario de Yucatán*, March 8, 2003, www.sureste.com.mx.

15. Graham H. Turbiville, Jr., "Mexico's Evolving Security Posture," *Military Review* (May-June, 2001), 4; Sergio Aguayo, "La seguridad nacional," *Diario de Yucatán*, August 2001, www.sureste.com.mx.

16. Jorge Fernández Menéndez, "México, su seguridad nacional y la guerra antiterrorista," *Milenio Semanal* September 23, 2001, www.milenio.com/nota.asp.

17. "Por malestar en el Ejército se aplaza la tercera presentación del gabinetazo," www.suracapulco.com.mx, November 26, 2000.

18. www.larevista.com.mx.

19. Richard L. Millet, "The Future of Latin America's Armed Forces," in *Beyond Praetorianism, the Latin American Military in Transition*, eds. Richard Millet and Michael Gold-Bliss (Miami, Fla.: North-South Center Press, 1996), 297.

20. Martin H. Greenberg, *Bureaucracy and Development: A Mexican Case Study* (Lexington, Mass.: Heath, 1970), 117.
21. Roderic Ai Camp, *Mexico's Mandarins, Crafting a Power Elite in the 21st Century* (Berkeley, Calif.: University of California Press, 2002), 265ff; and "Political Recruitment, Governance, and Leadership, Has Democracy Made a Difference?," Paper presented at the Conference on Pathways to Power: Political Recruitment and Democracy in Latin America," Wake Forest University, April 2004.
22. Personal interview, Mexico City, 1990.
23. In 2003, the figures were 53,000 navy (1,671 civilians) and 188,143 army/air force, for a total of 241,143. Secretaria de Marina, Unidad de Enlance, oficio numero 169/2003, August 22, 2003.
24. Personal interview, Mexico City, 1991.
25. "Testimony of General Gerardo Clemente Vega García before the 59th Session of Congress, October 13, 2004, p. 13.
26. Raúl Benítez Manaut, "México: doctrina, historia y relaciones cívico-militares a inicios del siglo xxi," in *Las relaciones cívico-militares en el mundo Iberoamericano* (Madrid: Instituto Universitario General Gutiérrez Mellado, 2003), np.
27. Douglas L. Bland, "A Unified Theory of Civil-Military Relations," *Armed Forces and Society*, Vol. 26 (Fall 1999), 13.
28. Rodney W. Jones and Steven A. Hildreth, eds., *Emerging Powers: Defense and Security in the Third World* (New York: Praeger, 1986), 387.
29. Personal interviews, Mexico City, 1991.
30. *Acción*, January 18, 1982, 8.
31. Senado, *Diario de Debates*, November 5, 2001, 6.
32. *Diario Oficial*, December 30, 2002, 11.
33. *Diario Oficial*, October 30, 2001, 5–6.
34. *Diario Oficial*, July 1, 2002, 4.
35. The article asserted that, by law, such individuals should not be awarded contracts. "Hay negocios turbios en el ejército mexicano," *Diario de Yucatán*, December 9, 2002, www.sureste.com.mx.
36. *Diario de Yucatán*, July 20, 2000, www.sureste.com.mx.; *El Financiero*, September 27, 1994, 53; *Proceso*, April 12, 1993, 7; *Proceso*, August 3, 1997, np; and www@debate.com.mx.
37. Roderic Ai Camp, *Militarizing Mexico, Where is the Officer Corps Going?* Policy Paper on the Americas (Washington, D.C.: CSIS, 1999), 2.
38. Benítez Manaut, "Las fuerzas armadas mexicanas a fin del siglo," 13.
39. *Diario Oficial*, April 2, 2001.
40. *Primer Informe*, September 1, 1995, www.zedillo.presidencia.gob.
41. Erubiel Tirado, "Relación civil-militar en México: Hacía la reformulación de un nuevo pacto." Center for Hemispheric Defense Studies, Washington, D.C., May 22–25, 2001, 6.
42. Sam C. Sarkesian, "Professionalism and Civil-Military Relations in the West," *International Political Science Review* 2, no. 3 (1981): 287.
43. For Fox's position on two controversial issues, see his speech "National Crusade Against Drug Trafficking and Organized Crime," Sinaloa, Mexico, January 2001, as cited in Turbiville, Jr., "Mexico's Evolving Security Posture," 2.
44. Sigrid Arzt, "The Shaping of Mexico's Civil-Military Relationship under the Fox Administration in Light of the Law Enforcement Challenges," Unpublished paper, Latin American Studies Association, Washington, D.C., September 2001, 14. The

latter mission has been completely ignored since Jorge Castañeda, Fox's first secretary of Foreign Relations, resigned.

45. Héctor Tobar, "Latin America Losing Faith in Democracy," *Los Angeles Times*. April 22, 2004, A3.

46. Sam C. Sarkesian, "Military Professionalism and Civil Military Relations in the West," *International Political Science Review* 2, no. 3 (1981): 287.

47. Moshe Lissak, "Center and Periphery in Developing Countries and Prototypes of Military Elites," in *Militarism in Developing Countries*, ed. Kenneth Fidel (New Brunswick, N.J.: Transaction Press, 1975), 49.

48. Jordi Diez "Political Change and Environmental Policymaking in Mexico," (Unpublished Ph.D. dissertation, University of Toronto, January 2004).

49. A rare case appearing in the legislative record is that of the Veterans Association of Campeche, which made it known to the Senate that it supported the veterans' legislation under consideration. Cámara de Senadores, *Memorias*, November 7, 1941, 5.

50. Michael J. Dziedzic, "The Essence of Decision in a Hegemonic Regime: The Case of Mexico's Acquisition of a Supersonic Fighter" (Ph.D. dissertation, University of Texas, Austin, 1986), 282.

51. Deborah Norden, "Democracy and the Military in Venezuela, From Subordination to Insurrection," *Latin American Research Review* 33, no. 2 (1998), 143–165; Fitch, *The Armed Forces and Democracy in Latin America*, 80.

52. Jorge Luis Sierra, "Las fuerzas armadas imponen su autonomía," *Proceso*, August 28, 2000, 5, www.proceso.com.mx.

53. *Diario de Yucatán*, March 26, 1999, www.sureste.com.mx.

54. Jorge Luis Sierra, *El ejército y la constitución mexicana* (Mexico: Plaza y Valdez, 1999), 12.

55. Hugo Martínez McNaught, "Piden a Sedena rendir cuentas," *Reforma*, April 28, 1998, np.

56. Sergio Aguayo, "Las fuerzas armadas y la alianza," *Diario de Yucatán*, August 3, 1999.

57. Hugo Martínez McNaught, "Pedirán explicar el gasto militar," *Reforma*, November 20, 1998, np.

58. "El PRD analizan la situación actual de la institución," *Diario de Yucatán*, December 24, 1999, www.sureste.com.mx.

59. *Diario de Yucatán*, September 7, 2000, www.sureste.com.mx.

60. Sergio Aguayo, "La seguridad nacional," *Diario de Yucatán*, August 30, 2001, www.sureste.com.mx. According to Division General Luis Garfias, who was president of the National Defense Committee in Congress in 1994, he attempted to arrange a meeting with the then secretary of national defense, General Enrique Cervantes Aguirre. However, members of PRI prevented him from arranging such a meeting. The only exception to this pattern prior to 2000 was General Juan Arévalo Gardoqui, who became the first secretary to come to the legislative palace during the 52nd legislative session (1982–1985). Personal correspondence from General Luis Garfias Magaña, January 27, 2005.

61. *El Universal*, August 27, 2001.

62. "Testimony of General Gerardo Clemente Vega García before the 59th Session of Congress," October 13th, 2004.

63. Interview with Division General Alfredo Ochoa Toledo, president of the national defense committee, Chamber of Deputies, Congressional Television Channel, March 1, 2002.

64. Personal interview with General Gerardo Clemente Vega García, Secretary of National Defense, Mexico City, February 26, 2004.
65. www.senado.gob.mx/comisiones.
66. Senado, *Diario de Debates*, No. 1, March 15, 2001, 3–4.
67. From 1964 through 1994, the percentage increases ranged from a low of 16 to a high of 37 percent. George W. Grayson, *Mexico's Armed Forces, A Fact book* (Washington, D.C., CSIS, 1999), 39; and Ernesto Zedillo, *Sexto Informe, Anexo Estadístico*, Disco 1, 2000, 5.
68. José Luis Piñeyro, "Presencia políticomilitar nacional y en el Distrito Federal," in *Distrito Federal, gobierno y sociedad civil*, ed. Pablo Gonzalez Casanova (Mexico: El Caballito, 1987, 70.)
69. In fact, General Vega García considers the loss of jobs to China, and the inability of Mexico's government to create sufficient new jobs, as a fundamental policy issue. Personal interview, February 26, 2004.
70. Personal interviews, Mexico City, 1990.
71. Personal interview, Mexico City, January 19, 1991.
72. Personal interview, Mexico City, August 23, 1990.
73. General Luis Garfías Magaña, "Las fuerzas armadas y la nueva política," email to the author, August 4, 2003.
74. Tirado, "Relación civil-militar en México," 7; and José Luis Sierra, "The Current Role of the Mexican Armed Forces," *Always Near, Always Far: The Armed Forces in Mexico* (San Francisco: Global Exchange, 2000), 38.
75. Benítez Manaut, "Las fuerzas armadas mexicanas a fin del siglo," 9.
76. "Secreto discrecionalidad en el gasto militar," *Diario de Yucatán*, February 24, 2002, www.sureste.com.mx.
77. Personal interview with President Miguel de la Madrid, Mexico City, August 23, 1990, who wanted to improve their salaries during his administration.
78. Luis Garfías Magaña, "Hacia un nuevo ejército para México," *Forum*, No. 67 (June 1988), 22.
79. Luis Garfías Magaña, "El problema de los retirados militares II," Unpublished essay, April, 2004.
80. Jorge Luis Sierra, "Mexico's Military in the War on Drugs," *Drug War Monitor* (Washington, D.C.: WOLA, April 2003), 2.
81. Ibid, 13.
82. Peter Andreas, *Border Games, Policing the U.S. Mexico Divide* (Ithaca, N.Y.: Cornell University Press, 2000), 65–66.
83. Sierra "Mexico's Military in the War on Drugs," 3.
84. Ibid, 2.
85. Sigrid Arzt, "Combating Transnational Organized Crime in Mexico, Only an Illusion?" Unpublished Paper, International Studies Association, Chicago, Illinois, February 2001, 15.
86. Sierra, "Mexico's Military in the War on Drugs," 4.
87. Interestingly, General Rafael Macedo de la Concha, the new attorney general, was the cousin of Liliana de la Concha, President Fox's first wife.
88. This violated the army-air force internal law because these individuals did not take the required leave of absence from the armed forces, during which time in grade credit stops.
89. Raúl Benítez Manaut, "Containing Armed Groups, Drug Trafficking, and Organized Crime in Mexico, The Role of the Military," in *Organized Crime and*

Democratic Governability: Mexico and the United States-Mexican Borderlands, eds. John Bailey and Roy Godson (Pittsburgh, Penn.: University of Pittsburgh Press, 2000), 136.
90. *Primer informe de gobierno, participación de la secretaria de marina*, 4, www.semar.gob.mx.
91. See Article 5, *Diario Oficial*, March 5, 2001, 5.
92. *Primer informe de gobierno*, 12.
93. www.sedena.gob.mx, transparency request, folios 2003000078 and 2003070024, August 8, 2003.
94. *Diario de Yucatán*, November 8, 2001, www.sureste.com.mx.
95. *Diario de Yucatán*, April 4, 2003, www.sureste.com.mx.
96. Turbiville, "Mexico's Evolving Security Posture," np.
97. Sergio Aguayo, "La seguridad nacional," *Diario de Yucatán*, August 30, 2001, www.sureste.com.mx.
98. Fernández Menéndez, "México, su seguridad nacional e la guerra antiterrorista," np.
99. Human Rights Watch, "Mexico, Military Injustice," 13, no. 4 (December 2001), 3.
100. Amnesty International, *Mexico: Justice Betrayed: Torture in the Judicial System* (New York: Amnesty International, 2001), 8, www.amnesty.org/library.
101. Benítez, "Containing Armed Groups," 131.
102. Millet, "The Future of Latin America's Armed Forces," 298.
103. Amnesty International, *Mexico: Justice Betrayed*, 4–5.
104. Organization of American States, Inter-American Commission on Human Rights, "Report on the Situation of Human Rights in Mexico," September 24, 1998, Chapter 11, 7.
105. Ginger Thompson, "12 Who 'Disappeared' in Mexico: A General's Sinister Story," *New York Times*, July 16, 2002.
106. Human Rights Watch, "Torture, 'Disappearance,' and Extra-judicial Execution in Mexico," January, 1999, 3. Carlos Montemayor discovered that the secretariat of national defense opposed the establishment of an International Red Cross office in Mexico in 1991–1992, and the acceptance of the Second Protocol to the Geneva Convention dealing with internal armed groups. He believes they opposed them because they already were well aware of the Zapatistas. "El ejército y la injerencia internacional," *Proceso*, archives, www.proceso.com.mx.
107. José Gil Olmos, "El ejército debe abrirse: General Garfias," *Proceso*, July 22, 2001, www.proceso.com.mx. General Vega García has stated that the secretariat of nacional defense has transferred all of the archival materials it had in its possession from the 1960s to the 1970s to the National Archives. He agrees, however, that it may not be complete, but it included everything they had when he took office. Personal interview, February 26, 2004.
108. "Sedena no coopera en el caso Digna Ochoa," *Diario de Yucatán*, January 31, 2002, www.sureste.com.mx.
109. For example, in the January–February 1998 report, 30 percent of the complaints involved the army, the highest figure for any single group. Comisión Mexicana de Defensa y Promoción de los Derechos Humanos, *Los Derechos humanos en México* (March–April 1998), 36.
110. Laurie Freeman, *Troubling Patterns, the Mexican Military and the War on Drugs* (Washington, D.C.: Latin American Working Group, 2002).
111. www.amnestyusa.org/news/july 10, 2001.
112. Rodrigo Vera, "Fox y Gallardo," *Proceso*, archives, www.proceso.com.mx.

113. Martin Edwin Anderson, "Civil-Military Relations and Internal Security in Mexico: the Undone Reform," in *The Challenge of Institutional Reform in Mexico*, ed. Riordan Roett (Boulder, Colo.: Lynne Rienner, 1995), 167.
114. Roderic Ai Camp, "Mexico's Armed Forces, Marching to a Democratic Tune?," in *The Dilemma of Mexican Politics in Transition*, ed. Kevin Middlebrook (London: Institute of Latin American Studies, University of London, 2004), 353–372.
115. Kevin Sullivan, "Freed Mexican Vows to Clear His Name," *Washington Post*, February 9, 2002, A21.
116. Email from reporter Ricardo Chacón, *Boston Globe*, January 20, 1999; Ginger Thompson, "Mexico Army Protester Goes Loudly into Hiding," *New York Times*, December 29, 1998. The legal rights issues raised by the group include the arbitrariness of military justice, the lack of constitutional protections enjoyed by ordinary citizens, and the inability of military personnel to appeal their cases to the high command. See *Proceso*, May 30, 1999, www.proceso.com.mx and Miguel A. Granados Chapa, "Plaza Pública," *Diario de Yucatán*, May 24, 1999, www.sureste.com.mx.
117. James Smith, "Mexican Army Officers' Protest is 'Wake-Up Call' for Military," *Los Angeles Times*, December 22, 1998.
118. Sam Dillon, "Dissidents in Mexican Army Criticize Government," *New York Times*, December 21, 1998, www.nyt.com.
119. *Proceso*, January 17, 1999.
120. Álvaro Delgado, "Según el general Garfías Magaña, los inconformes están equivocados," *Proceso*, December 27, 1998, 2, www.proceso.com.mx. General Mota Sánchez presently is chairman of the Senate committee on nacional defense affairs.
121. *Diario de Yucatán*, April 17, 1999, www.sureste.com.mx.
122. Anthony W. Pereira, "Virtual Legality, Authoritarian Legacies and the Reform of the Military Justice in Brazil, the Southern Cone, and Mexico," *Comparative Political Studies* 34, No. 5 (June 2001), 571.
123. *Revista de Ejército y Fuerza Aérea* July 1999; and June 2001, 21–27.
124. *Diario Oficial*, Chapter IV, 11–12, May 6, 2002.
125. www.sedena.gob.mx/leytrans/petición/julio/2003.
126. "Que debería limitarse la obediencia militar," *Diario de Yucatán*, February 24, 2002, www.sureste.com.mx.
127. Diario de Yucatán, December 9, 1999, www.sureste.com.mx.
128. "Figueras de la 'guerra sucia,' no investigados," *Diario de Yucatán*, April 21, 2003.
129. He points out that everyone from sergeant on up receives repeated formal training in human rights. Every soldier is required to carry a card in their pocket outlining those rights. Each unit commander is required to review those rights on a regular basis. Personal interview, February 26, 2004.
130. Sergio Aguayo, "El juicio a dos generales," *Diario de Yucatán*, March 10, 2002, www.sureste.com.mx; and Mary Jordan and Kevin Sullivan, "Mexican Generals Charged in '70s Deaths," *Washington Post*, September 28, 2002, A19. The army formed a Council of War on the guerrilla dirty war, its version of a court martial board, made up of Generals Tomás Angeles Dauhajere, Rigoberto Rivera Hernández, Roberto Badillo Martínez, Carlos E. Adam Yabur, and Juan A. Oropeza Garnica, the first of its kind to judge this topic. "Abren un Consejo de Guerra contra dos generales," *Diario de Yucatán*, October 29, 2002, www.sureste.com.mx.
131. Kate Doyle, "The Militarization of the Drug War in Mexico," *Current History*, February 1993, 87.
132. Turbiville, Jr., "Mexico's Evolving Security Posture," 2.

133. *Diario de Yucatán*, November 10, 1999, www.sureste.com.mx.
134. www.fas.org/asmp.
135. Caesar Sereseres, "The Mexican Military Looks South," in *The Modern Mexican Military: A Reassessment*, ed. David Ronfeldt (La Jolla, Calif.: Center for United States-Mexican Studies, University of California, San Diego, 1984), 211.
136. Edward J. Williams, "Mexico's Central American Policy: National Security Considerations," in *Rift and Revolution: Central American Imbroglio*, ed. Howard J. Wiarda (Washington, D.C.: American Enterprise Institute, 1984), 303–328.
137. For an outline of its potential role on civil-military relations, see David R. Mares, "U.S. Drug Policy and Mexican Civil-Military Relations: A Challenge for the Mutually Desirable Democratization Process," *Crime, Law and Social Change* 40, No. 1 (July 2003), 61–75.
138. Interestingly, the Mexican army views the petroleum industry as the primary target of terrorism in their country.
139. Stephan Dinan, "Border Patrol Agent Fired On," *Washington Times*, May 23, 2002, www.asp.washtimes.
140. Leonarda Reyes, "Comando Norte: Las expectaciones de Washington," *Proceso*, www.proceso.archivos.com.mx.
141. *Diario de Yucatán*, August 28, 2002, www.sureste.com.mx.
142. Personal interview, Mexico City, February 26, 2004.
143. Tirado, "Relación civil-militar en México," 23–24.
144. See *Excelsior*, August 25, 1990 and January 3, 1991. Also see Monica Serrano, "The Armed Branch of the State: Civil Military Relations in Mexico," *Journal of Latin American Studies* 27, no. 2(1995), 436, note 38.
145. Tirado, "Relación civil-militar en México," 9.
146. Hugo Martínez McNaught, "Destacan nueva era en la ayuda militar," *Reforma*, December 12, 1999, 2.
147. Oscar Rocha, "México ante el nuevo paradigma de las relaciones internacionales: la seguridad," in *En la frontera del imperio*, ed. Rafael Fernández de Castro (Mexico: Planeta, 2003), 290. For a contrary view, see General Luis Garfías Magaña, "Las fuerzas de paz (cascos azules)," Manuscript, November 2004.
148. *Diario de Yucatán*, December 14, 2001, www.yucatan.com.mx.
149. *Diario de Yucatán*, May 28, 2002, www.sureste.com.mx.
150. Ibid.
151. *Gaceta Parlamentaria*, No. 63, September 26, 2002.
152. Serrano, "The Armed Branch of the State," 436–437.
153. Sergio Zermeño, "De Echeverría a de la Madrid: Las clases altas y el estado mexicano" (Paper presented at the Latin American Program, Woodrow Wilson International Center for Scholars, 1982), 27.
154. Roderic Ai Camp, *Mexico's Mandarins, Crafting a Power Elite for the 21st Century*, 265–266.
155. When he retired, General Garfias initially joined the PRD, and with the help of General Agustín Alvarez Castillo, set up a small office called the Special Commission on Armed Forces Research, which produced a number of recommendations and studies, which had little impact on the party's policies. They did sponsor, for the first and only time, a public symposium on the armed forces. Personal letter to the author, January 20, 2005.
156. Personal letter from Raúl Benítez Manaut, November 6, 2004. Benitez Manaut argues that the army is sending the message that if the PAN and PRD want the military's support it should desist from supporting these investigative reforms.

157. Irving Louis Horowitz expressed a similar view on democracy itself: "Democracy is not a function of civilian authority any more than of military authority. It is a consequence of openness versus closure in the systems." "Militarism and Civil-Military Relationships in Latin America: Implications for the Third World," *Research in Political Sociology*, vol. 1 (Greenwich, Conn.: JAI Press, 1985), 96.

158. William S. Ackroyd, "Descendants of the Revolution: Civil-Military Relations in Mexico" (Ph.D. dissertation, University of Arizona, 1988), 27.

159. Army/Air Force Organic Law, *Diario Oficial*, December 26, 1986, 2–3.

160. See Article 6, Ley Orgánica de la Armada de México, www.semar.gob.mx.

161. Note the possible, emerging exception on past human rights abuses discussed above.

162. Kenneth Kemp and Charles Hudlin, "Civil Supremacy over the Military: Its Nature and Limits," *Armed Forces and Society* Vol. 19 (No. 1 1992), 7–26.

163. A third condition is that military officials are willing to relinquish control once a capable civilian organization emerges. See David Pion-Berlin and Craig Arceneaux, "Decision-Makers or Decision-Takers? Military Missions and Civilian Control in Democratic South America," *Armed Forces and Society*, Vol. 26 (Spring 2000), 433.

Bibliographic Essay

Since 1992, when I published my first book on the Mexican military, little has changed in the caliber of scholarly research on the Mexican armed forces. As I suggested then, literature on the Mexican military remains at best sketchy and sparse. Much of what has been written in the 1970s and 1980s is repetitive in content, often slightly modified reprints of earlier versions. The work published in the 1990s, with the exception of several notable essays by Mexican scholars, is based on secondary research. Thus, it is accurate to conclude that much of this work, for better or worse, perpetuates interpretations from the past. Almost no empirical research on the Mexican military exists about its relationship to civilian authorities, its interlocks with civilian political elites, its specific military and political activities, its prestige in society, its self-image, its composition, or its internal affairs. This is especially true of the navy. These lacunae have led to speculations and, occasionally, to gross inaccuracies about the armed forces and its relationship to civil society. The weak analytical nature of the literature on the Mexican military has generally excluded it from a richer literature on the Latin American military, and from theoretical comparative perspectives. With the democratization of Latin America in the late 1980s and the attempts to establish a new framework for civil-military relations in the region, some authors have proffered new theoretical interpretations.

In the 1990s, tensions developing between the Clinton administration and the armed forces produced, for the first time in many years, some reexaminations of broad issues in civil-military relations. Prior to this decade, a fairly voluminous literature provided a theoretical backdrop for examining the Mexican case. Nevertheless, the uniqueness of Mexico's military and its civil-military relations, limited this literature's applicability. This unfortunate situation has not disappeared in the context of the more recent Latin American theoretical arguments. Some useful interpretations, however, can be drawn from the United States literature. Strangely, an equally large literature on military sociology in the United States and Canada has rarely been used to draw comparisons with Latin American militaries. This study corrects that deficiency by incorporating, where appropriate, extensive comparative sociological literature that sheds light on the comparability or uniqueness of the Mexican case, especially in the chapters on professionalization.

I initiated my theoretical overview with two classic works in the literature, S. E. Finer's, *The Man on Horseback: The Role of the Military in Politics*, 2nd ed. (Boulder, Colo.: Westview Press, 1988), and Samuel P. Huntington's, *The Soldier and the State, The Theory and Politics of Civil-Military Relations* (Cambridge, Mass.: Harvard University Press, 1964). A number of books published after those two works were found to be particularly useful. The revised edition of Finer is highly recommended because the author surveys the literature since his original interpretation and incorporates new theoretical views into his own analysis. A more relevant theory for today's armed forces, one that borrows from Western examples and deals directly with the concept of professionalism, is that of Sam C. Sarkesian, who primarily focuses on the United States. His *Beyond the Battlefield, The New Military Professionalism* (New York: Pergamon Press, 1981), and "Military Professionalism and Civil-Military Relations in the West," *International Political Science Review* 2, no. 3 (1981): 283–298, provide a challenging and realistic model of civil-military relations. I have adapted Sarkesian's theory to the Mexican case and integrated elements from a newly argued model. Another author whose work offers a helpful analysis of the political role of the military is Amos Perlmutter. Of particular note is his "The Military and Politics in Modern Times; A Decade Later," *Journal of Strategic Studies*, 9 (March 1986): 5–15. Finally, one of the best overall analyses, which reinterprets the literature through the end of the 1980s, is Martin Edmonds's clearly written *Armed Services and Society* (Leicester, U.K.: Leicester University Press, 1988). An equally superior but more recent update of the broader issues is provided in Peter D. Feaver, in "The Civil-Military Problematique: Huntington, Janowitz, and the Question of Civilian Control," *Armed Forces and Society* 23, no. 2 (Winter 1996): 149–178.

The most useful recent theoretical contributions applicable to Mexico from western societies are Kenneth Kemp and Charles Hudlin, "Civil Supremacy over the Military: Its Nature and Limits," *Armed Forces and Society* 19, no. 1 (1992): 7–26, Douglas L. Bland's excellent "A Unified Theory of Civil-Military Relations," *Armed Forces and Society* 26, no. 1 (Fall 1999): 7–26, and James Burk, "Theories of Democratic Civil-Military Relations," *Armed Forces and Society* 29, no. 1 (Fall 2002): 7–29. All of these provide fresh elements to my own eclectic framework. Felipe Aguero has written an excellent comparative study of Spain, but it offers insights more appropriate to South America: *Soldiers, Civilians, and Democracy: Post-Franco Spain in Comparative Perspective* (Baltimore, Md.: Johns Hopkins University Press, 1995).

The two most useful theorists of Third World countries who have some applicability to Mexico are Morris Janowitz and Claude E. Welch, Jr. Janowitz's work, *The Military in the Development of New Nations* (Chicago: University of Chicago Press, 1964), is a classic in its own right. Like Janowitz, Welch examined the Third World, but he has contributed a great deal to sorting out the comparative theoretical issues, especially for countries where military disengagement from politics has been long term. His analyses are particularly useful to Mexico. Among them are his *Civilian Control of the Military: Theory and Cases from Developing Countries* (Albany, N.Y.: State University of New York Press, 1976); "Civil-Military Relations: Perspectives from the Third World," *Armed Forces and Society* 11 (Winter 1985): 183–198; and *No Farewell to Arms? Military Disengagement from Politics in Africa and Latin America* (Boulder, Colo: Westview Press, 1987).

Numerous articles and collected essays on the Latin American military are available. Generally their focus has been on South and Central America which, in terms of political and party structure, had little in common with Mexico between 1930 to 2000. The most helpful theoretical literature can be found in J. Samuel Fitch's, *The Armed Forces and Democracy in Latin America* (Baltimore, Md.: Johns Hopkins University Press, 1998). Chapter 2 of this book lays out a typology on civil-military relations in the post democratic transition period. It is followed by a chapter which provides valuable insights on attitudes towards the military's role in these societies. The most ambitious collection is David Pion-Berlin's *Civil-Military Relations in Latin America, New Analytical Perspectives* (Chapel Hill, N.C.: University of North Carolina Press, 2001). Three other works are helpful but, again, are more relevant to South America. They are Douglas L. Bland, "What Officers Need to Know about Civil-Military Relations," Latin American Studies Association, Miami, March 2000; Richard L. Millet, "The Future of Latin America's Armed Forces," in Richard Millet and Michael Gold-Biss, eds., *Beyond Praetorianism: The Latin Military in Transition* (Miami, Fla.: North-South Center Press, 1996), 291–300; and Bruce W. Farcau, *The Transition to Democracy in Latin America: The Role of the Military* (Westport, Conn.: Praeger, 1996). Mark J. Ruhl provides important interpretations of the recent literature, focusing on the issue of the military's decline or continued dominance, in his review essay "Changing Civil-Military Relations in Latin America,"

Latin American Research Review 33, no. 3 (1998), 257–269. Finally, John T. Fishel, offers a highly original exploration of "The Organizational Component of Civil-Military Relations in Latin America: The Role of the Ministry of Defense," Latin American Studies Association, Miami, March 2000.

One work from a historical angle having utility for Mexico is John J. Johnson's classic, *The Military and Society in Latin America* (Stanford: Stanford University Press, 1964). This book provides a single author's interpretation, including interviews from that era. The most helpful early interpretations of the Latin American scene, as they relate to Mexico's civil-military relations, are those by J. Samuel Fitch, "Armies and Politics in Latin America: 1975–1985," in Abraham Lowenthal and Samuel Fitch's collection, *Armies and Politics in Latin America* (New York: Holmes and Meier, 1986), 26–58; Irving Louis Horowitz, "Militarism and Civil-Military Relationships in Latin America, Implications for the Third World," *Research in Political Sociology* (Greenwich, Conn.: JAI Press, 1985); and Frederick M. Nunn. Nunn is the only author who has incorporated Mexico's experience in any detail within the broad sweep of Latin American literature. See his provocative "On the Role of the Military in Twentieth-Century Latin America: The Mexican Case," in *The Modern Mexican Military: A Reassessment*, ed. David Ronfeldt (La Jolla, Calif.: Center for United States-Mexican Studies, University of California, San Diego, 1984), 33–49.

The best place to initiate research on the Mexican military through the 1980s is two excellent bibliographical essays. The most complete list of Mexican sources is provided by Palmira Olguín Pérez's "Los militares en México: Bibliografía introductoria," *Revista Mexicana de Sociologia* 36 (April–June 1976): 433–490. For United States sources, especially useful because it identifies many government publications, there are two versions of librarian Harold Colson's essay. The first is his *Civil-Military Relations and National Security in Modern Mexico: A Bibliography* (Auburn, Ga: Auburn University, September 1987). The second version, *National Security Affairs and Civil-Military Relations in Contemporary Mexico: A Bibliography* (Monticello, Ill.: Vance Bibliographies, 1989), is more readily available. Both are annotated. Unfortunately, no more recent bibliographies have been published. For the period prior to 1935, the Secretaria de Guerra y Marina published its own excellent *Apuntes para una bibliografía militar de México, 1536–1936* (Mexico, 1937), organized by year. This is, however, without annotations.

The literature that deals specifically with the Mexican military tends to focus on two broad themes: the historical evolution of armed forces institutions and contemporary civil-military relations. The historical literature has received better treatment qualitatively and quantitatively in terms of book-length works. Standard political analyses on Mexico basically ignore the military, making only passing mention at best, with the exception of my own general work *Politics in Mexico, the Democratic Transformation* 4th edit (New York: Oxford University Press, 2003). The only book-length historical work in English is that of Edwin Lieuwen, *Mexican Militarism, the Political Rise and Fall of the Revolutionary Army, 1910-1940* (Albuquerque, N.M.: University of New Mexico Press, 1968). But Lieuwen's study, which analyzes the military only through the 1940s, focuses primarily on the immediate postrevolutionary period and was never updated. A more complete analysis, providing excellent insights into Mexican civil-military relations prior to 1940, is Gordon C. Schloming's unpublished Ph.D. dissertation, "Civil-Military Relations in Mexico, 1910-1940. A Case Study" (Columbia University, 1974). Mexican scholars have been more interested in the military than their North American counterparts. A work complementary to Lieuwen's is Jorge Alberto Lozoya's *El ejército mexicano (1911-1965)* (Mexico: El Colegio de México, 1970), which went through three editions (the most recent is from 1984), but with the exception of a new chapter on foreign policy, contains only superficial changes and little new research. An outstanding addition to the historical literature can be found in Elisa Servín's carefully researched *Ruptura y oposición, el movimiento henriquista, 1945-1954* (Mexico: Cal y Arena, 2001). This is an essential work for understanding the last efforts of the military to participate directly in presidential politics.

Other Mexicans have provided a more thorough look at the post-1960s military. The first of these, Guillermo Boils, published *Los militares y la política en Mexico, 1915-1974* (Mexico: El Caballito, 1975), with a useful update in the *Revista Mexicana de Sociología* 47 (January–February 1985): 169–185. The most prolific Mexican scholar in the last two decades is José Luis Piñeyro, who published a small monograph *Ejército y sociedad en México: pasado y presente* (Puebla: Universidad Autónomo de Puebla, 1985), but whose earlier article offered his essential ideas: "The Mexican Army and the State: Historical and Political Perspective," *Revue Internationale de Sociologie* 14 (April–August 1978): 111–157. This was followed by his helpful revision in "The Modernization of the Mexican Armed Forces," in *Democracy under Siege, New Military Power in Latin America*, ed. Augusto Varas (Westport, Conn.: Greenwood Press, 1989), 115–130. More recently, Piñeyro analyzed the 1995–1996 period under President Zedillo in "Las fuerzas armadas en la transición política de México," *Revista Mexicana de Sociología* 59, no. 1 (January–March, 1997), 163–189, followed by an insightful interpretation of the military's relationship with Fox during his first year in office: "Gobernabilidad democrática y fuerzas armadas en México con Fox," Latin American Studies Association, Washington, D.C., September, 2001. In the 1990s, Piñeyro has been joined by another adept colleague, Raúl Benítez Manaut, whose most comprehensive contribution is "Fuerzas armadas mexicanas a fin de siglo, misiones," in *Control civil y fuerzas armadas en las nuevas democracias latinoamericanas*, ed. Rut Diamint (Buenos Aires: Grupo Editorial Latinoamericano, 1999), 469–513. His other excellent essays appear in the following sections. An adviser to the secretary of government, Erubiel Tirado, has produced an extremely useful account of civil-military relations into the Fox administration, "Relación civil-militar en México: Hacia la reformulación de un nuevo pacto," Center for Hemispheric Defense Studies, Washington, D.C., May 2001.

Except for the work of Piñeyro and Benitez Manaut, American authors have provided the bulk of specific analysis of the recent Mexican military, and some of the best work remains unpublished. The only early work with a political bent is that of Virginia Prewett, whose pre-World War II assessment of Mexico's army in "The Mexican Army," *Foreign Affairs* 19 (April 1941): 609–621, was a first. About the period Lieuwen published his historical monograph, Karl Schmitt contributed a timely assessment in his "The Role of the Military in Contemporary Mexico," in *The Caribbean: Mexico Today*, ed. Curtis A. Wilgus (Gainesville, Fla.: University of Florida Press, 1964), 52–62. The first work to provide any empirical information on Mexican military sociology is that of Lyle N. McAlister, whose excellent chapter "Mexico," in *The Military in Latin American Socio-political Evolution: Four Case Studies* (Washington, D.C.: Center for Research in Social Systems, 1970); has been the source of successive interpretations often using outdated, if useful, information. The other early article-length work, offering an incisive focused interpretation of the military's political role, was David Ronfeldt's *The Mexican Army and Political Order since 1940* (Santa Monica: Rand Corporation, 1973). Ronfeldt is the only American scholar other than the author who has produced contributions on the Mexican military since the 1970s. Ronfeldt's short essay, republished several times but essentially unmodified, received more attention than McAlister's. He provided a helpful overview in the collection edited for the Center for United States-Mexican Studies, *The Modern Mexican Military; A Reassessment* (1984), later appearing in the Abraham Lowenthal and J. Samuel Fitch 1986 collection, and incorporated into a 1985 Rand publication. He co-authored a brief analysis of its relationship to civilian leadership with Kevin McCarthy and Kevin O'Connell, in another Rand publication, *Engaging the Mexican Military: Prospects and Policy* (February 1998).

The other author who initially raised the visibility of Mexican military studies, offering several important theses, was Franklin D. Margiotta, a career Air Force officer who completed an M.A. thesis at Georgetown University, "The Mexican Military, A Case Study in Non-intervention" (1968).

His work combined the theoretical interpretations of Ronfeldt with the type of empirical research found in McAlister's article. Margiotta offered a concise version of his ideas in a paper presented to the American Political Science Association in 1973 and published as "Civilian Control and the Mexican Military: Changing Patterns of Political Influence" in Claude E. Welch, Jr.'s, 1976 edited collection.

Four other authors have made significant contributions through their Ph.D. dissertations. Michael J. Dziedzic, another Air Force officer, analyzed the first case study of Mexican military decision-making influence in his excellent "The Essence of Decision in a Hegemonic Regime: The Case of Mexico's Acquisition of a Supersonic Fighter" (University of Texas, Austin, 1986). He followed his dissertation with an equally important unpublished essay, "Mexico's Converging Challenges: Problems, Prospects, and Implications," United States Air Force Academy, April 1989. The second individual, William S. Ackroyd, began presenting papers as early as 1980. The papers were based on dissertation research entitled "Descendants of the Revolution: Civil-Military Relations in Mexico" (University of Arizona, 1988) prepared under the direction of Edward J. Williams, another contributor to this literature. A synopsis of Ackroyd's basic views on military socialization appeared in published form in "Military Professionalism, Education and Political Behavior," *Armed Forces and Society*, 18 (Fall 1991). Ackroyd deserves special mention for organizing the first conference on the Mexican military. The conference led to the collection published in 1984 under the editorship of David Ronfeldt. A third individual who has contributed significantly to recent literature in the 1980s and 1990s is Stephen J. Wager, an army officer and West Point professor (retired) who began writing on the Mexican military as a graduate student at Stanford University. His unpublished paper, "The Mexican Military 1968–1978: A Decade of Change" (June 1979), was followed by an excellent dissertation. Helped by personal insights gained as an exchange officer at the Escuela Superior de Guerra, Wager continued writing unpublished papers at West Point, finally publishing his ideas in "Basic Characteristics of the Modern Mexican Military," 87–105, in the Ronfeldt collection, and throughout the text of Robert Wesson's *The Latin American Military* (Westport, Conn.: Greenwood Press, 1986).

The best overviews of the military's political role in the 1980s are Phyllis Greene Walker's "The Modern Mexican Military: Political Influence and Institutional Interests in the 1980s" (M.A. thesis, American University, 1987) which, like the works of Wager, Ackroyd and Dziedzic, includes some interviews with Mexican officers, and Edward J. William's "The Evolution of the Mexican Military and Its Implications for Civil-Military Relations," in *Mexico's Political Stability: The Next Five Years*, ed. Roderic Ai Camp (Boulder,

Colo.: Westview Press, 1986), 143–165. A Ph.D. dissertation by Richard James Kilroy, Jr., "Crisis and Legitimacy: the Role of the Mexican Military in Politics and Society" (University of Virginia, 1990), provides a broad overview.

The number of high caliber broadly focused essays on Mexican civil-military relations increased in the 1990s. These include Martin Edwin Anderson's "Civil-Military Relations and Internal Security in Mexico: the Undone Reform," in *The Challenge of Institutional Reform in Mexico*, ed. Riordan Roett (Boulder, Colo.: Lynne Rienner, 1995), 155–180, and Monica Serrano's more developed "The Armed Branch of the State: Civil Military Relations in Mexico," *Journal of Latin American Studies* 27, no. 2 (1995), 423–448. My own work, capturing various moments in civil-military relations during the last ten years, include "Civilian Supremacy in Mexico: The Case of a Post-Revolutionary Military," in *Military Intervention and Withdrawal*, ed. Constantine P. Danopoulous (London: Routledge, 1991), "Mexico," in *The Political Role of the Military, An International Handbook*, eds. Constantine P. Danopoulous and Cynthia Watson (Westport: Greenwood Press, 1996), 271–282; "Militarizing Mexico, Where Is the Officer Corps Going?," *Policy Paper on the Americas* (Washington, D.C.: CSIS, 1999); and "Mexico's Armed Forces, Marching to a Democratic Tune?," in *The Dilemma of Mexican Politics in Transition*, ed. Kevin Middlebrook (London: Institute of Latin American Studies, University of London, 2004), 353–372.

Considerable literature, some of it outstanding, also exists on specific facets of the Mexican military. Enlisted ranks and the air force and navy are neglected altogether. For army/air force officer corps composition, background, and education, some work is available. My own early studies of officers represented in "Mexican Military Leadership in Statistical Perspective since the 1930s," in *Statistical Abstract of Latin America*, vol. 20, eds. James W. Wilkie and Peter Reich (Los Angeles: Latin American Center Publications, University of California, Los Angeles, 1980), 595–606, is the first empirical collection of data about career army and political-military officers. This was followed by my "Generals and Politicians in Mexico: A Preliminary Comparison," 107–155, in the Ronfeldt collection. The most helpful comparative work, suggesting certain similarities in military cultures across boundaries, is Maureen Mylander's *The Generals* (New York: Dial Press, 1974), which remains the most detailed analysis of United States generals. James J. Dowd, "Connected to Society: The Political Beliefs of U.S. Army Generals," *Armed Forces and Society* 27 no. 3 (Spring 2001): 343–372, adds wonderful insights from 62 generals in the 1990s.

Other excellent empirical studies on top United States officers, in some cases with comparable data on political or business elites, include W. Lloyd

Warner et al., *The Federal Executive: A Study of the Social and Personal Characteristics of the Civilian and Military Leaders of the United States* (New Haven, Conn.: Yale University Press, 1963); Bruce M. Russell, "Political Perspectives of U.S. Military and Business Elites," *Armed Forces and Society* I (Fall 1974): 79–108; R. F. Schloemer and G. E. Myers, "Making It at the Air Force Academy, Who Stays? Who Succeeds?" in *The Changing World of the American Military*, ed. Franklin D. Margiotta (Boulder, Colo.: Westview Press, 1978), 321–344; and Charles H. Castes, "America's New Officer Corps," in *The American Military*, ed, Martin Oppenheimer (New Brunswick, N.J.: Transaction, 1971), 46–53.

For a comparative perspective from the Third World, the best survey remains George Kourvetaris and Betty Dobratz, *Social Origins and Political Orientations of Officer Corps in a World Perspective* (Denver, Colo.: Graduate School of International Studies, University of Denver, 1973). The best comparable Latin America country study of officer corps composition is the work of Frank D. McCann, whose preliminary findings appear in his "Brazilian Officers Biography Project," Latin American Studies Association, Miami, December 1989 and some of which are reported throughout his *Soldiers of the Patria, A History of the Brazilian Army, 1889–1937* (Palo Alto, Calif.: Stanford University Press, 2004).

The subject of professionalization has led to some important scholarship. The most useful places to start are with Serge Guimond, "Encounter and Metamorphosis: The Impact of Military Socialization on Professional Values," *Applied Psychology: An International Review* 44, no. 3 (1995), 251–275, and Sarkesian, "An Empirical Reassessment of Military Professionalism," in *The Changing World of the American Military*, ed. Franklin D. Margiotta (Boulder, Colo.: Westview Press, 1978), 37–56. The most comprehensive general institutional analysis, with many relevant insights, is Marion J. Levy, Jr.'s classic "Armed Forces Organization," in *The Military and Modernization*, ed. Henry Bienen (Chicago: Aldine-Atherton, 1971), 41–78. For a Latin American perspective, the most relevant political/historical analysis is Frederick M. Nunn's outstanding "The South American Military and (Re) Democratization: Professional Thought and Self-Perception," *Journal of Inter-American Studies and World Affairs* 37, no. 2 (Summer 1995): 1–56. This is a work unduplicated by any other source. For the historical controversy about professionalization, a question introduced by Alfred Stepan, see his reevaluation, *Rethinking Military Politics, Brazil and the Southern Cone* (Princeton, N.J.: Princeton University Press, 1988); a critique of his initial ideas, in John Markoff and Silvio Baretta, "Professional Ideology and Military Activism in Brazil: Critique of a Thesis of Alfred Stepan," *Comparative Politics* 17 (January 1985): 175–191; and the excellent study by Christopher Brogan, "Military Higher Education and the Emergence of 'New Professionalism': Some Consequences for Civil-Military Relations in Latin America," *Army Quarterly and Defense Journal*, no. 112 (January 1982): 20–30. My own work on this topic includes: "The Education and Training of the Mexican Officer Corps," in *Forging the Sword, Selecting, Educating, and Training Cadets and Junior Officers in the Modern World*, vol. 5, Military Historical Symposium Series, United States Air Force Academy, ed. Elliot V. Converse (Chicago: Imprint Publications, 1998), 336–346. Aside from Ackroyd's essays, the only other work which provides important insights into Mexican military professionalization is that of Daniel Mora. This work is based on his fifteen-month experience with forty-four company grade officers at the Escuela Superior de Guerra. It was presented at the Rocky Mountain States Latin American Conference, Tucson, 1984, as "Profile of the Mexican Company Grade Officers," and supplemented by the unpublished reports of other U.S. officers assigned to Mexico. For the impact of international training, especially in the United States, see the comprehensive analysis by Jennifer M. Taw, "The Effectiveness of Training International Military Students in Internal Defense and Development," (Santa Monica, Calif.: Rand Corporation, 1993), 15–22. John A. Cope also addresses this issue in his *International Military Education and Training: An Assessment* (Washington, D.C.: Institute for National Strategic Studies, 1995).

It is difficult to come by data of any sort regarding Mexican military weaponry, internal budget expenditures, salaries, and pensions. This has changed dramatically with the implementation of the transparency law in Mexico in June 2003. Salary information and annual budget reports are now available directly from the secretary of national defense and navy websites (www.sedena.gob.mx and www.semar.gob.mx). A complete list of military units, transport, and weaponry is also available in General Vega Garcia's testimony before congress, October 13, 2004. For other information, one has to make a request through the governmental transparency website. This can be done either through the respective military sites, or directly through the transparency site, www.informacionpublica.gob.mx. For some projections that put Mexico into a larger comparative context in the past see Charles Wolf, Jr., *Long-Term Economic and Military Trends, 1950–2010* (Santa Monica: Rand Corporation, 1989); Rodney W. Jones and Steven A. Hildreth, eds., *Emerging Powers, Defense and Security in the Third World* (New York: Praeger, 1980), 371–399; Lind L. Reif "Seizing Control: Latin American Military Motives, Capabilities, and Risks," *Armed Forces and Society* 10 (Summer 1984): 563–582, and Merilee S. Grindle, "Civil Military Relations and Budgetary Politics in Latin America," *Armed Forces and Society* 13 (Winter 1987): 255–275. For Mexico budgetary information and equipment specifically, see George Grayson, *Mexico's Armed Forces, A Factbook*, Military Studies Report

(Washington, D.C.: CSIS, 1999). One analyst, Vicente Ernesto Pérez Mendoza, a Mexican naval officer, also has examined the potential influence of the armed forces in Mexico's economy in his M.A. thesis, "The Role of the Armed Forces in the Mexican Economy in the 1980s" (Naval Graduate School, Monterey, California, 1981).

Two of the topics associated with the Mexican military receiving the most attention in recent years are its ties to the United States and its role in foreign policy. The subject can be generally placed in a broader regional setting through J. Samuel Fitch, "The Decline of US Military Influence in Latin America," *Journal of Inter-American Studies and World Affairs* (Summer 1993), 1–49. The most comprehensive and thorough discussion of these issues can be found in John A. Cope, "In Search of Convergence: U.S.-Mexican Military Relations into the Twenty-first Century," in *Strategy and Security in U.S.-Mexican Relations Beyond the Cold War*, eds. John Bailey and Sergio Aguayo (La Jolla, Calif.: Center for U.S.-Mexican Studies, UCSD, 1996), 179–209. On border issues which sometimes involve the armed forces, see Peter Andreas, *Border Games, Policing the U.S. Mexico Divide* (Ithaca, N.Y.: Cornell University Press, 2000). A superb analysis, focused on national security, can be found in Donald E. Schulz's "Between a Rock and a Hard Place: the United States, Mexico and the Agony of National Security," United States Army War College, SSI, Carlisle Barracks, Pennsylvania, 1997. The broadest, most insightful historical source on Mexico's armed forces' relationship with the United States is Donald F. Harrison's "United States-Mexican Military Collaboration during World War II" (Ph.D. dissertation, Georgetown University, Washington, D.C., 1976). The best general analysis of its role in foreign policy remains Edward J. Williams's "The Evolution of the Mexican Military and Its Implications for Civil-Military Relations," in *Mexico's Political Stability: The Next Five Years*, ed. Roderic Ai Camp (Boulder, Colo.: Westview Press, 1986), 143–158. In addition, Williams has written several articles on the military's role in Mexico's Central American policy in the 1980s. These include "Mexico's Central American Policy: National Security Considerations," in *Rift and Revolution: The Central American Imbroglio*, ed. Howard J. Wiarda (Washington, D.C: American Enterprise Institute, 1984), 303–328. Equally valuable from this time period is Caesar Sereseres's "The Mexican Military Looks South," in Ronfeldt's *Modern Mexican Military: A Reassessment*, 201–213.

The subject which has attracted the most scholarship on the Mexican armed forces, however, is its national security roles. The best recent comprehensive work is that of Mexican security expert, Sergio Aguayo Quezada, titled "The Uses, Misuses, and Challenges of Mexican National Security: 1946–1990," in *Mexico, In Search of Security*, eds. Bruce M. Bagley and Sergio Aguayo (New Brunswick, N.J.: Transaction Publishers, 1993), 97–142. Theoretically, the best presentation is that of Luis Herrera-Lasso and Guadalupe González G., "Reflections on the Use of the Concept of National Security," 339–359, in the Bagley and Aguayo volume. Equally outstanding in providing a comprehensive framework is Manuel Carrillo Poblano's, "Cambios y retos en el sistema de seguridad nacional mexicano," Unpublished manuscript, 1991. Other useful essays from the 1980s include: Olga Pellicer de Brody "National Security in Mexico: Traditional Notions and New Preoccupations," in *U.S.-Mexico Relations, Economic and Social Aspects*, ed. Clark W. Reynolds and Carlos Tello (Stanford, Calif.: Stanford University Press, 1983), 181–192. The most helpful article describing the changing missions in the 1980s is that of Alden M. Cunningham, "Mexico's National Security in the 1980s/1990s," 157–178, in Ronfeldt's collection.

National security missions related to guerrilla warfare, suppression of political leftists, and human rights abuses, has received significant attention since 1990. Sergio Aguayo has provided a wealth of new archival information on the military's actual role in the 1968 student massacre, clarifying many events from that period. See his *1968, los archivos de la violencia* (Mexico: Grijalbo, 1998). A work which provides excellent documents and the point of view of the then secretary of nacional defense, is Julio Scherer García and Carlos Monsiváis, *Parte de guerra, Tlatelolco 1968* (Mexico: Aguilar, 1999). Aguayo complements his other fine work with an original analysis and history of the Mexican intelligence service, in *La charola, una historia de los servicios de inteligencia en México* (Mexico: Grijalbo, 2001). A broad picture of nacional security issues is provided by Raúl Benítez Manaut and Stephen J. Wager in "National Security and Armed Forces in Mexico: Challenges and Scenarios at the End of the Century," Latin American Program, Woodrow Wilson International Center for Scholars, October 1998.

For the Zapatista uprising, with a focus on the military's role, one of the most useful resources is José Luis Piñeyro, "Chiapas: la seguridad nacional y la corta guerra," Latin American Studies Association, Washington, D.C., September 1995. For an equally insightful interpretation, see Stephen J. Wager and Donald E. Schulz, *The Awakening: the Zapatista Revolt and its Implications for Civil-Military Relations and the Future of Mexico*, United States Army War College, SSI, Carlisle Barracks, Pennsylvania, 1994. Finally, David Ronfeldt, et al. have added a unique strategic look in their highly original and provocative *The Zapatista Social Netwar in Mexico* (Santa Monica: Rand, 1998), which was prepared for the US Army. The emergence of small, violent guerrilla groups has not received equal scholarly attention. The most comprehensive analysis of the Popular Revolutionary Army can be found in Mark R. Wrighte, "The Real Mexican Terrorists: A Group Profile of the *Pop-*

ular Revolutionary Army (ERP)," *Studies in Conflict and Terrorism* 25 (2002), 207–225, which includes their original communiqué. Equally informative are Graham H. Turbiville, Jr., "Mexico's Multimission Force for Internal Security," *Military Review* (July–August 2000), 41–49, and "Mexico's Other Insurgents," *Military Review* (June–July 1997), 81–89.

For human rights abuses and guerrilla groups, see the Canadian Immigration and Refugee Board, "Mexico: Armed Insurgent Groups," Research Directorate Documentation, Ottawa, Canada, May 1997. For the military specifically, see Human Rights Watch, "Mexico, Military Injustice," 13, no. 4 (December 2001), as well as their "Torture, 'Disappearance,' and Extra Judicial Execution in Mexico," January 1999, and *Implausible Deniability, State Responsibility for Rural Violence in Mexico* (New York: Human Rights Watch, 1997). Amnesty International also explores this issue in depth, focusing on the public security structure and the new legal system, in *Mexico: Justice Betrayed: Torture in the Judicial System* (2001), www.amensty.org/library. On the legal front, which has attracted little attention, Anthony Pereira provides a comparative analysis of military justice in "Virtual Legality, Authoritarian Legacies and the Reform of Military Justice in Brazil, the Southern Cone, and Mexico," *Comparative Political Studies* 34 (No. 5, June 2001), 555–574.

Drug trafficking, as a major national security issue, has attracted increased scholarly attention. The best historical account of the evolution of this issue is that of Richard B. Craig, "Mexican Narcotics Traffic: Binational Security Implications," in *The Latin American Narcotics Trade and U.S. National Security*, ed. Donald J. Mabry (Westport, Conn.: Greenwood Press, 1989), 27–41. Equally perceptive on the evolution of this issue from a Mexican perspective is Jorge Chabat's "Seguridad nacional y narcotráfico: vínculos reales e imaginarios," *Política y Gobierno* 1, no. 1 (enero–junio 1994): 97–123. For the Mexican military's role in this nacional security mission, see two detailed analyses. The first is by Raúl Benítez Manaut, "Containing Armed Groups, Drug Trafficking, and Organized Crime in Mexico, the Role of the Military," in *Organized Crime and Democratic Governability: Mexico and the U.S.-Mexican Borderlands*, eds. John Bailey and Roy Godson (Pittsburgh, Penn.: University of Pittsburgh Press, 2000), 126–160. The second is Jorge Luis Sierra Guzmán's "Mexico's Military in the War on Drugs," *Drug War Monitor* (Washington, D.C.: WOLA, April 2003). For the U.S. role, see David R. Mares insightful "U.S. Drug Policy and Mexican Civil-Military Relations," *Crime, Law & Social Change* 40 (July 2003), 61–75. For two different perspectives, see Stefan J. Wray's MA thesis, which is excellent on information warfare, "The Drug War and Information Warfare in Mexico," University of Texas, Austin, August 1997; and Patrick O'Day, who explores the army's own role in drug trafficking, in "The Mexican Army as Cartel," *Journal of Contemporary Criminal Justice* 17, no. 3 (August 2001): 278–295.

Media sources are few indeed, but this has begun to change in the last few years. This pattern is explained by former reporter Sallie Hughes in her "The Pen and the Sword: Mexican Mass Media Coverage of the Armed Forces, 1986–1996," unpublished paper, Tulane University, 1999, the only essay of its type ever written about the Mexican armed forces. A small number of original, investigative articles have appeared in *Proceso, Milenio,* and other magazines, including revealing interviews with top defense officials. For example, journalists provided the best information on the national defense ministry succession in 2000. Newspapers do not cover the military with any regularity.

Much of the original material on Mexico's armed forces in this new work comes from unpublished Mexican sources. The internet has expanded these dramatically. Today, there is no question that the most comprehensive source for information on the armed forces is their own transparency programs, referred to above. Most of the relevant legislation, because of such requests, is now available on the defense and navy websites or through links to relevant legislation. Also, the National Security Archives website, available at George Washington University, maintains a section on Mexico which includes numerous valuable declassified documents from the U.S. Embassy and the Defense Intelligence Agency. The official army and air force magazine, *Revista de Ejército y Fuerza Aérea,* is critical to any analysis of the Mexican military. Historical volumes are found in the Library of Congress collection, but the only complete set of recent volumes in the United States are located at the International Relations Library, University of California, San Diego. This journal provides information irregularly on promotions, reassignments, sometimes biographical data, and, most importantly, the philosophy of the officer corps and its educational program. Equally important for details on budget and weaponry, as well as promotions to general, are the Secretaria de Defensa Nacional *Memorias* and its antecedents. The Nettie Lee Benson Latin American Library, University of Texas, maintains the best collection of such documents. To gain a much better understanding of elite political and military relations, especially during the transition years of the 1940s and 1990s and 2000s, the yearly Senate *Memorias* are invaluable. The most recent documents are on line through the Senate website, and can be partially searched for discussion of military affairs. The *Memorias* also provide a complementary promotion record above the rank of colonel. In the last decade, in addition to the promotion, the record contains the individual's graduation date from the Heroico Colegio Militar and the Escuela Superior de Guerra.

In addition, the Secretariat of National Defense itself, or through another publisher, has provided several essential sources. The first of these, José María Dávila, *El ejército de la revolución* (Mexico: SLYSE, 1938), contains important promotion data, biographies, and information on zone commands. It is available at the Colegio de México. Uncirculating, but in the Bancroft Collection, University of California, Berkeley, are the *Memoria gráfica del cincuentenario de la reapertura del Heroico Colegio Militar* (Mexico: SHCP, 1970), including detailed information on graduating classes, instructors, and directors of Mexico's West Point; and Félix Galván López, *Escuela Superior de Guerra, 1932-1982* (Mexico: SDN, 1982), which presents the names and photographs off all the Higher War College graduates from its founding through 1982, as well as all the graduates of the Higher Arms curriculum. The Navy has provided an equally important source of data in Enrique Cárdenas de la Peña, *Educación Naval en México*, Vol. 2 (Mexico: Secretaria de Marina, 1967), which includes a detailed listing of graduates from each class at the Escuela Naval Militar, the navy's equivalent of the Heroico Colegio Militar. The Navy has issued a *Reseña fotográfica del Centro de Estudios Superiores Navales, 1970-2000* (Mexico: Secretaria de Marina, 2000) which offers complete lists of graduates from the many different staff and command and specialty war college courses. A valuable semi-official source is the history of the Military Medical School by a leading graduate and politically connected physician, Jesús Lozoya Solís, *La Escuela Médico Militar de México* (Mexico, 1977), which includes a comment on nearly every graduate from the school.

Collective Biographical Data

The collective biographical data have been acquired during 35 years of research in newspapers, magazines, government organization manuals, biographical directories, interviews, secondary literature and the internet. *The Mexican Military Biography* data bank now includes complete biographies for 670 officers who have reached brigade (two star) or division rank (three star), or their naval and air force equivalents, most of whom were at the highest rank and were on active duty after 1940. It is probably the most complete and up to date data set on the top officers in any Third World country today. A complete examination of promotion records suggests that the data bank provides a broad and even sample of leading generals and admirals from each of the years covered by the study, including those individuals who have held influential staff positions and commanded the most important naval and army/air force units. The most complete biographies are those where assignments are taken from the official personnel files. Nearly half of the biographies in this study include such information, available from published official records or military journals. However, despite recent protestations to the contrary, the Mexican military's secretiveness extends to biographical information. Even in recent official biographies on their website (www.sedena.gob.mx), or in such government sponsored publications as the *Diccionario biográfico del gobierno mexicano* 1984, 1987, 1989, 1993 and 1994, the majority of officers have purposely left out their military assignments, including zone commands and early military education, and the relevant dates, despite official requests for the information. The government discontinued official directories after 1994, making the task of acquiring accurate information all that more difficult. Their service records (hojas de servicios), which have appeared in recent senate memorias, only contain the date they joined the service, and their attendance at the military academy.

These limitations mean that data are most complete for date of entry into the service, promotions, geographic origin, military training in Mexico and abroad, and all foreign assignments. Data are also fairly complete for staff assignments above the level of department head, especially since 1947, which have been obtained through multiple transparency requests from the navy and the army. We also have complete information on their military education, again from official records and transparency requests. The most difficult to obtain data are, of course, data on social background, including parents' occupation and ties to other leaders. These data contain the most complete information ever published on the social backgrounds of Mexican officers, but it is probable that lower socioeconomic backgrounds are slightly under-reported in official biographies because a person is less likely to include a father's occupation if it is nonprofessional.

In addition to this military biographical data set, two other data sets provided the information for many of the empirical comparisons cited in this study. The two sources are part of the *Mexican Political Biography Project*. The first, covering the years 1884 through 1991, provides information about political-military officers and civilian politicians who served in top national positions. Comparable data sets now exist for Mexican intellectuals and leading entrepreneurs from the 1920s through 1993. Data on politicians and political military officers is analyzed extensively and from a generational perspective in my *Political Recruitment across Two Centuries, Mexico, 1884–1991*. The most recent data set is a collective biography of the period from 1970 through 2000. This source explores comparatively the backgrounds and experiences of the most influential Mexican politicians, clergy, intellectuals, capitalists, and military officers, including their transformation under changing economic and political models. That data is explored comparatively in my *Mexico's Mandarins, Crafting a Power Elite for the 21st Century*. These data sets were not available for use in the prior book, *Generals in the Palacio, the Military in Modern Mexico*. Many of the biographies of older military and political figures are now available from the author's *Mexican Political Biographies, 1935–1993* (Austin, Tex.: University of Texas Press, 1995) and Mexican Political Biographies, 1884–1934 (Austin, Tex.: University of Texas Press, 1991).

Index

Ackroyd, William S., 341
Age-in-grade limits, 206
Age limits for military service, 21, 45
Aging, of political-military officers, 48–49
Aguayo, Sergio, 268
Aguilar Zinzer, Adolfo, 249
Air force, foreign training of personnel, 195, 198
Air Tactics, 169
Alemán, President Miguel
   abuse of military promotions, 207–209, 213
   Federal Security Department, establishment of, 104–105
   military promotion rates, 210–212
   military representation in political office, reduction in, 75–76
   presidency of, 25–27
   PRI and, 90
Alliances
   between civil population and military, 17
   between political parties and military, 141–142
Amaro, Joaquín, 208, 233
Angel Godínez, General Miguel, 253
Anti-drug programs. *See* Drug trafficking, anti-drug programs
Applied schools, 169
Arévalo Gardoqui, General Juan, 167, 224
abuse of military promotions, 215–216
Army and Air Force Development Program (1995), 123
   decentralization of the command hierarchy, 126
   Escuela Superior de Guerra, changes at, 200
   kinship ties, 234
   zone commanders, role in military training, 153
Army medical corps, channel for political-military communication, 78–79
Assistant secretary of national defense, 236–237
Attaché assignments. *See* Diplomatic missions
Authentic Party of the Mexican Revolution (PARM), 90
Authoritarianism, factors affecting, 65
Autonomy of military
   protection from civilian scrutiny, 7–8, 10
   subordination to civilian control, 11, 271–276
Avila Camacho, General Manuel
   advisory role of military, preference for, 22
   civilian supremacy during presidency, 24–25
   military promotion rates, 210–212
Azteca directive, 261

Bacilio Gómez, Lt. Colonel Hildegardo, 266–267
Ballesteros Prieto, General Mario, student suppression at Tlatelolco Plaza, 29–31
Banks, nationalization of, 35
Baz, Gustavo, 78–79
Benítez Manaut, Raúl, 253, 339–340
Bermúdez Dávila, General Carlos Humberto, 231
Bland, Douglas, theory of shared responsibility, 2
Border security, 269, 345
Brazil
   generational division in military, 161
   Higher War College, 174, 177
Brigada Blanca (White Brigade), 32
Budget, military
   oversight of, 138, 258–261
   professionalization level and, 153–154

Cabinet agencies
   military officers in, 76, 77
   on national security, 81–82, 106
Calles, President Plutarco Elias, 20
   and Colegio Militar, 19
   professional requirements for military officers, 45
Cárdenas, Cuauhtémoc, 36
   political activities of, 96, 97
   supporter of Henríquez Guzman, 92–93
Cárdenas, President Lázaro, 19
   enlisted ranks, institutionalization of, 54
   and limits on military career spans, 45
   military promotion rates, 210–212
   and mustangs, disappearance of, 55
   political-military combat veteran, 46–47
   professionalization of military, 20–21, 206
   restructuring of political party, role in, 89
   secretary of national defense during World War II, 25
Cardona Marino, Arturo, 214, 231
Career military officers. *See* Orthodox professional officers
Carillo Olea, Jorge, 106–107
Caste mentality in the military
   background variables of military recruits and, 43–44
   elimination of, 7, 11
   and political-military officers, 51
Castrejón, Adrian, 208
Catholic Church, societal attitudes on role of, 141
Center for Army Air Force Studies, 169–170
Center for Hemispheric Defense Studies, 198
Center for National Security and Investigation, 262
Center for Research and National Security (CISEN), 106
Center for the Planning of Drug Control (CENDRO), 112, 262
Centro de Estudios Superiores Navales, 152, 179–181
   teachers, benefits for, 186–187
   training during 1950s and 1960s, 152
Centro de Instrución de Jefes y Oficiales, 54
Cervantes Aguirre, General Enrique, 215–216, 248, 249
   background of appointees of, 228
Chiapas, rebellion in (1994), 37–39. *See also* Zapatista movement
Chief of Staff, presidential, 230–231
China, social revolution in, 4
Civic actions by the military, 100–102
Civilian supremacy
   Avila Camacho, during presidency of, 24–25
   effectiveness, limited, 9
   establishment of, 15

Index 355

Mexican Revolution, role of, 40
military presidents, attributed to, 40
and political-military officer graduates, 52
Porfirio Díaz, influence of, 16
of post-revolutionary era, 5, 18–21
and socialization process in the military, 130–131
Civil leadership
budgetary control of military, 138
declining respect for, 127
dependence on military, 41
education of, 52
military affairs, non-intervention in, 11
at military institutions, 105, 107
military leadership, shared attributes with, 161
responsibilities of, 3
Civil society
Church involvement in politics, views on, 141
confidence in military, 134–136
democratic institutions, 246–247, 250, 273–274
drug trafficking, response to military control of, 115–116
isolation of the military from, 133–134, 247, 250, 255–256
militarization of, 100–101
participation in government of military, views on, 139–141
Colegio Aire, admission procedure, 67–68
Colegio de Defensa Nacional, 58, 59, 168
civil-military relationships, improvement of, 86–89, 190
curriculum of, 187, 189
enrollment, 187–188
public servants in, 98
Colegio Militar. *See also* Heroico Colegio Militar

and Calles, during presidency of, 19
Porfirio Díaz, during presidency of, 17
Colombia, provision of military training for Mexico, 198–199
Colosio, Luis Donaldo, assassination of, 217, 221–222
Combat experience, influence on military advancement, 224–226, 237
Command hierarchy, decentralization of, 126
Communications, military specialty of, 57
Compadrazco, 213
Compensation in the military. *See* Military salaries and retirement pay
Conference of American Armies, 145
Constitutional Army, 18
Constitution of Mexico, responsibilities of military, 101
Cooptation of the military, partisan politics and, 91
Corruption, drug-driven, 112, 113–115, 116–117, 146–147, 263
Cristero rebellion (1920s), 62
Cuenca Díaz, General Hermenegildo, 46, 164

Decentralization of military, 126–127
Obregón, during presidency of, 18–19
Defense specialists, civilian
recruiting and hiring of, 142–143
reduced role of, 85–86, 88
shortage of, 8
Democratic Revolutionary Party (PRD), 273
military representation in, 94
Democratization process, role of Tlatelolco Plaza in, 33
Department heads, 235–236

Díaz. *See* Díaz Ordaz, President Gustavo; Porfirio Díaz, President José de la Cruz
Díaz Ordaz, President Gustavo, 231
  military promotion rates, 210–212, 219
  and student suppression at Tlatelolco Plaza, 28–31
Diplomatic missions
  influence on military advancement, 232–233
  Mexican military attachés, 235–236
  political-military communication, role in, 81–82
  U.S. military attachés, 144
Directorate of Federal Security, 26
Disaster relief, role of military, 102, 138
Discipline
  in military academies, 10
  socialization process, instilled during, 127–128
Dishonesty. *See* Corruption; Professional dishonesty
Dissension within armed forces, 253, 266–267
  over promotions and advancement, 240–243
  public disclosure of, 122–123, 128
Diversity, of military and political leadership and education, 154
Drug trafficking, 261–262, 269
  anti-drug programs, 36, 37
  Cananea Corporation and control of, 37
  civilian response to military intervention, 115–116, 135–136
  and corruption in civil and military agencies, 112, 113–115, 116–117, 146–147, 263
  crop production, eradication of, 110, 111, 112, 114, 115
  and human rights abuses, 264–265
  literary work on role of military, 347–348
  de la Madrid administration, control under, 36
  militarization of control efforts, effects of, 117, 261–262
  military resources, use of, 111, 112, 146
  and military role in foreign policy, 269
  reservations of military of its role, 112, 115
  Salinas administration, control under, 37
  United States, effect in controlling of, 13, 111, 145–146
Dziedzic, Michael J., 341

Echeverría, President Luis
  military promotion rates, 210–212, 219–220
  presidency of, 33–34
  and student suppression at Tlatelolco Plaza, 29
Education
  advancement, military, 223–224
  authoritarianism, effect on, 65
  of civilian political leaders, 52
  civilians, in military academies, 190–193
  discipline in military academies, 10
  and diversity of military and political leadership, 154
  foreign military training (*see* Foreign military education)
  mentor relationships, 162
  military institutions (*see individual institution*)
  military sociology and strategy, lack of preparation in, 8
  of mustangs, 54–55
  of navy officer corps, 162
  networking interlocks and, 86–89
  non-military institutions, higher education of officers, 152

of political-military officers, 51–52
of politicians, foreign training, 186
preparatory training for military, 157–158
private institutions, 165–166
and professionalism, literary work on, 343–344
socialization, effect on, 154–155
teachers, military officers as, 155–156
U. S. military, influence of, 13, 25, 144–145
war colleges, and interventionist tendencies, 173
Ejército Zapatista de Liberación Nacional (EZLN). *See* Zapatista movement
Election violence, during Salinas administration, 37
Entrepreneurial leadership, apolitical nature of, 89–90
Escuela Constitucionalista Médico Militar, 168
Escuela Militar de Transmisiones, 168
Escuela Naval Militar, 170–171
Escuela Náutica Mercante of Mazatlán, 171
Escuela Superior de Guerra, 58, 59
  alums in defense posts, 179
  attrition rates, 181–182, 183, 184
  benefits of attendance, 175, 179, 196
  civilians, critical attitude toward, 184–185
  curriculum of, 160, 176–178
  enrollment levels, 178
  establishment of, 174, 176
  graduates, data on, 175–176
  internal national defense document, changes following, 200
  interservice rivalries, potential for, 181
  military families, officers from, 70–71
  political-military officer graduates, 52
  post-revolutionary generation, training of, 151
  principles of, 124–125
  socialization process at, 182
  socioeconomic composition of graduates, 67–68
  student cheating, 183–184
  teachers, benefits for, 186
  training during 1950s and 1960s, 152
EZLN. *See* Zapatista movement

Factionalism, military, 12, 252–253, 275
  during Zapatista movement, 38
Familial relationships in the military, 83–86, 104–105, 233–234
  in Federal Security Department, 104–105
Federal Army of Mexico, after Mexican Revolution of 1910, 18
Federal bureaucracy, military officers in, 48
Federal Judicial Police, 262
Federal Preventative Police, 118
Federal Security Department, 104–105
Federation of Peoples Party of Mexico, 92
Finer, S.E., 336
Foreign military education, 159, 174
  and career success, 195–196, 224, 229
  for naval officers, 194
  during post-revolutionary years, 193
  received in the United States, 193–194
Foreign policy, 345
  military influence on, 131–132, 268–271
Fort Leavenworth, Staff and Command School, 197
Fox, President Vicente, 245, 247–250
  age structure of leaders and, 49, 60
  civil-military agenda of, 254
  dissatisfaction of military during presidency of, 123, 129
  drug-related corruption during presidency of, 116–118
  and drug war, 262

Fox, President Vicente (*continued*)
  foreign military training during presidency, 195
  military officers in cabinet, 76
  military promotion rates, 210–212
  military role, expansion of, 116, 117–118, 262–264
  praise for the military, 7
  presidential logistics and security, role of military in, 95
  Vega García, selection as national defense secretary, 248–250
French Intervention (1862–1867), 16

Gallardo, José Francisco, 216, 222–223, 265–266
Galván, General Félix, abuse of military promotions, 215–216
García Barragán, General Marcelino, 215–216, 231
  career of, 46
  and student suppression at Tlatelolco Plaza, 28–31
García Elizalde, General José A., 239
García Reyes, Brigade General Domiro R., 48, 217
Garfias Magaña, General Luis, 215, 260
Gastelum Salcido, Division General Juan José, 224
General Directorate of Investigation and National Security, 105
Geographical composition of officer corps, 51, 56–57
  orthodox professional officers, 60–64
Godínez Bravo, General Miguel Angel, 230
Governorships, military officers in, 76, 77, 239
Guerilla warfare, 263–264, 269
  and censorship, military, 108
  and drug trafficking, 112
  first reference in military publications, 103–104
  literary work on military involvement, 346
  as source of combat experience, 225–226
Guinart López, Modesto A., 238
Gulf region, representation in military, 62
Gutiérrez Barrios, Fernando, 104, 107
Gutiérrez Oropeza, Colonel Luis, 231
  and student suppression at Tlatelolco Plaza, 29–31
Gutiérrez Rebollo, Division General Jesús, 263
  and drug-related corruption, 113–114, 126–127

Halcones, Los, 34
Henríquez Guzmán, General Miguel, presidential candidacy of, 27, 92–93
Heroica Escuela Naval Militar, 152, 170
Heroico Colegio Militar, 59
  admission procedure, 67–68
  curriculum, 160
  declining importance of, 168
  enlisted soliders as cadets, 54–55
  enrollment levels, 156, 157
  military families, cadets from, 69
  Porfirio Díaz, during presidency of, 150
  preparatory education, role in, 157
  recruitment function of, 163–164, 166–167
  socioeconomic composition of graduates, 67–68
  subordination to authority, goal of, 125
Homogeneity of leadership, 7
  and discipline during training, 10
Huerta, Victoriano, 218
Human rights violations
  arbitration, suppression of, 222–223, 264
  drug trafficking, related to, 113

guerilla activity, related to, 109
literary work on military involvement, 346
in the 1970s, 9
School of the Americas training and, 199
Huntington, Samuel P., 336

Institutionalized army, 20
Institutional Revolutionary Party (PRI), 246. *See also* Cuauhtémoc Cárdenas
election of 1988, 36
President Alemán and, 90
Intelligence sharing, between military and civilian agencies, 106, 107
Inter-American Defense College, 197
Internal military matters, non-intervention by civil leadership, 11
Internal security, combination of military and police functions, 26. *See also* National security
Internal suppression, by military forces, 107–110
International Military Education and Training (IMET) funds, 144
International military forces, participation in, 269–270
Ireta Viveros, Division General Félix, 238

Johnson, John J., 338
Juárez, Benito, 16

Kinship ties, 69–71, 233–234
in Federal Security Department, 104–105
Kumate Rodríguez, Jesús, 79

Labastida, Francisco, 249
Labor battalions, 101
Labor unions, military repression of, 26, 27, 108
Lara Preciado, Jesús Armando, 222

Latin America
civil-military relations compared to Mexico, 254, 273
empirical studies of officers, 343
military theory of, 337–338
Leave policy for military officers, 82
Legislative branch of government
budgets for military, oversight of, 258–261
interactions with military, 256–258
military officers in, 76–78
Lerdo de Tejada, Sebastian, 16
Liberal Conservative conflicts (mid-1800s), 16
Limón, Gilberto R., 208
Line officers, 233
López Mateos, President Adolfo,
military promotion rates, 210–212, 219
López Portillo, José, 251, 253, 260
military promotion rates, 210–212, 220–221
presidency of, 34–35
unification of military services concept, 244
Lorenzo Franco, Admiral José Ramón, 232
Los Halcones, 34
Loyalty
of military, 9–10, 19
political, 19

Madero, Francisco (1911–1913), 17
de la Madrid, President Miguel, 260
military promotion rates, 210–212, 220–221
military representation in political office, preference for, 79–80
national security policy, 131
presidency of, 35
Margiotta, Franklin, 213, 340–341
civilian supremacy, 74
Martínez Perea, General Ricardo, 263
McAlister, 229

Media
    control of, 108
    coverage of military, 138–139
    criticism of the military, 39
    literary work on coverage of military, 348
Medical corps, Army. *See* Army medical corps; Military Medical School
Memorias, 348
Mentor-disciple relationships, 162, 234
Mexican military, organizational structure of, 251–254, 237–238
Mexican Revolution (1910s), 3–4
    and centralization of political power, 49–50
    and civilian supremacy, 40
    Federal Army of Mexico, post-revolutionary, 18
    leadership skills, post-revolutionary, 6
    military subordination, concept of, 5
    and peace, desire for, 18
    political office, military representation in, 75
Mexico
    constitution of, 101
    empirical studies of officers, 344–345
    United States, leadership compared with, 164–165
Mexico City
    centralization of military power, 60–62
    earthquake of 1985, 36, 102
    emergency relief by the military, 36
Milenio, internal survey of the army, 123
Militarization of civil society, 100–101
Military and Society in Latin America, The, 338
Military Code of Justice (Mexico), 264
Military expenditures, reduction during presidency of Avila Camacho, 25
Military families, children of. *See* Familial relationships in the military

Military institutions, functions of, 149. *See also individual institution*
Military intervention
    citizen values concerning, 6, 115–116, 135–136
    professionalism and, 11
Military leadership
    civil leadership, shared attributes with, 161
    civil population, alliances with, 17
    family ties in networking, 69–71
    homogeneity, education and, 154
    political leadership, distance from, 64–65, 71
    positive recognition by citizens, 136
    social inferiority, perception of, 64, 71
    social problems, homogeneity in attitudes towards, 88
    socioeconomic composition of, 66–68, 70
    sources of contact with political leadership, 72
    stability of office, 88
    teaching, role in, 155–156
    United States, trained in, 144
Military Medical School, channel for political contacts, 79
Military officers
    leave policies for, 82
    mustangs, 53–57
    types of, 44–45
Military pay. *See* Military salaries and retirement pay
Military professionalism, 10–11, 233
    Alemán, during presidency of, 25–27
    attributes of, 122
    Cárdenas, as secretary of national defense during World War II, 25
    Cárdenas, under presidency of, 21
    and class linkages, 123
    historic expansion of, 40–41
    independence from the United States, desire for, 143–144
    literary work on, 336, 343

Index

and military budget, 153–154
in the navy, 85
Porfirio Díaz, during presidency of, 17
restructuring of the military, 33, 38–39
techniques of improvement, 21
United States, assistance from, 25
during Zedillo administration, 194–195
Military rebellions, of the 1920s, 20
Military repression of civilians, 26, 27
student suppression at Tlatelolco Plaza, 28–31
Military salaries and retirement pay, 243, 261
moonlighting, effect on, 80
Military theory, literary work in
border issues, related to, 345
foreign policy, related to, 345
guerilla warfare, related to, 346–347
human rights violations, related to, 346–347
on Latin America, 337–338
of Mexico, 338–342
national security, related to, 345–346
professionalism, 343–344
Sarkesian, Samuel P., 1, 336
in Third World countries, 337, 343
Miranda Sánchez, Roberto, 214, 231
Modified Equilibrium Model of civil-military relations, 2–3, 4, 5, 6, 8–9, 11–13, 254–255
Moonlighting by military staff, 80–81
Mora, Daniel, 344
Mota Sánchez, Ramón, 267
Mustangs, 53–57
parental ideological influence, 130

National Action Party (PAN)
alleged alliances with religious and military groups, 142
military contacts of, 96
National Commission on Human Rights, 113

National Defense College. *See* Colegio de Defensa Nacional
National Defense Secretariat. *See* Secretariat of National Defense (army and air force)
National Development Plan, 131
National Federation of Popular Organizations, 90
National Institute to Combat Drugs, 262
National Public Security Council, 114
National Revolutionary Party (PNR), 15
institutionalization of, 21–24
membership statute, 23
officer corps representation in, 23
restructuring of, 22
National security
border security, 269
cabinet agencies and, 81–82, 106 (*see also individual agencies*)
drugs, importance in (*see* Drug trafficking)
guerilla conflicts and (*see* Guerilla warfare)
and human rights violations, 264–268
internal security, trend toward, 103–104, 105, 106, 107
Latin America, doctrine in, 103
literary work on, 345–346
and military politics, 12
military, role of, 35, 131
Tlatelolco Plaza, effect of, 31–32
National University
in civil training and recruitment, 165
post-revolutionary generation, training of, 151
Nava Castillo, Major Antonio, 90
Navy, the
educational institutions of, 170
education of officer corps, 162
foreign training of personnel, 194, 198
merchant marine program, 171
Organic Law, 242, 252, 274
organization of, 238, 241–242

Navy, the (*continued*)
  as source of information to public, 349
Networking interlocks
  through education, 86–89, 104–105
  of family, 83–86, 104–105, 233–234
Non-bargaining behavior, 255–256
North American Free Trade Agreement (NAFTA), 270–271
North American invasion (1846–1848), 16

Obregón, General Alvaro, 18–19
  labor battalions, creation of, 101
  professional requirements for military officers, 45
Occupational specialty, and military promotions, 226–229
Ochoa, Digna, 265
Organic Law of armed forces, 132
  of the navy, 242, 252, 274
Organization of American States, 145
Orthodox professional officers
  authoritarianism of, 65
  generational pattern, 58
  geographical composition of, 60–64
  political leadership, distance from, 64–65
Ortiz Rubio, Pascual, 19
Otal Briseño, Admiral, 209

Palmerin Cordero, General Delfino M., 249
PAN. *See* National Action Party (PAN)
Paramilitary organizations, Los Halcones, 34
Partisan politics
  cooptation of military and, 91
  military officers in opposition parties, 92–93
  military sector, inclusion of, 89–90
Party of the Mexican Revolution (PRM)
  corporate sectors, 22–23
  origins of (*see* National Revolutionary Party (PNR))

restructuring of, 22, 89
Pencillinos, 122–123
Pereira, Anthony, 267
Peyrot González, Admiral Antonio, 232, 241, 249, 270
Piña Soria, Alémán's favoritism of, 208–209
Piñeyro, José Luis, 339
Plan de Tuxtepec rebellion (1876), 16
Plan Huicot (pilot development program), 101
Pluralism, political, 9
PNR. *See* National Revolutionary Party (PNR)
Political crisis, military factionalism during, 12
Political leadership
  discipline, self-imposed, 128
  and distance from military leadership, 64–65, 71
  diversity, education and, 154
  interpersonal relationships, 185–186
  legitimizing of civilian leadership, 73–74
  monopolistic, 9
  pluralism, 9
  revolutionary experiences, 3–4
  socioeconomic composition of, 66, 67
  sources of contact with military leadership, 72
  university education of, 158
Political led strategy toward the military, 6
Political-military officers, 44–45
  aging of, 48–49
  caste mentality and, 51
  centralization of political power, effect on, 50
  characteristics of military and, 48
  civil-military relations, role in, 97
  diversity of leadership, effect on, 48–52
  education of, 51–52, 151
  lessening of role, 47

Index 363

professional officers vs. combat
  veterans, 46–47
revolutionary veterans and, 45–46
Political participation of military, 11
Political professionalism
  Alemán, during presidency of, 25
  Cárdenas, during presidency of,
    21–24
  Porfirio Díaz, during presidency
    of, 17
Popular Revolution Army, compared to
  Zapatista movement, 109
Porfirio Díaz, President José de la Cruz
  institutionalization of military, 150
  and military participation in politics,
    16–17
  and military promotions, 218
Portes Gil, Emilio, 19
Powell, Colin (Secretary of State), 269
Praise for the military, 7
Presidential campaigns
  civil-military interactions during, 95
  1988 elections, political
    consequences of, 36–37
  officer corps support during, 92–93
  of PRI, military involvement in, 95
  violence during, 37
Presidential military staff, 26,
  229–232
PRI. *See* Institutional Revolutionary
  Party
PRM. *See* Party of the Mexican
  Revolution (PRM)
Professional dishonesty, 124, 184
Professionalism. *See* Military
  professionalism; Political
  professionalism
Promotions, military, 206
  abuse of, by Alémen, 207–209, 213
  civilian interference in, 217–223
  to colonel, 216
  and combat experience, 224–226,
    237
  and educational level, 223–224,
    228–229

formal variables influencing,
    223–234
  and occupational specialty, 226–229
  and personal contacts, 233–234,
    236–237
  and presidential staff service,
    229–232
  rates of, for 1939–2003, 210–212,
    217–223
  reform of, 213–215, 241–243
  and teaching experience, 229
  time to attain rank, 209–213
Provincial security issues, military
  officers in political office, 77
Public opinion polls on military,
  134–136, 139–141
Public Security, secretariat for, 118

Quirós Hermosillo, General Francisco,
  215–216

Ramos Santos, Matías, 208
Rapid Response Force, 254
Regime differences between states,
  3–4
Regionalism, 44
  and centralization of political power,
    49–50
Reserve Officer Training Corps (ROTC),
  165
Reta Trigos, General Rodolfo, 215
Retirement pay, 243, 261
Revista de Ejército y Fuerza Aérea, 348
Revolutionary military versus regular
  army, 4
Revolutionary Party of National
  Unification (PRUN), 24
Revolutionary People's Army (ERP),
  264
Revolutionary Popular Democratic
  Party (PDRP), 109
Rivalries between and in armed services,
  181, 243, 252–253, 275
  between presidential staff and regular
    army, 231

Riviello Bazán, General Antonio, 167, 243, 215–216
    background of appointees of, 228
    kinship ties of, 234
Ronfeldt, David, 340
Royal Canadian Military College, military professionalization in, 124
Ruiz Cortines, President Adolfo, military promotion rates, 210–212
Ruiz Pérez, Division General Victor Manuel, 238
Rumsfeld, Donald (Defense Secretary), 269

Salinas de Gortari, President Carlos
    drug trafficking, control of, 111, 112
    international military force, offer of, 269–270
    military promotion rates, 210–212, 221–222
    national security policy, 131
    presidency of, 36–37
    and Zapatista movement (*see* Zapatista movement)
Salinas Leal, Bonifacio, 208
Sarkesian-Bland Model, 1–2
Sarkesian, Samuel P.
    equilibrium model of civil-military relations, 1
    literary work of, 336
School of the Americas, 198
    training, and human rights violations, 199
Secretariat of National Defense (army and air force), 21, 237
    centralization of authority, 125–126
    defense plans, current, 100
    drug trafficking control, budget for, 115
    enlisted officer program, 54–55
    intelligence, source of, 106
    leaders of, 45, 47
    mustangs in, 55
    non-PRI supporters, reprimand of, 93–94
    Party of the Mexican Revolution, delegation to, 23
    as source of information to public, 348–349
Secretariat of the Navy, 21
Secretariat of War and Navy, 21
Serrano, General Francisco R., assassination of, 91–92
Serrano, Monica, 270
Shared responsibility, theory of, 2
Social ideology of military officers, 129–130
Social inferiority, perception of military careers, 83, 136–137
Social isolation of Mexican military, 7–8
Socialization
    and civil supremacy, 130–131
    education, effect of, 154–155, 158, 160
    of elite groups, 43–44, 65
    foreign military training, consequences of, 200–201
    at military institutions, 124–125, 182–183
    of military leaders, 65
    of mustangs, 56, 57
Social mobility
    career choice of military, 136, 140
    economic growth and, 68
    in military service, 68–69
Social revolution, military disengagement and, 4–5
Socioeconomic background
    authoritarianism, effect on, 65
    of officer corps, 64–69
South Florida Task Force, on drug trafficking through Mexico, 110
Special Forces units, 253–254
Staff officers, 233, 235–238
Structural changes to the military, under presidency of Cárdenas, 20–21
Student organizations
    Halcones, Los, suppression by, 34

importance of, 126
literary work on military
 involvement, 346
military repression of, 27, 108

Tamayo Casillas, General José, 231
Teaching experience of officers,
 155–156, 229, 236
Third World countries
 empirical studies on officers, 343
 military theory of, 337
Tlatelolco Plaza, student repression at,
 28–31, 108
 outcomes of, 31–32
 Zapatista movement, effect on,
  32–33
Transparency law, and data availability,
 344–345, 348

United States
 bilateral military assistance pact,
  rejection of, 27
 domestic military training, 163
 drug trafficking in Mexico, effect on,
  13, 111
 empirical studies on officers,
  342–343
 ideological conflicts, 132
 influence on Mexico, 13
 literary work on Mexican military,
  340
 Mexican defense strategy, effect on,
  103, 143
 Mexican leadership compared with,
  164–165
 military training, provision of, 13, 25,
  193–194, 195, 196–198, 199–201
 Reserve Officer Training Corps
  (ROTC), 165
 socioeconomic composition of
  military, 68
 Tlatelolco Plaza student suppression,
  report on, 30–31
Urbanization, of military leadership,
 63–64

U.S. Air Force bases, 198
U.S. Border Patrol, 269
U.S. Military Academy, West Point, 196
U.S. Naval War College, 198

Vega García, General Gerardo
 Clemente, 58, 233, 251, 257–258
 age similarity with political leaders,
  60
 background of appointees of,
  227–228
 border security with the United
  States, 269
 educational institutions, role in,
  86–87
 human rights violations, punishment
  reintroduced by, 267–268
 on moonlighting by military officers,
  80
 national defense secretary,
  appointment as, 248–250
 new promotions and commendations
  law, 242–243
 Zapatista movement, need for
  dialogue with, 264
Véjar Vázquez, Octavio, trial of, 94–95
Violent conflicts, chronology of, 75

Wager, Stephen J., 233, 341
West Central region, low military profile
 in, 62
Williams, Edward J., 345
World War II, orthodox professional
 officers during, 59

Zamorano Esparza, General Fausto M.,
 267
Zapatista movement (Ejército Zapatista
 de Liberación Nacional),
 263–264, 269
 Chiapas rebellion (1994), 37–39
 factionalism of military and, 38
 foundation for, 32–33
 literary work on military
  involvement, 346

Zapatista movement (*continued*)
   and military education, changes in, 202–203
   Popular Revolution Army, compared to, 109
   and regionalism, 50
   and Salinas de Gortari, presidency of, 36
Zedillo, President Ernesto, 248
   administration of, 10
   drug-related corruption during presidency, 113–115, 147
   and drug war, 261–262
   international military forces, participation in, 270
   military promotion rates, 210–212, 222
Zone commanders, 235, 238–240
   relationship to state governors of, 239
Zone system, military, 237–239

About the Author

RODERIC AI CAMP is the Philip McKenna Professor of the Pacific Rim at Claremont McKenna College. He serves as an adjunct fellow of the Mexico Program, Center for Strategic and International Studies in Washington, D.C., and on the Advisory Board, Mexico Institute, Woodrow Wilson Center for International Scholars. He is the author of numerous articles and twenty books on Mexico. His recent publications include *Politics in Mexico: the Democratic Transformation* (2003), *Mexico's Mandarins: Crafting a Power Elite for the 21st Century* (2002), and *Citizen Views of Democracy in Latin America* (2001).